MW01488656

SUSTAINABLE LIFEWAYS: CULTURAL PERSISTENCE IN AN EVER–CHANGING ENVIRONMENT

Penn Museum International Research Conferences
Holly Pittman, Series Editor, Conference Publications

Volume 3: Proceedings of "Forces of Nature:
Risk and Resilience as Factors of Long-term Cultural Change,"
Philadelphia, January 29–February 3, 2008

PMIRC volumes

1. *Landscapes of Movement. Trails, Paths, and Roads in
Anthropological Perspective*, edited by James E. Snead,
Clark L. Erickson, and J. Andrew Darling, 2009
2. *Mapping Mongolia: Situating Mongolia in the World from
Geologic Time to the Present*, edited by Paula L.W. Sabloff, 2011

SUSTAINABLE LIFEWAYS

Cultural Persistence in an Ever-changing Environment

EDITED BY

Naomi F. Miller, Katherine M. Moore, and Kathleen Ryan

University of Pennsylvania Museum of Archaeology and Anthropology
Philadelphia

Library of Congress Cataloging-in-Publication Data

Sustainable lifeways : cultural persistence in an ever-changing environment /
edited by Naomi F. Miller, Katherine M. Moore, and Kathleen Ryan.
p. cm. — (Penn Museum international research conferences v.3)
"Proceedings of "Forces of Nature: Risk and Resilience as Factors
of Long-term Cultural Change," Philadelphia, January 29-February 3, 2008."
ISBN-13: 978-1-934536-19-3 (hardcover : alk. paper)
ISBN-10: 1-934536-19-9 (hardcover : alk. paper)
1. Sustainable living—Cross-cultural studies—Congresses. I. Miller, Naomi Frances.
II. Moore, Katherine M. III. Ryan, Kathleen.
GF78.S87 2011
333.72—dc22
2010049978

Published for the University of Pennsylvania Museum of Archaeology and Anthropology
by the University of Pennsylvania Press.

This book was printed in the United States of America on acid-free paper.

Contents

Figures

Tables

Contributors

Lee Arco
Dept. of Anthropology
Washington University
St. Louis, MO 63130-4862

Lois Beck
Dept. of Anthropology
Washington University
St. Louis, MO 63130-4862

Maria Bruno
Dept. of Anthropology
Washington University
St. Louis, MO 63130-4862

Katherine Grillo
Dept. of Anthropology
Washington University
St. Louis, MO 63130-4862

Julia Huang
Dept. of Anthropology
The London School of Economics and Political Science
Houghton Street
London WC2A 2AE
United Kingdom

Scott Ingram
School of Human Evolution and Social Change
Arizona State University
Tempe, AZ 85287-2402

Karega-Munene
United States International University
Nairobi, Kenya

Timothy A. Kohler
Dept. of Anthropology
Washington State University
Pullman, WA 99164-4910

Fiona Marshall
Dept. of Anthropology
Washington University
St. Louis, MO 63130-4862

Naomi F. Miller
University of Pennsylvania Museum
3260 South Street
Philadelphia, PA 19104-6324

Katherine M. Moore
University of Pennsylvania Museum
3260 South Street
Philadelphia, PA 19104-6324

Margaret Nelson
School of Human Evolution and Social Change and Barrett Honors College
Arizona State University
Tempe, AZ 85287-2402

Matthew A. Peeples
School of Human Evolution and Social Change
Arizona State University
Tempe, AZ 85287-2402

Charles Reed
Dept. of Anthropology
Washington State University
Pullman, WA 99164-4910

Neil Roberts
Quaternary Environments Research Group
School of Geography
University of Plymouth
Plymouth Devon PL4 84A
UK

Arlene Rosen
Institute of Archaeology
University College London
31–34 Gordon Sq.
London WC1H 0PY
UK

Kathleen Ryan
University of Pennsylvania Museum
3260 South Street
Philadelphia, PA 19104-6324

Katherine A. Spielmann
School of Human Evolution and Social Change
Arizona State University
Tempe, AZ 85287-2402

Peter Stahl
Dept. of Anthropology
Binghamton University
Binghamton, NY 13902-6000

Penn Museum International Research Conferences

Foreword

For more than a century, a core mission of the University of Pennsylvania Museum of Archaeology and Anthropology has been to foster research that leads to new understandings about human culture. For much of the 20th century, this research took the form of worldwide expeditions that brought back both raw data and artifacts whose analysis continues to shed light on early complex societies of the New and Old worlds. The civilizations of pharaonic Egypt, Mesopotamia, Greece, Rome, China, Mexico, and Central America are represented in galleries that display only the most remarkable of Penn Museum's vast holding of artifacts. These collections have long provided primary evidence for many distinct research programs engaging scholars from around the world.

As we moved into a new century, indeed a new millennium, Penn Museum sought to reinvigorate its commitment to research focused on questions of human societies. In 2005, working with then Williams Director Richard M. Leventhal, Michael J. Kowalski, Chairman of the Board of Overseers of the Penn Museum, gave a generous gift to the Museum to seed a new program of high-level conferences designed to engage themes central to the Museum's core research mission. According to Leventhal's vision, generating new knowledge and frameworks for understanding requires more than raw data and collections. More than ever, it depends on collaboration among communities of scholars investigating problems using distinct lines of evidence and different modes of analysis. Recognizing the importance of collaborative and multidisciplinary endeavors in the social sciences, Penn Museum used the gift to launch a program of International Research Conferences that each brought together ten to fifteen scholars who have reached a critical point in their consideration of a shared problem.

During the three years until the spring of 2008, it was my privilege to identify, develop, run, and now to oversee the publication of eight such conferences. The dozen or so papers for each conference were submitted to all participants one month in advance of the meeting. The fact that the papers were circulated beforehand meant that no time was lost introducing new material to the group. Rather, after each paper was briefly summarized by its author, an intense and extended critique followed that allowed for sustained consideration of the contribution that both the data and the argument made to the larger questions. The discussions of individual papers were followed by a day discussing crosscutting issues and concluded with an overarching synthesis of ideas.

Sustainable Lifeways: Cultural Persistence in an Ever-Changing Environment is the edited proceedings of a conference entitled "Forces of Nature: Risk and Resilience as Factors of Long-term Cultural Change," held in the winter of 2008. It is the third of the conferences to see publication. As Series Editor, I look forward to five more volumes that will appear over the next few years. The publication of the results of these conferences allows the new knowledge and understanding that they achieved to be shared broadly and to contribute to the uniquely human enterprise of self understanding.

HOLLY PITTMAN
Series Editor
Deputy Director for Academic Programs Penn Museum 2005–2008
Curator, Near East Section
Professor, History of Art
Bok Family Professor in the Humanities,
University of Pennsylvania

Preface

In the winter of 2008, the Penn Museum International Research Conference series sponsored a four-day symposium, "Forces of Nature: Risk and Resilience as Factors of Long-term Cultural Change." We gathered specialists working in at least one of four areas of the world with significant archaeological and paleoenvironmental databases: West Asia, the American Southwest, East Africa, and Andean South America. The participating scholars have made contributions to research within at least one of three broad time scales: long-term (spanning millennia), medium-term (archaeological time—centuries or a few thousand years), and recent (ethnohistoric or ethnographic—years or decades). In addition to the authors whose work appears in this volume, Richard Redding participated in the conference and presented a case study at a medium time scale in Egypt. This volume addresses forces of conservatism and innovation at work in societies dependent on the exploitation of aquatic and other wild resources, agriculture, and specialized pastoralism.

By bringing an archaeological eye to an examination of human response to unpredictable environmental conditions that is informed by an understanding of contemporary traditional peoples, the symposium participants attempted to develop a more detailed picture of how societies perceive environmental risk, how they alter their behavior in the face of changing conditions, and under what challenges the most rapid and far-reaching changes in adaptation have taken place.

We are particularly grateful to Mike Kowalski, Chairman of the Board of Overseers of the Museum, who provided funding for the Penn Museum International Research Conference series. As co-ordinator for the series, Prof. Holly Pittman was especially enthusiastic about our proposal, and was very attentive to our needs at all stages of the conference and production. Teagan Schweitzer provided essential logistical assistance during the conference. We would also like to thank Jennifer Quick for shepherding the volume toward publication.

Naomi F. Miller, Katherine M. Moore, and Kathleen Ryan
Philadelphia, 2010

Introduction:
Sustainable Lifeways

NAOMI F. MILLER AND KATHERINE M. MOORE

All organisms and species respond to unpredictable variability in their environment. For individual humans and for the societies in which they live, cultural responses to environmental risk are embedded in technology, practice, and ideology. By their collective actions, societies can mitigate or exacerbate immediate and long-term risk in their environment. In addition, all societies, ancient and modern, have to deal with risk on several time scales. The most limited temporal scales concern annual and interannual variability in weather, pests, and other short-term risks. Over decades and longer (referred to here as medium scale), changes in climate, soil conditions, and vegetation cover can be perceived and recorded in intergenerational time. Even longer-term changes in environmental conditions or extremely rare events, like volcanic eruptions, are least likely to be recognized by social groups. Even so, they have a material effect on the ability of those groups to persist. The 2008 Penn Museum International Research Conference "Forces of Nature: Risk and Resilience as Factors of Long-term Cultural Change" addressed these issues. In this volume, we bring the archaeological record to the forefront in understanding the human experience of dynamic environments (Figs. 0.1, 0.2). Even a sustainable system will not be static, because it must respond to changing external conditions and internally generated stresses. But a subtle shift in our focus occurred in the course of the session's discussions: although societies and individuals confront many uncertainties, success requires continuity of tradition.

The contributors to this volume are aware that the concept of nature in the context of human societies and their traditions is problematic; that even foragers and low-level cultivators manage, and thereby create, their environment (see, for example, Ford and Nigh 2009; Smith 2007; Weiser and Lepofsky 2009). Nevertheless, from the perspective of the individual agent, it is frequently analytically useful to separate certain kinds of conditions,

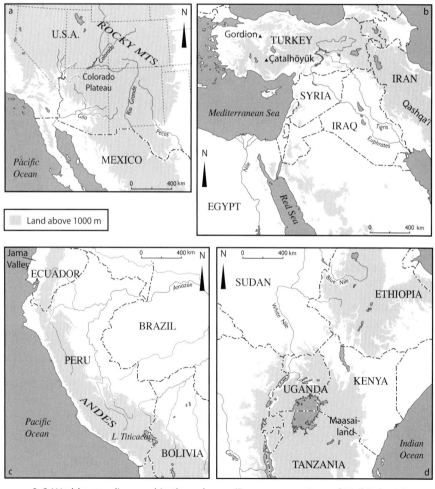

0.1 World areas discussed in the volume. (Base map courtesy of Neil Roberts)

such as climate or volcanism, as independent variables. That said, the chapters in this volume are more concerned with the underlying processes that condition cultural responses to the vagaries of nature.

This subject is a perennial one.[1] The 2010 earthquake in Haiti was unprecedented in memory; the Indian Ocean tsunami in 2004 was unusual in the territory it covered, but the affected societies had experienced tsunamis before; in 2005, Hurricane Katrina was an admittedly severe example of an ordinary seasonal climate event that virtually all residents of the region had experienced many times. Thus, we can see that Haiti endured an event predictable only on a long time scale, the tsunami in Asia might have been predicted based on a medium scale record, and Hurricane Katrina, though horrific in its impact, has already been followed by other storms on a short-term, annual cycle. In the past few years, the world has witnessed many such "natural" disasters whose effects were exacerbated by pre-existing interrelated social and environmental conditions (Leroy 2006).

One way that events at these different time scales interact is when the response to a short-term environmental fluctuation results in irrevocable social or environmental changes. For example, British colonial agriculture policy in Kenya was established during a brief phase of favorable climate. It created an unsustainable system when normal drier conditions returned, the results of which are still being felt (Roberts, Chapter 1). If a period of favorable climate is long enough, new technologies may emerge associated with new social structures, as Rosen (Chapter 5) proposes for the Pre-Pottery Neolithic B of the Levant. After a similar short-term climate amelioration permitted a more secure living from farming, agropastoralists at Gordion returned to their prior practices, with lower population densities and a less energy-intensive agricultural system (Miller, Chapter 11). Conversely, volcanic eruptions in the Jama Valley of lowland Ecuador destroyed the original agroecological system by covering the floodplain with tephra. Later-period farmers created a productive, diverse forest mosaic in the uplands that supported larger populations and was less vulnerable to volcanic ashfall (Stahl, Chapter 10).

Periods of perceived stability in the archaeological record may be interpreted as the results of effective risk management in the face of varying conditions. Insofar as these factors relate to the 'natural' environment, these cultural systems have demonstrated their resilience in the face of risks. Archaeological evidence of environment and land use can then help

	Ch. 1 East Africa	Ch. 2 East Africa	Ch. 3 East Africa	Ch. 4 Iran	Ch. 5 Levant
AD 1000 (1100 bp)	Historic period droughts		Maasai, historic to present	Qashqa'i 17th c. to present	
BC/AD (2100 bp)					
		Southern Settlement Phase (SSP)			
1000 BC (2800 bp)					
5000 BC (5700 bp)	4.2 ka (BP) Event	Exploratory Northern Pastoral (ENP)			
	"8.2 ka" (BP) Drought				Early PPNB
10,000 BC (~11,000 bp)	Younger Dryas				PPNA Natufian

0.2 Timeline for chapters. (Radiocarbon calibration extrapolated from Stuiver et al. 1998)

Ch. 6 US Southwest	Ch. 7 US Southwest	Ch. 8 Andes	Ch. 9 Andes	Ch. 10 Northern Andes	Ch. 11 Anatolia
	Mimbres & Salinas	Aymara, historic to present	Late Horizon	Muchique 4	Medieval
				Muchique 3	
Pueblo I			Middle Horizon		
Basketmaker III				Muchique 2	
			Late Formative		
				Muchique 1	
					Hellenistic
			Middle Formative		Late Phrygian
					Middle Phrygian
					Early Phrygian
			Early Formative= Middle & Early Chiripa	Late Formative	Early Iron Age Late Bronze Age
				Early Formative	Middle Bronze Age

us identify long-term developmental processes that allowed ancient societies to persist and change (Redman and Kinzig 2003). Moore (Chapter 9) shows how despite fluctuating water levels, the aquatic richness of Lake Titicaca allowed for flexible responses to climate shifts through the integration of the agropastoral system with the use of fish and birds. In contrast, well-documented periods of rapid change, depopulation, or abandonment may represent cases where risk management strategies were overwhelmed by the magnitude of change (as in the cases of rapid landform changes and floods) or by the cumulative effects of smaller scale changes, such as the abandonment of lower Mesopotamia (see Redman 2005).

The quality of stability in social and ecological contexts arose repeatedly as a methodological issue in conference discussions. The perception of stability that could be inferred from the location of archaeological sites or the record of subsistence practices from deposits in sites appeared to risk an error of circular reasoning: a site's surface would not collect an archaeological record of an adaptation that was no longer possible at that location. This weakness of reading adaptation from the on-site archaeological record is countered here primarily with comparison to off-site deposits such as pollen cores, ice cores, tephra records, tree rings, lake varves, and so on. Yet, how can such records be linked convincingly with site deposits? Each of the chapters addressing archaeological sequences demonstrates careful attention to chronology, and makes intensive use of absolute dating to link site location and contents to specific environmental records. A side effect of this approach is that the location and details of smaller, open, ephemeral sites cannot be linked to the larger, well-dated sites that are the focus of these chapters, even though mobility and dispersal are routinely cited as a response to declining resources. In the case of the effect of volcanic ash falling on sites in the Jama Valley (Stahl), the off-site record does link tightly with the on-site record with ashfalls literally blanketing the sites. In the basin of present-day Lake Titicaca, the off-site record of lake-level change suggests repeated dramatic alterations of the landscape over the period of intensive occupation (Moore). The stability of site location and ecological relationships from the on-site archaeological record contrasts with the picture of climate and vegetation changes from the lake cores, calling the relationship between the two records into question. In other chapters, the off-site record shows slighter amounts of change over time, though the social effects may have been profound. By contrasting the off-site to on-site relationships between studies in the volume, the range of threshold values that bring about change in economic and ecological systems can be estimated. Even so, we were repeatedly reminded of how multiple aspects of traditional practice combined to dampen the effect of changing rainfall or temperature.

One of the challenges for archaeologists is incorporating the effect of ancient people's knowledge of their environment. Ryan and Karega-Munene's (Chapter 3), Beck and Huang's (Chapter 4), and Bruno's (Chapter 8) case studies point to the kinds of information we may miss in trying to understand ancient practices. Agent-based modeling can provide a virtual link between ethnographic understanding and archaeological inference. For example, in the U.S. Southwest, Kohler and Reed (Chapter 6) create an infinite variety of alternative scenarios for an extended period. While behavioral ecology models would predict site location oriented toward agricultural fields, Kohler and Reed demonstrate that the model with the "best fit" to actual site distribution is one in which the subsistence system favored wild deer over cultivated maize. At Çatalhöyük in Turkey, retention of old ways of subsistence seems like a better explanation for site location in proximity to the fields of this Neolithic site. Roberts and Rosen (2009) suggest that the familiar and diverse resources of the marshland might have secured the transition to full agriculture. Ancient TEK (Traditional Ecological Knowledge) is but one part of the picture. The high value of domesticated cattle among the Maasai (Ryan and Karega-Munene) may give some insight into the cultural significance of deer in the Southwest (Kohler and Reed) and aurochs at Çatalhöyük (Twiss et al. 2009). One reality of traditional agricultural practice to which archaeologists have poor access is the effect of diseases and parasites. Both crop pests (nematodes in potato crops, see Bruno) and animal disease (cattle pests, see Ryan and Karega-Munene) were emphatically identified as central forces in determining the location and nature of settlements. Of course, the distribution of these risks reflects the experience of humans with those plants and animals over time.

Archaeology and long-term ethnographic information provides time depth unavailable in short-term actualistic studies. With the perspective of different chronological and spatial scales within each region, several archaeologically useful parameters of risk and resilience that acted in the past were investigated. Within archaeological assemblages, measures of changing representation of taxa were used as proxies for changing adaptation.

These comparisons included ones where rank orders of important taxa were reversed (Marshall, Grillo, and Arco, Chapter 2) and ones where smaller changes were consistent across a region (Kohler and Reed; Miller; Moore). This use of relatively robust quantitative measures will allow the incorporation of more archaeological sites into such regional studies, particularly sites excavated or analyzed long ago (Amorosi et al. 1996).

Over the four days of the conference, we kept returning to some important concepts. Superficially, adapting to climate is a key variable. Indeed, in choosing the world areas, we considered relatively arid regions of west Asia and Andean South America as supporting societies dependent on domesticated plants and animals; East Africa, with full time pastoralists; and the U.S. Southwest, with societies based on domesticated plants. Arid regions are intrinsically important in studying response to climate change as they are more prone overall to short- and long-term variability in rainfall and are likely to suffer most from the changing climates in the near future compared to regions in more favorable climes (see Solomon et al. 2009:1706). With the exception of Stahl's contribution, therefore, drought is a directly limiting factor, though temperature changes may also have had a key role in bringing cultural change in Kohler and Reed's case in the northern edge of the American Southwest. But it should be understood that climate merely creates conditions. As the "natural" environment changes, humans respond to those changes, thereby creating new conditions. The responses, therefore, are to the conditions, whether of weather, vegetation, soil, or society.

"Climate change" is sometimes used as a shorthand for the whole set of conditions in which people operate and that is not itself stable. Humans and other animals persist by creating circumstances favorable to their survival—"niche construction" (see Smith 2007). "Sustainability" implies "risk minimization," so that "critical thresholds" forcing qualitative systemic changes are not reached. Though change is inevitable, "ecological inheritance" constrains responses. Using Traditional Ecological Knowledge and "management" of the local environment, small-scale societies create the conditions for their own perpetuation. Several other mechanisms of risk reduction also kept recurring in the discussions: mobility (cyclical movement), migration (one-way movement), exchange, cooperation, raiding and warfare, intensification, and subsistence resource diversification.

The broad concept of diversity unites these mechanisms of risk reduction, and thereby helps focus attention on how ancient societies dealt with risk and sustainability. Our discussions revolved around the interconnections among diversity of place, subsistence, and society. In the category of diversity of place, mobility is an important strategy for many foraging societies (see Rosen), as well as transhumant and nomadic pastoral societies (Beck and Huang; Marshall, Grillo, and Arco; Ryan and Karega-Munene). Strategies for movement include using social as well as natural environmental resources (Beck and Huang; Marshall, Grillo, and Arco; Ryan and Karega-Munene). A farming society may be able to survive even sudden, periodic massive devastation of field and forest in place (Stahl). Yet, Spielmann, Nelson, Ingram, and Peeples (Chapter 7) point out that occasional abandonment in the Southwest actually *is* the response to an uncertain environment! Similar histories and abandonment and reorganization are suggested by Marshall, Grillo, and Arco. But even sedentary people take advantage of small-scale spatial diversity, as the Lake Titicaca farmers discussed by Maria Bruno (Chapter 8) take advantage of different soil types.

Diversity of subsistence choices, including technology, is also an important strategy. Moore shows that overall resource productivity may be stable if you are willing to be flexible in your reliance on particular species of plants and animals. As Boserup (1965) pointed out, some technologies may be known long before they are "needed"; irrigation at Gordion is an example of this. Another point where social relationships intersect with technology is in the creation and maintenance of storage. Beyond the obvious cases of storing crops and wild plant foods, we can see examples of social storage in the case of the African pastoralists' history of gift obligations, and we also note the nature of storage of economic value in herds, or even in fisheries and other wild resources. Strategies for manipulating and prolonging the usefulness of stored resources of all kinds have clearly been key for the ancient societies studied in this volume. We also were conscious of memory, a kind of mental and cultural storage, as an essential process in resilient societies: memories of cattle and their donors, memories of where crops had done well and how long ago a certain field had been sown, memories of other ways to manipulate water and to make tools and supplies for long-dormant practices. In the short-term of the contemporary societies in this volume, diversification by the adoption of new crops or new economic roles seems to be a way to buffer a society against further change and loss of the part of the identity that is held most dear, as Qashaq'i pastoralists tend orchards of fruit and nut trees to support their herds, or as the Aymara farmers adopt European crops to keep working their land. The economic accommodations they are willing to make shows the value they put on fundamental ties to place and way of life.

Cultural and social systems show obvious diversity. Whether through full-time nomadic transhumance or specialized exchange, relationships of individuals and groups to those beyond their immediate subsistence catchment can allow a social group to survive. These practices permit diversity of knowledge and of place to benefit both parties to the exchanges. Yet, exchange is not necessarily to mutual advantage; raiding and warfare always create losers, and sometimes winners. Culturally transmitted TEK is also diversity-enhancing. Successful (i.e., sustainable) systems accumulate wisdom over time that can be applied to recurring or new conditions.

The examples discussed in this volume mostly deal with small-scale rather than expansive societies. In that sense, they are not directly analogous to those of today. Unrestricted mobility as a solution to resource stress has been crippled by the disappearance of open, non-commercial space in modern nations. High population densities constrain movement and the migration of whole populations, despite the fact that the number of individual migrants and length of their journeys is greater now than at any time in the past. Human impacts on the atmosphere, biosphere, and geosphere that are the result of our modern high per capita energy consumption, as well as the high absolute number of people the earth is now expected to support also have no analogy with the past. Perhaps the most profound statement about the limits of resilience comes in Beck and Huang's assessment of the possibility of nomadic life in modern Iran: the Qashaq'i herders know well how to deal with hail, disease, market conditions, and drought, but their flexibility was useless in the face of tight control by an autocratic state. Self-determination and the employment of individual knowledge and experience of the environment is more accessible as a goal in democratic societies than in autocratic ones, and this fact may offer cosmopolitan readers of this volume an avenue for political and social engagement.

Insofar as we are dispassionate scholars, these archaeological, ethnoarchaeological, and ethnographic studies can inform discussion of sustainable practice in the modern world. Yet the contributors to this volume have long-term commitments to physical and conceptual research areas. The data of archaeology and ethnography demonstrate the many alternative lifeways that have sustained humanity, and it is up to people alive today to use that hard-earned knowledge stored in the memory of peoples, places, and things.

NOTE

1. Recent volumes taking somewhat different perspectives include Bawden and Reycraft (2000), Fisher, Hill, and Feinman (2009); McAnany and Yoffee (2009).

REFERENCES CITED

Amorosi, Thomas, James Woolett, Sophia Perdikaris, and Thomas McGovern. 1996. Regional Zooarchaeology and Global Change: Problems and Potentials. *World Archaeology* 28:126–57.

Bawden, Garth, and Richard M. Reycraft, eds. 2000. *Environmental Disaster and the Archaeology of Human Response*. Maxwell Museum Anthropology Papers no. 7. Albuquerque: University of New Mexico Press.

Boserup, Ester. 1965. *The Conditions of Agricultural Growth: The Economics of Agrarian Change under Population Pressure*. Chicago: Aldine.

Fisher, Christopher T., J. Brett Hill, and Gary M. Feinman, eds. 2009. *The Archaeology of Environmental Change: Socio-Natural Legacies of Degradation and Resilience*. Tucson: University of Arizona Press.

Ford, Anabel, and Ronald Nigh. 2009. Origins of the Maya Forest Garden: Maya Resource Management. *Journal of Ethnobiology* 29:213–36.

Leroy, Susan A. G. 2006. From Natural Hazard to Environmental Catastrophe: Past and Present. *Quaternary International* 158:4–12.

McAnany, Patricia A., and Norman Yoffee, eds. 2009. *Questioning Collapse. Human Resilience, Ecological Vulnerability, and the Aftermath of Empire*. Cambridge: Cambridge University Press.

Redman, Charles L. 2005. Resilience Theory in Archaeology. *American Anthropologist* 107:70–77.

Redman, C. L., and A. P. Kinzig. 2003. Resilience of Past Landscapes: Resilience Theory, Society, and the *longue durée*. *Conservation Ecology* 7(1): 14. [online] URL: http://www.consecol.org/vol7/iss1/art14/.

Roberts, Neil, and Arlene Rosen. 2009. Diversity and Complexity in Early Farming Communities of Southwest Asia: New Insights into the Economic and Environmental Basis of Neolithic Çatalhöyük. *Current Anthropology* 50:393–402.

Smith, Bruce D. 2007. The Ultimate Ecosystem Engineers. *Science* 315:1797–98.

Solomon, Susan, Gian-Kaspar Plattner, Reto Knutti, and Pierre Friedlingstein. 2009. Irreversible Climate Change due to Carbon Dioxide Emissions. *Proceedings of the National Academy of Sciences* 106:1704–9.

Stuiver, M., P. J. Riemer, E. Bard, J. W. Beck, G. S. Burr, K. A. Hughen, B. Kromer, G. McCormac, J. van der Plicht, and M. Spurk. 1998. INTCAL98 Radiocarbon Age Calibration, 24,000–0 cal BP. *Radiocarbon* 40:1041–83.

Twiss, Katheryn C., Amy Bogaard, Michael P. Charles, Jennifer Henecke, Nerissa Russell, Louise Martin, and Glynis Jones. 2009. Plants and Animals Together: Interpreting Organic Remains from Building 52 at Çatalhöyük. *Current Anthropology* 50:885–95.

Weiser, Andrea, and Dana Lepofsky. 2009. Ancient Land Use and Management of Ebey's Prairie, Whidbey Island, Washington. *Journal of Ethnobiology* 29:184–212.

1

"Living with a Moving Target": Long-term Climatic Variability and Environmental Risk in Dryland Regions

NEIL ROBERTS

INTRODUCTION: ON TIME SCALES

People, both individually and collectively, prefer the natural world around them to be stable over time periods longer than the march of the seasons. A property owner with a sea view is surprised that the shoreline does not always stay in its appointed position, but moves alarmingly closer due to coastal erosion. An Andean Indian farmer tills fields ever higher up the slopes of the volcano notwithstanding the risk of life-threatening explosive eruption. Nature has a dangerous habit of being volatile and dynamic. This is manifested particularly clearly in the world's drylands, whose climates are notoriously variable from one year (or one decade) to the next, and whose water resources are consequently often unreliable.

Human societies have developed a wide range of strategies for coping with a variable natural environment that produces, for example, episodes of drought and flood. For any strategy to be sustainable, maximization of resource use has to be balanced against risks of crop or livestock failure. Over annual to decadal time scales—that is, within a single human lifetime—environmental variability is normally perceived to occur about a stable mean, for example, the 30-year average rainfall. Under these conditions, direct individual experience is likely to be used as a guide for managing future environmental risk. This often proves to be a reasonably trustworthy basis for decision-making. Over these relatively short timescales "expert" western opinion will draw on information derived primarily from observation and monitoring, for example, from ethnographic survey or from Earth-orbiting satellites.

Extending back from an individual to an intergenerational time frame increases the probability that we encounter extreme or higher magnitude events, such as a one-in-a-hundred-year flood, or a multiyear drought. It also alters the sources used to judge environmental risk away from personal experience to communal memory and oral tradition. Sources change for the academic specialist too, from direct observation to documentary records, such as colonial archives or historical meteorological data. The availability of written documentary evidence varies greatly from one region to another. Of the four case study regions represented in this volume, three (Andes, American Southwest, East Africa) have historical records extending back less than five centuries, while the fourth (Southwest Asia) has historical documentary evidence extending back to 3000 BC, one of the longest written records anywhere.

Over still longer centennial or millennial timescales, memory becomes transformed into myth. The one-in-a-thousand-year flood becomes the Flood Myth of the Epic of Gilgamesh and the Biblical Old Testament. These are "longue durée" timescales back beyond our oldest traceable ancestors. They are not easily comprehended in terms of human experience and consequently fade in importance as a basis for environmental decision-making. Our data sources also shift from direct observation and participation, through written documentary records, to archaeological investigation and proxy methods of reconstructing environmental history, such as pollen analysis and radiocarbon dating (Fig. 1.1). Drawing back in time therefore shifts the disciplinary emphasis from the social anthropologist first to the historian and then to the prehistorian and the paleoclimatologist.

Of course, events seem more important because they occurred nearer to us in time, but nature is immune to these changing human perceptions of time receding into the distance. It is not only the magnitude and frequency of extreme climatic events that alter as timescales are extended. Over centennial to millennial periods climate—and the environment in general—becomes non-stationary; that is, it exhibits underlying trends through time from one mean state to another different one. The early to

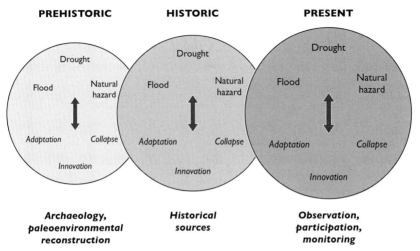

1.1 Schematic model for changing data sources regarding human-environment relations over different timescales.

mid-Holocene climate in most the world's dryland regions was significantly different from that of recent times, for instance. On archaeological timescales, therefore, past experience would have become an ever more unreliable basis for achieving sustainable strategies, and risks of environmental crisis consequently increased.

CONSEQUENCES OF SECULAR CLIMATE CHANGE

Figure 1.2a illustrates a hypothetical, but typical, 60-year rainfall time series in a dryland region showing year-to-year variations but no overall trend in climate through time. Drought events—arbitrarily assumed to be those years with rainfall below 200 mm—occur on average every 8–9 years, and they occur randomly through time. Crop yields (which are assumed to be zero below 200 mm rainfall—i.e., complete crop failure—and to increase linearly above this) fluctuate greatly between years, with some back-to-back years when harvests were seriously inadequate. At these times, food would have to be obtained from stored surpluses or from exchange, and hunger or even starvation would be prevalent. None the less, subsequent years see a return to fat years of good harvests. Figure 1.2b shows the same rainfall data as Figure 1.2a, but with a 20% decline in the mean rainfall during the second half of the series. In years 31–60, the frequency of drought years and crop failure now increases to one year in three, although the duration of droughts does not rise significantly but remains at a maximum of three consecutive bad years. In fact, one of the most notable consequences of the falling average rainfall is a decline in crop yields during "good" years, which would mean less food being available for storage or exchange to tide over the intervening lean years.

At what point in this particular story would it become clear to agrarian communities that the underlying climatic conditions had changed, as opposed to simply being part of natural variability? Even with the benefit of hindsight and seeing the full 60-year sequence in Figure 1.2b, it is far from obvious whether the increase in bad years represents a temporary or a permanent shift in conditions. Only a recognition of the latter would be likely to lead to a change in human lifeways and food procurement strategies. Figure 1.2c represents a real example of declining rainfall over a 60-year period, namely the Sahel drought of the 1970s and 1980s, which was the most extreme experienced by any dryland region of the world during the last century (see Dai et al. 2004 and Hulme 1992 for details). In this case, the decline in rainfall during the period 1960–1990 compared to the preceding 30-year period was all too clear and its human consequences (although compounded by many other factors) all too tragic, through famine and loss of livelihoods (Mortimore 1989). Notwithstanding this, the period since 1990 has seen farming systems in the Sahel showing signs of recovery. However, and significantly, people have made new adaptations since the Sahel crisis, such as diversifying livelihoods in order to mitigate the effects of future droughts and food shortage (Mortimore and Adams 2001). As a result, the cultural–ecological system has evolved rather than simply returning to its previous condition.

DEMONSTRATING THE LONG ZOOM

Using multiple different types of archives allows us to create a long temporal focus, and pull our lens back from recent to historic to Holocene timescales, and potentially beyond. I will use the environmental history of part of the East African Rift Valley to illustrate how this long zoom operates.

In 1963, Kenya became an independent nation state after almost 70 years of British colonial rule. In most of East Africa, the early to mid-1960s

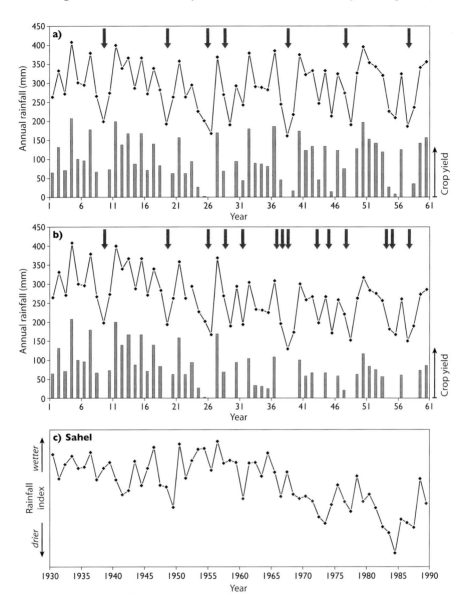

1.2 Sixty-year dryland rainfall time series, drought events (arrowed), and crop yields; (a) hypothetical case with inter-annual variations but no overall trend; (b) the same data as a but with a 20% step decline in mean precipitation during the second 30 years of the series; (c) actual rainfall in the Sahel, 1930–1990. (Normalized deviations, source: UNEP)

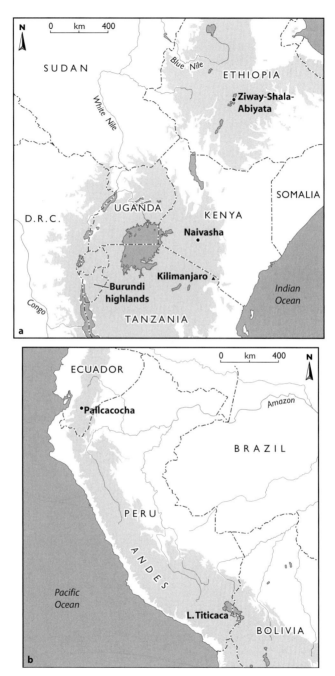

1.3a–d Location maps of sites in East Africa, northern Andean South America, Southwest Asia, and U.S. Southwest.

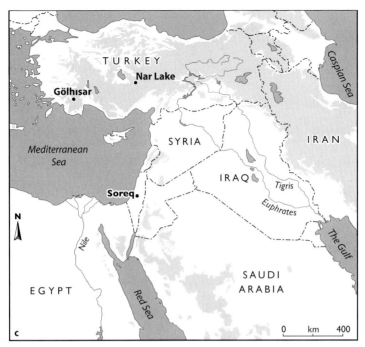

Land above 1000 m

witnessed heavy rains, causing rising lake levels and floods along rivers such as the Tana (Roberts and Barker 1993). The dry years that followed across much of Africa south of the Sahara helped burst a balloon of postcolonial optimism that may have contained over-inflated expectations. International opinion, taken by surprise by these droughts and associated famines, particularly in the Sahel region, led directly to the UN Desertification Programme which was established following a conference in Nairobi in 1977. It raised questions about what should be considered "normal" rainfall, the magnitude and frequency of drought events, and the long-term sustainability of human occupancy in drylands. This in turn, demanded a longer-term perspective than that possible from contemporary political ecology. Analysis of historical meteorological records showed that the Sahel was probably the only dryland region of the world to experience a drought during the 1970s and 1980s that was exceptional by 20th-century standards (see Fig. 1.2c). For the Maasai pastoralists of Kenya's central Rift Valley, for example, climatic variations during the postcolonial period would have been unexceptional in comparison with their previous collective experience. What had changed over previous decades were their traditional access rights to wetlands—critical for cattle grazing and watering in dry years—many of which had been removed due to land alienation during colonial times (Anderson 1984; see Ryan and Karega-Munene, this volume).

The danger of drawing on short-term experience in developing a sustainable land-use strategy is well-illustrated by Kenya's Naivasha district (Fig. 1.3), which was settled by white colonial farmers at the turn of the 20th century. This happened to coincide with the wettest climatic period of the last two centuries, reflected in high water levels of Lake Naivasha (Verschuren, Laird, and Cumming 1999) (Fig. 1.4a). These unusually favorable conditions were out of balance with long-term trends in water-resource availability, and subsequent water usage for cropland has almost certainly become unsustainable without degrading ecosystems such as nearby Lake Nakuru, a World Heritage site. Lakes such as these lacking a surface outlet can act as giant rain gauges, with their water levels rising (and their salt content decreasing) at times of high rainfall, and lake levels falling (and their salinity increasing) during periods of drought. This was the case, for instance, in Oloidien Bay, which was alternately connected to and isolated from the main Lake Naivasha by water-level fluctuations, so changing its salinity dramatically.

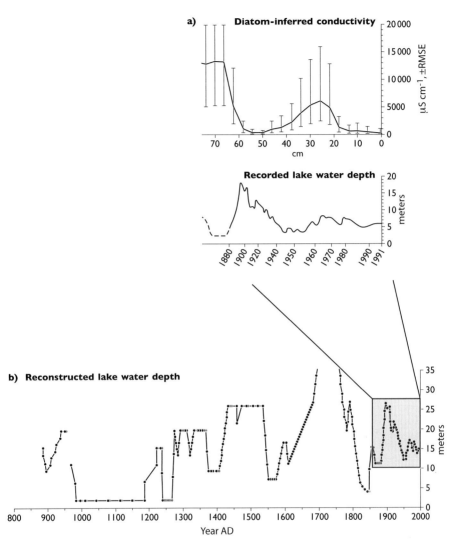

1.4 Lake levels and drought events in Naivasha, Kenya; (a) Recorded observations of lake water level and diatom-inferred lake salinity from a core in Oloidien Bay, since ca. AD 1850; (b) inferred lake level fluctuations and drought events from a core in Crescent Island Crater since AD 800. (Sources: Verschuren et al. 1999; Verschuren, Laird, and Cumming 2000)

Proxy indicators of lake level and salinity can therefore extend our knowledge of climate in dryland regions back to periods before instrumental records were kept. In this way the long zoom can be extended back to archaeological as well as historical timescales of culture change. In the case of Lake Naivasha, a continuous and well-resolved record of lake-level changes has been reconstructed from diatom and midge fossils in lake sediments spanning the last 1100 years (Verschuren, Laird, and Cumming 2000). This shows that droughts occurred prior to around AD 1270, and again around 1380–1420, 1560–1620, and 1760–1840, some of which were much more severe than those known from historical times. The droughts of the mid-20th century caused failing harvests which fuelled the social unrest that ultimately led to Kenya's drive for independence, but these climatic events were far from exceptional when viewed from a long-term perspective. In pre-colonial times, it has been argued that extended periods of drought coincided with evidence from oral traditions for political unrest and large-scale migration of indigenous peoples (Webster 1979), although clearly famines were contingent not only on rainfall (Robertson et al. 2004).

Over still longer timescales, tropical African lakes experienced even more massive and sustained changes in water level, notably during the first half of the Holocene when Naivasha was over 100 m deep and almost four times larger in area than it is today (Bergner, Trauth, and Bookhagen 2003). Water balance calculations for this and other East African lakes (e.g., Dühnforth, Bergner, and Trauth 2006) indicate a mean precipitation increase of at least 16% during the early Holocene, linked to a strengthened and expanded monsoon system across Africa and South Asia (Gasse 2000). If we were to pull back in time even further to the Plio-Pleistocene, we would see even more spectacular expansions and contractions in lakes occupying this portion of the East African rift (e.g., Trauth et al. 2005), driven by large-scale alternations of aridity and humidity. These, in turn, acted as key drivers for early hominin evolution within, and radiation out of, Africa.

GLOBAL CLIMATE CHANGE
SINCE THE LAST GLACIAL MAXIMUM

The climate and water resources available to pastoralists, agriculturalists, and forager-hunters in dryland regions such as East Africa during the early to mid-Holocene were evidently quite different from those that have existed during modern times. In contrast to the last 2000 years, climates of the early to mid-Holocene and preceding Pleistocene were controlled by boundary conditions (e.g., solar radiation, ice cover) that differ substantially from those currently prevailing. None the less, these chronologically more distant climates are no more different from today's than those that are projected to occur by the end of the 21st century (IPCC 2007). As such, they provide valuable insights into how human beings have coped with climate changes in the past. In order to provide a long-term context for variations in the climate of dryland regions over archaeological timescales, it seems appropriate to outline briefly how the Earth's climate has changed since the Last Glacial Maximum (LGM). At various points in this outline, I will make brief excursions into examples illustrating proposed relations between climate and culture.

Twenty-thousand years ago[1] major ice sheets covered large parts of the northern hemisphere continents and caused a glacio-eustatic sea-level fall of around 120 m. A colder climate also weakened the global hydrological cycle so that with a few exceptions, such as the American Southwest, the glacial Earth was also an arid Earth. Deserts such as the Sahara expanded far south of their present position and tropical forests were greatly reduced in extent. On tropical mountains such as the Andes, temperature depression led to the elevation of vegetation zones being lowered by around 1000 m. Glacial-interglacial climate cycles of similar magnitude and frequency had occurred repeatedly during the last million years or so, with their timing apparently regulated by minor but regular variations in the Earth's orbit around the Sun, the so-called Milankovitch cycles. Glacial and interglacial periods of the Pleistocene were synchronous over the whole planet, even though direct orbitally induced changes in radiation operated differently in the northern and southern hemispheres. In effect, first-order global climatic changes during the Quaternary period were driven by the build-up and decay of land ice over Canada and Scandinavia. Significantly, this is the shortest timescale for which there is definite evidence of past climatic changes being synchronous across the whole planet. Although orbital changes in solar radiation took place gradually, the Earth's climate responded much less smoothly. Due to complex interactions between factors including greenhouse gas concentrations, ice-ocean albedo effects, and sea levels, the global climate has tended to switch abruptly between glacial and interglacial modes. Thus, a gradual shift in radiation balance after the LGM was manifest in rapid warming steps, initially soon after 15,000 BP in the northern hemisphere. This was accompanied by similarly rapid wetting of the climate in regions such as East Africa and the Mediterranean, and by cultural shifts such as the Kebaran–Natufian transition in Southwest Asia (see Rosen, this volume).

Orbital changes may have acted as the pacemaker for climatic fluctuations over multi-millennial time periods, but there have been other drivers of climate change over shorter timescales. "Sub-Milankovitch" climatic variations were clearly in evidence during the last glacial to interglacial transition in the form of reversals of climate that interrupted the last great global warming. The best-known of these is the Younger Dryas event, between 12,900 and 11,700 BP, when conditions became once again cold and dry. This climatic event involved a partial shutdown in the oceanic heat and salt "conveyor" due to glacial meltwater flux into the North Atlantic Ocean from the surrounding ice sheets. The Younger Dryas stadial was most clearly felt in adjacent land areas such as northwest Europe, but its footprint extended across the northern hemisphere and into the tropics. It did not, however, affect the southernmost parts of the southern hemisphere (e.g., New Zealand, Patagonia) which were instead affected by an Antarctic Cold Reversal that preceded the Younger Dryas by about a thousand years. The Earth's polar regions thus experienced a climate seesaw during the last Glacial-Interglacial transition.

In many dryland regions, including East Africa and Southwest Asia, the Younger Dryas seems to have been characterized by extended drought conditions. The transition from a cold, dry to a warm, wetter interglacial climate 11,700 years ago took place in less than a century, and apparently simultaneously over high and low latitudes (Rasmussen et al. 2006; Roberts et al. 1993). This major shift in climate thus occurred over a timescale that would have been easily detected by individual humans; in fact, it would have been impossible for any human group not to notice this radical shift in their natural world and available water resources, even though subsequent cultural adjustment would undoubtedly have taken time. One of those adjustments involved the adoption of plant and animal domesticates. While the relationship between climate change and domestication seems unlikely to have been a simple matter of cause and effect, it is equally true that farming evolved independently in at least three major centers during the first half of the Holocene, having failed to develop previously. The emergence of agriculture may have been possible only in an interglacial world populated by anatomically modern humans (Feynman and Ruzmaikin 2007; Richerson, Boyd, and Bettinger 2001).

One of the characteristic features of the Holocene climate has been its stability relative to, for example, the high-frequency variability that characterized much of the last glacial stage. None the less, climate has varied on a hierarchy of timescales and for a variety of different causes. Some have been abrupt in character, although none was as dramatic as the Younger Dryas. Probably the most important comparable event occurred around 8200 years ago, when there was a 100–150 year long cooling across much of the northern hemisphere (Alley and Ágústsdóttir 2005). The cause was again a pulse of glacial meltwater into the North Atlantic ocean, in this case from the final break-up of the Laurentide (Canadian) ice sheet over Hudson Bay. This event caused major drought in the Old World tropical drylands, as indicated by an abrupt fall in East African lake levels (Gasse 2000; Street-Perrott and Roberts 1983). The "8.2 ka" event probably also affected Southwest Asia, although independent palaeoclimatic records of it in this region are not common. Other centennial-scale abrupt climatic events have been identified for later periods of the Holocene (e.g., Lamb et al. 1995), but it is unclear how widespread these were. One such drought event has been recognized around 4200 BP in Southwest Asia with links postulated to the collapse of the Akkadian Empire and the Egyptian Old Kingdom (Cullen et al. 2000; Dalfes et al. 1997). Its spatial extent may have extended to the Indian Ocean monsoon weather system, since the Blue Nile flood is controlled by summer rainfall over Ethiopia; however, its ultimate cause is unknown.

Dramatic though these abrupt drought events may have been, they would have been less significant in the long run than underlying trends in Holocene climate linked to orbital changes in the receipt of solar radiation. This led to a gradual weakening of the African and Asian monsoon systems, and a significant decline in rainfall in many areas of the Old World tropics and subtropics between 6000 and 4000 BP (Fig. 1.5a–d). This was also the period of major cultural transformation that saw the rise of the first Near Eastern civilizations. As summer monsoon rains weakened and retreated, so the modern-day Saharan and Arabian deserts came into existence. Cattle-raising pastoralists were pushed southward into sub-Saharan Africa for the first time, to create cultures ancestral to the modern Maasai and Fulani (Hassan 2002; Marshall et al., this volume). Other human groups responded to mid-Holocene climatic desiccation by relocating from the eastern Sahara into well-watered "oases," notably along the river Nile, where flood irrigation developed to provide the economic basis for pre-Dynastic Nilotic civilization (Kuper and Kröpelin 2006). The decline in rainfall during mid-Holocene times was not gradual, but oscillatory, and indeed the 4200 BP drought event may have been no more than one of several fluctuations during a period of long-term climatic desiccation.

In East Africa, the "African Humid Period" came to an end around 6000–5000 BP, but there were important variations in the speed and timing of climatic desiccation at different sites (deMenocal et al. 2000; Gasse 2000). Some of this variability is likely to be due to dating imprecision and to differences of the response rate of different climate archives, such as pollen vs. isotopes, or small vs. large lake basins (Kiage and Liu 2006). However, given the complex spatial mosaic of different climatological regions in East Africa, part of the variability is also likely to reflect regional differences in climate history (Nicholson 1996). The Ethiopian Highlands provide the most detailed climate records for the northern sector of East Africa (see Umer et al. 2004 for a review). For basins such as Ziway-Shala-Abiyata, there is both lake-level evidence from marginal shorelines and sedimentary facies, and water chemistry reconstructions from diatom and stable isotope analyses of sediment cores (Fig. 1.5c–d). They show that a major decline in rainfall occurred around 5500 BP, with a return to less saline lake conditions and a wetter climate around 4000 BP and again around 2500 BP. A related sequence of events is evident farther south in the equatorial Great Lakes region from lake sediment cores and from pollen analysis from montane peat bogs (see Barker et al. 2004 for a review). Climatic calibration of the pollen data (Bonnefille and Chalié 2000) implies that after 4000 BP climate became more variable and therefore less reliable (Fig. 1.5e). Africa's only ice cores, from the top of Kilimanjaro (Thompson et al. 2002), also provide valuable data on higher-frequency climatic variability. This sequence also contains a

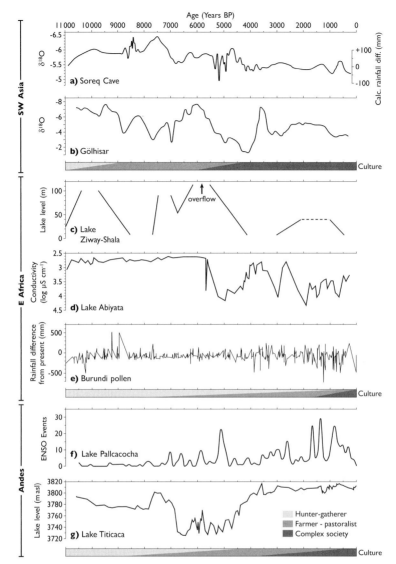

1.5 Selected proxy climate records and shifts in cultural complexity for Southwest Asia, East Africa, and Andean South America during the Holocene (complex society implies state formation, monumental architecture, writing, etc.). (a) stalagmite $\delta^{18}O$ and inferred change in rainfall from present-day, Soreq Cave, Israel (Bar-Matthews, Ayalon, and Kaufman 1998); (b) $\delta^{18}O$ from carbonates in Lake Gölhisar, Turkey (Eastwood et al. 2007); (c, d) lake-level and diatom-inferred salinity fluctuations in the Ziway-Shala-Abiyata basin, Ethiopian rift (Chalié and Gasse 2002; Gillespie, Street-Perrott, and Switsur 1983); (e) pollen-inferred rainfall changes, Burundi Highlands (Bonnefille and Chalié 2000); (f) frequency of El Niño events inferred from laminated sediments in Laguna Pallcacocha, Ecuador (Moy et al. 2002); (g) water level fluctuations in Lake Titicaca and inferred percent change in precipitation (Rowe and Dunbar 2004).

30 mm-thick accumulation of dust within the Northern Ice Field core dating to ca. 4000 BP that may be coincident with the 4200 BP drought event in Southwest Asia.

In Andean South America, the overall sequence of wet and dry periods during the Holocene is different from that in intertropical Africa, with a marked mid-Holocene phase of low lake water levels and rainfall. Lake Titicaca, for example, fell by about 85 m between 7000 and 4000 BP, representing a basin-wide precipitation on average about 11% lower than today (Rowe and Dunbar 2004) (Fig. 1.5f). This aridity in the northern Andean region coincided with a period when positive ENSO (El Niño–Southern Oscillation) mode conditions were less frequent in the circum-Pacific region (Markgraf and Diaz 2000). El Niño events are known to have occurred even in glacial times, but analysis of Pacific corals, varved lake sediments from Ecuador, mollusk species found at Peruvian archaeological sites, and other proxy climate records shows that their frequency and amplitude altered significantly during the Holocene (Donders, Wagner-Cremer, and Visscher 2008; Moy et al. 2002). These data indicate that key changes occurred at around 5000 and again at 3000 BP towards more active ENSO cycles in the equatorial Pacific that were comparable to the high-amplitude fluctuations known in recent decades (Fig. 1.5g). As at Kilimanjaro, cores have been drilled and analysed from the tropical ice caps on the highest Andean mountains, such as Quelccaya and Huascarán (Thompson, Mosley-Thompson, and Henderson 2000). These data, along with a suite of other paleoclimate data, have been integrated on a Pole-Equator-Pole (or PEP I) transect through North and South America (Markgraf and Seltzer 2001). A similar synthetic north-south PEP III transect was undertaken through Africa, Southwest Asia, and Europe (Battarbee, Gasse, and Stickley 2004).

During the last two millennia, the boundary conditions controlling global climate have been essentially the same as today, except for the sharp rise in atmospheric greenhouse gas concentrations during the last three centuries. Nonetheless, climate was far from constant as a result of secular variations in the receipt of solar radiation (e.g., due to sunspot cycles), the effects of large volcanic eruptions, and other factors (NRC 2006; Wanner et al. 2008; Stahl, this volume). Late Holocene climate changes include those associated with the Little Ice Age (ca. AD 1400–1850) and the preceding medieval climate anomaly (ca. AD 800–1400). While these periods are well-marked in the circum-North Atlantic region, their spatial extent and manifestation elsewhere on the planet are much less certain (Bradley, Hughes, and Diaz 2003). In many dryland regions such as East Africa and the American West, the medieval period was characterized by extended droughts (Cook et al. 2004; Laird et al. 1996; Stine 1994; Verschuren, Laird, and Cumming 2000), although in Southwest Asia, it was the time of the Little Ice Age that saw more arid conditions (Jones et al. 2006). In the American Southwest three major droughts between AD 990 and 1300 meant frequent failure of the maize harvest for the Ancestral Pueblo Indians, and seem likely to have contributed to the abandonment of settlements such as Mesa Verde (Benson et al. 2007; see also Kohler and Reed, this volume).

In addition to long-term climate trends linked to orbital forcing, there is also evidence of changes in climate variability through time, with many records, such as those recording ENSO events, suggesting that in mid- to late Holocene times climate became increasingly variable with frequent oscillations between wetter and drier conditions. The Soreq cave speleothems, for example, appear to show that the transitional period 6000 to 4000 BP was also one of greater climatic instability (Fig. 1.5a). As Rosen (2007) has pointed out, the greater variability of rainfall at this time, and consequent increasingly unreliable water supply, may have been as important as the amount of rainfall *per se* in stimulating technical innovation and cultural change. In South America, as in Southwest Asia, increased variability in climate and flood risk, along with unpredictable freshwater resources, seem to have been associated with a quickening pace of cultural development in the northern Andean region during the late Holocene (Dillehay, Kolata, and Pino 2004; Sandweiss et al. 2001), notwithstanding the difference in the overall trajectory of climate in this region towards wetter conditions after 5000 BP. Along with fluctuating water resources caused by quasi-cyclical changes in rainfall over decadal-centennial timescales, late Holocene landscapes became increasingly transformed by human agency. Forest clearance and other forms of land-use conversion added to the non-stationarity of environmental resources (Oldfield 2005; Roberts 1998), and may even have influenced the evolution of global climate by altering greenhouse gas fluxes (Ruddiman 2005).

COMPARING THE ARCHIVES

Natural archives for reconstructing long-term changes in climate and environment derive primarily from off-site, non-archaeological contexts, such as ice cores, lake sediments, and cave carbonates. Past human strategies for managing environmental risk in drylands can be inferred from archaeological excavation and systematic site survey, supplemented in regions such as Southwest Asia by significant documentary records. Comparing and combining these various archives poses nontrivial methodological challenges, for instance in terms of reliably correlating records. This is often best attempted via integrated regional multidisciplinary field projects (e.g., Gilbertson et al. 2007). Accurate dating plays a key role for comparisons between different archives, because past causal relations are commonly inferred from serial relations, i.e., the timing of events. As it is not possible for societal consequences to have *preceded* a purported environmental (or other) cause, we can use this logic to falsify or verify hypothesized relationships. In the case of 11th- to 13th-century AD droughts in the American Southwest, annual dating precision has been possible through dendrochronology. The same tree rings—often from timbers in archaeological sites—also provide evidence of past rainfall levels in the form of ring widths and densities. The chronological tie-in between climatic variability and cultural change in this case is therefore a well-founded one. In many other cases, however, such dating accuracy and precision may not be possible.

For most of prehistoric and early historic times, ^{14}C dating provides the main basis for sequence chronologies, both paleoclimatic and archaeological. After allowing for standard statistical errors and the time-varying additional uncertainty introduced by the need for ^{14}C calibration, the precision attributed to any individual date almost always rises to more than ±50 years. This is longer than the sub-centennial duration of most Holocene drought events recorded in continuous high-resolution paleoclimatic sequences. The statistical uncertainty in establishing whether two events have the same age can be reduced somewhat by using Bayesian methods on multiple age determinations through both time sequences (Blaauw et al. 2007). Even so, chronological uncertainties of non-annually resolved climate records are too large to answer decadal timescale questions; that is, those of most direct societal relevance. Instead there is a real danger that the problem of "suck-in and smear" can lead to erroneous—or at least not proven—correlations (Baillie 1991), with obvious consequences in terms of correctly or wrongly inferred causal relationships. For example, the 4200 BP drought event has been linked to ^{14}C-dated sediment cores from the Arabian-Persian Gulf, archaeological site abandonment in Upper Mesopotamia, a dust layer in the Kilimanjaro ice cap, and historical records of failing Nile floods in Egypt. But does the dating precision allow us to be sure that these are all recording the same event? The geopolitical consequences of water and food shortage occurring simultaneously throughout the ancient Near East would have been very different from those if Egypt suffered famine and social unrest while Mesopotamia was still well-stocked with food, and then vice versa (see Butzer 1997).

One way to test the synchronicity, or otherwise, of climatic and cultural changes is by using multiple techniques on the same stratigraphic sequence. In this case, pollen or sedimentological parameters can provide an index of human land-use change, while stable isotope or other geochemical/biological indicators offer a proxy for past climate. Because these can be derived from the same sediment records, there is no possibility of mis-correlation between them, even if their absolute age is not known precisely. For example, an annually varved late Holocene sedimentary sequence from Nar crater lake in central Anatolia shows pollen evidence for the latter stages of the Beyşehir Occupation cultural land-use phase (England et al. 2008). This phase came to an end during early Byzantine times and was followed by apparent landscape abandonment. The inferred age of its termination varies between about AD 400 and 700 in different individual pollen diagrams based on ^{14}C dating (e.g., Eastwood, Roberts, and Lamb 1998; Kaniewski et al. 2007). Did the inferred societal "collapse" in this region coincide with a period of drought conditions? The Nar record has also been analyzed for stable isotopes (Jones et al. 2006) which show that markedly dry climatic conditions prevailed between AD 400 and 500. With a ±150-year dating uncertainty for the end of the Beyşehir Occupation phase, it would be tempting to align intersite chronologies so that drought and landscape abandonment were synchronized. In fact, cultural pollen indicators in the Nar record do not decline until around AD 670 based on varve count ages, that is, two centuries later than the period of greatest aridity in the same record (Fig. 1.6). Examination of climatic and cultural history from the same sedimentary archive provides a rigorous test of the hypothesis that the late Antique societal crisis was prompted or inflamed by climatic stress, and it has been shown not to be the case.

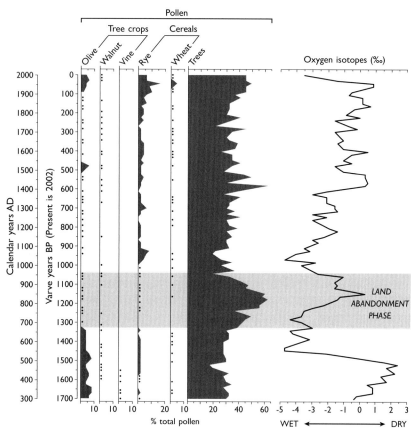

1.6 Stable isotope record of wet-dry climate shifts, and pollen record of human land-use change in Cappadocia, Turkey, for the last 1720 years from Nar lake. (Source: England et al. 2008; Jones et al. 2006).

CONCLUDING REMARKS

It can become temptingly easy to use climatic fluctuations as a catch-all explanation for socioeconomic changes in premodern times (see deMenocal 2001; Weiss and Bradley 2001), when in reality non-environmental factors were at least as important (Crumley 2000; Robertson et al. 2004). Societies were perfectly capable of "bucking" the climatic trend under appropriate circumstances, as shown by the example above from early Byzantine Anatolia. On the other side, it would be equally naïve to deny the possibility of a role for climatic variations in past human affairs. What is clear is that societal responses to environmental stresses and opportunities have not been predetermined in the past, but have been chosen from within a range of constraints, based on belief systems, economic dependency, social organization, and governance (Diamond 2005; Erickson 1999; Rosen 2007).

Understanding different societal choices in the past can help inform contemporary responses to present or future environmental risk, such as predicted human-induced climate change. Arguably we are better placed now than ever before to understand environmental changes over timescales longer than the human lifespan, such as the evolution of climate. On the other side, the pace of societal change is now faster than during times past, which may diminish the authority of experience as a guide to decision-making. More than ever before, we live in the "now." The timescales for policy-making and implementation by governments and corporations and the timescales of environmental change are still a long way from being aligned.

Acknowledgments

I am grateful to a number of colleagues who contributed to, or commented on, this chapter, particularly David Gilbertson, Fiona Marshall and Warren Eastwood. Diagrams were drawn by Brian Rogers at the Plymouth University Cartographic Unit.

NOTES
1. All dates in calendar years Before Present (BP).
2. See Zettler (2003, pp. 17ff.) and Marro and Kuzucuoğlu (2007) for a detailed chronological assessment of climatic and cultural changes in northeastern Syria for this time interval.

REFERENCES CITED

Alley, R.B., and A.M. Ágústsdóttir. 2005. The 8k Event: Cause and Consequences of a Major Holocene Abrupt Climate Change, *Quaternary Science Reviews* 24:1123–49.

Anderson, D. 1984. Depression, Dust Bowl, Demography, and Drought: The Colonial State and Soil Conservation in East Africa during the 1930s. *African Affairs* 83:321–44.

Baillie, M. G. L. 1991. Suck-in and Smear: Two Related Chronological Problems for the 90s. *Journal of Theoretical Archaeology* 2:12–16.

Barker, P., M. R. Talbot, F. A. Street-Perrott, F. Marret, J. Scourse, and E. Odada. 2004. Late Quaternary Climatic Variability in Intertropical Africa. In *Past*

Climate Variability through Europe and Africa, ed. R. W. Battarbee, F. Gasse, and C. Stickley, pp. 117–38. Dordrecht: Kluwer.

Bar-Matthews, M., A. Ayalon, and A. Kaufman. 1998. Middle to Late Holocene (6,500 Yr. Period) Paleoclimate in the Eastern Mediterranean Region from Stable Isotopic Composition of Speleothems from Soreq Cave, Israel. In *Water, Environment and Society in Times of Climatic Change*, ed. A. S. Issar and N. Brown, pp. 204–14. Dordrecht: Kluwer.

Battarbee, R. W., F. Gasse, and C. Stickley, eds. 2004. *Past Climate Variability through Europe and Africa*. Dordrecht: Kluwer.

Benson, L. V., M. S. Berry, E. A. Jolie, J. D. Spangler, D. W. Stahle, and E. M. Hattori. 2007. Possible Impacts of Early-11th-, Middle-12th-, and Late-13th-century Droughts on Western Native Americans and the Mississippian Cahokians. *Quaternary Science Reviews* 26:336–50.

Bergner, A. G. N., M. H. Trauth, and B. Bookhagen. 2003. Paleoprecipitation Estimates for the Lake Naivasha Basin (Kenya) during the Last 175 k.y. Using a Lake-balance Model. *Global and Planetary Change* 36:117–36.

Blaauw, M., J. A. Christen, D. Mauquoy, J. van der Plicht, and K. D. Bennett. 2007. Testing the Timing of Radiocarbon-dated Events between Proxy Archives. *The Holocene* 17:283–88.

Bonnefille, R., and F. Chalié. 2000. Pollen-inferred Precipitation Time-series from Equatorial Mountains, Africa, the Last 40 kyr BP. *Global and Planetary Change* 26:25–50

Bradley, R. S., M. K. Hughes, and H. F. Diaz. 2003. Climate in Medieval Time. *Science* 302:404–5.

Butzer, K. W. 1997. Sociopolitical Discontinuity in the Near East c. 2200 B.C.E.: Scenarios from Palestine and Egypt. In *Third Millenium BC Climate Change and Old World Collapse*, ed. H. N. Dalfes, G. Kukla, and H. Weiss, pp. 245–96. Berlin: Springer.

Chalié, F., and F. Gasse. 2002. Late Glacial–Holocene Diatom Record of Water Chemistry and Lake Level Change from the Tropical East African Rift Lake Abiyata (Ethiopia). *Palaeogeography, Palaeoclimatology, Palaeoecology* 187:259–83.

Cook, E. R., C. Woodhouse, C. M. Eakin, D. M. Meko, and D. W. Stahle. 2004. Long-term Aridity Changes in the Western United States. *Science* 306:1015–18.

Crumley, C. L. 2000. From Garden to Globe: Linking Time and Space with Meaning and Memory. In *The Way the Wind Blows: Climate, History, and Human Action*, ed. R. J. McIntosh, J. A. Tainter, and S. K. McIntosh, pp. 193–208. New York: Columbia University Press.

Cullen, H. M., P. D. deMenocal, S. Hemming, G. Hemming, F. H. Brown, T. Guilderson, and F. Sirocko. 2000. Climate Change and the Collapse of the Akkadian Empire: Evidence from the Deep Sea. *Geology* 28:379–82.

Dai, A., P. J. Lamb, K. E. Trenberth, M. Hulme, P. D. Jones and P. Xie. 2004. The Recent Sahel Drought Is Real. *International Journal of Climatology* 24:1323–31.

Dalfes, H. N., G. Kukla, and H. Weiss, eds. 1997. *Third Millennium BC Climate Change and the Old World Collapse.* Proceedings of NATO ASI Series I, vol. 49. Berlin: Springer Verlag.

deMenocal, P. B. 2001. Cultural Responses to Climate Change during the Late Holocene. *Science* 292:667–73.

deMenocal, P., J. Ortiz, T. Guilderson, J. Adkins, M. Sarnthein, L. Baker, and M. Yarusinsky. 2000. Abrupt Onset and Termination of the African Humid Period: Rapid Climate Responses to Gradual Insolation Forcing. *Quaternary Science Reviews* 19:347–61.

Diamond, J. 2005. *Collapse. How Societies Choose to Fail or Succeed.* London: Allen Lane.

Dillehay, T., A. L. Kolata, and M. Q. Pino. 2004. Pre-industrial Human and Environment Interactions in Northern Peru during the Late Holocene. *The Holocene* 14:272–81.

Donders, T. H., F. Wagner-Cremer, and H. Visscher. 2008. Integration of Proxy Data and Model Scenarios for the Mid-Holocene Onset of Modern ENSO Variability. *Quaternary Science Reviews* 27:571–79.

Dühnforth, M., A. G. N. Bergner, and M. H. Trauth. 2006. Early Holocene Water Budget of the Nakuru-Elmenteita Basin, Central Kenya Rift. *Journal of Paleolimnology* 36:281–94.

Eastwood, W. J., M. J. Leng, N. Roberts, and B. Davis. 2007. Holocene Climate Change in the Eastern Mediterranean Region: A Comparison of Stable Isotope and Pollen Data from Lake Gölhisar, Southwest Turkey. *Journal of Quaternary Science* 22:327–41.

Eastwood, W. J., N. Roberts, and H. F. Lamb. 1998. Palaeoecological and Archaeological Evidence for Human Occupance in Southwest Turkey: The Beyşehir Occupation Phase. *Anatolian Studies* 48:69–86.

England, A., W. J. Eastwood, C. N. Roberts, R. Turner, and J. F. Haldon. 2008. Historical Landscape Change in Cappadocia (Central Turkey): A Palaeoecological Investigation of Annually Laminated Sediments from Nar Lake. *The Holocene* 18(8): 1229–45.

Erickson, C. L. 1999. Neo-environmental Determinism and Agrarian "Collapse" in Andean Prehistory. *Antiquity* 73:634–42.

Feynman, J., and A. Ruzmaikin. 2007. Climate Stability and the Development of Agricultural Societies. *Climatic Change* 84:295–311.

Gasse, F. 2000. Hydrological Changes in the African Tropics since the Last Glacial Maximum. *Quaternary Science Reviews* 19:189–211.

Gilbertson, D., G. Barker, D. Mattingly, C. Palmer, J. Grattan, and B. Pyatt. 2007. Archaeology and Desertification: The Landscapes of the Wadi Faynan. In

Archaeology and Desertification: The Degradation and Well-being of the Wadi Faynan Landscape, Southern Jordan, ed. G. Barker, D. Gilbertson, and D. Mattingly, pp. 397–421. Oxford: Oxbow Books.

Gillespie, R., F. A. Street-Perrott, and R. Switsur. 1983. Post-glacial Arid Episodes in Ethiopia Have Implications for Climate Prediction. *Nature* 306:681–83.

Hassan, F. 2002. *Droughts, Food, and Culture: Ecological Change and Food Security in Africa's Later Prehistory*. New York: Kluwer.

Hulme, M. 1992. Rainfall Changes in Africa—1931–1960 to 1961–1990. *International Journal of Climatology* 12:685–99.

IPCC. 2007. *Climate Change 2007—The Physical Science Basis. Working Group I Contribution to the Fourth Assessment Report of the Intergovernmental Panel on Climate Change*. Cambridge: Cambridge University Press.

Jones, M. D., N. Roberts, M. J. Leng, and M. Türkeş. 2006. A High-resolution Late Holocene Lake Isotope Record from Turkey and Links to North Atlantic and Monsoon Climate. *Geology* 34(5): 361–64.

Kaniewski, D., E. Paulissen, V. De Laet, K. Dossche, and M. Waelkens. 2007. A High-resolution Late Holocene Landscape Ecological History Inferred from an Intramontane Basin in the Western Taurus Mountains, Turkey. *Quaternary Science Reviews* 26:2201–18.

Kiage, L. M., and K.-B. Liu. 2006. Late Quaternary Paleoenvironmental Changes in East Africa: A Review of Multiproxy Evidence from Palynology, Lake Sediments, and Associated Records. *Progress in Physical Geography* 30(5): 633–58.

Kuper, R., and S. Kröpelin. 2006. Climate-controlled Holocene Occupation in the Sahara: Motor of Africa's Evolution. *Science* 313:803–7.

Laird, K. R., S. C. Fritz, K. A. Maasch, and B. F. Cumming. 1996. Greater Drought Intensity and Frequency before AD 1200 in the Northern Great Plains, USA. *Nature* 384:552–54.

Lamb, H. F., F. Gasse, A. Benkaddour, N. el-Hamouti, S. van der Kaars, W. T. Perkins, N. J. Pearce, and N. Roberts. 1995. Relation between Century-scale Holocene Arid Intervals in Tropical and Temperate Zones. *Nature* 373:134–37.

Markgraf, V., and H. F. Diaz, eds. 2000. *El Niño and the Southern Oscillation: Multiscale Variability and Global and Regional Impacts*. Cambridge: Cambridge University Press.

Markgraf, V., and G. Seltzer. 2001. Pole-Equator-Pole Paleoclimates of the Americas Integration: Towards the Big Picture. In *Interhemispheric Climate Linkages*, ed. V. Markgraf, pp. 433–22. San Diego, CA: Academic Press.

Marro, C., and C. Kuzucuoğlu, eds. 2007. *Sociétés humaines et changement climatique à la fin du troisième millénaire: une crise a-t-elle eu lieu en Haute-Mésopotamie?* Varia Anatolica. Paris: De Boccard.

Mortimore, M. J. 1989. *Adapting to Drought: Farmers, Famines and Desertification in West Africa*. Cambridge: Cambridge University Press.

Mortimore, M. J., and W. M. Adams. 2001. Farmer Adaptation, Change and "Crisis" in the Sahel. *Global Environmental Change* 11:49–57.

Moy, C. M., G. O. Seltzer, G. T. Rodbell, and D. M. Anderson. 2002. Variability of El Niño/Southern Oscillation Activity at Millennial Timescales during the Holocene Epoch. *Nature* 420:162–65.

NRC. 2006. *Surface Temperature Reconstructions for the Past 2,000 Years*. Washington, DC: National Academies Press.

Nicholson, S. E. 1996. A Review of Climate Dynamics and Climate Variability in Eastern Africa. In *The Limnology, Climatology and Paleoclimatology of the East African Lakes*, ed. T. C. Johnson and E. Odada, pp. 25–56. The International Decade for the East African Lakes (IDEAL). Amsterdam: Gordon and Breach.

Oldfield, F. 2005. *Environmental Change*. Cambridge: Cambridge University Press.

Rasmussen, S. O., K. K. Andersen, A. M. Svensson, J. P. Steffensen, B. M. Vinther, H. B. Clausen, M.-L. S. Andersen, et al. 2006. A New Greenland Ice Core Chronology for the Last Glacial Termination. *Journal of Geophysical Research* 111:D06102.

Richerson, P. J., R. Boyd, and R. L. Bettinger. 2001. Was Agriculture Impossible during the Pleistocene but Mandatory during the Holocene? A Climate Change Hypothesis. *American Antiquity* 66:387–411.

Roberts, N. 1998. *The Holocene: An Environmental History*. 2nd ed. Oxford: Blackwell.

Roberts, N., and P. Barker. 1993. Landscape Stability and Biogeomorphic Response to Past and Future Climatic Shifts in Africa. In *Landscape Sensitivity*, ed. D. Thomas and R. Allison, pp. 65–82. Chichester: John Wiley & Sons.

Roberts, N., M. Taieb, P. Barker, B. Damnati, M. Icole, and D. Williamson. 1993. Timing of Younger Dryas Climatic Event in East Africa from Lake-level Changes. *Nature* 366:146–48.

Robertson, P., D. Taylor, S. Doyle, and R. Marchant. 2004. Famine, Climate and Crisis in Western Uganda. In *Past Climate Variability through Europe and Africa*, ed. R. W. Battarbee, F. Gasse, and C. Stickley, pp. 535–49. Dordrecht: Kluwer.

Rosen, A. M. 2007. *Civilizing Climate. Social Responses to Climate Change in the Ancient Near East*. Lanham, MD: Altamira Press.

Rowe, H. D., and R. B. Dunbar. 2004. Hydrologic-energy Balance Constraints on the Holocene Lake-level History of Lake Titicaca, South America. *Climate Dynamics* 23:439–54.

Ruddiman, W. F. 2005. *Plows, Plagues and Petroleum. How Humans Took Control of Climate*. Princeton, NJ: Princeton University Press.

Sandweiss, D. H., K. A. Maasch, R. L. Burger, J. B. Richardson, III, H. B. Rollins, and A. Clement. 2001. Variation in Holocene El Niño Frequencies: Climate Records and Cultural Consequences in Ancient Peru. *Geology* 29:603–6.

Stine, S. 1994. Extreme and Persistent Drought in California and Patagonia during Mediaeval Time. *Nature* 369:546–49.

Street-Perrott, F. A., and N. Roberts. 1983. Fluctuations in Closed Basin Lakes as an Indicator of Past Atmospheric Circulation Patterns. In *Variations in the Global Water Budget*, ed. F. A. Street-Perrott, M. Beran, and R. A. S. Ratcliffe, pp. 331–45. Dordrecht: Reidel.

Thompson, L. G., E. Mosley-Thompson, and K. A. Henderson. 2000. Ice-core Palaeoclimate Records in Tropical South America since the Last Glacial Maximum. *Journal of Quaternary Science* 15:377–94.

Thompson, L. G., E. Mosley-Thompson, M. E. Davis, K. A. Henderson, H. H. Brecher, V. S. Zagorodnov, T. A. Mashiota, P.-N. Lin, V. N. Mikhalenko, D. R. Hardy, and J. Beer. 2002. Kilimanjaro Ice Core Records: Evidence of Holocene Climate Change in Tropical Africa. *Science* 298:589–93.

Trauth, M. H., M. A. Maslin, A. Deino, and M. R. Strecker. 2005. Late Cenozoic Moisture History of East Africa. *Science* 309:2051–53.

Umer, M., D. Legesse, F. Gasse, R. Bonnefille, H. F. Lamb, M. J. Leng, and A. Lamb. 2004. Late Quaternary Climate Changes in the Horn of Africa. In *Past Climate Variability through Europe and Africa*, ed. R. W. Battarbee, F. Gasse, and C. Stickley, pp. 159–80. Dordrecht: Kluwer.

Verschuren, D., K. R. Laird, and B. F. Cumming. 2000. Rainfall and Drought in Equatorial East Africa during the Past 1100 Years. *Nature* 403:410–14.

Verschuren, D., J. Tibby, P. R. Leavitt, and N. Roberts. 1999. The Environmental History of a Climate-sensitive Lake in the Former "White Highlands" of Central Kenya. *Ambio* 28:494–501.

Wanner, H., J. Beer, J. Bütikofer, T. J. Crowley, U. Cubasch, J. Flückiger, and H. Goosse. 2008. Mid- to Late Holocene Climate Change—An Overview. *Quaternary Science Reviews* 27:1791–1828.

Webster, J. B. 1979. Noi! Noi! Famines as an Aid to Interlacustrine Chronology. In *Chronology, Migration and Drought in Interlacustrine Africa*, ed. J. B. Webster, pp. 1–37. Dalhousie: Longman and Dalhousie University Press.

Weiss, H., and R. S. Bradley. 2001. What Drives Societal Collapse? *Science* 291:609–10.

Zettler, R. L. 2003. Reconstructing the World of Ancient Mesopotamia: Divided Beginnings and Holistic History. *Journal of the Economic and Social History of the Orient* 46:3–45.

2

Prehistoric Pastoralists and Social Responses to Climatic Risk in East Africa

FIONA MARSHALL, KATHERINE GRILLO, AND LEE ARCO

INTRODUCTION

Holocene climate change has long been thought to have played a major role in societal transformations such as the beginnings of food production and the decline of ancient cities and polities. Temporally and spatially large-scale climatic change, such as the desertification of the Sahara, may admit a limited range of human responses. The effects of more common smaller scale variability, though, have been much debated. Some scholars emphasize catastrophic societal declines in the face of climatic fluctuations, but others stress the extent to which climatic variability has stimulated successful technological and cultural innovation and resilience (Fagan 2004; Hassan 2002; McIntosh, Tainter, and McIntosh 2000; Rosen 2007; Weiss and Bradley 2001). The reactions of African pastoralists to medium- and small-scale environmental risks provide an interesting counterpoint to studies based on sedentary, agricultural, and village-based societies.

Pastoralism developed more than 8000 years ago in northeastern Africa and was the earliest form of food production on the continent (Gifford-Gonzalez 2005; Marshall and Hildebrand 2002; Neumann 2005). The earliest pastoralists relied on cattle and subsequently integrated sheep, goat, and donkeys into their herds (Close and Wendorf 1992; Linseele et al. 2009;

Marshall 2007). Savanna environments such as those in which the earliest African pastoralism developed and spread are, however, especially vulnerable to climatic perturbations (Sala et al. 2000; Sankaran et al. 2005). In these settings pastoral social and economic systems have allowed long-term and flexible approaches to coping with environmental risk. As the African Humid phase ended and hyperarid conditions developed in the Sahara between 6000 and 5000 years ago, herders moved more frequently, and ultimately most abandoned the Sahara, migrating long distances to better watered areas such as those of the Sahel and as far south as the equator in eastern Africa (di Lernia 2002; Kuper and Kropelin 2006; Marshall and Hildebrand 2002). It was only after ca. 4000 years ago that African plants were domesticated (D'Andrea et al. 2007; Neumann 2005).

East Africa is an especially interesting place in which to examine long-term responses of African pastoralists to medium- and short-term climatic fluctuations because unlike the Sahara it was never abandoned. Pastoralism has, therefore, a five thousand year history in the region. During a low rainfall period between 5000 and 4000 years ago small numbers of herders moved into East Africa from the Sudan and Ethiopia (Ambrose 1998; Barthelme 1985; Phillipson 1977; Robbins 1972). A more favorable modern climatic regime developed by 3400 years ago and at this time more numerous and more varied pastoral groups settled southern Kenya (Ambrose 1984b, Marshall 1990) (Table 2.1). Early prehistoric pastoral sites, however, are concentrated in savanna grasslands characterized by relatively unpredictable rainfall.

In this chapter we examine the changing nature of climatic and ecological challenges and East African pastoral responses during the "Exploratory Northern Pastoral Phase" (ENP), 5500–3500 BP and the later "Southern Settlement Phase" (SSP) <3500–2000 BP of the Pastoral Neolithic. The distribution of key northern and southern sites is illustrated in Figure 2.1. Table 2.1 summarizes the culture-historical sequence of the region and provides a framework for understanding the temporal, geographic, and local variability that underpins differing environmental risks and responses. Unless otherwise indicated all dates used in this paper follow regional conventions and are presented in uncalibrated ^{14}C years before present (BP). For arbitrary time periods conventionally delineated by BP intervals we use intercal medium probability estimates to provide alternative calibrated BC estimates (Table 2.2). Readers should be aware that these dates do not imply

Table 2.1. Cultural History of the Pastoral Neolithic in East Africa

EXPLORATORY NORTHERN PASTORAL PHASE

REGIONAL TRADITIONS	ORIGINS/LINGUISTIC AFFILIATION	TEMPORAL RANGE	SUBSISTENCE ECONOMY	MATERIAL CULTURE	NOTES/DEFINING CHARACTERISTICS
Nderit	Southern Cushitic?	5000–3500 BP	Generalized pastoralism, including sheep, goats, and some cattle; hunting and fishing	"Nderit" ceramic tradition including figurines, obsidian microliths, exotic ornamentation	Megalithic pillar sites near Lake Turkana, group cemeteries. Later sites with Nderit pottery found throughout Central Rift
Ileret	Southern Cushitic?	4000–? BP	Unknown, likely generalized pastoralism	"Ileret" ceramic tradition, stone bowls	Connection with Nderit tradition poorly understood, either contemporary or Ileret may be derivative

SOUTHERN SETTLEMENT PHASE

REGIONAL TRADITIONS	ORIGINS/LINGUISTIC AFFILIATION	TEMPORAL RANGE	SUBSISTENCE ECONOMY	MATERIAL CULTURE	NOTES/DEFINING CHARACTERISTICS
Elmenteitan	Southern Nilotic?	3000–1200 BP	Specialized cattle, sheep, and goat pastoralism	Blade-based obsidian lithic technology, undecorated or lugged ceramic vessels	Highland western and southwestern Kenya, Loita/Mara plains, western side of central Rift

Savanna Pastoral Neolithic (SPN)	Southern Cushitic?	3300–1200 BP	Specialized cattle, sheep, and goat pastoralism	Highly diverse lithic and ceramic industries (including Narosura, Akira, Marangishu), stone bowls	Highland central and southwestern Kenya, Serengeti/Mara plains
Eburran Phase 5	Indigenous early Holocene populations	5000–1200 BP	Hunting/gathering, gradual adoption of domestic stock	Blade-based obsidian lithics with characteristic platform preparation, range of ceramic types found in association (including Akira, Salasun, Marangishu)	Sites found in Naivasha and Nakuru basins of the central Rift, intensive interaction with SPN groups, avoidance of Elmenteitan?
(Late) Kansyore	Indigenous early Holocene populations	3000–? BP	Hunting/gathering/fishing, some adoption of domestic stock	Highly decorated "Kansyore" ceramics	Contemporary with food producers, domestic fauna found at few later Kansyore sites

Source: Ambrose 2001; Dale 2007; Nelson n.d. 1995; Prendergast 2008

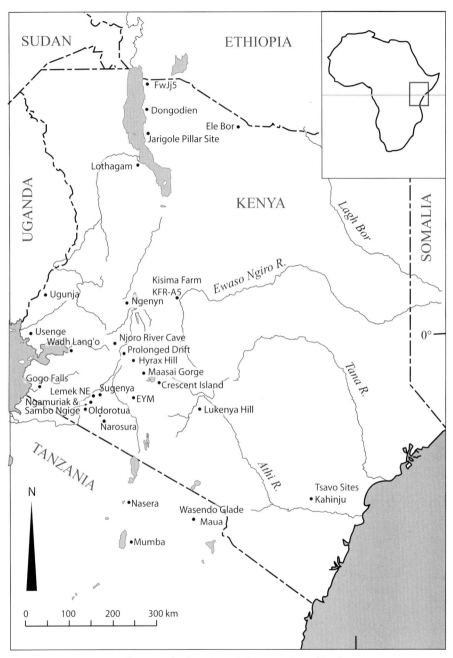

2.1 Map showing the location of sites mentioned in the text.

Table 2.2 Radiocarbon Dates for Select Pastoral Neolithic Sites*

EXPLORATORY NORTHERN PASTORAL PHASE

SITE	BP	CAL BP	BC/AD	MATERIAL	LAB ID	REFERENCE
Dongodien	3945±135	4824–4000	2875–2051 BC	charcoal	SUA-637	(Barthelme 1985)
	3890±60	4513–4104	2564–2155 BC	charcoal	P-2610	(Barthelme 1985)
Il Lokeridede	4180±60	4849–4531	2900–2582 BC	charcoal	TO-4911	(Koch et al. 2002)
Ileret Stone Bowl Site	4000±140	4843–4090	2894–2141 BC	bone apatite (mammal)	GX-4643A	(Barthelme 1985)

SOUTHERN SETTLEMENT PHASE

SITE	BP	CAL BP	BC/AD	MATERIAL	LAB ID	REFERENCE
Ngamuriak (Elmenteitan)	2135±140	2485–1740	536BC–210 AD	charcoal	GX-8533	(Robertshaw 1990)
	1940±140	2305–1555	356BC–395 AD	charcoal	GX-8534	(Robertshaw 1990)
Njoro River Cave (Elmenteitan)	2900±75	3319–2851	1370–902 BC	charcoal	Y-220	(Merrick and Monaghan 1984)
	3165±100	3636–3082	1687–1133 BC	charcoal	Y-222	(Merrick and Monaghan 1984)
Crescent Island	2045±125	2331–1737	382BC–214 AD	bone apatite	GX-4319/A	(Bower et al 1977)
Causeway (SPN)	2795±155	3360–2500	1411–551 BC	bone gelatin	GX-4587-G	Onyango-Abuje 1977)
Narosura (SPN)	2430±115	2758–2163	809–214 BC	charcoal	N-700	(Odner 1972)
	2840±120	3322–2751	1373–802 BC	charcoal	N-702	(Odner 1972)
Enkapune ya Muto (Eburran 5)	4680±70	5589–5290	3640–3341 BC	charcoal	ISGS-1742	(Ambrose 1998)
	2680±70	2964–2547	1015–598 BC	charcoal	ISGS-1733	(Ambrose 1998)
KFR-A5 Porcupine Cave	2320±160	2750–1990	801–41 BC	bone?	HEL-852	(Siiriäinen 1977)
	2830±120	3320–2748	1371–799 BC	charcoal	HEL-532	(Siiriäinen 1977)

*All calibrated ages BP and calendrical BC/AD dates calculated using IntCal 09, OxCal v4.1 (Bronk Ramsey 2009), 95.4% confidence (two-sigma range). Note: Charcoal dates reported where possible; only earliest and latest dates from each site are reported here.

precision. For key radiocarbon dates we calculated calibrated BC/cal BP dates using IntCal 09, OxCal v4.1 (Bronk Ramsey 2009).

Scholars have not previously focused on diachronic differences in social and economic strategies available to prehistoric East African pastoralists for coping with environmental risk. In order to model these, therefore, we first review ethnographic data on environmental risks and examine the range of coping strategies employed by contemporary African herders. New information on global ENSO oscillations, more fine-grained data from African lake cores, and data acquired from the Kilimanjaro ice core also provide fresh perspectives on spatial and temporal climatic fluctuations and the challenges that these posed for prehistoric pastoralists in East Africa. We argue that two factors, climatic variability across space and through time, and fluctuations in the densities and the social organization of early East African herders determined the strategies available to ancient East African pastoralists for countering climatic risk.

CONTEMPORARY PASTORALIST AND RISK

African pastoralism has been defined as a social and economic system where people are primarily dependent on their livestock and rely on spatial mobility as a survival strategy (Dyson Hudson and Dyson Hudson 1980:16). Livestock is also of central social and symbolic importance (McCabe 2004:46; Spear and Waller 1993). Historically, African pastoralist populations have moved to obtain forage and water for their herds and to take advantage of differences in local topography, rainfall patterns, and vegetation (Behnke et al. 1993; Galvin et al. 2001; Mace 1991). In most of Africa, pastoralist groups have also relied on broad and flexible subsistence bases, focusing on strategic management of sheep, goat, and cattle herds, hunting, fishing, seasonal cultivation, and exchange of goods and services with hunter-gatherers and neighboring agriculturalists (Dahl and Hjort 1976; Homewood 2008; Spear and Waller 1993). Over the long term the greatest hazards for African pastoralists have been the effects of drought and disease and risks associated with livestock raiding and conflict (McCabe 2004).

It has been argued that there are fundamental differences, however, between the risks associated with more arid or disequilibrium (<400 mm/yr) and wetter or equilibrium savanna ecosystems (>800 mm/yr) (Behnke, Scoones, and Kerven 1993). Rangeland ecologists view the arid grasslands as persistent but inherently unstable ecosystems with especially unpredictable and variable rainfall and frequent droughts (Coppock 1993; Behnke, Scoones, and Kerven 1993). Distinctive, opportunistic, and highly mobile pastoral systems with frequent stock crashes are considered characteristic of disequilibrium savannas (Behnke and Scoones 1993; Le Houérou, Bingham, and Skerbek 1988; Mortimore 1998). Success in these areas is dependent on the ability of pastoral households to move over large areas and access diverse terrains (McCabe 2004). Savanna grasslands with rainfall of >800 mm/yr, on the other hand, are more vulnerable to bush encroachment and increased disease risk as a result of tsetse fly infestation (Coppock 1993; Sankaran et al. 2005). Pastoralists in these areas are typically less mobile. In wetter regions complex relationships also exist between both the cycles of increased bush and wooded cover _versus_ open grassland and the effects of fire, grazing by domestic stock, and browsing by giraffe, elephants, and other wild ungulates (Dublin 1986, 1995; Lamprey and Waller 1990; Sankaran et al. 2005). Up to a point, heavier pastoral grazing and burning along with higher giraffe and elephant populations result in more open grasslands and lower disease threats. Beyond this point woody encroachment increases, tsetse populations rise, and environmental impacts are longer term.

These relationships between savanna ecosystems and environmental risks provide the basis for further consideration of social and economic coping strategies, the most fundamental of which is mobility. Scholars have debated relations between mobility and African pastoral social systems since the 1940s (Evans-Pritchard 1940; Dyson-Hudson and McCabe 1985; McCabe 2000). It is clear, though, that the social organization of African pastoralists provides complex and flexible frameworks for addressing environmental risks. Although diverse, they are responsive to the exigencies of mobility and day-to-day demands and perturbations of pastoral systems. Most are non-hierarchical and decentralized but have resilient mechanisms in place for economic and social exchange. Nested relations among lineages and clans create regional coalitions and age set systems allow long-distance contacts, cooperative social and political links, exchange of information, and access to distant water and pastures and refuge grazing areas (Homewood 2008; Little 1999; Ryan et al. 2000; Salzman 1999; Schneider 1979). Decision-making by individual households, in combination with clan and age set–based systems, allow rapid individual and group reactions to changing circumstances (McCabe 1999, 2004; Tavakolian 1999).

Cooperative actions such as giving or loaning livestock to friends and relatives, sharing, and exchanging information reinforce social bonds within families, clans, and between age sets and are often considered mechanisms of risk management (Legge 1989; Robinson 1989; Ryan et al. 2000; Ryan this volume). Communities work together to preserve and access grazing for drought years in montane forests or far from permanent water (McCabe 2004). On the other hand, use of warfare and raiding to gain access to lands, grazing, and cattle are common but less discussed approaches to recouping stock and combating drought-related losses (Fukui and Turton 1979; McCabe 2004). Violence of this kind is usually small scale, however, involving fewer than 20 people, and is spontaneous and relatively uncoordinated. Nevertheless, the impact can be significant, with hundreds or even thousands of head of livestock stolen.

A complex relationship exists among the many proximate causes for raiding. There has been much discussion of the relative roles of social structure and age set institutions, as well as historic contingencies, including colonialism and the introduction of firearms in the history of raiding, but there is good evidence for increases in debt-related disputes and raiding during times of climate change, drought, and famine (Almagor 1979; Tornay 1979; Turton 1977, 1979). Some scholars have argued that conflict is inevitable in unstable, non-equilibrium pastoral systems (Cousins 1996). Moreover, as a result of long-term studies of raiding in arid regions of eastern Africa, Turton (1977, 1979) argues that ecologically and economically motivated raiding and warfare play a significant role in creating and maintaining separate pastoral identities.

Emigration out of the pastoral system is another uncommon but consistent response of contemporary herders to climate change, drought, and disaster. Contemporary Sahelian pastoralists maintain relationships with agricultural groups or sectors of their own societies in the better-watered south and depend on these ties during droughts (Nicolaisen 1963). In eastern Africa there are historic cases of pastoral families taking refuge with hunter-gatherers, situations which entail long- or short-term identity shifts (Kenny 1981; Spencer 1973; Waller 1988). In times of disaster pastoralists today often rely on food aid distributed to settled communities; for some individuals agriculture or wage-labor in cities offer alternatives to nomadic pastoral life.

Key ecological factors that affect the nature of environmental risks include the distribution of equilibrium versus non-equilibrium savannas, the availability of permanent water, and the proximity of diverse environments. McCabe (2004:236) notes that specific strategies used by present-day pastoralists to combat risk resulting from climatic change and drought are contingent on a range of factors but are complex and nonlinear. They vary from household to household depending upon numerous factors: other families with whom the group is cooperating, labor availability, memory or knowledge of successful responses to similar disasters, family growth, evaluation of forage patches in relation to types, numbers, and ages of family herds, as well as access to water and grazing, threat of disease, predators, and of raiding and warfare. There is, therefore, a great deal of variability within and between years in individual responses to climatic fluctuations. Nevertheless, a range of common patterns is discernible. These include employing various scales of mobility, herding diverse livestock species over large and varied terrain, maintaining clan- and age set–based social systems discussed above, engaging in raiding and warfare, increasing cultivation or other economic diversification, and emigration out of the pastoral system to towns or cities (Galvin et al. 2001; Homewood 2008; McCabe 2004; Fukui and Turton 1979). These social and economic responses are contingent on a wide range of specific factors, but are broadly constrained by the number of people using a particular landscape, political relations among them, and resultant access to large areas and varied terrain.

Similarities among past and present pastoralist landscapes, the productivity of savanna biomes, dependence on donkeys, cattle, sheep, and goat, and patterns of land use all suggest that aspects of these contemporary strategies for managing environmental risks are relevant (*sensu* Wylie 1985) to understanding ancient pastoralism. On the other hand, the presence of large cities and integration into market economies and world systems are obvious differences. The information reviewed here demonstrates that the ecology of savanna grasslands greatly influences threats of both drought and disease and that relational analogies exist between operation of these mechanisms in the present and the past. Similarly, rainfall and topography and density of people and livestock on the landscape affect the range of contemporary pastoral responses to environmental threats, constraining possibilities for cooperative stock-sharing, combative raiding, access to refuge grazing, or possibilities for refuge. As a result, we argue that two factors, the precise nature of climatic variability across space and through time, and fluctuations in the densities and the social organization of early East African herders, are key to modeling the strategies available to ancient East African pastoralists for countering climatic risk. Furthermore, differences between the present and the past in options for economic diversification, including the lack of plant cultivation or ancient cities during the Pastoral Neolithic, lead us to hypothesize that ancient pastoral solutions to environmental or climatic stress in East Africa would have been more socially and politically than economically varied.

ARCHAEOLOGICAL FRAMEWORK AND CLIMATIC VARIABILITY

Following Bower et al. (1977), the term Pastoral Neolithic is used to refer to East African societies with a Later Stone Age lithic technology, ceramic vessels, and an economic base relying on domestic stock. We focus on changing environmental risks encountered by archaeologically visible earlier vs. later stone-using pastoral groups (see Tables 2.1, 2.2). The earlier "Exploratory Northern Pastoral Phase" (ENP) as defined here encompasses Nderit, Ileret, and other northern Kenyan archaeological entities dating between 5000 and 3500 BP. The later "Southern Settlement Phase" (SSP) groups date to the Savanna Pastoral Neolithic (SPN) (<3500–2000 BP) and include Elmenteitan, later Kansyore, Eburran 5a, and other contemporary archaeological "cultures." This framework is useful for contrasting earlier and later pastoralists, but does not imply cultural continuity between northern and southern regions. The date 2000 BP is an arbitrary, but useful, end point for this study because it allows us to focus on responses of stone-using pastoralists to environmental change prior to the activities of and interactions with Iron Age agriculturalists in the region.

East African pastoralists of the ENP are best known from sites dating to 5000–4000 BP in the Lake Turkana basin associated with use of Nderit or Ileret ceramics (Tables 2.1, 2.2). Two types of early pastoral sites have been found in northern Kenya: open domestic sites and stone pillar cemetery and ceremonial sites (Barthelme 1985; Nelson 1995; Robbins 2006). At the Jarigole Pillar Site burials, diverse ceramic vessels, ornaments, and figurines were found (Nelson 1995; Grillo pers. obs. 2008) but there is no evidence of domestic settlement. Domestic sites such as Dongodien, on the other hand, preserve hearths, lithics, and diverse faunas but contain no structures or stratigraphic evidence for long-term settlement (Barthelme 1985; Marshall,

Barthelme, and Stewart 1984). The settlement and faunal data are consistent with relatively high residential mobility and a broad subsistence base including sheep, goat, some cattle, fishing, and hunting (Table 2.3) (see also Kiura 2005). Northern Kenyan sites predate current evidence for African plant domesticates (D'Andrea et al. 2007; Neumann 2005). There is no direct information on wild plant use, however, because of poor preservation and retrieval of plant remains. Contemporary hunter-gatherer sites have not been documented close to Lake Turkana, and site distributions suggest that mobile early pastoralists moved at low densities into a lightly populated or uninhabited region and lacked forager neighbors (Barthelme 1985).

Numerous pastoral sites demonstrate that a variety of herders with diverse origins successfully settled the southern regions 3500–2000 BP. Differences in the geography and populations significantly affected risks faced by stone-using pastoralists. Northern Kenya is significantly less topographically diverse than regions to the south, rivers are seasonal, and Lake Turkana is the only major body of water. By contrast, southern Kenya and northern Tanzania are dominated by significant well-watered highlands and bisected by the Rift Valley with western regions adjacent to Lake Victoria.

Table 2.3. Relative Proportions of Wild and Domestic Fauna in Savanna Pastoral Neolithic and Elmenteitan Sites

	WILD MAMMALS	DOMESTIC MAMMALS	BIRDS %	REPTILES %	FISH %	N = TAXONOMIC NISP
Kadero, Sudan	21.0	79.0	rare	rare	v. common	1815 mammals
Dongodien, Nderit	0.5	4.4	0.3	0.2	94.6	2576
Narosura, SPN	7.0	93.0	0.0	0.0	0.0	1215
Crescent Island Main, SPN	18.4	81.4	0.2	0.0	0.0	526
Prolonged Drift, SPN	81.2	18.8	0.0	0.0	0.0	163840
Lemek NE, SPN	0.0	100.0	0.0	0.0	0.0	838
Ngenyn Phase 3, SPN	30.2	66.7	3.1	0.0	0.0	96
Ngamuriak, Elmenteitan	0.5	99.6	0.0	0.0	0.0	4653
Sambo Ngige Elmenteitan	0.9	99.1	0.0	0.0	0.0	214
Sugenya Elmenteitan	1.9	98.1	0.0	0.0	0.0	1774
Oldorotua Elmenteitan	1.6	98.4	0.0	0.0	0.0	2127
Maasai Gorge Elmenteitan	4.3	96.7	0.0	0.0	0.0	115
Gogo Falls Elmenteitan	8.3	6.1	0.0	0.0	85.6	MNI 444

Sources: Gautier 1984, 1989; Gifford-Gonzalez 1998; Marshall 1990; Marshall and Stewart 1995; Marshall, Barthelme, and Stewart 1984; Simons 2004

Furthermore, in southern Kenya, pastoralists lived at higher densities than in the north and the social context of pastoral settlement was more heterogeneous, comprised of at least two contemporary pastoral and several hunter-gatherer groups (Table 2.1).

Mobility, however, remained a key response to environmental risks among later East African pastoralists. The pastoral occupants of Savanna Pastoral Neolithic (SPN) (3100–1200 BP) and Elmenteitan (3300–1295 BP) sites occupied adjacent and sometimes overlapping areas of the central Rift Valley and Loita-Mara plains of southern Kenya (Tables 2.1, 2.2). Elmenteitan and SPN material culture is differentiated by lithic technology, lithic sources, ceramic styles, and burial practices (Ambrose 1984b, 2001; Bower and Nelson 1978; Nelson 1980; Wandibba 1977, 1980). It has been hypothesized that these groups also had differing linguistic affiliations (Ambrose 1982). Subsistence was based on domestic stock, with variable reliance on wild resources. There is no evidence for cultivation on any of these sites, but domestic pearl millet and cowpeas were farmed during this period in West Africa (D'Andrea et al. 2007; Neumann 2005). The number and size of sites suggests higher population densities than in northern Kenya and considerable variability in the extent of mobility. In drier, non-equilibrial environments sites were also located close to permanent water as at SPN sites in Tsavo (Wright 2007). In the equilibrial rangelands of southwestern and western Kenya settlement was somewhat longer term at Elmenteitan sites such as Ngamuriak or Gogo Falls (Robertshaw and Marshall 1990; Robertshaw 1991). Unlike northern Kenya, however, ceremonial sites are less evident in the south. The dead, when buried, were interred in rockshelters, crevasses, or cairns; large open ceremonial or pillar sites are unknown.

In central Kenya Eburran hunter-gatherers occupied the high altitude forests of the Mau Escarpment, close to both Elmenteitan and SPN herders of the Central Rift Valley and Loita Plains (Ambrose 1984a). Kansyore hunter-gatherer sites were located adjacent to Elmenteitan sites near Lake Victoria (Dale 2007; Lane et al. 2007; Kusimba and Kusimba 1995). In northern Tanzania the zone bounded by the southern Serengeti, Lake Eyasi, and Maasai Steppe marks the border between northeastern Africa, which was successfully colonized by substantial numbers of stone-using pastoralists, and regions to the south, which were not (Fig. 2.1). This constitutes a rare, long-term frontier between stone-using pastoralists and hunter-gatherers (see Lane 2004). Archaeologists argue that high densities of pastoral sites have never been found south of northern Tanzania because the heavier rainfall, increased bush cover, and Miombo vegetation of the south constituted a tsetse fly zone with an increased risk of trypanosomiasis (Gifford-Gonzalez 2000; Lambrecht 1964; Lamprey and Waller 1990; Marshall and Stewart 1995).

Taken together, the archaeological data demonstrate significant differences between the ENP and the later SSP in population densities and social and political relations. Early pastoralists lived at low densities on the landscape, appear tethered to permanent water (*sensu* Wright 2007), and lacked hunter-gatherer neighbors. During the SSP, on the other hand, diverse pastoral groups lived adjacent to one another in savanna grasslands while varied hunter-gather groups occupied nearby rockshelters, high altitude forests, and bushy areas along the rivers and shores of Lake Victoria.

CLIMATIC VARIABILITY AND RISK

Early pastoralists first moved into East Africa at a time when East African paleoclimatic archives document a transition to a long-term trend of greater aridity in the region corresponding to the end of the African Humid Phase (Gasse 2000). Diverse proxy data sets (isotopic, geochemical, sedimentological, and palynological data) derived from research of the East African Lakes constitute a large portion of the extant paleoclimatic data from the region. Figure 2.2 illustrates regional variability and outlines those periods during which aridity was widespread throughout eastern Africa.

High-resolution isotopic data from the Kilimanjaro ice cores provide a new archive of Holocene paleoclimate data ca. 6500–2000 BP (Fig. 2.2). Significant reduction of $\delta^{18}O$ values 6500–5200 BP, immediately before the record of the earliest herders in Kenya, is thought to represent the driest period of the Holocene (Gasse 2002; Thompson et al. 2002a, 2002b). Higher $\delta^{18}O$ values, signifying a wetter phase, are present between 5000 and 4000 BP (Gasse 2002; Thompson et al. 2002b). The appearance of the earliest Nderit and Ileret pastoral sites, such as Dongodien east of Lake Turkana, at ca. 4000 BP is co-incident, however, with a large amplitude globally documented period of severe aridity and 30 cm of dust accumulation in the Kilimanjaro core (Gasse 2002; Thompson et al. 2002a, 2002b) (Table 2.3, Fig. 2.2). A shift in diatom assemblages and isotopic signatures in cores from Lake Turkana also reflects decreasing lake levels and a dramatic shift to more

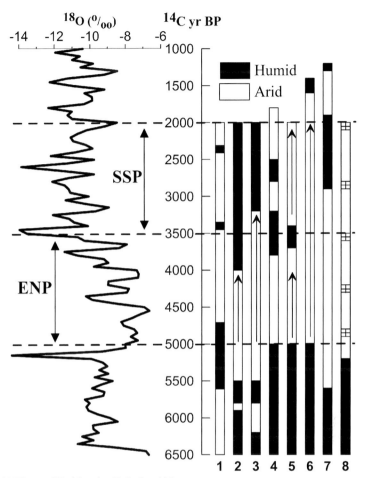

1) Tigray Highlands; 2) Lake Abhe;
3) Ziway-Shala Basin; 4) Lake Abiyata; 5) Lake Tilo; 6) Lake Turkana;
7) Mount Kenya Alpine Lakes; 8) Lake Edwards

2.2 Data from the Kilimanjaro Ice Core, East African Lakes, and stratified paleosols in highland Ethiopia show that the Southern Settlement Pastoral Phase (SSP) of the Pastoral Neolithic was associated with a generally more humid interval than was the earlier Exploratory Northern Phase (ENP). Kilimanjaro ice core $\delta^{18}O$ isotope data from Thompson et al. 2002a. Proxy paleoclimate data on East African Lakes from Barker et al. 2001; Chalié and Gasse 2002; Gasse 1977, 2000; Gasse and Street 1978; Gillespie, Street-Perrott, and Switzur 1983; Lamb et al. 2000; Ricketts and Johnson 1996; Russell et al. 2003; Street and Grove 1979; Street-Perrott et al. 1997; Telford and Lamb 1999. Data on radiocarbon dated sequence of stratified paleosols from the highlands of Ethiopia from Dramis et al. 2003.

arid conditions at this time. These data support hypotheses of drying in the north 5500–4200 BP, which might have precipitated southward movement of early pastoralists into East Africa. To the south, sediment cores from the Laikipia Plateau floodplain suggest climatic aridification and increased seasonality between 6000 BP and 4000 BP (Taylor et al. 2005), reinforcing a picture of arid conditions and risks for early East African pastoralists associated with desert conditions and arid disequilibrium savanna environments.

During the Southern Settlement Phase, the East African paleoclimatic data as a whole support reconstructions of a wetter, more modern climatic regime after 4000 BP (Fig. 2.2). In line with global El Niño Southern Oscillation events (ENSO) data, though, a variety of lines of evidence suggests more seasonal rainfall and greater fluctuations between wet and dry years (Fig. 2.3). Pollen records, isotopic data, and lake level transgressions indicate a switch to wetter, but still variable, climate conditions in Ethiopia ca. 3800–1400 BP (Fig. 2.2). This is supported by diatom and isotopic studies of Mount Kenya alpine lakes, which provide evidence for wetter conditions especially from 2900–1900 BP (Barker et al. 2001; Rietti-Shati, Shemesh, and Karlen 1998). Lake Turkana, however, remained dry. Aridity there at ca. 4000 BP was followed by a 2000 year long period of significant changes in isotopic composition as the lake became increasingly lower and more saline (Ricketts and Johnson 1996; Rietti-Shati et al. 1998). This microclimatic difference between regions provides obvious motivation for settlement of wetter southern Kenya and northern Tanzania.

A rare high-resolution data set of annual rainfall estimates is provided by a recent reconstruction of Holocene precipitation levels derived from pollen data from peat bogs and swamps in the highlands of nearby Burundi (Fig. 2.3) (Bonnefille and Chalié 2000; Vincens et al. 2003). The marked increase in larger amplitude fluctuations between low and high annual precipitation levels after ca. 4000 BP (Bonnefille and Chalié 2000) is especially significant and provides regional expression of an increase in the periodicity of ENSO events (Moy et al. 2002a; Sandweiss et al. 2001; Wright 2007). This is consistent with a global record that shows a heightened rate of increase of ENSO event frequency between 4000–3000 BP, with a marked increase in the frequency and intensity of events after ca. 3000 BP (Riedinger et al. 2002).

Today, El Niño events typically result in heavy rainfall in equatorial East Africa, with regional variation (Mutai and Ward 2000; Nicholson 2000; Nicholson and Kim 1997). The greatest increase in precipitation occurs within the

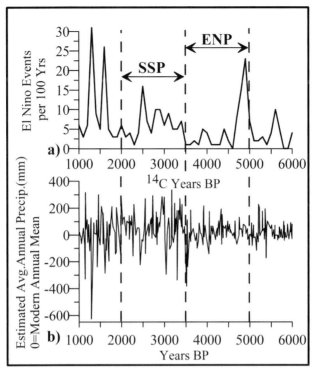

2.3 Climatic variability in eastern Africa over the last 5,000 years, showing greater variability in the Southern Settlement Phase (SSP) than in the earlier Exploratory Northern Phase (ENP) of the Pastoral Neolithic: (a) El Niño event periodicity (after Moy et al. 2002a, 2002b); (b) pollen-derived annual precipitation estimates from highland swamps and peat bogs in Burundi. (After Bonnefille and Chalié 2000)

easternmost regions. In Kenya, precipitation in the coastal plains and Lake Victoria Basin is anomalously high. Conversely, northern Tanzania and the western Rift Valley receive below-average levels of rainfall (Clark, Webster, and Cole 2003; Indeje, Semazzi, and Ogallo 2000; Wright 2007). Similar variability in the past would have had a significant effect on regional and local environmental risk, worsening already arid conditions for early pastoralists in northern Kenya, and increasing rainfall and the prevalence of equilibrium savanna ecosystems in areas occupied by Elmenteitan pastoralists and Kanysore hunter-gatherers. In other regions, including northern Tanzania, SPN groups are likely to have experienced increased episodes of aridity.

As a whole, East African climatic archives suggest that both earlier and later pastoralists experienced relatively arid and risky conditions, but considerable differences in predictability. Exploratory northern pastoralists faced predictably dry and hostile climatic conditions. Later pastoralists, with the exception of herders living in northern Kenya, benefited from increased rainfall. Climate and environmental risks during the Southern Settlement phase were significantly more temporally and spatially variable and less predictable, however, than those of the Exploratory Northern Pastoral phase.

SOCIAL, POLITICAL, AND ECONOMIC APPROACHES TO ENVIRONMENTAL STRESS

The archaeological and climatic data demonstrate that both early northern pastoralists (ENP) and later herders of the south (SSP) coped with arid to semi-arid rangelands and significant risks of drought by moving domestic herds to pasture and relying on a wide range of wild resources. The precise nature of climatic variability and social and economic responses appears, however, situationally variable. The question remains therefore—to what extent did social, political, and economic strategies for coping with environmental risk, or the possibilities for such strategies, differ between the ENP and the SSP?

During the ENP, pastoral settlement at sites such as Dongodien at Lake Turkana ca. 4000 BP is associated with a period of extreme aridity and low lake levels. Early pastoralists faced disequilibrium environments and severe multi-year droughts. Regional conditions were extremely dry and the topography relatively uniform, providing few opportunities for high-elevation microhabitats and refuge grazing. Close to permanent lakes and rivers, northern Kenya provided sufficient, but not ample, grazing grounds for drought-stricken pastoralists of the north. As immigrants, early herders were also confronted with lack of indigenous knowledge of local ecosystems, raw material sources, and disease vectors. Just as in the Sudan, northern Kenyan pastoralists depended on their herds and a wide range of wild resources to cope with unpredictable episodes of drought and disease. Cultivation was not an option, though, which limited the range of economic strategies available for coping with disastrous stock loss.

Furthermore, the archaeological evidence indicates that earlier pastoralists had relatively few social and political strategies available to them for coping with ongoing environmental risks. Low densities of pastoralists on the landscape constrained opportunities for risk-reduction based on co-operative social actions, such as animal exchange and gift giving (Gifford-Gonzalez 1998, 2000; Marshall and Hildebrand 2002). The widespread nature of aridity in the ENP reduced chances of herders finding people with livestock herds unaffected by drought and thus restricted restocking efforts through exchange after catastrophic livestock losses. The low numbers of pastoralists in the regions also limited the effectiveness of combative strategies such as raiding for recouping pastoral losses. Furthermore, opportunities for exiting the pastoral system were hampered by the lack of agricultural neighbors and low densities of nearby hunter-gatherers.

Given the shortage of safety nets available to in-migrating herders in northern Kenya, we hypothesize that the exigencies of drought and migration into a lightly populated hunter-gatherer landscape resulted in the creation and maintenance of institutional frameworks for enhancing cooperation among geographically dispersed herders. The appearance of stone circle sites in northern Kenya 5000-4000 BP suggests that public and monumental ceremonial sites could have been important places for meeting and mobilizing support across highly dispersed pastoral communities. In Ethiopia Brandt and Carder (1987) have suggested a similar role for pastoral rock art sites. Meetings or ceremonies at these venues may have facilitated access to water and grazing, breeding stock, and may have allowed exchange of scarce resources such as obsidian or chert, marine shells, and incense. Long-distance and regional exchange likely played a role in the economic lives of early pastoral communities, and shells and beads from as far as Ethiopia and the East African coast were found at Jarigole (Nelson n.d., 1995; see also Ndiema, Dillian, and Braun 2009). Perhaps as importantly, pastoralists could come together to discuss issues related to the accessibility of water and pasture and the breeding of domestic stock. Essential social negotiations around marriage, territorial claims, and social and political relations with hunter-gatherers may likewise have taken place at these ceremonial sites. In many places burials signify land-claims, and the presence of burials at these stone pillar ceremonial stone circle sites is almost certainly significant in regards to the creation of a politically and socially complex pastoral landscape.

During the SSP, on the other hand, rainfall was higher and climatic variability greater. Herders still moved animals to pasture, but site structure suggests that mobility was more varied—lower in equilibrium and higher in disequilibrium savannas. Herders at sites such as Wasendo Glade (Mturi 1986) and the Remnant site (Nelson 1980) took advantage of more varied terrain and refuge grazing available at higher altitudes on the slopes of Mt. Kilimanjaro, the Rift escarpments, and western highlands. Permanent lakes and rivers were also more common in the south than the north and hunter-gatherers more numerous and diverse. Most—but not all—southern Kenyan pastoralists depended on a wide range of wild and domestic animals, and probably on wild plants. Just as in the north, however, there is no evidence for cultivation in the SSP. The presence of higher population densities, greater social variability, and territorial overlap, though, changed the character of social strategies for coping with environmental risk in the south.

Social actions dependant on cooperation among settlements across the region, such as animal exchange and gift giving, as well as maintenance of healthy breeding stock and restocking of herds after population crashes were facilitated by higher densities of pastoralists. The higher rainfall, greater heterogeneity of terrain, and variety of microclimates also increased the chances of finding people with livestock herds unaffected by drought for restocking after catastrophic livestock losses. Compared to northern Kenya, though, in southern Kenya there is little evidence for large-scale communal ceremonial activity suggestive of regionally cohesive institutions. Burials are rare and inconspicuous and there are no open ceremonial sites with readily visible architecture.

Competition for grazing, on the other hand, is evidenced by the El-menteitan occupation of non-optimum grazing near Lake Victoria, an area already occupied by Kansyore hunter-gatherers and vulnerable to tsetse fly (Marshall and Stewart 1995). This picture is reinforced by the temporal and spatial overlap of Elmenteitan and SPN pastoralists in the Lemek Valley (Marshall 1994). Historic differences between Elmenteitan and SPN groups are indicated by the differentiation of lithic and ceramic traditions (Ambrose 1984b). Choice of obsidian sources and the extent of specialization on livestock provide evidence, however, for ongoing construction of diverse local identities and contexts for more combative approaches to environmental risk.

Intentional group differentiation is especially evident in human-animal relations. Elmenteitan sites of the Lemek-Mara region are almost entirely dominated by domestic livestock (Marshall 1990, 1994; Simons 2004, 2005) (Table 2.1). This is surprising because the Mara ecosystem, which forms the northern part of the Serengeti, is known for having the world's highest biomass of wild ungulates. These faunas contrast with those accumulated on Elmenteitan sites such as Gogo Falls close to Lake Victoria in western Kenya, where people had a more flexible approach to food, eating domestic livestock, fish, and wild ungulates. It has been argued that the equilibrial rangeland of the Loita Mara, and the advent of a bimodal rainfall system, may have made specialization possible, because in this region enough milk can be obtained year round to survive on livestock alone (Marshall 1986, 1990). The choice not to hunt and to rely only on meat, milk, and blood from domestic animals must nonetheless have been a social one. The proximity of Eburran hunter-gatherer groups on the Mau Escarpment of the Rift Valley and neighboring SPN pastoralists together, we hypothesize, provided impetus for social differentiation in an environment of social heterogeneity and pastoral competition in the Loita-Mara.

Patterns of obsidian procurement are also consistent with a larger pattern of intentional differentiation of Elmenteitan from SPN groups. Herders from the SPN settlements of Narosura or Lemek-North East consistently obtained green obsidian from distant southern Naivaisha, Njorowa Gorge sources (Fig. 2.4; Merrick and Brown 1984; Merrick, Brown, and Connelly 1990; Merrick, Brown, and Nash 1994). By contrast, Elmenteitans, living on other sites in the Lemek Valley such as Ngamuriak or Sambo Ngige, consistently used gray obsidian from sources located on the slopes of Mt. Eburru above Lake Naivaisha. These differences were maintained regardless of the proximity of SPN or Elmenteitan sites to Njorowa Gorge or Mt. Eburru (Merrick, Brown, and Connelly 1990).

Turton (1979; Fukui and Turton 1979) emphasizes the role of warfare in creating and maintaining pastoral identity today. On the basis of these data and studies that link raiding to disequilibrium environments (Cousins 1996), we argue that higher population densities and increasing competition and differentiation among ancient pastoral groups led to growing hostility, including raiding. Archaeologists in East Africa have not previously considered this issue or the role that combative strategies may have played in replenishing herds lost to drought or disease. The only case of violence currently known from the East African Pastoral Neolithic comes from the site of KFR-A5 in Laikipia (Siiriäinen 1977). These data are suggestive, but further research is needed on this topic and until then the use of violence to recoup stock losses is only a hypothesis.

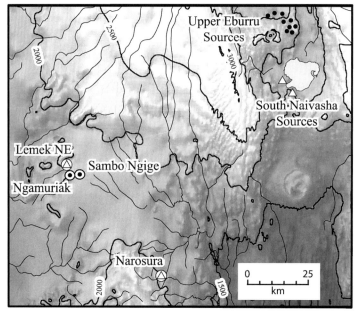

2.4 Map showing distances from preferred obsidian sources in the Central Rift Valley to Elmenteitan and Savanna Pastoral Neolithic sites in southwestern Kenya.

The nature of social and political relations with hunter-gatherers is another factor that influenced the access of southern herders to better watered regions, reserve grazing, and possibilities of refuge (Gifford-Gonzalez 1998; Lane 2004; Mutundu 1999, Kusimba and Kusimba 2005). In the well-watered lowlands of the southeast Lake Victoria basin, pastoralists from Elmenteitan sites interacted with delayed-return Kansyore hunter-gatherers (Dale, Marshall, and Pilgram 2004; Dale 2007). Fauna from some later Kansyore sites also suggest that transitions to herding were taking place at this time (Karega-Munene 2002; Lane et al. 2007; Prendergast 2008). In central Kenya Eburran hunter-gatherers occupied the high-altitude forests of the Mau Escarpment, close to both Elmenteitan and SPN herders of the Central Rift Valley and Loita Plains (Ambrose 1984a). Domestic stock is well documented in some Eburran sites after 3500 BP (Ambrose 1998). It has also been argued that at the SPN site of Prolonged Drift, large quantities of wild fauna indicate herder-hunter interactions possibly related to recovery of pastoralists after disastrous herd loss (Gifford-Gonzalez, Isaac, and Nelson 1980).

Comparing economic with social and political approaches to coping with environmental stress emphasizes the lack of variability in economic strategies employed by prehistoric East African pastoralists through time. Both earlier (ENP) and later (SSP) pastoralists relied on mobility and dependence on a range of stock including varying proportions of cattle, sheep, goat, and donkeys. A broader range of subsistence strategies is documented among later herders—including specialized dependence on domestic stock—but flexible and opportunistic dependence on domestic and available wild resources remains the dominant approach to coping with environmental risk. There are significant diachronic differences, on the other hand, in the range of social and political strategies available to prehistoric East African pastoralists for coping with environmental risk. Earlier groups (ENP) lived at low population densities and necessarily relied on cooperation among far-flung settlements. In southern Kenya, by contrast, the presence of significant and diverse hunter-gatherer populations and the coexistence of both Elmenteitan and SPN herders allowed more varied cooperative and combative approaches to environmental risk. As a whole, the archaeological data indicate that ancient pastoral solutions to environmental or climatic stress in eastern Africa were more socially and politically than economically varied.

CONCLUSION

The nature of historic relationships between people and climate change are of profound interest to contemporary societies but remain controversial. It is clear, though, that at certain times and places interactions among technological, economic, social, and political factors promoted resilience rather than failure to cope with climatic challenges (Fagan 2004; Hassan 2002; Rosen 2007). Most scholars agree, however, that more information on diverse and regionally specific global cases is needed in order to better understand situational vs. institutional factors affecting outcomes. Theoretical perspectives on human responses to climatic stress have been largely based on settled village societies (but see Hassan 2002). Through this comparison of earlier northern and later southern Holocene East African pastoralists we identify some of the factors that constrained or facilitated pastoral responses to medium- and small-scale climatic and environmental fluctuations in East African grasslands.

Early northern Kenyan pastoralists 5000–3500 years ago employed similar technologies, economies, attitudes to what constituted food, and patterns of use of the environment to those of later herders who settled southern Kenya 3500–2000 years ago. Both groups were relatively egalitarian, did not rely on cultivation, interactions with cities, or long-distance trade, and had subsistence economies based on cattle, sheep, and goat, donkeys, and wild resources. The earliest herders of northern Kenya, though, responded differently than the herders who settled southern Kenya to the challenges of moving into and surviving in the East African landscape under conditions of highly variable rainfall and frequent droughts. We think that this is due, in large part, to differences between them in the density of neighboring pastoralists and hunter-gatherers. Other factors that provided opportunities for, or constrained, options open to prehistoric East African herders for coping with environmental risk were local and temporal variation in rainfall, terrain, the availability of equilibrial versus disequilibrial rangelands, and threats of disease.

High-amplitude fluctuations in rainfall and periodic severe droughts, such as that of ca. 4000 BP, constituted significant climatic risks for the earliest northern Kenyan pastoralists. Potential disasters included flooding, disease, stock-loss, and the threat of starvation. Savanna environments and pastoral systems in northern Kenya at this time were disequilibrial and high risk and there were very few herders or hunter-gatherers present. As a result options for replenishing stock or for refuge were few. Mobility was a key strategy employed for reducing risks. Early pastoralists engaged in long-distance migration into southern Kenya, exploratory mobility, and as at Lake Turkana, sited settlements close to permanent water. Another long-term approach used by East African pastoralists in drier areas was reliance on a broad resource base including sheep and goat, some cattle, wild mammals, reptiles, wild plants, and large quantities of fish. Stone circle ceremonial sites are a distinctive feature of the archaeological record of early northern Kenyan pastoralism and provide one of the few insights into the social, political, and spiritual rather than the economic lives of early herders. We hypothesize that these locales served as a focus for events that would have enhanced social and economic cooperation, exchange of information and livestock among the few and widely spread early herders of the region through participation in life-event ceremonies. Taken as a whole, the northern Kenyan archaeological record shows that mobility and economic diversification were key strategies used to combat environmental risks and there are strong suggestions that social and ceremonial institutions promoted cooperative relations among early herders.

Significantly more diverse risks existed for later pastoralists during the settlement of southern Kenya and northern Tanzania. After 3500 BP rainfall was higher in East Africa, though except at high altitude or close to Lake Victoria, grasslands remained semi-arid. It is during this wetter period that pastoralists moved into southern Kenya in some numbers. This coincided also with a period of increased variability in rainfall and more frequent ENSO events. As a result, although rainfall was higher, climatic conditions were challenging. Like earlier northern Kenyan herders, the pastoralists who settled southern Kenya faced generally disequilibrial dry savanna environments in much of the region. But potentially equilibrial conditions existed in the wetter Loita-Mara plains of southwestern Kenya, near southeastern Lake Victoria, and at higher elevations. Equilibrial conditions were not, however, always favorable for later pastoralists. Densities of wildlife and domestic stock, as well as fire and pastoral activity, determined whether wetter rangeland was open or closed. Bushy vegetation favored tsetse fly and created a threat to pastoralists. The archaeological record suggests that cattle and sheep and goat flourished in the Loita-Mara, but did not thrive in the Lake Victoria region. South of northern Tanzania, closed bush put an end to grasslands, archaeologically visible numbers of herders, and the successful pastoral settlement of northeast Africa.

Compared to conditions faced by northern Kenyan pastoralists a thousand years earlier, the increased rainfall, regionally varied ENSO effects, diverse terrain and vegetation, and higher densities of people in southern Kenya contributed to expanded options for coping with disasters. Increased pastoral settlement densities meant that gift-giving, stock exchange, and other social approaches could be more easily undertaken. The likelihood of someone, somewhere, having stock that survived any given disaster was greater and chances for restocking were greatly increased. Similarly, the chances of recouping stock through raiding were also improved by higher pastoral populations. Higher rainfall resulted in less risky land use with lower incidence of drought, and frequent ENSO events meant more well-watered years in eastern East Africa in later periods than in earlier ones. The more varied terrain of southern Kenya resulted in greater possibilities for refuge grazing and microclimates unaffected by particular episodes of drought or disease. In southern Kenya after 3500 BP, exit strategies from the pastoral system were enhanced, compared to those available earlier in northern Kenya, by the presence of varied Eburran and Kansyore hunter-gatherer groups.

On the other hand, in contrast to earlier periods, increased numbers of people on the landscape and contiguous and overlapping distributions of Savanna Pastoral Neolithic and Elmenteitan pastoralists also meant more competition for refuge grazing or prime pastoral lands. Our analysis suggested that long-distance social networks were actively maintained during the earlier pastoral period through ceremonies held at stone circle sites, but conscious social fragmentation was the hallmark of later Savanna Pastoral Neolithic and Elmenteitan pastoralists in southern Kenya. We conclude that, as a result, later pastoralists were able to use a wider range of social strategies, cooperative as well as combative, to cope with environmental risks.

The East African case provides strong support for theoretical perspectives that emphasize successful and long-term social and economic responses to spatial and temporal climatic variability. It also provides specific information about long-term strategies employed by East African pastoralists to cope with environmental risk. Interestingly, though, the East African archaeological record also demonstrates environmental limits to the resilience of ancient pastoralists. Broad subsistence strategies and close relations with hunter-gatherers were used to cope with spatial and temporal variability in bush and forested locales, subject to tsetse fly and the threat of sleeping sickness, in western and southern Kenya. But the termination of open grasslands and extensive, long-term closed vegetation that extended from Tanzania to southern Africa constituted a disease threat and scale of environmental variability that was never successfully met by ancient African pastoralists.

In arid and semi-arid grasslands of eastern Africa, pastoralism and mobility are still viable responses to climatic uncertainty, just as they were during earlier periods of reduced and unpredictable rainfall. But strategies for maintenance of successful mobile pastoral societies are complex. They necessitate extensive land tenure systems with widespread access to water and grazing including preservation of refuge areas, mechanisms for flexible contingency-based decision-making regarding movement of herds and settlements, arrangements for livestock sharing, and other societal conditions that allow mobilization of labor. Present-day pastoral societies in Sudan and eastern Africa reflect a legacy of 5000 years of adjustments to environmental risk, and they retain finely tuned social, political, and economic structures that permit flexible responses to changing climatic conditions, increasing aridity, and unpredictable rainfall. Nevertheless, current governments routinely advocate cultivation and settled agriculture as economic approaches more suited to the modern world. Given that current climatic fluctuations associated with global warming are projected to increase aridity and climatic unpredictability in eastern Africa, however, consideration of mobility and the strengths of long-term social and economic strategies used by African herders for coping with environmental risk is timely.

Acknowledgments

We are most grateful to Naomi F. Miller, Katherine Moore, and Kathleen Ryan for inviting us to participate in the Forces of Nature conference and for providing both intellectual challenges and practical assistance. Participants of the conference provided insightful comments and two anonymous reviewers greatly improved this paper. We thank Tim Schilling for both illustrations and comments and T. R. Kidder for broad climatic perspectives. We are entirely responsible for any errors.

REFERENCES CITED

Almagor, U. 1979. Raiders and Elders: A Confrontation of Generations among the Dassanetch. In *Warfare among East African Herders*, ed. K. Fukui and D. Turton, pp. 119–46. Senri Ethnological Studies. Osaka, Japan: National Museum of Ethnology.

Ambrose, S. H. 1982. Archaeological and Linguistic Reconstructions of History in East Africa. In *The Archaeological and Linguistic Reconstruction of African History*, ed. C. Ehret and M. Posnansky, pp. 104–57. Berkeley: University of California Press.

—— 1984a. Holocene Environments and Human Adaptations in the Central Rift Valley, Kenya. PhD diss., Univ. of California, Berkeley.

—— 1984b. The Introduction of Pastoral Adaptations to the Highlands of East Africa. In *From Hunters to Farmers: The Causes and Consequences of Food Production in Africa*, ed. J. D. Clark and S. Brandt, pp. 212–39. Berkeley: University of California Press.

—— 1998. Chronology of the Later Stone Age and Food Production in East Africa. *Journal of Archaeological Science* 25:377–92.

—— 2001. East African Neolithic. In *Encyclopedia of Prehistory*. Vol. 1, *Africa*, ed. P. N. Peregrine and M. Ember, pp. 97–109. New York: Kluwer Academic.

Barker, P. A., F. A. Street-Perrott, M. J. Leng, P. B. Greenwood, D. L. Swain, R.

A. Perrott, R. J. Telford, and K. J. Ficken. 2001. A 14,000-year Oxygen Isotope Record from Diatom Silica in Two Alpine Lakes on Mt. Kenya. *Science* 292:2307–10.

Barthelme, J. 1985. *Fisher-Hunters and Neolithic Pastoralists in East Turkana, Kenya.* BAR International Series 254. Oxford.

Behnke, R. H., and I. Scoones. 1993. Rethinking Range Ecology: Implications for Rangeland Management in Africa. In *Range Ecology at Disequilibrium: New Models of Natural Variability and Pastoral Adaptation in African Savannas,* ed. R. H. Behnke, I. Scoones, and C. Kerven, pp. 1–30. London: Overseas Development Institute.

Behnke, R. H., I. Scoones, and C. Kerven, eds. 1993. *Range Ecology at Disequilibrium: New Models of Natural Variability and Pastoral Adaptation in African Savannas.* London: Overseas Development Institute.

Bonnefille, R., and F. Chalié. 2000. Pollen-inferred Precipitation Time Series from Equatorial Mountains, Africa, the Last 40 kyr BP. *Global and Planetary Change* 26:25–50.

Bower, J. R. F., and C. M. Nelson. 1978. Early Pottery and Pastoral Cultures of the Central Rift Valley, Kenya. *Man* 13:554–66.

Bower, J. R. F., C. M. Nelson, A. F. Waibel, and S. Wandibba. 1977. The University of Massachusetts' Later Stone Age/Pastoral "Neolithic" Comparative Study in Central Kenya: An Overview. *Azania* 12:119–46.

Brandt, S. A., and N. Carder. 1987. Pastoral Rock Art in the Horn of Africa: Making Sense of Udder Chaos. *World Archaeology* 19(2): 194–213.

Bronk Ramsey, C. 2009. Bayesian Analysis of Radiocarbon Dates. *Radiocarbon* 51(1): 337–60.

Chalié, F., and F. Gasse. 2002. Late Glacial-Holocene Diatom Record of Water Chemistry and Lake Level Change from the Tropical East African Rift Lake Abiyata (Ethiopia). *Palaeogeography, Palaeoclimatology, Palaeoecology* 187:259–83.

Clark, C. O., P. J. Webster, and J. E. Cole. 2003. Interdecadal Variability of the Relationship between the Indian Ocean Zonal Mode and East African Coastal Rainfall Anomalies. *Journal of Climate* 16:548–54.

Close, A., and F. Wendorf. 1992. The Beginnings of Food Production in the Eastern Sahara. In *Transitions to Agriculture in Prehistory,* ed. A. B. Gebauer and T. D. Price, pp. 63–72. Madison, WI: Prehistory Press.

Coppock, D. L. 1993. Vegetation and Pastoral Dynamics in Southern Ethiopian Rangelands: Implications for Theory and Management. In *Range Ecology at Disequilibrium: New Models of Natural Variability and Pastoral Adaptation in African Savannas,* ed. R. H. Behnke, I. Scoones, and C. Kerven, pp. 42–61. London: Overseas Development Institute.

Cousins, B. 1996. Conflict Management for Multiple Resource Users in Pastoral and Agro-pastoral Contexts. *IDS Bulletin* 227:41–54.

D'Andrea, A. C., S. Kahlheber, A. L. Logan, and D. J. Watson. 2007. Early

Domesticated Cowpeas (*Vigna unguiculata*) from Central Ghana. *Antiquity* 81:686–98.

Dahl, G., and A. Hjort. 1976. *Having Herds: Pastoral Herd Growth and Household Economy.* Stockholm Studies in Social Anthropology 2. Stockholm: University of Stockholm.

Dale, D. 2007. An Archaeological Investigation of the Kansyore, Later Stone Age Hunter-Gatherers in East Africa. PhD diss., Dept. of Anthropology, Washington Univ., St. Louis.

Dale, D., F. Marshall, and T. Pilgram. 2004. Delayed-return Hunter-Gatherers in Africa? Historic Perspectives from the Okiek and Archaeological Perspectives from the Kansyore. In *Hunter-Gatherers in Theory and Archaeology*, ed. G. M. Crothers, pp. 340–75. Center for Archaeological Investigations Occasional Paper 21. Carbondale: Southern Illinois University.

di Lernia, S. 2002. Dry Climatic Events and Cultural Trajectories: Adjusting Middle Holocene Pastoral Economy of the Libyan Sahara. In *Droughts, Food, and Culture: Ecological Change and Food Security in Africa's Later Prehistory*, ed. F. Hassan, pp. 209–25. New York: Kluwer.

Dramis, F., M. Umer, G. Calderoni, and M. Haile. 2003. Holocene Climate Phases from Buried Soils in Tigray (Northern Ethiopia): Comparison with Lake Level Fluctuations in the Main Ethiopian Rift. *Quaternary Research* 60:274–83.

Dublin, Holly. 1986. Decline of the Mara Woodlands: The Role of Fire and Elephants. PhD diss., Univ. of British Columbia, Vancouver.

Dublin, H. 1995. Vegetation Dynamics in the Serengeti-Mara Ecosystem. In *Serengeti II: Dynamics, Management and Conservation of an Ecosystem*, ed. A. Sinclair and P. Arcese, pp. 71–90. Chicago: University Press.

Dyson-Hudson, R., and N. Dyson Hudson. 1980. Nomadic Pastoralism. *Annual Review of Anthropology* 9:15–61.

Dyson-Hudson, R., and J. T. McCabe. 1985. *South Turkana Nomadism: Coping with an Unpredictably Varying Environment.* HRAFlex Books, FL17-001. Ethnography Series. New Haven, CT: Human Relations Area Files.

Evans-Pritchard, E. E. 1940. *The Nuer: A Description of the Modes of Livelihood and Political Institutions of a Nilotic People.* Oxford: Oxford University Press.

Fagan, B. M. 2004. *The Long Summer: How Climate Changed Civilization.* New York: Basic Books.

Fukui, K., and D. Turton, eds. 1979. *Warfare among East African Herders.* Senri Ethnological Studies. Osaka, Japan: National Museum of Ethnology.

Galvin, K. A., R. B. Boone, N. M. Smith, and S. J. Lynn. 2001. Impacts of Climate Variability on East African Pastoralists: Linking Social Science and Remote Sensing. *Climate Research* 19:161–72.

Gasse, F. 1977. Evolution of Lake Abheh (Ethiopia and T.F.A.I.) from 70,000 B.P. *Nature* 2:42–45.

—— 2000. Hydrological Changes in the African Tropics since the Last Glacial Maximum. *Quaternary Science Reviews* 19:189–211.

—— 2002. Kilimanjaro's Secrets Revealed. *Science* 298:548–49.

Gasse, F., and F. A. Street. 1978. Late Quaternary Lake-level Fluctuations and Environments of the Northern Rift Valley and Afar Region. *Palaeogeography, Palaeoclimatology, Palaeoecology* 25:145–50.

Gautier, A. 1984. The Fauna of the Neolithic Site of Kadero (Central Sudan). In *Origin and Early Development of Food-producing Cultures in North-Eastern Africa*, ed. L. Kryzaniak and M. Kobusiewicz, pp. 317–19. Poznan: Polish Academy of Sciences and Poznan Archaeological Museum.

—— 1989. A General Review of the Known Prehistoric Faunas of the Central Sudanese Nile Valley. In *Late Prehistory of the Nile Basin and the Sahara*, ed. L. Krzyzaniak and M. Kobusiewicz, pp. 352–57. Poznan: Poznan Archaeological Museum.

Gifford-Gonzalez, D. P. 1998. Early Pastoralists in East Africa: Ecological and Social Dimensions. *Journal of Anthropological Archaeology* 17:166–200.

—— 2000. Animal Disease Challenges to the Emergence of Pastoralism in Sub-Saharan Africa. *African Archaeological Review* 17(3): 95–139.

—— 2005. Pastoralism and Its Consequences. In *African Archaeology: A Critical Introduction*, ed. A. Stahl, pp. 187–224. Cambridge: Blackwell.

Gifford-Gonzalez, D. P., G. L. Isaac, and C. M. Nelson. 1980. Evidence for Predation and Pastoralism from a Pastoral Neolithic Site in Kenya. *Azania* 15:57–108.

Gillespie, R., F. A. Street-Perrott, and R. Switzur. 1983. Post-glacial Arid Episodes in Ethiopia Have Implications for Climate Prediction. *Nature* 306:680–83.

Hassan, F. 2002. Paleoclimate, Food and Culture Change in Africa: An Overview. In *Droughts, Food, and Culture: Ecological Change and Food Security in Africa's Later Prehistory*, ed. F. A. Hassan, pp. 11–26. New York: Kluwer.

Homewood, K. 2008. *Ecology of African Pastoralist Societies*. Oxford: James Currey.

Indeje, M., F. H. M. Semazzi, and L. J. Ogallo. 2000. ENSO Signals in East African Rainfall Seasons. *International Journal of Climatology* 20:19–46.

Karega-Munene. 2002. *Holocene Foragers, Fishers and Herders of Western Kenya.* BAR International Series 1037. Oxford: Archaeopress.

Kenny, M. G. 1981. Mirror in the Forest: The Dorobo Hunter-Gatherers as an Image of the Other. *Africa: Journal of the International African Institute* 51(1): 477–95.

Kiura, P. 2005. *Ethnoarchaeological and Stable Isotopes in the Study of People's Diets.* Germany: VDM Verlag Dr. Müller.

Koch, C. P., L. A. Pavlish, R. M. Farquhar, R. G. V. Hancock, and R. P. Beukens. 2002. INAA of Pottery from Il Lokeridede and Jarigole, Koobi Fora Region, Kenya. In *Archaeometry 98: Proceedings of the 31st International Symposium Budapest, April 26–May 3 1998*, ed. E. Jerem and K. T. Biró, pp. 587–92. Oxford: Archaeopress.

Kuper, R., and S. Kropelin. 2006. Climate-controlled Holocene Occupation in the Sahara: Motor of Africa's Evolution. *Science* 313:803.

Kusimba, C. M., and S. B. Kusimba. 2005. Mosaics and Interactions: East Africa, 2000 B.P. to the Present. In *African Archaeology: A Critical Introduction*, ed. A. Stahl, pp. 392–419. Cambridge: Blackwell.

Lamb, A. L., M. J. Leng, H. F. Lamb, and M. U. Mohammed. 2000. A 9000-year Oxygen and Carbon Isotope Record of Hydrological Change in a Small Ethiopian Crater Lake. *The Holocene* 10(2): 167–77.

Lambrecht, C. L. 1964. Aspects of Evolution and Ecology of Tsetse Flies and Trypanosomiasis in Prehistoric African Environment. *Journal of African History* 5:1–24.

Lamprey, R., and R. Waller. 1990. The Loita-Mara Region in Historical Times: Patterns of Subsistence, Settlement and Ecological Change. In *Early Pastoralists of South-Western Kenya*, ed. P. Robertshaw, pp. 16–35. Nairobi: British Institute in Eastern Africa.

Lane, P. 2004. The "Moving Frontier" and the Transition to Food Production in Kenya. *Azania* 39:243–64.

Lane, P. C., O. Ashley, P. Seitsonen, S. Harvey, S. Mire, and F. Odede. 2007. The Transition to Farming in Eastern Africa: New Faunal and Dating Evidence from Wadh Lang'o and Usenge, Kenya. *Antiquity* 81:62–81.

Legge, K. 1989. Changing Responses to Drought among the Wodaabe of Niger. In *Bad Year Economics: Cultural Responses to Risk and Uncertainty*, ed. P. Halstead and J. O'Shea, pp. 81–86. London: Cambridge University.

Le Houérou, H. N., R. L. Bingham, and K. Skerbek. 1988. Relationships between the Variability of Primary Production and the Variability of Annual Precipitation in World Arid Lands. *Journal of Arid Environments* 15:1–8.

Linseele, V., E. Marinova, W. Van Neer, and P. M. Vermeersch. 2009. Sites with Holocene Dung Deposits in the Eastern Desert of Egypt: Visited by Herders? *Journal of Arid Environments* 74(7): 818–28.

Little, P. D. 1999. Comment on "Is Inequality Universal?" by P. C. Salzman. *Current Anthropology* 40(1): 50–51.

Mace, R. 1991. Overgrazing Overstated. *Nature* 349:280–81.

Marshall, F. 1986. Aspects of the Advent of Pastoral Economies in East Africa. PhD diss., Univ. of California, Berkeley.

—— 1990. Origins of Specialized Pastoral Production in East Africa. *American Anthropologist* 92(4): 873–94.

—— 1994. Archaeological Perspectives on East African Pastoralism. *African Pastoralist Systems*, ed. E. Fratkin, J. Galvin, and E. Roth, pp. 17–44. Boulder, CO: Lynne Rienner.

—— 2007. African Pastoral Perspectives on Domestication of the Donkey: A First Synthesis. In *Rethinking Agriculture: Archaeological and Ethnoarchaeological Perspectives*, ed. T. P. Denham and L. Vrydaghs, pp. 537–94. London: UCL Press.

Marshall, F., and E. Hildebrand. 2002. Cattle before Crops: The Beginnings of Food Production in Africa. *Journal of World Prehistory* 16(2): 99–143.

Marshall, F., and K. Stewart. 1995. Hunting, Fishing, and Herding Pastoralists of Western Kenya: The Fauna from Gogo Falls. *Zooarchaeologia* 7:7–27.

Marshall, F. B., J. W. Barthelme, and K. Stewart. 1984. Early Domestic Stock at Dongodien. *Azania* 19:120–27.

McCabe, J. T. 1999. Comment on "Is Inequality Universal?" by P. C. Salzman. *Current Anthropology* 40(1): 51–52.

—— 2000. Patterns and Processes of Group Movement in Human Nomadic Populations: A Case Study of the Turkana of Northwestern Kenya. In *On the Move: How and Why Animals Travel in Groups*, ed. S. Boinsky and P. Garber, pp. 649–77. Chicago: University of Chicago Press.

—— 2004. *Cattle Bring Us to Our Enemies: Turkana Ecology, Politics, and Raiding in a Disequilibrium System*. Ann Arbor: University of Michigan Press.

McIntosh, R. J., J. A. Tainter, and S. K. McIntosh, eds. 2000. *The Way the Wind Blows. Climate History, and Human Action*. New York: Columbia University Press.

Merrick, H. V., and F. H. Brown. 1984. Obsidian Sources and Patterns of Source Utilization in Kenya and Northern Tanzania: Some Initial Findings. *African Archaeological Review* 2(1): 129–52.

Merrick, H. V., and M. C. Monaghan. 1984. The Date of the Cremated Burials in Njoro River Cave. *Azania* 19:7–11.

Merrick, H. V., F. H. Brown, and M. Connelly. 1990. Sources of the Obsidian at Ngamuriak and Other South-western Kenyan Sites. In *Early Pastoralists of South-western Kenya*, ed. P. Robertshaw, pp. 173–82. Nairobi: British Institute in Eastern Africa.

Merrick, H. V., F. H. Brown, and W. P. Nash. 1994. Use and Movement of Obsidian in the Early and Middle Stone Ages of Kenya and Northern Tanzania. In *Society, Culture, and Technology in Africa*, ed. S. T. Childs, pp. 29–44. MASCA Research Papers in Science and Archaeology, suppl. to vol. 11. Philadelphia: Museum Applied Science Center for Archaeology, University of Pennsylvania Museum of Archaeology and Anthropology.

Mortimore, M. 1998. *Roots in the African Dust: Sustaining the Drylands*. Cambridge: Cambridge University Press.

Moy, C. M., G. O. Seltzer, D. T. Rodbell, and D. M. Anderson. 2002a. Laguna Pallcacocha Sediment Color Intensity Data. *IGBP PAGES / World Data Center for Paleoclimatology, Data Contribution Series #2002-76*. Boulder, CO: NOAA/ NGDC Paleoclimatology Program.

—— 2002b. Variability of El Niño/Southern Oscillation Activity at Millennial Timescales during the Holocene Epoch. *Nature* 420:162–65.

Mturi, A. A. 1986. The Pastoral Neolithic of West Kilimanjaro. *Azania* 21:53–64.

Mutai, C. C., and M. N. Ward. 2000. East African Rainfall and the Tropical Circulation/Convection on Interseasonal to Interannual Timescales. *Journal of Climate* 13:3915–39.

Mutundu, K. K. 1999. *Ethnohistoric Archaeology of the Mukogodo in North-Central Kenya*. BAR International Series 775. Oxford: Archeopress.

Ndiema, E., C. D. Dillian, and D. R. Braun. 2010. Interaction and Exchange across the Transition to Pastoralism, Lake Turkana, Kenya. In *Trade and Exchange: Archaeological Studies from History and Prehistory*, ed. C. D. Dillian and C. L. White, pp. 95–110. New York: Springer.

Nelson, C. M. 1980. The Elmenteitan Lithic Industry. In *Proceedings of the 8th Panafrican Congress of Prehistory and Quaternary Studies Nairobi, 5 to 10 September 1977*, ed. R. Leakey and B. Ogot, pp. 275–78. Nairobi: TILLMIAP.

—— 1995. The Work of the Koobi Fora Field School at the Jarigole Pillar Site. *Kenya Past and Present* 27:49–63.

—— n.d. Evidence for Early Trade between the Coast and Interior of East Africa. Paper prepared for the WAC Mombasa Intercongress Conference Volume, 1993.

Neumann, K. 2005. The Romance of Farming: Plant Cultivation and Domestication in Africa. In *African Archaeology: A Critical Introduction*, ed. A. Stahl, pp. 249–75. Cambridge: Blackwell.

Nicholson, S. E. 2000. The Nature of Rainfall Variability over Africa on Time Scales of Decades to Millennia. *Global Planetary Change* 26:137–58.

Nicholson, S. E., and E. Kim. 1997. The Relationship of the El Niño-Southern Oscillation to African Rainfall. *International Journal of Climatology* 17:117–35.

Nicolaisen, J. 1963. *Ecology and Culture of the Pastoral Tuareg*. Copenhagen: National Museum of Copenhagen.

Odner, K. 1972. Excavations at Narosura, a Stone Bowl Site in the Southern Kenya Highlands. *Azania* 7:25–92.

Onyango-Abuje, J. C. 1977. Crescent Island: A Preliminary Report on Excavations at an East African Neolithic Site. *Azania* 12:147–59.

Phillipson, D. W. 1977. Lowasera. *Azania* 7:1–32.

Prendergast, M. E. 2008. Forager Variability and Transitions to Food-Production in Secondary Settings: Kansyore and Pastoral Neolithic Economies in East Africa. PhD diss., Dept. of Anthropology, Harvard Univ., Cambridge.

Ricketts, R. D., and T. C. Johnson. 1996. Climate Change in the Turkana Basin as Deduced from a 4000 Year Long Delta 18 Record. *Earth and Planetary Science Letters* 142:7–17.

Riedinger, M. A., M. Steinitz-Kannan, W. M. Last, and M. Brenner. 2002. A 6100 14C Record of El Niño Activity from the Galapagos Islands. *Journal of Paleolimnology* 27:1–7.

Rietti-Shati, M., A. Shemesh, and W. Karlen. 1998. A 3000-Year Climatic Record from Biogenic Silica Oxygen Isotopes in an Equatorial High-Altitude Lake. *Science* 281:980–82.

Robbins, L. H. 1972. Archaeology in Turkana District, Kenya. *Science* 176:359–66.

—— 2006. Lake Turkana Archaeology: The Holocene. *Ethnohistory* 53:71–93.

Robertshaw, P. 1990. *Early Pastoralists of South-western Kenya*. Memoir 11. Nairobi: British Institute in Eastern Africa.

—— 1991. Gogo Falls: A Complex Site East of Lake Victoria. *Azania* 26:63–195.

Robertshaw, P., and F. Marshall. 1990. Ngamuriak. In *Early Pastoralists of South-western Kenya*, ed. Robertshaw, pp. 54–72. Nairobi: British Institute in Eastern Africa.

Robinson, P. W. 1989. Reconstructing Gabbra History and Chronology: Time Reckoning, the Gabbra Calendar, and the Cyclical View of Life. In *Coping with Drought in Kenya: National and Local Strategies*, ed. T. E. Downing, K. W. Gitu, and C. M. Kamau, pp. 151–68. Boulder, CO: Lynne Rienner.

Rosen, A. M. 2007. *Civilizing Climate.* Lanham, MD: Alta Mira.

Russell, J. M. 2006. Mid- to Late Holocene Climate Change in Tropical Africa: Regional Patterns, Rates, and Timing. *Eos Trans. AGU 87(52): Fall Meeting Suppl., Abstract PP42A-06.*

Russell, J. M., T. C. Johnson, K. R. Kelts, T. Lærdal, and M. R. Talbot. 2003. An 11,000-year Lithostratigraphic and Paleohydrologic Record from Equatorial Africa: Lake Edward, Uganda-Congo. *Palaeogeography, Palaeoclimatology, Palaeoecology* 193:25–49.

Ryan, K., K. Munene, S. M. Kahinju, and P. N. Kunoni. 2000. Ethnographic Perspectives on Cattle Management in Semi-arid Environments: A Case Study from Maasailand. In *The Origins and Development of African Livestock: Archaeology, Genetics, Linguistics, and Ethnography*, ed. R. M. Blench and K. C. MacDonald, pp. 462–77. London: UCL Press.

Sala, O. E., F. S. Chapin, III, J. J. Armesto, E. Berlow, J. Bloomfield, R. Dirzo, E. Huber-Sanwald, et al. 2000. Global Biodiversity Scenarios for the Year 2100. *Science* 287:1770–74.

Salzman, P. C. 1999. Is Inequality Universal? *Current Anthropology* 40(1): 31–61.

Sandweiss, D. H., K. A. Maasch, R. L. Burger, J. B. Richardson, III, H. B. Rollins, and A. Clement. 2001. Variation in Holocene El Niño Frequencies: Climate Records and Cultural Consequences in Ancient Peru. *Geology* 29:603–6.

Sankaran, K., N. P. Hanan, R. J. Scholes, J. Ratnam, D. J. Augustine, B. S. Cade, J. Gignoux, et al. 2005. Determinants of Woody Cover in African Savannas. *Nature* 438:846–49.

Schneider, H. K. 1979. *Livestock and Equality in East Africa: The Economic Basis for Social Structure.* Bloomington: Indiana University Press.

Siiriäinen, A. 1977. Later Stone Age Investigation in the Laikipia Highlands, Kenya: A Preliminary Report. *Azania* 12:161–86.

Simons, A. 2003. Sugenya: A Pastoral Neolithic Site in South-western Kenya. *Azania* 38:169–73.

—— 2004. The Development of Early Pastoral Societies in South-Western Kenya: A Study of the Faunal Assemblages from Sugenya and Oldorotua 1. PhD diss., La Trobe Univ., Victoria, AU.

—— 2005. Exchange Networks, Socio-political Hierarchies, and the Archaeological Evidence for Differential Wealth amongst Pastoralists in Southwestern Kenya. *Nyame Akuma* 64:36–40.

Soper, R. 1982. Archaeo-astronomical Cushites: Some Comments. *Azania* 17:45–165.

Spear, T. 1993. Being "Maasai," but not "People of Cattle": Arusha Agricultural Maasai in the Nineteenth Century. In *Being Maasai*, ed. T. Spear and R. Waller, pp. 120–36. London: James Currey.

Spear, T., and R. Waller, eds. 1993. *Being Maasai*. London: James Currey.

Spencer, P. 1965. *The Samburu: A Study of Gerontocracy in a Nomadic Tribe*. Berkeley: University of California Press.

—— 1973. *Nomads in Alliance*. London: Oxford University Press.

Street-Perrott, F. A., Y. Huang, R. A. Perrott, G. Eglinton, P. A. Barker, L. Khelifa, D. D. Harkness, and D. O. Olago. 1997. Impact of Lower Atmospheric Carbon Dioxide on Tropical Mountain Ecosystems. *Science* 278:1422–26.

Street, F. A., and A. T. Grove. 1979. Global Maps of Lake-level Fluctuations since 30,000 Years BP. *Quaternary Research* 12:83–118.

Tavakolian, B. 1999. Comment on "Is Inequality Universal?" by P. C. Salzman. *Current Anthropology* 40(1): 54.

Taylor, D., P. J. Lane, V. Muiruri, A. Ruttledge, R. Gaj McKeever, T. Nolan, P. Kenny, and R. Goodhue. 2005. Mid- to Late-Holocene Vegetation Dynamics on the Laikipia Plateau, Kenya. *The Holocene* 15(6): 837–46.

Telford, R. J., and H. F. Lamb. 1999. Groundwater-Mediated Response to Holocene Climatic Change Recorded by the Diatom Stratigraphy of an Ethiopian Crater Lake. *Quaternary Research* 52(1): 63–75.

Thompson, L. G., E. Mosley-Thompson, M. E. Davis, K. A. Henderson, H. H. Brecher, V. S. Zagorodnov, T. A. Mashiotta, et al. 2002a. Kilimanjaro Ice Core Oxygen Isotope, Ion, and Dust Data. *IGBP PAGES/World Data Center for Paleoclimatology Data Contribution Series,* #2002-071. Boulder, CO: NOAA/NGDC Paleoclimatology Program.

—— 2002b. Kilimanjaro Ice Core Records: Evidence of Holocene Climate Change in Tropical Africa. *Science* 298:589–93.

Tornay, S. 1979. Armed Conflicts in the Lower Omo Valley, 1970–1976: An Analysis from within Nyangatom Society. In *Warfare among East African Herders*, ed. K. Fukui and D. Turton, pp. 97–118. Senri Ethnological Studies. Osaka, Japan: National Museum of Ethnology.

Turton, D. 1977. Response to Drought: The Mursi of Southwestern Ethiopia. *Disasters* 1:275–87.

—— 1979. War, Peace and Mursi Identity. In *Warfare among East African Herders*, ed. K. Fukui and D. Turton, pp. 179–210. Senri Ethnological Studies. Osaka, Japan: National Museum of Ethnology.

Vincens, A., D. Williamson, F. Thevenon, M. Taieb, G. Buchet, M. Decobert, and N. Thouveny. 2003. Pollen-based Vegetation Changes in Southern Tanzania during the Last 4200 Years: Climate Change and/or Human Impact. *Palaeogeography, Palaeoclimatology, Palaeoecology* 198:321–33.

Waller, R. 1988. Emutai: Crisis and Response in Maasailand 1883–1902. In *The

Ecology of Survival, ed. D. Johnson and D. Anderson, pp. 73–114. Boulder, CO: Westview Press.

Wandibba, S. 1977. The Definition and Description of Ceramic Wares of the Early Pastoralist Period in Kenya. Paper presented at the Staff Seminar, Kenyatta University College, Department of History, Nairobi.

—— 1980. The Application of Attribute Analysis to the Study of Later Stone Age / Neolithic Pottery Ceramics in Kenya (Summary). In *Proceedings of the 8th Panafrican Congress of Prehistory and Quaternary Studies, Nairobi, 5 to 10 September 1977*, ed. R. Leakey and B. Ogot, pp. 283–85. Nairobi: TILLMIAP.

Weiss, H., and R. S. Bradley. 2001. What Drives Societal Collapse. *Science* 291:609–10.

Wright, D. K. 2007. Tethered Mobility and Riparian Resource Exploitation among Neolithic Hunters and Herders in the Galana River Basin, Kenyan Coastal Lowlands. *Environmental Archaeology* 12(1): 25–47.

Wylie, A. 1985. The Reaction against Analogy. *Advances in Archaeological Method and Theory* 8:63–110.

3

Spreading Risk in Risky Environments: An East African Example

KATHLEEN RYAN AND KAREGA–MUNENE

INTRODUCTION

East African pastoralism has been characterized mainly by the ability of successive or continuing groups of people to adapt to, and survive in, an unpredictable but potentially productive environment. This has been made possible by the adoption/development of a diversity of adaptations: environmental, biological, behavioral, social and/or political. A hallmark of success has been flexibility. Some examples can be seen in opportunistic use of pastures and water sources; ability to opt in and out of a pastoral lifestyle as the need arises; biological adaptations of people to diet and nutritional seasonal stress and of animals to heat stress and low water intake; biobehavioral adaptations, as control of fertility in humans, or human reinforcement/facilitation of animals' biological adaptations to scarcity of water and to disease. Insurance against times of stress can be seen in exchanges between groups (agricultural or hunting products in exchange for livestock), and within the group (gift exchanges, loans, and bridewealth).

When we began research in Maasailand in 1990, we posed two related questions: How do pastoral groups, such as the Maasai, manage to survive, and often prosper, in harsh and unpredictable environments? And can their strategies of survival provide analogs for the behavior of pastoral groups living in similar environments in the historic and prehistoric past? In this chapter we concentrate on the present and recent past, that is, the last 150 years. The primary focus is on cattle; how they are integrated into both the biological and social environments of their caretakers; and how social relationships, cemented through cattle, are an essential part of pastoralists' survival strategy.

ENVIRONMENTAL CONTEXT

Although straddling the equator, environment and climate vary considerably throughout East Africa, ranging from the hot and semi-arid areas of northern Kenya to the cool conditions of the highlands. Several environmental/climatic zones can be distinguished on the basis of vegetation, which reflects both general environment and climate (Hamilton 1982; Lind and Morrison 1974). Cultivation practices are determined by the amount and predictability of rainfall.

Mobile pastoralists can cope in areas of lower and less predictable rainfall because livestock can be moved to within reach of locally remaining water sources when dry conditions are prolonged, and distributed widely in the aftermath of the rains when grasses are both abundant and most nutritious. Higher altitude grasslands, generally in areas with rather higher annual rainfall, would suit stock even better, but in those areas herders and agriculturalists compete over land. Most of the nomadic or semi-nomadic groups of East Africa inhabit arid or semiarid landscapes.

Maasailand today straddles the border of southern Kenya and northern Tanzania. Census figures for Maasai in Kenya in 1989 were estimated at 377,089. Figures based on Maa speakers estimated 453,000 in Kenya (1994) and 430,000 in Tanzania (1993) for a total population estimate of close to 900,000 between the two countries (http://en.wikipedia.org/wiki/Maasai). Our study locations were in Kajiado District which covers 21,105 km^2 with a human population in 1979 of approximately 107,000, of whom 70,000 were Maasai (Meadows and White 1979:2). The elevation varies from 600 m to 2,400 m, but open plains lying between 1,000 m to 1,500 m predominate. Precipitation is inadequate for rainfed agriculture except for two pockets of high rainfall, one on the lower northern slopes of Kilimanjaro in the southeast of the District in the area around Loitokitok, and the other around Ngong where the District borders Nairobi suburbs.

Rainfall in Kajiado is bimodal, with the long rains normally between March and June and the short rains between October and December. However, they are unpredictable in terms of their onset and duration. In some years no rain comes in the short rains season and too little, if any, in the long rains season. It is important to have well distributed rainfall in any year in order to increase productivity; heavy rain all at once is less favorable to pastoral herds.

PREHISTORIC BACKGROUND TO
EAST AFRICAN PASTORALISM

The beginnings of the pastoral mode in eastern Africa have been the focus of interest in archaeology for many decades. However, it is only in the last 20 years that these studies of long-term trends in evolutionary history have been incorporated into the anthropological literature on pastoralism. Pastoralism began in northeastern Africa around 9,000 years ago (Gifford-Gonzalez 2005; Hanotte et al. 2002; Stokstad 2002; Marshall et al. this volume). Unlike in the Near East and Europe, it developed among hunter-gatherers before the establishment of settled agricultural communities in the area (Marshall 1994; Marshall and Hildebrand 2002).

Marshall calls attention to the implications of the establishment of the modern climatic regime in East Africa with a bimodal rainfall system around 4,000 years ago (Marshall et al. this volume; Roberts this volume). The resultant burgeoning of the rangelands of East Africa presented opportunities for pastoral expansion onto the savannas that had not been possible previously. The absence of a lengthy dry season improves the chances of adequate grass growth and conservation, and facilitates cattle lactation year round. This is what differentiates East African pastoral adaptations from those in other parts of Africa (Marshall 1994:34, citing Dahl and Hjort 1976 and Western and Finch 1986; Marshall and Hildebrand 2002).

Ambrose (1982), taking the example of Kenya today, points to the extreme heterogeneity of ethnic and linguistic groups in a very diverse landscape. An examination of prehistoric/historic climatic, archaeological, and linguistic sequences (post-5000 BP; Ambrose 1984:fig. 6) suggests that a high degree of diversity pertained in the past also.

RECENT HISTORY OF MAASAI

Ancestors of the Maasai are believed to have originated somewhere between Lake Turkana and the Ethiopian Highlands, perhaps as early as AD 500, and spread southwards and westwards into Kenya and Tanzania by AD 1000–1500. Between the 16th and 19th centuries AD Maa-speaking peoples extended their influence from Lake Turkana, southward through the Rift Valley, and into northern Tanzania (Homewood and Rodgers 1991:58–59). The 19th-century history of the Maasai is normally drawn from accounts of contemporary observers (Hollis 1905; Merker 1904) and from detailed reconstructions of events presented by Lamprey and Waller (1990), Waller (1985, 1988), and Waller and Sobania (1994). During the British colonial period, which ended in 1963 with Kenyan independence, many of the lands that Maasai used as refuge areas during the dry season or during prolonged drought were confiscated and turned into wildlife reserves, for example, Nairobi National park, Amboseli, Masai Mara.

Until the introduction of group ranch formations in the 1960s through 1990s, traditional systems of section, clan, and age-set provided a framework for Maasai social and economic cooperation, particularly in management, transactions, and redistribution of livestock (Homewood and Rodgers 1991:43). Our study coincided with the continuing formation of group ranch systems in Kajiado District where several extended families became members and acquired tenure over a designated group ranch that had specific boundaries. Not all group ranches were equal, either in extent or pasture. Kitengela group ranch, set up in the mid-1970s, covered 18,292 ha with 215 registered Maasai members. It was subsequently subdivided in 1988 into approximately 101-ha plots to 215 landowning households (Nkedianye et al. 2008:129–30). This trend towards privatization spread throughout Maasailand and still continues today. Many individual land holders wanted to raise fences around their plots, which posed serious risks to wildlife in an area like Kitengela that was on the pathway of herd migrations in and out of Nairobi National Park. Local groups worked to persuade landowners to leave the range open in return for monetary compensation. Many have accepted this option. In addition, Kitengela's proximity to the capital city of Nairobi offered a variety of wage-earning opportunities not available in other parts of Maasailand. More southern areas of Kenya's Maasailand tended to fall into a middle range, with a much more limited range of options than at Kitengela, and several group ranching families found themselves cut off from their traditional grazing areas and water sources, especially the refuge areas resorted to in the dry seasons.

The Case Study

Our initial ethnographic/ethnohistoric case study, which began in 1990 and continued through 2002, focused on how Maasai pastoralists utilized cattle and other livestock to mediate the vicissitudes inherent in their environment. We gathered recent histories of the study families as well as the histories of their cattle herds embedded in cattle genealogies dating back to the war against the Laikipia in 1875, before the British took control of the area. Our inquiries sought to elucidate the ways in which the requirements of the cattle shaped Maasai life. Notably, the mobility necessary to provide cattle with a diversity of grazing ranges, in order to spread the risks inherent in periodic drought and/or disease, has led to a complex system of cattle acquisition, redistribution, and exchange.

We deliberately chose families in the middle range of economic opportunity and concentrated on those who continued to live with their livestock within a traditional *boma* settlement. These families typically herded up to 50 cattle, which is the number generally deemed manageable by a family group. In addition, each family also kept sheep and goats. Many of our consultants were senior elders (ranging in age from 50 to 100) who still practiced traditional herd management, even within the new constraints of their designated group ranches. We did include the extended families (wives, sons, daughters) in our discussions, but it was clear that it would be the older men who retained the knowledge of their "traditional" risk management and survival strategies. It was these elders who first alerted us to the significance of social transactions related to cattle that allowed herders and their livestock to successfully mediate their physical environment.

MAASAI POLITICAL AND SOCIAL ORGANIZATION

Sections, clans, and age-grades are important organizing principles in Maasai society. Under British colonial rule Maasai groups in northern areas such as Laikipia were forced to move southwards. The Maasailand Reserves (set up by the British) were divided into separate geographically based Maasai sections occupied by Ilkisongo, Ilpurko, Iloitai, Imatapato, Iloodokilani, Ilkeekonyokie, Ilkaputiei, Ildamat, Ilsiria, Ilwuasinkishu, Ildalalekutuk, and Ilaitaytok. The largest sectional group was the Ilkisongo, who occupied parts of southern Kenya and northern Tanzania (Saitoti and Beckwith 1980:19) (Fig. 3.1). Each section occupied a specific territory with well-defined boundaries within which all members of that section were free to graze their cattle; to cross into another section with cattle, permission had to be sought from that section (Hedlund 1971:1). Each section was divided into localities (*enkutoto*, pl. *inkutot*): self-contained ecological units with contiguous areas of wet and dry season pastures.

Maasai may belong to any one of five clans whose members are spread throughout the sections. Clans have no formal clan leaders and are not organized as local geographically cohesive groups (Hedlund 1971:45). Clan members are dispersed throughout Maasailand, thereby providing a wide network of potential support and obligation which supercedes section boundaries.

In addition, Maasai are organized according to age-grade and age-set systems. Each age-set has its own spokesman appointed from among the group. Men proceed through different age-grades as members of named cohorts or age-sets that are formed every 14 or 15 years. Age grades determine the formal political structure and the system is based on the primacy of elder males over younger males and men over women. Women do not have an independent age-set system but automatically join the age-set of their husbands when they marry.

SETTLEMENT PATTERN

Pastoralist settlements are clearly designed to reduce risk to humans and herds. Western and Dunne (1979:75–98) confirm that Maasai settlements are "distributed in a pattern which reflects various physical and biological characteristics of the landscape." For example, they avoid steep hill slopes, as well as lower sections of long hillsides likely to be in the path of large amounts of run-off. Steep slopes are also difficult for weakened cattle to negotiate at the end of the dry season so that even well-drained steep slopes are avoided.

Mbae (1986) identified five major site types: boma (*enkang*), butchery sites, seasonal cattle camps, meat feasting sites (*il puli*), and *manyatta*.

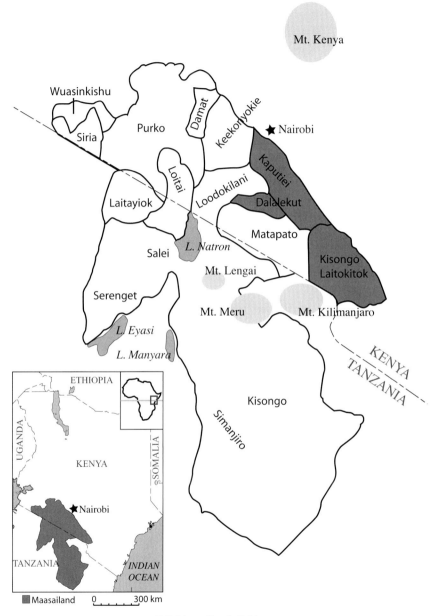

3.1 Maasailand divisions.

The Boma (*enkang*)

The boma is considered the main home settlement. It is normally occupied by a number of families who may or may not be related. It is occupied year round by at least some members of each family. Bomas range in size and in resident population depending on the economic status of the owners and the labor requirements for caring for the herd at the boma or that needed seasonally at other satellite settlements such as the seasonal cattle camps or *manyatta*. Women construct houses within the boma of sticks and daub, and cow dung. The roofs are made waterproof with a mixture of cow dung, soil, and ashes (Mbae 1986:158; Ryan 2004; Shahack-Gross, Marshall, and Weiner 2003; Shahack-Gross et al. 2004). Figure 3.2 shows a house under construction.

Bomas may be abandoned and reoccupied several times, not necessarily by the same people. Reasons for abandonment vary: death of a family member; death of many livestock associated with that site; disagreements between boma members; or when accumulated dung becomes unmanageable (Mbae 1990:281). The last is sometimes resolved by either building a new boma or just building an extension of the existing one, right next to the original settlement. That way the animals can be moved, allowing the dung in the central area to dry out and become compacted, as our Maasai consultants in Ol Girra did in 1996. This same boma was inundated by flooding and was completely abandoned in 1998.

Butchery Sites

Butchery is normally carried out in designated places hidden by bushes and preferably under a tree (Mbae 1986:163) and may be as much as 30 to 150 m from the boma. A butchery site has two areas: the area designated for skinning and dismemberment and the hearth area.

The Seasonal Camp

During the dry season, Maasai set up transient seasonal camps in areas where there is pasture. Their placement may be as much as 35 km from the home boma and is dependent on the intensity and extent of dry conditions (Mbae 1990:285). Wet season camps are also set up to take advantage of fresh pastures and to spare the grazing around the home boma.

3.2 House under construction.

Meat Feasting Sites (*il puli*)

Mbae (1990:286) identifies two variations of meat or soup feasting enclosures. The first is used by all family members of a man who has slaughtered an animal for family consumption (Mbae 1990:fig. 13.7). The second type of *ol pul* is reserved exclusively for warriors (*ilmurrani*) and is located from a half to one km away from the nearest bomas (Mbae 1990:fig. 13.8) and always near water.

The *Manyatta*

The *manyatta* is a settlement similar to, but larger than, a home boma, specifically built to accommodate warriors during their moranhood. Selected elders act as mentors to the warriors. It is in these surroundings that young men are instructed in their future role as elders and caretakers of the herds. Traditionally the warriors stayed apart for up to 10 years in the manyatta. The introduction of formal schooling, however, has constrained the time that warriors can spend there. Some of our families sent their children to formal schools but allowed them to stay in the manyatta for short periods of time during school vacations.

LIVESTOCK ECOLOGY AND FOOD SECURITY

Cattle, camels, sheep, and goats are the domesticates of choice in arid and semi-arid regions of East Africa today (Dahl and Hjort 1976; Homewood and Rodgers 1991; Wilson 1984). These species have played a prominent role in the area for several thousand years. Their choice of vegetation and their requirements for water, forage, and minerals such as salt differ, as does their ability to survive periods of scarcity. Differences in reproductive capacity; dietary requirements; production of milk, blood, and meat; resistance to disease; heat tolerance, etc., differentially affect their own chances of survival and the survival of the humans who care for them and depend on them for their livelihood. The potential value of these species to their owners, therefore, varies considerably with vegetation and climate.

Although Maasai are perceived as "people of cattle" they also herd sheep and goats as part of their risk management strategy. It is generally these small stock that supply meat for family consumption. They also can be relied on for limited amounts of milk when cow's milk is in short supply.

Cattle

Reproductive capacity. Fertility and fecundity rates among cattle, as well as the timing of the beginning and end of their fertile period, are dependent on their nutritional status (Ryan 2005) and are closely correlated with availability and quality of forage or fodder, water, and other environmental conditions (Dahl and Hjort 1976:33).

Lactation. Lactation is dependent on regular calving. Calving frequency correlates with a cow's fecundity, which in turn is dependent on nutritional status. In general, cattle lactation on marginal drylands lasts on average 8 months (Dahl and Hjort 1976:142), but can be as little as 3 months under bad conditions. In areas with two rainy seasons a year, cattle have a better chance of prolonging lactation than in areas with only one. In addition, this bimodal rainfall pattern can lead to bimodal patterns of conception and calving, thus facilitating lactation in some of the cows in the herd at every season of the year.

Milk production. While individual yields of milk from cows in arid and semi-arid zones of eastern Africa are low, the milk is of high quality. For example, Orr and Gilks (1931), in their study of the diet of Maasai pastoralists during the 1930s, estimated milk composition of 5.5% fat, 3.7% protein, 4.9 % lactose, and 0.73% ash. In comparison to traditional East African herding systems, the average European cow's milk contains 3.5% fat, 3.5% protein, and 5.0% lactose (Orr and Gilks 1931:154).

Water needs. Access to water limits both the number and species that can be herded successfully. Cattle require frequent watering although they can adapt to watering every 2–4 days depending upon the environment (Dahl and Hjort 1976: 238). According to Baxter (1954), the ideal distance between settlement and water is five herding hours at 4.8–5.6 kms/hour (3–3.5 miles). In our study area, in order to preserve the grazing area around the settlement after the rains in June 1999, cattle traversed 20 km per day. They grazed along the way to keep up their strength, spending 10 hours to complete the journey.

Mortality. The average age at death is given as 9–15 years (Grunnet 1962, for Dinka cows; Prole 1967, for Maasai cows). The number of calves per dam over her lifetime then could range from 5–12 live births. One of the cows in a Maasai herd in our study area had given birth to 13 calves and died at the age of 18+ years.

SYMBIOTIC RELATIONSHIPS

Cattle provide the Maasai with meat, bone marrow, milk, and blood. In return, Maasai protect and care for their cattle.

Food Security for Humans

Meat. Although cattle provide herders with meat, they are seldom slaughtered to supply food for the family alone, rather they tend to be part of a ceremony or celebration, with the meat shared among a number of participants. Mature, fattened steers are chosen for most ceremonies. Slaughter of a malnourished animal is avoided unless the animal is near death and likely to die anyway. Every effort is made to keep an animal alive so that it can be fattened for more nutritive consumption at a later time. This choice of only animals in good condition fits well with Speth's (1987) and Speth and Spielmann's (1983) evidence of seasonal consumption of meat among hunter-gatherers.

Maasai, who suffer weight loss and general nutritional stress during the yearly dry seasons or during prolonged drought, would have reason to limit their consumption of lean meat protein and seek out fat. When one of our elderly consultants became ill he asked us to purchase large amounts of beef breast and stomach fat which was boiled down to liquid so that he could drink it. He was also fed stews made from mutton to build up his strength. Digestive aids derived from plants are normally added to boiled fat or fatty stews to emulsify the fat and aid digestion.

Bone marrow. Bone marrow is an important addition to the human diet, supplying much needed fat. Marrow cavities act as fat and energy storage units and are the final reserve drawn upon by nutritionally stressed animals (Blumenschine and Madrigal 1993:557). Fat is mobilized first from the proximal long bones (humerus and femur); therefore, distal long bones, especially metapodials, increase in importance as energy sources as stress progresses, whether it be in response to seasonal shortages of forage and water and/or reproductive state. Fat is redeployed in reverse order under nutritionally favorable conditions (Speth 1990:152).

Blood. Many pastoralist groups consume limited amounts of blood from living animals. Dahl and Hjort (1976:172, citing French 1970:185) report that cattle blood contains 7.6% protein, 0.06% fat, 0.05% glucose. It also contains some valuable minerals such as iron, and small amounts of calcium and phosphorus. A limited supply of blood is drawn from living cattle, especially during the dry season when milk is scarce, usually from male animals. It is often mixed with milk or maize meal and boiled or, more rarely, drunk raw on ritual occasions.

Milk. Cattle also supply milk, a main staple of the Maasai diet. The amount of milk that an animal produces over a year is heavily dependent on length of lactation. This in turn is constrained by the environment in which the animal subsists. In years of "normal" rainfall, taken for Maasailand as a long and short rainy season, cow nutrition will be good, conception likely, and healthy calves produced.

Advantages for Livestock

Protection. In return, humans offer cattle and other livestock protection from predators, in the case of the Maasai, vigilant herding during the day and a safe haven within an enclosure at night (Fig. 3.3).

Health and nutrition. Herders' extensive knowledge of the vegetation on their range enhances livestock's ability to survive. Grasses from the field study area that are important for animal nutrition appear in varying sequence throughout the year. Some at the beginning of the wet season ensure quick recovery from near starvation after a long dry season or help

3.3 Settlement enclosure.

to put on weight; while others are particularly useful in promoting lactation and maintaining an overall healthy state; and yet others act as last resort forage towards the end of a long dry season or during prolonged drought. In May/June 1999, at the end of the rainy season, our Maasai consultants pointed out variations in vegetation cover.

Prevention or treatment of disease. Maasai herders spend a lot of time and effort on animal disease prevention by avoidance of disease-infested areas, or quarantining healthy animals in refuge areas. Some acquire animals that have a resistance to certain diseases. Maasai and many other pastoralist groups in East Africa use a wide variety of plant-derived medicines to prevent or treat livestock disease (see Fratkin 1996; Glover, Stewart, and Gwynne 1966; Heine, Heine, and König 1988; Kokwaro 1976; Kokwaro and Herlocker 1982; McCorkle and Mathias-Mundy 1992; Morgan 1981; Watt and Breyer-Brandwijk 1962). Even application of an insecticide can make a difference. The gum from the olchilchili tree (*Commiphora* sp.) and/or a solution derived from boiling the bark is very effective against fleas and ticks.

CATTLE MANAGEMENT AND SOCIAL TRANSACTIONS

To explore the links between the special needs of cattle and some features of Maasai social relations, we concentrated on three aspects of cattle management: how cattle are acquired; how they are exchanged or redistributed; and how, and under what circumstances, they die.

What follows was drawn from interviews conducted with Maasai elders and their families between 1990 and 2002. Elders were chosen because they exercise the ultimate control over the family herds, but wives and older children were also consulted, particularly when we discussed milk yields, animal health, or behavior of individual animals. In conducting these interviews we were strongly supported by our Kenyan collaborators from the National Museums of Kenya and our Maasai interpreter.

Cattle Naming

The classificatory system embedded in the naming of individual cows is discussed in detail by Galaty (1989:218–30). He identifies distinct modes of signification, using symbols of social transactions (such as "in exchange," "gift from a friend," or "bridewealth") and forms of visual description (such as "speckled," or "without horns") or a combination of both (such as "exchanged for reddish-brown ox"). All cattle in a particular lineage are named after a matriarch cow. Her name tends to commemorate the event or transaction by which she was acquired and her descendants continue to take that name. For further discussion of cattle-naming systems, see Rigby (1969) and Schoenbrun (1993:46). In Table 3.1, we give examples of names given to cattle in our consultants' herds. Figure 3.4 shows an elder and his brother in Isynia with Noomaroro "first cow from father."

Table 3.1. Names Given to Consultants' Cattle (heifers)*

	NAME	MEANING	HOW OR WHY OBTAINED
Named for transaction	Noontoyie	for girls	Bridewealth received for sister
	Entoua	of love	Gift from age-mate
	Pokurot	after a struggle	From a cattle raid
	Kereti	blessing	Brought in by informant's mother
	Naoli	exchanged one	Adopted into family matriarch line
Received from	Nolmongi	reminder of an ox	Exchanged for steer
	Mongio	exchanged for	Received in exchange for steer
	Sampu	brown-striped ox	
	Nesingo	from Singo in Kambaland	Bought for disease resistance
Descriptive/ behavioral names	Meshuri**	no cover: brownish with no horns	Cattle raid; first cow received from father
	Noomaroro**	named after maroro tree; long ears	First cow received from father
	Kilera**	named after acacia tree	Paid for by selling dead elephant tusk found in acacia bush in Amboseli; first cow received from father
	Nkeyi	speckled, black and white	Descendant of main family matriarch
	Naimai	no horns and small hump	Descendant of main family matriarch
	Merurai	troublesome, cried at night when a calf, doesn't allow people to sleep	Descendant of main family matriarch

*Following classifications used in Galaty 1989

**Main family matriarch descended from "first cows" given to informants

3.4 Maasai brothers pose with Noomararoo, descendent of "first cow from father" at Isynyia.

A typical Maasai family cattle herd is approximately 50, the number a family can manage in terms of labor and grazing. Ideally the herd comprises 80% females and 20% males, including castrates, although there is quite a lot of variation in these ratios even within Maasailand. These may be subdivided into as many as 10 cattle matrilineages or lines. Cattle are allotted to specific matricentric households in the polygynous Maasai family. Each animal can therefore be classified genealogically (from the matriarch), spatially (to a household), and by individual description (gender, age, color, and behavior) (Galaty 1989). A detailed examination of naming and genealogical data, undertaken from 1991 to 1995 (Ryan et al. 1991; 2000) in an attempt to record strategies of herd management, led us to examine more closely the social significance of cattle transactions in Maasai society and to identify those actions which we suggest have a direct causal link to animal welfare and therefore overall risk management.

Acquisition of Cattle

Cattle are acquired through inheritance, bridewealth, gift-giving, raiding, and purchase. Avenues of acquisition are different for men and women.

Acquisition here does not imply ownership but simply rights in an animal (Oboler 1985 discusses this differentiation). Although both sexes eventually acquire herds, they do so in a different sequence and they maintain different levels of authority over their allotted animals. In constructing the genealogies we started with the first cow given to each man when he was a small boy, usually by his father, recording her name and how she was acquired, how many female and male calves were born to her, how many of those females produced offspring of their own, how many males were kept whole and how many castrated, and how and under what circumstances the castrates were disposed of. In 1991, our oldest Maasai consultant clearly remembered the first cow given to him by his father, over 90 years before when he was 2 years old (ca. 1900). That cow was a descendant of one raided by our consultant's father in 1875 from the Laikipia Maasai, and renamed Meshuri (meaning "no defence" or "no cover" from driving rain) in memory of the hardship endured during the arduous but successful raid. This original Meshuri matriarch had seven female and three bull calves. All but one of the female calves were given to my consultant and his brothers; one remained in the father's herd.

The calf shown in the center of the picture in Figure 3.5 follows in the line of the original Meshuri matriarch and carries the Meshuri line name, although she will not be officially recognized until she produces her first calf. This line remains dominant in the herd today. Males do not get named for the line as females do; they are given individual descriptive names, although it is known from which matriarch's line they descend. In some cases where the direct blood line of a matriarch (particularly the "first cow" line) dies out, one of the male offspring of that line is exchanged for a heifer from another herd and that heifer is "adopted" into the line and given the matriarch's name, although she has no direct blood link to that line. In fact, all of our consultant's Meshuri line derive from this kind of exchange because his second generation Meshuri heifer produced only bull calves. Other direct blood line Meshuri cattle continue in his brothers' children's herds.

Everyone remembered his "first cow" and at least one or two generations of offspring. Between the third or fourth generation and the recent past, as a man's herds increased and cattle were allocated to wives' households, redistributed to sons, sent out as bridewealth or dowry, or given or received as gifts, memories were less exact. However, because our consultants

3.5 Young calf cohort at Isajiloni; Meshuri "first cow from father" is second from the left.

came from different age-sets, the time of confused memories for one often coincided with the clear "first cow" stage of another and so we were able to collect family cattle histories spanning 130 years.

More animals can be given by a father at any time; the number given depends on the love between father and child, and a father's wealth. Other avenues of acquisition include animals given from a mother's herd, starting from when a boy is old enough to herd; and sons eventually inherit a share of their mother's herd. At the time of marriage, parents and relatives try to give gifts to build up a son's herd. Some of these are reallocated to his bride's herd but he retains a residual unallotted portion to which he has sole rights. Animals acquired through special gift or purchase generally are added to his personal herd.

Daughters are also given a heifer from the family line and it is descendants of this animal, usually a cow and calf, that go out with the girl when she marries. Unlike a boy, she does not inherit all of the progeny. However, she will be allotted cattle by her husband, and her husband's relatives and her co-wives are expected to give her gifts according to their means. These gifts are intended to cement a special bond with the new wife. They are always remembered by donor and recipient and are reflected in the reciprocal terms of

respect they use when addressing each other (see Spencer 1988:31). Our oldest consultant still remembered the names and colors of the heifers he gave
to his eldest son's two wives at marriage; they were both heifers descended
from his "first cow" lineage. The new wife's herd then will be made up from
the cow and calf from her own family; the allotment from her husband; and
other gift animals (from relatives and co-wives). From her herd, her sons will
build up herds of their own. She cannot give any cattle outside the family.

In addition, animals received by parents, as bridewealth for a daughter,
can be reallocated to her brother's herd; or a father can keep an animal from
his daughter's bridewealth in his own herd. Each of these animals is named
after the bridewealth transaction as *noontoyie* although each is identified and
remembered as a separate line. In Table 3.2, we list the noontoyie transactions for one elder in the southern area, who had one for a sister and three
for his daughters. All marriage contract animals are included here, not just

Table 3.2. *Noontoyie* (bridewealth) Lines

WHAT	HOW ACQUIRED	DISPOSITION OF BRIDEWEALTH ANIMALS OR THEIR OFFSPRING		
		FEMALES	BULLS	CASTRATES (STEERS)
Noontoyie 1 　1 mature cow	From sister's bridewealth	4 heifers; 1 "exch. heifer"	1 bull: remained in herd	3 steers: 1st exch. for 1 heifer; 2nd exch. for 2 steers*; 3rd sold
Noontoyie 2 　1 mature cow 　with male 　calf; 5 heifers; 　1 steer	From 1st daughter	1 mature cow: died of drought; 5 heifers: 2 given to informant's brothers		1 male calf: died; 1 steer
Noontoyie 3 　1 mature cow 　with male 　calf; 3 heifers; 　1 steer	From 2nd daughter	1 mature cow 3 heifers		1 male calf: castrated, slaughtered eve of daughter's initiation ceremony; 1 steer: slaughtered during wedding ceremony
Noontoyie 4 　1 mature cow 　with male 　calf; 3 heifers; 　2 steers	From 3rd daughter	1 mature cow; 3 heifers: 2 given to informant's brothers; 1 "exch. heifer"		1 male calf: died of EC fever; 2 steers: 1 exch. for 1 heifer

*1st "exch. Steer" exchanged for 6 sheep and 4 goats; 2nd "exch. steer" exchanged for 1 female donkey the one cow and calf plus a heifer that are given to the bride's parents when the bride officially goes to her husband's boma, but only the official cow and calf and their descendants are named noontoyie. Twenty-three animals in the herd in 1993 derived from bridewealth transactions.

A third category, *sotua* (a gift from a friend), includes gifts between age-mates, between brothers or half brothers, from a man to his future father-in-law, or from a rich man to a poorer relative. These are often reciprocal, with the original recipient returning the favor at some future time. Examples of sotua transactions are given in Table 3.3.

Table 3.3. *Sotua* Transactions

1	Given by friend and age-mate when they were morans
	Informant gave back a steer after second marriage (offspring: 8 calves—5 females, 3 males)
2	Given by friend one age-set older than informant
	Informant gave a daughter in return as second wife
	Just before marriage, informant gave his future father-in-law a heifer (offspring: 6 calves—3 females, 3 males)
3	Given by son of first wife's father (offspring: 6 calves—3 females, 3 males)
4	Given by sister's husband when informant married second wife (offspring: 10 calves—7 female, 3 male)

Cattle raiding, although illegal since colonial times, was, until quite recently, an acceptable means of increasing one's herd. Cattle were raided from other adjoining ethnic groups or from rival Maasai sections, as in the case of the raid on the Laikipia that garnered the matriarch Meshuri. Today, however, purchase has largely replaced this option.

The sources for typical lines in a herd from the southern area are shown in Table 3.4. All the matriarch lines (except the descendants of the one purchased animal) derive from social transactions enacted over a considerable period of the herd owner's lifetime: from the first cow received from his father; bridewealth from his sister; a gift from an age-mate while they were both young men; gifts from the fathers of his two wives; gifts from a stepbrother and son; and finally bridewealth from a daughter and a gift from a son-in-law. These transactions occurred sequentially over a period of 40 to 50 years, but all are still remembered through the matriarch lines. An example here is the gift from an elder brother to his young stepbrother (our consultant) that forged a special

Table 3.4. Source of Typical Herd Lines from the Southern Area

SOURCE	MAASAI TERM	DESCRIPTION
Gift from parent	*Kilera*	"first cow"
Bridewealth	*Noontoyie*	from sister
Bridewealth	*Noontoyie*	from oldest daughter
Other gift	*Sotua*	from age-mate during moranhood
Other gift	*Sotua*	from father of first wife
Other gift	*Sotua*	from father of second wife
Other gift	*Sotua*	*from older step-brother*
Other gift	*Sotua*	from son of same step-brother
Other gift	*Sotua*	from son-in-law
Purchase	(none)	(typically from Kambaland)

bond between the two and was reinforced in the next generation by a gift from the older man's son.

In Table 3.5, we summarize the differences in avenues of acquisition between men and women. Sons can inherit animals from both father and mother. A mother's herd is reserved for her sons and those sons, in particular the last-born, are responsible for their mother's welfare—especially in her widowhood or old age. A father is initially responsible for a daughter's acquisition in that he gives her an animal from the family herds that she is expected to care for until she leaves in marriage, taking with her perhaps one or two animals from the progeny. The bulk of the herd she will care for over her lifetime is given to her by her future husband and his relatives and her co-wives and will pass on to her sons. Gifts probably account for a majority of exchanges, marking social transactions that form special bonds and hence the reciprocal ties necessary to a family's survival.

Table 3.5. Avenues towards Cattle Acquisition for Men and Women

	MEN	WOMEN
Inheritance	from father and mother	from father
Bridewealth	from sister or daughter	from daughter
Gift	from friends, relatives	from husband, relatives, co-wife
Purchase	option open to men	rarely option for women
Cattle-raiding	men-only activity	may get re-allocated cattle

Redistribution and Exchange

Animals are redistributed and exchanged through inheritance, bridewealth, gift, loan, purchase or sale and, until recently, cattle-raiding. The

genealogical charts show that cattle are seldom exchanged for mainly economic reasons such as the sale of a steer to pay for food or school fees.
Most exchanges also fulfill social obligations or mark social transactions,
as providing bridewealth; making a gift to bind a friendship; exchanging
steers for heifers to put in the care of a new wife entering the home-
stead; or exchanging heifers for steers to obtain the latter for ceremonial
slaughter.

Even sales of animals often have an underlying social significance: one
of our consultants sold one steer to pay for initiation ceremony expenses
and another for his father's burial expenses. Of course, most exchanges tend
to combine social and economic rationale—such as the exchange of a mature steer for a heifer and a small steer, when one has no immediate ceremonial or monetary use for that mature steer.

Risk Reduction and Temporary Exchange

Besides these exchanges, animals are redistributed in other ways. Parts
of a herd are often lodged temporarily at other bomas in an attempt to
spread risk from predators or cattle-raiders, while the home boma may have
some additions from outside. Labor requirements may necessitate moving
animals to other bomas when labor is scarce at the home boma. Another
strategy is to move children to labor-scarce settlements. Animals are also
moved temporarily (or, in some cases, semi-permanently) to other settlements in times of drought or when disease in one area reaches proportions
that threaten the herds severely. Our oldest consultant moved his whole
herd for an extended period when East Coast Fever hit his home range
in 1990. Usually animals are moved to kin settlements or to those of age-
mates; in future years the herder will reciprocate by accepting animals from
his friends or relatives when they are in trouble.

In early September 1991, at the end of two years of drought, one of
our southern consultants had moved most of his herd to other settlements,
keeping only a few lactating cows and calves to provide milk for the small
children at his own boma. He also retained his female sheep and goats but
by the end of the month he had to move them also. Many of the lactating cows with calves held at the home boma died that year. Under severe
drought conditions, elders recognize that some animals must be exposed to
almost certain death for the good of the family.

Exchanges or purchases made outside of the home locality bring in new breeding stock into the herds. Borana bulls are especially prized. In addition, purchases are often arranged for health reasons. Animals are especially preferred from areas known to produce animals with immunity to certain diseases, such the Kamba area where cattle are believed to be resistant to East Coast fever (currently the main cause of death among our consultants' herds). One such animal already mentioned above, Nesingo (meaning "from Singo"), was purchased from the town of Singo in Kambaland. She died at the age of 18+ and may have passed on her immunity to 13 offspring.

Herd Mortality

To maintain a herd balance of approximately 80% female and 20% male, culling strategies have to be employed. Throughout the lifetime of Maasai men or women, as they pass from one life stage to the next, each stage is marked by a distinctive ceremony, many involving the slaughter of an animal. The animal chosen is almost always a mature castrated male, preferably fattened. Because the beauty and health of the sacrificed animal enhances the status of the family, there is an incentive to keep male animals to maturity rather than cull them at a young age, as is done in many modern dairy economies. Retaining male animals to maturity also allows use of blood from the living animal when milk is scarce. Although cows may stay in the herd until they are well over 15 years of age, old or sick female animals are culled (slaughtered, or sold, for meat). These cullings represent deliberate decisions under unstressed conditions.

However, prevalence of drought and disease in most of Maasailand often tips the balance. Under conditions of stress, as during a prolonged drought, young animals are more vulnerable than mature ones since they depend on continued lactation of their dams. A whole generation can be lost. Strategies of care may favor young female calves over males by allowing them longer access to their mother's milk although Homewood and Rodgers (1991:168) found no such bias in mortality data for Maasai herds they studied in Tanzania. Division of the adult herd into male and female grazing units favors the selection of better quality forage for the breeding cows but, weakened by drought and starvation, even mature cows succumb to disease. Great efforts are made to save animals by dispersing them to better watered and pastured areas or disease-free zones but, inevitably, under extreme stress, many of the herd will die; in some cases all may be lost.

It is under extreme conditions such as loss of the majority of the herd that other less palatable strategies are tried, such as selling of small stock to buy grain and resorting to wage labor or labor in exchange for food. Reverting to hunting and gathering, one of the options employed in the past, is hardly an option today in our area. However, the most successful strategies are those that utilize those social bonds already enacted during a man's lifetime. During the immediate crisis, these may include moving all or some of the family in with relatives; fostering children at other bomas; borrowing milking cows from relatives or age-mates. In order to rebuild a herd, a man will have to call on his reciprocal ties with his own relatives, or with age-mates and in-laws, contracted over the years in many sotua and noontoyie transactions. When Maasai herds were decimated by epizootics and drought in the early 1930s, our oldest consultant lost the best part of his herd, so he called on his father's Kikuyu relatives who supplied him with the means to acquire the nucleus of a new herd. A son-in-law will be expected to come to the aid of his father-in-law, father-in-law to aid a son-in-law; brothers, half brothers, brothers-in-law, and age-mates are all potential donors, provided they have not themselves suffered a similar loss. When asked why he so freely gave a cow to an age-mate in trouble, an elder said: "Today I am well off but who knows about tomorrow?" Delayed payments of those "extra" animals contracted as part of a bridewealth settlement can be called in many years later. One elder in our group delegated his senior wife to travel to a far-off boma to negotiate the release of a contracted animal. Meantime he traveled many miles in the other direction to make arrangements to lodge his few remaining animals at an age-mate's boma.

Impact of Disease and Disaster

Since coping with disease and natural disaster was such a significant part of our informants' herd management concerns, we expanded the case study in order to concentrate more fully on the mechanisms of cause, transmittal, treatment, and consequences of disease. Disease and natural disaster are interlinked since many of the deaths we recorded were of animals that had succumbed to disease after they had been subjected to long periods of drought or nutritional stress. For example, a cow and calf from the Kilera line (Fig. 3.6), belonging to our main consultant in the south, were the victims of prolonged drought during the early to mid-1990s and both animals

3.6 The first wife of our consultant at Ol Girra picured with her husband's "first cow from father."

died before the long rains in 1993. The calf died first, and the mother was sold for slaughter because she was weak from starvation and no longer producing milk. This is an example of a loss that had social as well as economic repercussions since the Kilera line is the elder's main matriarch line, i.e., descended from "first cow from father." The calf had already been allocated to the first son of the second wife as part of his inheritance from his father. Its loss disrupted the natural growth of the boy's herd but it also cut off the remembered link to his father and grandfather through this gift from the Kilera line. Although there were severe losses in this family's herds, they were able to survive and build up their herds again by 1997 mainly because they had the option of redistributing part of the herd to a supplementary family boma in the hills some distance away and were able to send other segments of the herd to be cared for by age-mates or relatives. Another consultant was not so lucky. His herd was practically wiped out between 1992 and 1995. All four of his matriarch lines were affected. The majority died from disease or starvation; the remainder, including his sheep and goats, had to be sold to pay for food for the family or for school fees. This man in effect became a non-herd owner and had to get work herding other people's animals until he could begin to rebuild a herd. In 1999 he still had not recovered from his losses. He still remained Maasai since he was tied by clan, age set, and family ties. It is a flexible system that allows him to remain Maasai with the option of recovering some of the role of herd ownership. Even Maasai who go through the full formal education system to a professional job in the city are still considered Maasai with or without cattle.

ACQUISITION OF KNOWLEDGE

At that point we turned our attention to how specific bodies of knowledge were transmitted from one generation to another. It became obvious that children were encouraged at a very young age to take note of their surroundings. Most elders said they learned from their fathers during walks over the range or while following the herds. In this open air classroom they were introduced to a diversity of grasses, trees, and herbs. For example, they learned to recognize what grasses attracted wild animals, such as *moloki*, a grass favored by rhinos, or trees such as olkiloriti, preferred by elephants, and so they knew to be wary in those areas. As they grew older and took on herding responsibilities, they learned to identify plants which were toxic and which nutritious; to search out specific grasses at different times of the year, such as certain highly nutritious post-rains grasses or specific plants that promoted lactation; in the dry season they had to be familiar with a range of grasses that enabled livestock to survive during drought. They learned about shrubs, berries, and fruits suitable for feeding different species of livestock or edible for humans. As they grew older, under the guidance of elders specifically chosen to teach them, their intensive education began. Dry land areas were examined for plants specific to dry conditions; wetland and riverine environments were equally scrutinized and each plant identified and memorized. Within this context boys were also taught to recognize a wide variety of plants used as medicine. Girls follow their mothers and learn how to take care of the stock when they are in the settlement. They learn how to milk the cows, process milk, make butter, or gye. They will often herd small stock and calves when boy labor is scarce. Although men generally process the medicines, women also know which plants to use and will often prepare medicines for their children.

CONCLUSIONS

The Maasai livestock management strategies we recorded from 1990 to 2002 had a direct relationship with social transactions within the culture. It was through cattle genealogies and the remembered transactions in cattle that past and present social relations of humans were preserved. In addition, however, the strategies of acquisition, exchange, and culling carried implications for the welfare of the herds. The acquisition of "first cow" from the father at a very young age facilitated bonding between child and animal; gradual increase in responsibility under adult supervision prepared a young man (or woman) for future cattle rearing responsibilities. While exchanges were often couched in social terms, they usually had a sound management rationale. Cattle not only served as biological, environmental filters for herding families but as a mnemonic for the social relations that enabled herders to spread risk in a risky environment.

Knowledge of their environment is a crucial element in the survival of families who continue to follow a pastoral lifestyle. Most Maasai recognize that conservation of the range is in their own interest. Indeed, they believe that they have always been conservationists in their efforts to preserve the range for domestic and wild animals. Their traditional management strategies, practised over long periods of time and transmitted from generation to generation, have preserved a diversity of plants in a fragile ecosystem long after they have disappeared from more developed landscapes. In a discussion of causes of overgrazing in Amboseli National Park, which now supports a smaller animal population as a wildlife reserve than it did when the Maasai still grazed their herds there, Balick and Cox (1997:197) quote David Lovett Smith, a former warden of the Park: "The demise has been brought about, in my opinion, by inept management and a total lack of communication with the local people . . . For it was the Maasai people who themselves looked after the wildlife until governments and wildlife authorities took over its management, and, from the 1970s on, proceeded to mismanage it so badly."

Since the 1990s Maasai have looked for ways to diversify their economic base while still keeping a foothold in cattle keeping. Once considered part of the problem of overgrazing, many now are involved in tourism and/or wildlife conservation (see Homewood, Kristjanson, and Chenevix Trench 2008; Simpson 2008). As this generation of Maasai moves forward to consider a diversity of options for successful use of their environment (as park rangers or tourist guides; as managers or owners of tourist lodges; as range ecologists or wildlife biologists; as livestock herders; or as agropastoralists), they can draw on a body of Maasai traditional knowledge that may help them to preserve the range and the animals who live on it for future generations.

REFERENCES CITED

Ambrose, S. H. 1982. Archaeology and Linguistic Reconstructions of History in East Africa. In *The Archaeological and Linguistic Reconstructions of African History*, ed. C. Ehret and M. Posnansky, pp. 104–57. Berkeley: University of California Press.

—— 1984. The Introduction of Pastoral Adaptations to the Highlands of East Africa. In *From Hunters to Farmers. The Causes and Consequences of Food Production in Africa*, ed. J. D. Clark and S. Brandt, pp. 212–39. Berkeley: University of California Press.

Balick, M., and P. A. Cox. 1997. Biological Conservation and Ethnobotany. In *Plants, People, and Culture: The Science of Ethnobotany*, ed. M. Balick and P. A. Cox, pp. 179–208. New York: Scientific American Library.

Baxter, P. T. W. 1954. The Galla of Northern Kenya. PhD diss., Oxford Univ.

Blumenschine, R. J., and R. C. Madrigal. 1993. Variability in Long Bone Marrow Yields of East African Ungulates and Its Zooarchaeological Implications. *Journal of Archaeological Science* 20:555–87.

Dahl, G., and A. Hjort. 1976. *Having Herds: Pastoral Herd Growth and Household Economy*. Stockholm Studies in Social Anthropology, No. 2. Stockholm: University of Stockholm.

Fratkin, E. 1996. Traditional Medicine and Concepts of Healing among Samburu Pastoralists of Kenya. *Journal of Ethnobiology* 16:63–97.

French, M. H. 1970. *Some Observations on the Goat*. Rome: FAO.

Galaty, J. G. 1989. Cattle and Cognition: Aspects of Maasai Practical Reasoning. In *The Walking Larder: Patterns of Domestication, Pastoralism, and Predation*, ed. J. Clutton-Brock, pp. 215–30. London: Unwin Hyman.

Gifford-Gonzalez, D. P. 2005. Pastoralism and Its Consequences. In *African Archaeology: A Critical Introduction*, ed. A. Stahl, pp. 187–224. Cambridge: Blackwell.

Glover, P. E., J. Stewart, and M. D. Gwynne. 1966. Masai and Kipsigis Notes on East African Plants. *East African Agricultural Forestry Journal* 32:184–207.

Grunnet, N. T. 1962. An Ethnographic-Ecological Survey of the Relationships between the Dinka and Their Cattle. *Folk* 4:5–20.

Hamilton, A. C. 1982. *Environmental History of East Africa: A Study of the Quaternary*. London: Academic Press.

Hanotte, O., D. G. Bradley, J. W. Ochieng, Y. Verjee, E. W. Hill, and J. E. O. Rege. 2002. African Pastoralism: Genetic Imprints of Origins and Migrations. *Science* 296(5566): 336–39.

Hedlund, H. G. B. 1971. *The Impact of Group Ranches on a Pastoral Society*. Staff Paper No. 100, Institute for Development Studies, University of Nairobi.

Heine, B., I. Heine, and C. König. 1988. *Plant Concepts and Plant Use: An Ethnobotanical Survey of the Semi-arid and Arid Lands of East Africa*. Part V, *Plants of the Samburu (Kenya)*. Saarbrücken: Verlag Breitenback.

Hollis, A. C. 1905. *The Maasai: Their Language and Folklore*. Oxford: Clarendon Press.

Homewood, K. M., and W. A. Rodgers. 1991. *Maasailand Ecology. Pastoralist Development and Wildlife Conservation in Ngorongoro, Tanzania*. Cambridge: Cambridge University Press.

Homewood, K., P. Kristjanson, and P. Chenevix Trench. 2008. *Staying Maasai? Livelihoods, Conservation and Development in East African Rangelands*. New York: Springer.

Kokwaro, J. O. 1976. *Medicinal Plants of East Africa*. Nairobi: East African Literature Bureau.

—— 1993. *Medicinal Plants of East Africa*. 2nd ed. Nairobi: Kenya Literature Bureau.

Kokwaro, J. O., and D. J. Herlocker. 1982. *A Check-list of Botanical Samburu and Rendille Names of Plants of the "IPAL" Study Area, Marsibit District, Kenya*. IPAL (Integrated Project in Arid Lands) Technical Report Number D-4. Nairobi.

Lamprey, R., and R. Waller. 1990. The Loita-Mara Region in Historical Times: Patterns of Subsistence, Settlement and Ecological Change. In *Early Pastoralists of South-western Kenya*, ed. P. Robertshaw, pp. 16–35. Nairobi: British Institute in Eastern Africa.

Lind, E. M., and M. E. S. Morrison. 1974. *East African Vegetation*. London: Longman.

Marshall, F. 1994. Archaeological Perspectives on East African Pastoralism. In *African Pastoralist Systems. An Integrated Approach*, ed. E. Fratkin, J. Galvin, and E. Roth, pp. 17–44. Boulder, CO: Lynne Rienner.

Marshall, F., and E. Hildebrand. 2002. Cattle before Crops: The Beginnings of Food Production in Africa. *Journal of World Prehistory* 16(2): 99–143.

Mbae, N. B. 1986. Aspects of Maasai Ethnoarchaeology: Implications for Archaeological Interpretation. Master's thesis, University of Nairobi.

—— 1990. The Ethnoarchaeology of Maasai Settlements and Refuse Disposal Patterns in the Lemek Area. In *Early Pastoralists of South-western Kenya*, ed. P. Robertshaw, pp. 279–92. Nairobi: British Institute in Eastern Africa.

McCorkle, C. M., and E. Mathias-Mundy. 1992. Ethnoveterinary Medicine in Africa. *Africa* 62:59–93.

Meadows, S. J., and J. M. White. 1979. *Structure of the Herd and Determinants of Offtake Rates in Kajiado District in Kenya 1962–1977*. London: Agricultural Administration Unit. Overseas Development Institute.

Merker, M. 1904. *Die Masai*. Berlin: D. Reimer.

Morgan, W. T. W. 1981. Ethnobotany of the Turkana: Use of Plants by a Pastoral People and Their Livestock in Kenya. *Economic Botany* 35:96–130.

Nkedianye, D., M. Radeny, P. Kristjanson, and M. Herrero. 2008. Assessing Returns to Land and Changing Livelihood Strategies in Kitengela. In *Staying Maasai? Livelihoods, Conservation and Development in East African Rangelands*, ed. K. Homewood, P. Kristjanson, and P. Chenevix Trench, pp. 115–49. New York: Springer.

Oboler, R. S. 1985. *Women, Power, and Economic Change: The Nandi of Kenya*. Stanford: Stanford University Press.

Orr, J. B., and J. L. Gilks. 1931. *Studies in Nutrition: The Physique and Health of Two African Tribes*. Privy Medical Research Council Special Report Series 155. London.

Prole, J. H. B. 1967. Pastoral Land Use. In *Nairobi—City and Region*, ed. W. T. W. Morgan, pp. 90–97. Oxford: Oxford University Press.

Rigby, P. 1969. *Cattle and Kinship among the Gogo*. Ithica, NY: Cornell University Press.

Ryan, K. 2004. Cattle Ecology and Human Survival in Unpredictable Environments: A Case from East Africa. PhD diss., Dept. of History, Univ. of Pennsylvania, Philadelphia.

—— 2005. Facilitating Milk Let-Down in Traditional Cattle Herding Systems: East Africa and Beyond. In *The Zooarchaeology of Fats, Oils, Milk and Dairying*, ed. J. Mulville and A. K. Outram, pp. 96–106. Oxford: Oxbow Books.

Ryan, K., Karega-Munene, S. M. Kahinju, and P. N. Kunoni. 1991. Cattle Naming: The Persistence of a Traditional Practice in Modern Maasailand. In *Animal Use and Culture Change*, ed. P. J. Crabtree and K. Ryan, pp. 90–96. MASCA Research Papers, Supplement to vol. 8. Philadelphia: Museum Applied Science Center for Archaeology, University of Pennsylvania Museum of Archaeology and Anthropology.

—— 2000. Ethnographic Perspectives on Cattle Management in Semi-arid Environments: A Case Study from Maasailand. In *The Origins and Development of African Livestock: Archaeology, Genetics, Linguistics, and Ethnography*, ed. R. M. Blench and K. C. MacDonald, pp. 462–77. London: UCL Press.

Saitoti, T. Ole, and C. Beckwith. 1980. *Maasai*. New York: Harry N. Abrams.

Schoenbrun, D. L. 1993. Cattle Herds and Banana Gardens: The Historical

Geography of the Western Great Lakes Region, ca. AD 800–1500. *The African Archaeological Review* 11:39–72.

Shahack-Gross, R., F. Marshall, and S. Weiner. 2003. Geo-ethnoarchaeology of Pastoral Sites: The Identification of Livestock Enclosures in Abandoned Maasai Settlements. *Journal of Archaeological Science* 30:439–59.

Shahack-Gross, R., F. Marshall, K. Ryan, and S. Weiner. 2004. Reconstruction of Spatial Organization in Abandoned Maasai Settlements: Implications for Site Structure in the Pastoral Neolithic of East Africa. *Journal of Archaeological Science* 31:1395–1411.

Simpson, David E. 2008. *Milking the Rhino. The Promise of Community-based Conservation in Africa*. Oley, PA: Bullfrog Films.

Spencer, P. 1973. *Nomads in Alliance. Symbiosis and Growth among the Rendille and Samburu of Kenya*. London: Oxford University Press.

—— 1988. *The Maasai of Matapato: A Study of Rituals of Rebellion*. Bloomington: Indiana University Press.

Speth, J. D. 1987. Early Hominid Subsistence Strategies in Seasonal Habitats. *Journal of Archaeological Science* 14:13–29.

—— 1990. Seasonality, Resource Stress, and Food Sharing in So-Called "Egalitarian" Foraging Societies. *Journal of Anthropological Archaeology* 9:48–188.

Speth, J. D., and K. Spielmann. 1983. Energy Source, Protein Metabolism and Hunter-Gatherer Subsistence Strategies. *Journal of Anthropological Archaeology* 2:1–31.

Stokstad, E. 2002. Early Cowboys Herded Cattle in Africa. *Science* 296 (5566): 236–38.

Waller, R. D. 1985. Ecology, Migration and Expansion in East Africa. *African Affairs* 84:347–70.

—— 1988. Emutai: Crisis and Response in Maasailand, 1883–1902. In *The Ecology of Survival*, ed. D. H. Johnston and D. M. Anderson, pp. 3–112. Boulder, CO: Westview Press.

Waller, R. D., and N. W. Sobania. 1994. Pastoralism in Historical Perspective. In *African Pastoral Systems. An Integrated Approach*, ed. E. Fratkin, K. A. Galvin, and E. A. Roth, pp. 45–68. Boulder, CO: Lynne Rienner.

Watt, J. M., and M. G. Breyer-Brandwijk. 1962. *The Medicinal and Poisonous Plants of Southern and Eastern Africa*. 2nd ed. Edinburgh: Livingstone.

Western, D., and T. Dunne. 1979. Environmental Aspects of Settlement Site Decisions among Pastoral Maasai. *Human Ecology* 7:75–98.

Western, D., and V. Finch. 1986. Cattle and Pastoralism: Survival and Production in Arid Lands. *Human Ecology* 14:77–94.

Wilson, R. T. 1984. *The Camel*. London: Longman.

4

Risk and Resilience among Contemporary Pastoralists in Southwestern Iran

LOIS BECK AND JULIA HUANG

The Qashqa'i tribal confederacy emerged in the middle 1700s as a prominent sociopolitical group in southwestern Iran, and the nomadic pastoralists affiliated with it have always faced risks stemming from their physical, political, economic, and social environments.[1] Comparisons with nomadic pastoralists in the wider region (Turkey, other parts of Iran, Afghanistan, and central Eurasia) over the past centuries indicate common features in their ecological, technological, political, economic, social, and cultural adaptations to similar semiarid, steppe, and high-altitude zones. Archaeologists suggest the presence of similar kinds of adaptations for the region for a longer period, including many millennia, on the basis of material and other evidence.[2]

Nomadic pastoralism in such often marginal territories has demonstrated, almost by definition, the necessity for its practitioners to cope with and adjust to varying ecological and other physical environmental factors, few of which the people could dependably rely on for the long term or even the short term. Pastoralists have continually faced, as their ancestors had done, unpredictable conditions. Despite these limitations, many of them (including many Qashqa'i) have preferred to persist with customary livelihoods and lifestyles rather than to choose alternative ones available in their regions, which for most of them would have meant settling in villages and towns and competing with growing numbers of residents there for scarce and/or undesirable jobs. Nomadic pastoralism for many Qashqa'i has continued in the early 2000s in some ways similar to centuries-old patterns and practices.

Still, many Qashqa'i have adopted some modern technology (such as trucks for transporting their livestock and mobile telephones for communicating with their spatially dispersed relatives and tribesmates), they have included new forms of agriculture (such as fruit orchards), and they have acquired new social skills (such as formal education leading to new types of jobs for some individuals). Perhaps not surprisingly, many of these new jobs relate to the people's past and still-current experiences with pastoralism and mobility and demonstrate the continuing importance of such strategies. Some Qashqa'i are now veterinarians, employees of the state agency responsible for protecting natural resources, teachers for mobile communities, and long-distance transporters.

For two and a half centuries, tribal organizations (particularly a highly developed leadership system) and identities have helped the Qashqa'i to defend their territorial and economic interests and to achieve some degree of continuity and stability for people during even the most turbulent times. Changes in central governments, in particular, have caused such disturbances and, most recently, have included the sudden end of a modernizing, secularizing despotic monarchy and the rapid transition to an Islamic republic bolstered by religious institutions and ideologies from the past. Despite and because of this turbulence, the Qashqa'i tribal system and the people's distinctive, politicized ethnolinguistic identity have helped many Qashqa'i to continue with the livelihoods and lifestyles of nomadic pastoralism. Many of the people's adaptive strategies (ecological, technological, political, economic, social, and cultural) have proven to be effective, especially under periods of rapid change, and many practitioners have preferred to pursue such strategies rather than to adopt alternative ones they observed in regional settlements.

Elsewhere, Beck (2003) discusses the specific ways that Qashqa'i nomadic pastoralists have used the physical environment over a 40-year span. She examines how their economic practices relate to such adaptations and offers details concerning the "forces of nature" and the factors of risk and resilience in various kinds of changes. She draws on her anthropological observations in the 1970s, 1990s, and early 2000s of the varying ecological adaptations and diversifying economic strategies of these tribal people as they exploited a vast section of the southern Zagros mountains. The people's practices include the use and protection of natural pastureland in varying ecological zones, mobility and migration, increased reliance on roads and motorized transportation, animal husbandry (including the growing use of modern veterinary science), investment in arable land, adoption and development of agricultural techniques, construction of water-control systems, building of shelters for people and animals, hunting, gathering, and closer ties with the national government and the market economy.

Although much of the land these nomadic pastoralists have used was not suitable for productive activities other than seasonal pastoralism, hunting, and gathering, the people have been increasingly forced to compete with nearby settled agrarian communities for scarce cultivable land on the margins of their pastureland and for access to water and rights of passage. They have enjoyed the competitive advantage of a continuing reliance on mobility and migration, which allowed them to exploit a succession of seasonal resources and to do so rapidly when necessary. Also, the primary products of pastoralism (meat, dairy items, wool, and weavings) have still been in high market demand throughout the country (and, in the case of wool and weavings, internationally) and have given the people an economic incentive to continue the livelihood.

In her previous article, Beck (2003) addresses the interests of archaeologists who want to draw data and insights from accounts of contemporary peoples so that they can gain a better understanding of the ways that physical evidence relates to actual human behavior and practice.[3] She focuses on the physical environment and the ways these nomadic pastoralists have interacted with and adjusted to it. Studies of comparable peoples in other parts of west Asia and in other times demonstrate similar patterns (Barfield 1993; Salzman 2004). Environmental studies in general too often underplay the role of the people who reside and subsist in any given territory and whose use of land is a vital part of their political, social, and cultural systems.

VARIATIONS IN CHANGE

Mobile residents of the slopes, valleys, plateaus, and foothills of the Zagros mountains of southwestern Iran, the Qashqa'i are members of a tribal confederacy of approximately a million individuals (unofficial estimate for 2010). They speak a form of Turkish derived from Central Asia, where some of their ancestors had once lived. Until the 1960s and 1970s, most Qashqa'i were tent-dwelling nomadic pastoralists who migrated semiannually hundreds of kilometers between winter pastures at low altitudes near the Persian Gulf and summer pastures high in the mountains to the north and east (Figs. 4.1, 4.2). Since then, many Qashqa'i have built small dwellings (usually one-room stone-and-reed huts and houses) in their pasturelands and/or have begun residing (often seasonally) in villages and towns. Yet, most of them have still retained migratory pastoralism as one of perhaps several means of livelihood and have continued to reside periodically in woven goat-hair tents during their travels and in their pasturelands. Despite the new places and patterns of residence for some people, most have remained socially and emotionally attached to their customary seasonal pastures, have regularly visited their kin there, have participated in communal activities, and have continued to exploit the natural resources, often in cooperation with these kin.

The Qashqa'i in the early 2000s can be divided into four socioeconomic categories based on their livelihoods and places of residence: mobile pastoralists who subsisted primarily on pastoralism, mobile pastoralists who also engaged in compatible pursuits such as arboriculture, wage and salaried workers in the private and public spheres (the work often connected with pastoralism and mobility), and residents abroad (a small number) who engaged in a variety of economic pursuits (Huang 2006, 2009).

For almost all of the Qashqa'i in these four categories, their ethnic, tribal, and kinship ties have remained strong, and the people have enhanced such bonds through frequent interaction and renewed interests in communal rituals and ceremonies. They have continued to perceive themselves as a distinctive sociopolitical, sociocultural, and sociolinguistic community in Iran, especially because they have seen that integration in the nation-state and assimilation in the Persian-dominant society and culture there have not offered them many advantages and in fact have sometimes impeded them in their pursuits.[4] During turbulent times in Iran, such as the disruptive aftermath of the disputed presidential election in 2009, the continuing separation of many Qashqa'i from the dominant society has benefited them.

How have the Qashqa'i handled the inherent environmental constraints

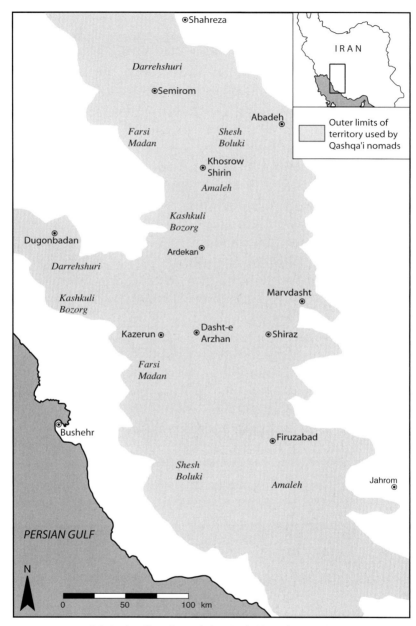

4.1 Qashqa'i territory. (After Beck 2003: fig. 28.1)

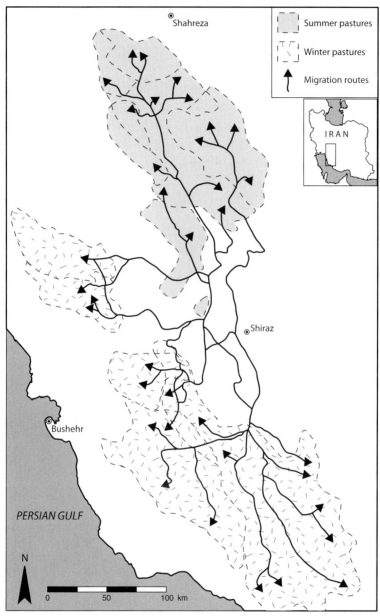

4.2 Qashqa'i winter pastures, summer pastures, and migration routes. (After Beck 2003: fig. 28.2)

of these rugged, mountainous, and semiarid lands? How and why have many of them continued with pastoralism and nomadism, despite increasing pressures to change their livelihoods and lifestyles? How and why have these pressures changed over time? Why has the current Islamic government (1979–), unlike previous Iranian governments during the 20th century, supported nomadic pastoralists and their livelihoods?

Three interrelating perspectives for examining the adaptations of Qashqa'i nomadic pastoralists to their physical and social environments are also helpful in understanding the ways they have maintained and adjusted the patterns and practices of the past.

First, the people have undergone periodic, profound changes since their emergence as a prominent sociopolitical group in the 1700s, many of them the result of political and economic forces stemming from wider domains (such as empires, states, armies, occupying foreign forces, and regional and global markets). Second, the people have always experienced many kinds of intra-seasonal, seasonal, and annual variations in their ecological, economic, and social circumstances. Third, despite these two kinds of changes (one periodic and of potentially major impact, the other constant and often less visible over the long term), the people have also demonstrated remarkable continuities in their society and culture. Their persisting success as a distinctive entity lies in the ways that people have handled these three situations simultaneously. They have maintained continuity with the past while at the same time adapting to different kinds of changing circumstances in varying spatial and temporal domains.

The archaeological record may offer some evidence for major, periodic shifts and for continuity but perhaps not for intra-seasonal, seasonal, and annual variation in patterns, which have remained a constant in the people's lives. These kinds of short-term alterations even in the contemporary period make the task of outside observers difficult.

Observers can document some of these recent changes, such as the first purchase of a motorized vehicle by anyone in a given tribal group. Yet, someone who bought a vehicle might have sold it a year later so that he could use the income to purchase ewes to augment his herd. Someone else who was the first person in his group to rent a truck to carry his household possessions from one seasonal territory to another might not have done so again for the next 10 years because of the high cost. A man who sold his camels because he no longer needed them for transport might have purchased camels several years later to respond to a growing demand for camel meat in urban areas.[5]

ECOLOGICAL RISKS

The Qashqa'i as well as other inhabitants of marginal environments in these semiarid, steppe, and high-altitude regions of western Asia have always relied on a variety of strategies to cope with the difficulties they encountered and to adapt to changing circumstances. They have faced significant physical, political, economic, and social risks, each of which has exerted an impact on other aspects of their lives, to the extent that it is sometimes difficult to separate them empirically and analytically.

Archaeologists who study past societies face additional challenges, especially because they derive their data primarily through archaeological methods and are limited to the physical evidence that survives over time. Cultural anthropologists observe a wide range of human and animal behaviors as well as the physical conditions and materials that are present. They see the place that these behaviors, situations, and materials occupy in daily life; they can discern their ecological, economic, political, social, and cultural significance; and they can assess any changes that occur (at least over the short term).

Each ecological risk for the Qashqa'i has had economic and social consequences. For instance, low levels of precipitation during the winter slowed the growth of essential springtime vegetation in Qashqa'i summer pastures. Aware of these conditions, a pastoralist might have decreased the size of his herd by selling some livestock (more sheep than goats) sooner than he had earlier intended. (Sheep need good-quality grazing while goats are more adaptive when faced with limited pasturage.) He might also have increased his use of supplemental fodder, depending on the land and water he had available to grow alfalfa and clover, the time and labor he had at hand for this activity, and the cost of buying fodder from nearby agricultural settlements. All these factors might have affected the timing of his plans to find spouses and arrange marriages for his son and his daughter, both ventures having their own high costs and affecting the household labor supply.

Some risks have been more threatening to people and their livelihoods and lifestyles than others, and changing circumstances have increased or decreased the severity of their impact. Drought conditions, for example, have forced pastoralists to alter herd sizes and grazing patterns, and yet a governmental agency could have constructed and supplied water reservoirs and reduced the drought's impact. The people's resilience in the face of these risks has derived from a combination of factors, which have also changed along with other circumstances. Such complex interrelationships are sometimes hard to distinguish (and to document), and cause-and-effect relationships may be difficult to determine, especially when people have valued non-material factors, such as social ties and cultural norms.

A Qashqa'i mobile pastoralist, for example, left his tent before dawn to spend the day in the rugged mountains hunting a wolf that had been killing the lambs of his campmates. His neighbors were puzzled by his enthusiasm, especially because he did not often put the interests of his campmates ahead of those of his own nuclear family. They knew he had just sold all of his livestock (including his lambs) in order to buy a pickup truck to be able to earn cash by transporting commodities for merchants and farmers. Many decisions (such as his) may have had these complex, interconnected, and possibly unknown ecological, economic, social, and even psychological components. In this man's case, he may have wanted to demonstrate (to himself and his kinship and tribal groups) that he still valued the notions of physical prowess and obligations toward family and neighbor, despite the seemingly contradictory change he had just made in his livelihood.

Another man, who considered the request of a suitor for his fourteen-year-old daughter, pondered a range of factors while making his decision. His stated reason for rejection (that he still needed his daughter at home because the labor-intensive period of milking and preparing milk products was approaching) had little to do with the circumstances he actually considered more weighty (that he was emotionally attached to her and was unwilling to let her join another family).

Qashqa'i pastoralists have faced the risks of climate and weather (key elements of the "forces of nature" for them) in ways similar to other pastoralists in these semiarid, steppe, and mountainous regions. Their primary adaptation has been mobility, and they have moved seasonally and intraseasonally to escape difficult conditions and to locate more suitable ones. Their winter and summer territories have usually been uninhabitable to the pastoralists and their livestock during the opposing seasons, and the ecological conditions there during the two transitional seasons of autumn and spring have been uncomfortable for them given their rudimentary dwellings and shelters and the physical needs of their livestock. Their winter pastures during the summer are hot, humid, and insect-ridden, and they lack water and much vegetation. Their summer pastures during the winter are cold, windy, and covered by meters of snow.[6]

The seasonal migrations of the pastoralists have come in the spring and the autumn, each journey lasting from one to three months, depending on the ecological conditions in three broad areas: the pastures they were leaving, the territories through which they would travel, and the pastures that were their destinations. The pastoralists have needed to make crucial decisions, often based on incomplete information, about staying longer in one locale or traveling quickly to the next one. Situations have also changed after people committed to a certain strategy, and they have needed to find solutions to these emerging problems as well.

The customary beginning of each trek has been the very first day of spring (the spring equinox) and the very first day of autumn (the autumn equinox). The first day of spring is also the first day of the New Year for many people in this part of the world, and the Qashqa'i share this holiday with other Iranians (and others). For cultural and symbolic reasons as well as physical ecological ones, Qashqa'i pastoralists have preferred to depart on these exact dates. Only when physical conditions have made their stay in one or the other seasonal territory difficult for the livestock (and only secondarily for the people) did they leave that territory earlier or later than usual. As elaborately as for their departure, they have marked with ritual and symbolic acts their arrival at the other seasonal territory. They could have entered this area earlier or later than customary, depending on the situation there and en route. During the migration, several men have traveled ahead to scout the status of the migratory route and the circumstances at their destination, and the group has delayed or expedited its journey based on the information it received. In one case, a group rushed ahead to occupy its summer campsites, not because of general ecological conditions there but because a rival group was already in residence and was exploiting the pasture that the group en route had planned to hold in reserve until mid-summer (Beck 1991:268–81).

The ecologies of the two periods of migration have been essential for the livestock. The vast terrain of varying altitudes and physical resources has supplied the needs of the animals in ways that the seasonal territories did not, especially in the autumn and spring. The vegetation along the route has provided for the nutritional needs of the animals without cost to or effort by the pastoralists (other than their traveling from one site to another). Practically every day of the spring migration, the pastoralists have climbed in altitude and have encountered new growth. Water has been plentiful from melting snow and ice. During the autumn migration, the pastoralists have not been as fortunate, even though their altitudinal descent offers them a way to escape the wind, cold, and snow of the changing seasons. Water has been scarce, and grazing has been limited to the residues of growth from months earlier. The expansion of other people's cultivation along the route has recently given the nomads' livestock an opportunity to browse on the stubble after the harvests were completed. The pastoralists have appreciated this reason for traveling overland during the autumn (as compared to a recent, expensive innovation for some, transporting the animals by truck) and for delaying their entry in winter pastures (which would not produce new growth until the onset of rain in the late autumn and early winter).

In addition to the first day of spring (the beginning of the New Year), the Qashqa'i have also marked with rituals the first day of the three other seasons (the summer solstice, autumn equinox, and winter solstice). They have viewed the beginning of each of the four seasons as an important transition. Each period has signified new ecological conditions, new stages in the life cycles of the animals (with corresponding changes in the people's labor and the animal products available), and new economic and social practices. The pastoralists have also marked the halfway point of each season (45 days into the season), each of which has its own corresponding ecologies, life-cycle changes, demands for labor, and accruing products. In addition, they have noted the passage of each of the six 15-day periods of winter, their most difficult, uncomfortable season in terms of climate, weather, shelter, and the vulnerability of their animals (especially newborn lambs, kids, and camel calves) and fodder crops.

Climate and weather have formed the context for the primary ecological risks faced by Qashqa'i pastoralists: finding adequate water and pasture. Water has sometimes been more problematic than pastoral vegetation. The people could have provided supplemental fodder to their animals without adjusting some of their other practices. Yet, transporting water (especially without having large containers and ways to carry them) and moving their livestock (and perhaps dwellings) closer to sources of water (where they have had to compete with other users) may have been more difficult. The pastoralists who have also engaged in agriculture (often to produce fodder crops) faced serious problems in finding adequate water, suitable soil, natural and other fertilizers, and weather appropriate for crop growth. They have competed for land and other natural resources with the growing populations in their regions and have tried to defend their interests (an often difficult task given their periodic absences and their frequent changes in locations). They have also needed to handle sometimes conflicting schedules for these varying pursuits, and they have relied on flexibility in the activities of their families and social groups and have depended on the values of mutual assistance.

The apple harvest for the Qashqa'i in summer pastures, for example, has fallen at the same time as the autumn migration to winter pastures hundreds of kilometers away. Some men have needed to stay behind to guard the crop, pick the ripened fruit, and transport the crates to market, while other men have continued on the migration with the livestock and set up camp in winter pastures. People have divided the labor available to them in their nuclear and extended families to meet such demands. They have stressed the importance of having large families and kin groups for this purpose and have valued the readiness of other people to help them.

Some newly married couples in the 1990s chose to form independent nuclear families instead of remaining in extended ones, as had been customary. New jobs for some men and women, new places of residence because of these jobs, and conflicting notions about how to spend any income were the primary reasons for the change.

A woman who was employed as a teacher needed to live near the school, while her natal family remained behind in seasonal pastures. When she married a kinsman (who was not also a teacher), his family members pressured the couple to live with them. She solved these two pressing demands by renting a house with other female teachers and returning home on the weekends. Later, when she had a baby, her husband came to live with her in the town and cared for the infant during the schoolday.

Many couples in the early 2000s were choosing to remain in extended families rather than to form their own nuclear ones, a decision they said better met the multiple labor needs of their diversifying economies and solved some of the social dilemmas as well (especially the care of young children).

RISKS FROM WIDER DOMAINS

Mobile pastoralists have pursued their economies within a national political context and a state and a government that might or might not have been supportive of them. In many instances, the risks for pastoralists have derived more from the wider political scene than from the physical environment. The pastoralists say that they have been able to adjust more easily to the latter than to the former. They have been more familiar with the range of ecological risks (and the varying strategies to cope with them) than the political ones, which tended to be unpredictable and not subject to any intervention by the pastoralists, who found that this wider domain was well beyond their reach and even beyond their comprehension.

Shifts in political regimes, especially unexpected ones (as in 1979), have raised many issues affecting the core livelihoods of the pastoralists. The people wondered, for example, if the new rulers in 1979 would uphold the enactments of the last shah to reform land ownership and to nationalize pastureland or if they would abolish his policies, introduce their own, and force the current occupants off the land.

Changes in regimes have also affected the relationships among Iran's citizens and have sometimes shifted the balance of power among their component groups. For example, the clergy of the Islamic Republic acted quickly against Iran's secularized, westernized upper class and drove many people into foreign exile. Political and especially economic problems have caused millions of Iranians to abandon rural agrarian areas and seek other livelihoods in towns and cities (a process that had also occurred under the shah and was a factor in the revolution against him). At the same time, the clergy claimed an interest in assisting the economies of the "disinherited," those the clergy defined as people whom the preceding shahs (1926–1979) had oppressed. The Ayatollah Khomeini had especially praised Iran's nomads as the "treasures of the revolution." Through governmental agencies and semi-independent foundations, the clergy offered the "disinherited" unprecedented economic incentives and in some places elevated the economic standing of some nomads over the country's (often nontribal) rural agriculturalists, many of whom had also undergone privations during the shahs' regimes.

Despite Khomeini's praise, Iran's nomads had played little or no role in the revolution. Khomeini and other clergy used the word *ashayer* for "tribes" as well as "nomads," thus complicating the issue of who should receive special state services. The confusion concerning the two terms continues to appear in the scholarly literature (despite decades of clarifications by anthropologists), where writers often incorrectly use them interchangeably. The Islamic government did not view "nomads" to be as politicized as "tribes" and preferred to use the former term for both entities (Beck and Huang 2008a, 2008b).

Political trends, combined with economic and social ones, within Iran have meant the increased integration of the Qashqa'i people in the state, government, and Persian-dominant society. The Qashqa'i have profited in some ways (such as in increased access to formal education and modern veterinary medicine), while they have been disadvantaged in others (such as when the state subjected young men to compulsory military service and engaged them in a fruitless, destructive war).

The pastoralists have also faced many risks stemming from the wider economy. The demands of the market have risen and fallen with regard to crucial commodities (including those the pastoralists sold and bought), and governmental subsidies for some consumer products have undercut the livelihoods of the primary producers. State subsidies for meat, for example, have lowered the price of live animals that the pastoralists received from regional slaughterhouses, and state imports of meat from abroad (Australia and New Zealand) have periodically reduced the scarcity and expense of this highly valued commodity. Rising inflation has affected all citizens in similar ways, but pastoralists and others who produced much of their own food and constructed many of their own goods (such as textiles, containers, and tools) have avoided inflationary pressures more than those who were not food producers and who depended on cash income to buy all the goods they needed. Market demands have often changed faster than most people could anticipate, and if people made appropriate changes in their economies one year, they might find that circumstances have changed by the following year.

Some Qashqa'i planted apple saplings, for example, in the hope of profiting from apple sales once the trees matured and began to produce marketable fruit (in the seventh year or so). Later they discovered that the prices they expected to receive for their first crops did not begin to cover the expenses (purchase or rental of land, irrigation, fertilizers, pesticides, transportation, and some labor) that they had incurred during the intervening years. A glut in the market caused by so many new producers lowered prices. When urban entrepreneurs expanded their efforts to export apples to the Persian Gulf states, the venture turned productive in ways that the pastoralists had not earlier predicted. Soon this new market was closed to most of them, because the entrepreneurs began to require the producers to store and refrigerate their apples from harvest time (in the late summer and early autumn) until the late winter or early spring, when prices in the gulf states were high. The pastoralists lacked any secure places for storage, protected from the physical elements for such a long period, and they could not afford any form of refrigeration.

Still, apple sales, even considering the low prices in local and regional markets within Iran, have subsidized the economies of many nomadic pastoralists and have enabled them to continue with their primary livelihood (pastoralism) and lifestyle (including mobility), especially at times when their annual earnings from the sales of animals and animal products were less than their major annual expenditures (pasture rental, salaries of hired shepherds, supplemental fodder, veterinary care, and transport). (These annual costs covered all their livestock, while the pastoralists sold only a portion of their animals in any given year.) The people have understood the growing importance of economic diversification; when needed, one venture could help to pay for the costs of another.

Modernization has offered further challenges for the pastoralists. For each change they have made, they said they moved further away from their customary, still-valued lifestyle. Some changes have seemed irreversible. Once people enjoyed certain innovations, such as piped water near their dwellings, they were no longer interested in carrying water long distances in goatskin bags loaded on donkeys. The acquisition of motorized vehicles (motorcycles, pickup trucks, Land Rovers, large-load trucks, and passenger cars) has changed people's lives substantially, and individuals without access to such equipment have found themselves economically (and socially) impeded.[7] Vehicles have meant that men could travel quickly from one economic pursuit to another (when necessary), such as irrigating apple trees in the early morning and transporting sheep to the market in the early afternoon. They could profit from both ventures, while men without rapid transport were limited in the range of pursuits they could follow.

New standards of comfort have changed people's attitudes about the money they now needed to buy an ever-growing list of new possessions.

Their economies had previously centered on barter and credit, but now they required livelihoods that produced reliable, recurring cash income. The change from tent-dwelling year-round to periodic residence in more permanent dwellings (no matter how humble) has led to other kinds of changes, such as the need to protect these new structures (and the growing number of goods they stored there) when they traveled and resided elsewhere.

Formal education, a major component of modernization globally, has changed the types of livelihoods that many youngsters planned to seek, and it has sometimes unrealistically raised the expectations of their families. Jobs for high school and even university graduates in Iran have been scarce. Those Qashqa'i who have taken new jobs often grew to dislike the accompanying alterations, such as expensive residences in towns and cities, new costs for transportation and telecommunications, new demands for consumer products, expanded obligations of hospitality, unwelcome governmental policies about dress and behavior (such as restricting the mobility of women), and physical separation from kin and tribal groups.

Social changes of many sorts interrelate with ecological, political, and economic ones. Population increases among the pastoralists have meant that a proportion of each residential community (a collection of nuclear and extended families) would be more likely than not to leave nomadic pastoralism (or reduce its activities) and to consider settled agriculture or urban employment. Expansion of regional populations has led to increased competition over vital resources for those individuals who persisted with pastoralism and those who adopted agriculture.

The policies of the Islamic government to force changes in people's behavior and dress have affected Iranian society in general. Yet, people who have been territorially distant from urban centers could often ignore or avoid following such restrictive measures. Qashqa'i women under some circumstances, for example, have not followed the codes of modest dress that the government imposed on most village women and all urban women (Beck 2004, Huang 2009).

Social discrimination within Iranian society against tribally organized people and ethnic minorities has negatively affected many Qashqa'i on both these grounds. Yet, these organizations and identities have also protected the Qashqa'i in some ways and have helped them to face and cope with other constraints.

RESILIENCE AND PERSISTENCE

Despite these many risks and problems, many Qashqa'i have preferred to persist with existing livelihoods and lifestyles.[8] The adjustments that the pastoralists have made have been similar to those of their predecessors. Most pastoralists have not found the alternatives appealing. Many have had little interest in settling in villages and towns and joining the large and expanding rural and urban proletariat, especially given the many problems they would face: high prices, rising inflation, scarcity of jobs, increasing unemployment, social discrimination, and political unrest. They have understood that income from new livelihoods would not be adequate to cover the costs of settlement, which have grown rapidly every year.

Many Qashqa'i, when they settled in villages, towns, and cities, have discovered that they were now part of Iran's lower class. As largely self-sufficient nomadic pastoralists and relatively isolated in their seasonal pastures, they had earlier perceived themselves differently; they had thought that they were adequately provisioned. Yet, under the new conditions, other Iranians considered them "poor" or even "impoverished." Mobility from the lower class to the middle class was possible for some settling Qashqa'i but only after many years and even decades, given the persisting economic problems in Iran as a whole. With their steady (but low) salaries and governmental benefits, some teachers and civil servants have had more opportunities to enter Iran's middle class (albeit at the lower level) than people who took other kinds of jobs, especially outside the public sector.

Many Qashqa'i have expressed displeasure about living in towns and cities where restrictive governmental policies were in effect and where discontent for the Islamic government has been widespread (especially after the disputed presidential election in 2009). Living in their seasonal pastures, they said they were glad to avoid contact with urbanites, who constantly complained about the government, the Muslim clergy, the repressive paramilitary forces, and the faltering national economy but who did not and would not take any concrete action to change the status quo.

The pastoralists did find themselves integrated in the state more than they had been in the past, but some changes had originated from their own choices to further their formal education and to take new kinds of jobs available outside of tribal territory. Although the state itself had changed dramatically since 1979 (from a modernizing, secularizing, despotic monarchy to an Islamizing, socially restrictive, clergy-controlled regime), the pastoralists (situated as they were at the periphery of the state) stressed the similarity of the two regimes. From their perspective, the urban Persians who have dominated in Iran have controlled both regimes. Both regimes have served urban populations, and both have been oriented toward and obsessed with Western powers and influences.[9]

Two sociopolitical factors—tribal organization and a politicized ethnolinguistic identity—help to explain the persistence of migratory pastoralism for the Qashqa'i during the past century or more. Such factors may have also played important roles in the more distant past. As before, people have continued to adjust to the various changing circumstances they confronted, and yet their success has rested more in sociopolitical factors than in the ways they strove to overcome the difficulties of the physical environment. As a tribally organized population and as a politicized ethnolinguistic minority in Iran, the Qashqa'i have held advantages over some other populations. These two factors have enabled them to be resilient when confronted by emerging threats. Their tribal organization, institutions of strong leadership, and military prowess have given them the structure and ability to protect and defend their territorial, economic, and social interests. Their ethnolinguistic identity has unified and strengthened them as a distinctive community. The region's dispersed, diffuse, settled agricultural populations and the lower and middle classes of towns and cities have lacked comparable systems of organization and leadership, military preparedness, and a politicized identity. From the perspective of the Qashqa'i, citizenship in Iran and a national identity as Iranians have not compared well with tribal and ethnic affiliations in terms of how such ties and notions have enhanced daily life, facilitated economic and social pursuits, and unified them politically. National loyalties have not served the people's interests in the ways that tribal and ethnic ones have done.[10]

The Iraq-Iran war (1980–1988) showed the Qashqa'i and some other national minorities the disadvantages of serving a nation-state rather than their own tribal and ethnic communities. Ironically, the military prowess that had derived from the experience of the Qashqa'i and similar groups as warriors, mountaineers, and hunters led to their incurring injuries and fatalities at a higher rate than among many other Iranian soldiers in the war. In battle they took more risks than many other soldiers, and many of them volunteered for special but dangerous duties (such as reconnaissance behind enemy lines). By paying special attention to Iran's nomads, the Islamic Republic in the 1980s had tried to integrate them into the country and to encourage their primary loyalties as Iranians (as compared to their primary loyalties as Kurds, Baluch, or Qashqa'i, for example). Yet, the devastating war demonstrated to the Qashqa'i and others the detriments of such national ideologies, even when Iran faced Iraq's military assaults.

Material evidence derived from archaeological methods may not address such often abstract notions as tribal, ethnic, and national identities and affiliations. If these notions have played important roles in the survival of the Qashqa'i as a distinctive society and culture and as long-term practitioners of mobile pastoralism and related pursuits, they may have left few or no physical remains.

Nomadic pastoralists seem to have been less subject than other rural peoples to risky conditions in their physical environment because of their reliance on mobility and their use of a wide territory consisting of differing ecological zones. Such patterns have always been an intrinsic part of the nomadic pastoral adaptation, and the people have often flourished under such circumstances. Most rural agriculturalists have lacked the opportunity to move elsewhere on short notice if local conditions were unsatisfactory or debilitating. For many of them, their only strategy under persistently poor conditions has been to relocate to urban centers, where jobs were already scarce and where they met many other economic and social difficulties.

The lower and middle classes of towns and cities have confronted the physical environment and its problems through protective permanent housing, piped water, and sources of heat, cooling, and light derived from electricity and petroleum products. Yet, these permanent residences have rendered the people vulnerable to risky political and economic conditions. Widespread, even local, political disturbances have disrupted daily life and harmed the economy, while such events may have had little immediate or even long-term impact on nomadic pastoralists in their relatively isolated locales and because of their often self-sufficient economies. Revolutionary conditions in Iran in 1978 and 1979, for example, disrupted life in the towns and cities and caused millions of people to change how and where they lived, while people in the countryside, especially mobile pastoralists, were relatively unaffected and have continued to be so three decades later.[11]

NOTES

1. We use the past continuous tense in much of this chapter to represent the past and often still present characteristics of nomadic pastoralism in Iran and the wider region. Lois Beck draws on cultural anthropological research conducted over a span of four decades (1969–2010) among, and concerning, nomadic pastoralists of the Qashqa'i tribal confederacy of southwestern Iran. Julia Huang uses her own experiences among the Qashqa'i from 1991 through 2010.

2. Mobile pastoralism has persisted as a form of environmental adaptation over a wide territory for millennia. Huang describes the herds of cattle and herds of horses that passed twice a day in the summer of 2006 by a Bronze Age archaeological site in mountainous eastern Kazakhstan, where Michael Frachetti and his team were excavating the habitations and cemeteries of mobile pastoralists who had occupied the same terrain thousands of years earlier. The animals, on their way to and from pastures at higher elevations, belonged to people who lived in a small village at a lower elevation. Frachetti studies 4000 years of nearly continuous use of this area by mobile pastoralists (Frachetti 2008; Frachetti and Mar'yashev 2007).

3. See the work of Hole (1978), Kramer (1982), and Watson (1979). Browman's book contains useful articles on arid land use and risk management in the Andes (Browman 1987).

4. In the 20th and early 21st centuries, 49 or 50% of Iran's population has consisted of ethnic Persians. The other 51 or 50% has contained ethnic and national minorities such as Turks, Kurds, Baluch, Arabs, Lurs, and Qashqa'i. Don Stilo (pers. comm., August 2007), a prominent sociolinguist of Iran, suggests these percentages.

5. These kinds of sometimes alternating practices are of special interest to Beck in her longitudinal research. She has documented economic and social changes within a single Qashqa'i tribe (400 households in 2004) over a span of four decades, and the data demonstrate innovations as well as long-term patterns of continuity. Between visits to Iran, Beck maintains contact with members of the tribe through letters, telephone calls, and e-mail messages and keeps informed and updated about their activities. Each household of the tribe chooses its own economic and social activities. Great variation occurs, and no unit has specific patterns identical to any others. Yet, many changes fall within a certain range, such as a lesser or a greater reliance on livestock or agriculture and residences alternating among seasonal pastures, villages, and towns. Overall, nomadic pastoralism is declining, not so much because of the depletion of pastoral resources or the competition over them but rather because of extraneous factors (Beck n.d.). Donald Cole (1975, 2006) is one of the few other cultural anthropologists who has conducted longitudinal research on a single nomadic community in the Middle East and Eurasia. The patterns he describes are quite different from the ones Beck and Huang document for the Qashqa'i.

6. In *Nomad: A Year in the Life of a Qashqa'i Tribesman in Iran* (1991), Beck describes in ethnographic detail the activities of the nomads in the autumn, winter, spring, and summer.

7. Passenger cars are unsuitable for the terrain (their axles close to the rocky, uneven ground) and the livelihood (no space for carrying livestock or gunny sacks of alfalfa), but some people purchased them because they were cheaper than other kinds of vehicles and more convenient than motorcycles for transporting many people at a time.

8. A study of material culture among Qashqa'i nomadic pastoralists, with a focus on weaving, documents the longevity and continuing existence (in 2010) of a well-integrated system drawing from the physical environment, multiple pastoral products, and sophisticated technologies and skill sets (Dareshuri and Beck, n.d.).

9. The Islamic beliefs and practices of the rulers and supporters of these two regimes seem to outside analysts to vary substantially. Yet, many Qashqa'i stressed the similarities (which they based on formal Islamic institutions) and contrasted them with their own beliefs and practices (which they said were based on each individual's personal ties to God).

10. The Qashqa'i tribal confederacy has been more successful than many other large tribal entities in Iran in these matters, especially in the 20th and early 21st centuries. After the 1920s, the Bakhtiyari tribal confederacy just to the north of the Qashqa'i had a lower level of political articulation than the Qashqa'i, and then and later its ethnolinguistic identity was less politicized (Garthwaite 1983). For comparisons of the attributes of tribes and states in Iran and the larger Islamic world, see Beck (1990) and Beck and Huang (2008a, 2008b, 2008c).

11. Millions of Iranians have fled Iran since 1978, and a sizable proportion of them (and their descendants) have not returned.

REFERENCES CITED

Barfield, Thomas. 1993. *The Nomadic Alternative*. Englewood Cliffs, NJ: Prentice Hall.

Beck, Lois. 1990. Tribes and the State in Nineteenth- and Twentieth-century Iran. In *Tribes and State Formation in the Middle East*, ed. Philip Khoury and J. Kostiner, pp. 185–225. Berkeley: University of California Press.

—— 1991. *Nomad: A Year in the Life of a Qashqa'i Tribesman in Iran*. Berkeley: University of California Press.

—— 2003. Qashqa'i Nomadic Pastoralists and Their Use of Land. In *Yeki Bud, Yeki Nabud: Essays on the Archaeology of Iran*, ed. Naomi Miller and Kamyar Abdi, pp. 289–304. Los Angeles: Cotsen Institute of Archaeology at UCLA.

—— 2004. Qashqa'i Women in Postrevolutionary Iran. In *Women in Iran from 1800 to the Islamic Republic*, ed. Lois Beck and Guity Nashat, pp. 240–78. Urbana: University of Illinois Press.

—— n.d. Nomads Move On: Qashqa'i Tribespeople in Post-Revolutionary Iran. Unpublished book manuscript.

Beck, Lois, and Julia Huang. 2008a. Nomads. In *Iran Today: An Encyclopedia of Life in the Islamic Republic*, Vol. 2, ed. Mehran Kamrava and Manochehr Dorraj, pp. 348–55. Westport, CT: Greenwood.

—— 2008b. Tribes. In *Iran Today: An Encyclopedia of Life in the Islamic Republic*, Vol. 2, ed. Mehran Kamrava and Manochehr Dorraj, pp. 481–88. Westport, CT: Greenwood.

—— 2008c. Tribes. In *Oxford Encyclopedia of the Islamic World*, Vol. 5, ed. John Esposito, pp. 390–98. Oxford: Oxford University Press.

Browman, David, ed. 1987. *Arid Land Use Strategies and Risk Management in the Andes*. Boulder, CO: Westview Press.

Cole, Donald. 1975. *Nomads of the Nomads: The Al Murrah Bedouin of the Empty Quarter*. Chicago: Aldine.

—— 2006. New Homes, New Occupations, New Pastoralism: Al Murrah Bedouin, 1968–2003. In *Nomadic Societies in the Middle East and North Africa: Entering the 21st Century*, ed. Dawn Chatty, pp. 370–92. Leiden: Brill Academic Publishers.

Dareshuri, Naheed, and Lois Beck. n.d. Bands, Ropes, Braids, and Tassels among the Qashqa'i in Iran. In *Warp-Faced Bands and Related Weavings of Nomadic Pastoralists in Iran*, ed. Fred Mushkat. In preparation.

Frachetti, Michael. 2008. *Pastoralist Landscapes and Social Interaction in Bronze Age Eurasia*. Berkeley: University of California Press.

Frachetti, Michael, and Alexei Mar'yashev. 2007. Long-term Occupation and Seasonal Settlement of Eastern Eurasian Pastoralists at Begash, Kazakhstan. *Journal of Field Archaeology* 32:221–42.

Garthwaite, Gene. 1983. *Khans and Shahs: A Documentary Analysis of the Bakhtiyari in Iran*. Cambridge: Cambridge University Press.

Hole, Frank. 1978. Pastoral Nomadism in Western Iran. In *Explorations in Ethnoarchaeology*, ed. Richard Gould, pp. 127–67. Albuquerque: University of New Mexico Press.

Huang, Julia. 2006. Integration, Modernization, and Resistance: Qashqa'i Nomads in Iran since the Revolution of 1978–1979. In *Nomadic Societies in the Middle East and North Africa: Entering the 21st Century*, ed. Dawn Chatty, pp. 805–39. Leiden: Brill Academic Publishers.

—— 2009. *Tribeswomen of Iran: Weaving Memories among Qashqa'i Nomads*. London: I. B. Tauris.

Kramer, Carol. 1982. *Village Ethnoarchaeology: Rural Iran in Archaeological Perspective*. New York: Academic Press.

Salzman, Philip. 2004. *Pastoralists: Equality, Hierarchy, and the State*. Boulder, CO: Westview Press.

Watson, Patty Jo. 1979. *Archaeological Ethnography in Western Iran*. Viking Fund Publications in Anthropology, no. 57. Tucson: University of Arizona Press.

5

Change and Stability in an Uncertain Environment: Foraging Strategies in the Levant from the Early Natufian through the Beginning of the Pre-Pottery Neolithic B

ARLENE M. ROSEN

"Climate is what we expect, weather is what we get."

—Mark Twain (1835–1910)

Climate change is much in the public mind today as we emerge from the early debates of "is it a real phenomenon?" to queries about "what is causing it, humans or nature?" and finally most recently "how should our modern society respond to climate change?" At all stages of these debates researchers—both natural and social scientists—have pointed to the past to emphasize instances in which climate change has impacted previous societies. In order to make the point that global warming is a very real and even urgent issue today, the case for the impact of climate change on past societies has sometimes been over-simplified and even exaggerated. Many researchers have pointed to the ups and downs of curves on graphs representing environmental proxies such as pollen, isotopes, and lake levels, and have loosely matched these up with graphs of fluctuating settlement patterns (Issar 2003). In some cases the match is reasonably good, in others, there is a lot of stretching to accomplish a measure of "wiggle-matching." All of this is usually done without considering ethnohistorical, historical, and archaeological examples of how past societies actually did adjust to climate change. Other researchers have demonstrated that social factors rather than natural ones determine whether or not a given society succeeds or fails to adapt to new and often stressful environmental and climatic conditions. The deciding factors relate to the specifics of social organization, economy, decision-making on the part of managers, technological level, political considerations, cosmology, and perceptions of the climate change (Hassan 1997; McGovern 1994; Rosen 1995, 2007a).

Without these social considerations, it is easy to overlook the significance of societies that have successfully adapted to the stress that climate change imposes on their subsistence systems. Such examples seem to be all but invisible in the archaeological record since the new subsistence strategies might leave only subtle physical indications of change, and population levels and even settlement patterns might appear to remain the same. However, the social, political, and economic adjustments might be visible by a targeted analysis of changes in the flora and fauna, as well as other archaeological remains such as storage installations. Furthermore, adverse climatic conditions might ultimately result in changes in social development towards more complexity rather than social devolution. In these cases, societies may shift to an economic system that buffers against risk, but one that becomes so successful it leads to more social and political complexity rather than less. Such might well have been the case in the rise of the first state in China (Rosen 2007b).

There is no doubt that secular changes in climate can have a pronounced impact on societies in the present as well as the past. However, this is a long way from considering climate change as a forcing agent that is the sole cause of social collapse. Climate change requires social, economic, technological, and even political adjustments depending upon the degree and magnitude of the change, but many previous societies have shown remarkable resilience in their responses to environmental stress.

Hunter-gatherers are among the most resilient type of society as is evident from the longevity of this style of life in the archaeological record. Therefore, foraging communities are not usually thought to have been adversely impacted by climatic change. One very significant exception to this is in the study of agricultural origins, and the possible role that climate change played as a forcing mechanism leading to the shift from foraging to food production. This is especially the case with the study of the origins of agriculture in the Near East, namely the impact of climate change on the Natufians who inhabited the Levant from ca. 14,500–11,700 BP. Climatically this period spans the change from the terminal Pleistocene to the early Holocene. Archaeologically, it is the phase that is on the threshold of change from complex hunter-gatherer to agricultural village societies.

This co-occurrence of climatic and social events has led a number of archaeologists to propose a direct causal link between climatic change and the origins of agriculture (Bar-Yosef 1996; Bar-Yosef and Belfer-Cohen 2002; Henry 1989; Hillman 1996; Moore and Hillman 1992). In this chapter I hope to demonstrate that the Natufians responded to climate change the way many ethnographically known hunter-gatherers respond to similar shifts in their environment, without heading on a trajectory towards agriculture. Rather, like more recent foragers, the Natufians initiated adjustments in subsistence strategies that led to a stable subsistence system lasting for over a thousand years. I will further argue that the climate change that did correspond with a shift to agriculture took place another thousand years after the Natufians, and was amelioration rather than a climatic deterioration. Furthermore, climatic amelioration was only one factor combined with equally important social elements which drove the change from a foraging to a food producing economy in the Pre-Pottery Neolithic B Period.

REVIEW OF CLIMATIC CONDITIONS IN THE NEAR EAST DURING THE PLEISTOCENE/HOLOCENE TRANSITION

The Southern Levant is located at the eastern periphery of the Mediterranean Sea (Fig. 5.1). It is characterized by classic Mediterranean climatic conditions with winter moisture and a summer drought. The temperatures range from averages of 26°C in the summer and 12°C in the winter. The annual average rainfall varies from ca. 100 mm in the south to ca. 1000 mm in the north, and falls almost exclusively in the months of October–April. Vegetation is composed of a mix of oak, pistachio, almond, carob, and olive in the Mediterranean woodland zone, steppic grasses and shrubs in the Irano-Turanian zone, and arid land vegetation in the Saharo-Arabian Zone.

The climate of the Late Pleistocene through the early Holocene experienced a major transition with the warming (beginning around 15,000 BP) that followed the Last Glacial Maximum (LGM) at around 23,000 BP. Numerous proxies from isotopes, lake levels, and pollen inform us about

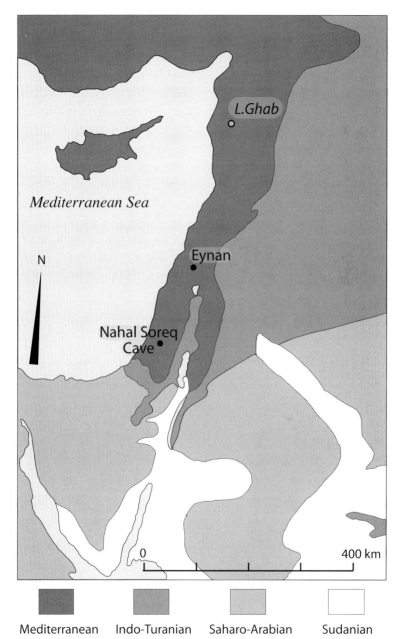

5.1 Map of the Southern Levant showing modern vegetation zones and the location of the Natufian site, Eynan. (Modified after Zohary 1973)

temperature, rainfall, and vegetation conditions of this period, although often this information seems contradictory and suffers from the imprecision of dating errors. The most useful high-resolution record for temperature and rainfall comes from oxygen and carbon isotope sequences. In the case of the Near Eastern Levant, the $\delta^{18}O$ isotope record from the Nahal Soreq Cave in central Israel is one of the most complete sequences covering the late Pleistocene through the Holocene (Bar-Matthews et al. 1999) (Fig. 5.2).

Oxygen isotopes are normally a proxy for temperature, but the Soreq Cave sequence has been calibrated to designate rainfall fluctuations through time. The general picture indicates markedly dry conditions at the height of the LGM, and then a rapid wetting up with the warming that corresponded to the Bølling-Allerød phase of glacial retreat in Europe (ca. 14,500–12,900 BP). The climatic reversal of the Younger Dryas event (ca. 12,900–11,700 BP) appears as a small raised plateau in the oxygen isotope diagram, which shows that the climate did indeed get drier during this cooling episode. The

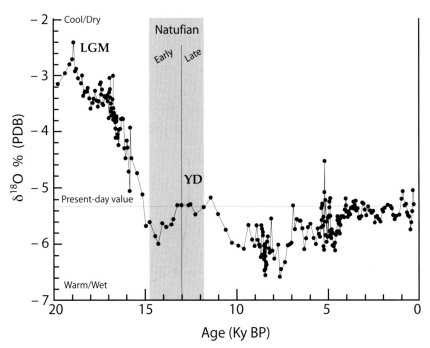

5.2 Oxygen Isotope curve from Nahal Soreq Cave showing fluctuations in climate from the Late Pleistocene through the Holocene. (Modified from Rosen 2007a, after Bar-Matthews et al. 1999)

Younger Dryas ended with the onset of the warmer, moister conditions in the early Holocene. At around 11,700 BP, the climate began to become warmer and wetter, but it is important to note that the climate at the start of the Holocene was not much moister than it is at the present, and although conditions became steadily more moist, the climate did not reach an optimum for warm/wet conditions until around 10,500 BP, the period of time that corresponds to the later phase of the preceramic Neolithic (the early Pre-Pottery Neolithic B).

Although estimates of rainfall and temperature are important, it is worthwhile looking beyond these and attempt to reconstruct the impact of these climate changes on the natural resources upon which the foraging populations in the Levant depended. Other environmental proxies provide us with more information about landscape, hydrology, and vegetation that helps to round out the picture of environmental conditions during the period leading up to the establishment of the first agricultural communities in the Levant. The Dead Sea record indicates that in spite of the very dry conditions of the LGM, the level of Lake Lisan (the precursor to the Dead Sea) had reached its maximum extent. This was probably a function of the cooler conditions that lowered the evaporation, despite the drier climate. The lake became much smaller during the Younger Dryas, and with the Holocene the modern Dead Sea was formed. Dead Sea levels began to increase with moister conditions of the mid-Holocene, and enhanced stream runoff into the basin (Bartov et al. 2002; Klinger et al. 2003; Machlus et al. 2000).

The streams also had a dynamic pattern of alluviation and downcutting that gives us insight into landscape and hydrological changes during this period. During the time of the Last Glacial Maximum, streams in the Southern Levant shifted from a regime of general alluviation and floodplain formation, to one of incision and valley erosion (Goldberg 1986; 2007a:61–64). This ended during the Bølling-Allerød period, at about 15,000 BP, when streams renewed their floodplain-building character, and there is evidence in these old floodplain deposits for high water tables and stable land surfaces. Some light soils began to form on the floodplains, although they were not as developed as the soils that formed prior to the LGM. The soils dating to around 14,000 BP suggest that the landscape and vegetation had stabilized. Down-cutting of the stream channels renewed during the Younger Dryas, leaving the former floodplains unwatered and incised. The streams appear to have stabilized with less erosive, slower but steadier flow in the early Holocene (Rosen 2007a:63–64, 78–80).

Pollen cores from Lake Hula have provided us with some insights into vegetation composition during the late Pleistocene/early Holocene (Fig. 5.3) (Baruch and Bottema 1999). If we accept the conventional dates with the Cappers correction for old carbon in Lake Hula (Cappers, Bottema, and Woldring 1998; Wright and Thorpe 2003), the pollen record suggests that

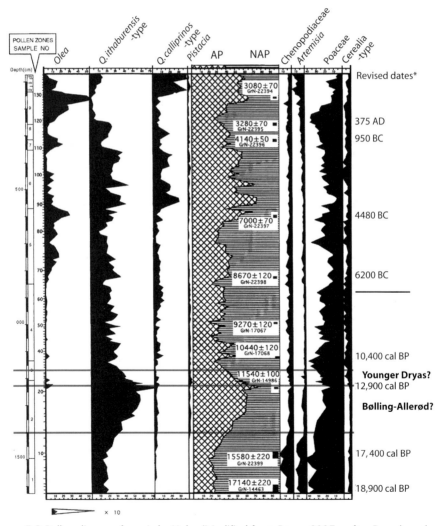

5.3 Pollen diagram from Lake Hula. (Modified from Rosen 2007a, after Baruch and Bottema 1999)

the LGM was characterized by steppic vegetation dominated by *Artemisia*, chenopods, and grasses. With the warming and increased moisture of the Bølling-Allerød, there was a rapid expansion of *Quercus* (oak), *Olea* (olive), *Prunus amygdalus* (almond), *Ceratonia siliqua* (carob), and *Pistacia* (pistachio) woodland vegetation. The pronounced spread of trees, especially *Pistacia*, at this early date is unusual around the Mediterranean, but if the Cappers, Bottema, and Woldring (1998) dates are correct, it may be a function of proximity to the Pleistocene refuge of these warm-loving plants in the Southern Levant. Although archaeobotanical evidence is thin, the early expansion of woodland could have provided Epipaleolithic populations with the nut resources that are a significant source of protein, fats, and oils found in acorns, almonds, and pistachio nuts. Carob and olive also might have been important resources for foragers.

With the onset of drier conditions during the Younger Dryas period, the woodland retreated and grasses became dominant, giving rise to moist steppic vegetation, which would have provided more starchy seed resources for foragers at that time (Bottema 1995, 2002). The arboreal component of the early Holocene pollen record remains relatively low despite the warming and increasing moisture. This apparent lack of response to new conditions might be an indicator of woodland clearance by the late Epipaleolithic and Neolithic populations. Roberts (2002) suggested this as a possibility for central Anatolia to explain the late appearance of the woodland vegetation after the start of the Holocene. A similar situation might be proposed for the Southern Levant as well. Some support for this comes from the relatively high microcharcoal levels reported from Lake Hula for the late Pleistocene and early Holocene (Turner et al. 2009).

NATUFIAN THROUGH PPNA: REVIEW OF THE EVIDENCE

The appearance of Early Natufian populations at around 14,500 BP in the Levant coincided with the beginning of the Bølling-Allerød warming and the expansion of Mediterranean forest vegetation. In northern Israel, traditionally considered the core area of the Early Natufians (Bar-Yosef 2002; Valla 1998), sites vary in size, but the largest have features which indicate that these sites may have been semi- or even fully sedentary. The site of Eynan (Ain Mallaha) on the shore of Lake Hula is significantly larger than any previous hunter-gatherer sites in the Levant (Fig. 5.4). Features that

indicate the population may have been semi- or even fully sedentary include structures with stone foundations and superstructures composed of
reeds (Rosen 2004), burials, possible storage installations, and the remains
of grinding stones (Olszewski 1993; Valla 1998; Wright 1994).

The chipped stone tool assemblages contain blades that are assumed
to have been sickles for harvesting cereals because they have typical sickle-
gloss polish. However, this polish also could have resulted from plant harvesting for basketry and matting as well. A well-developed basketry and
matting technology is evident from abundant phytolith remains of reeds

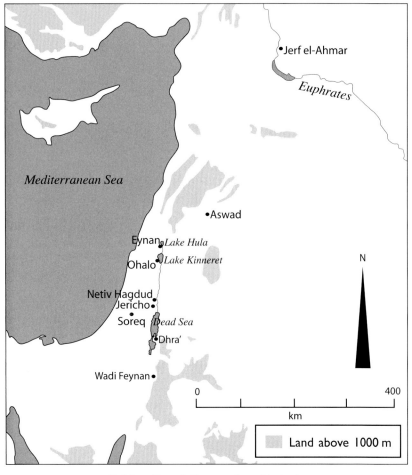

5.4 Location of sites mentioned in text.

and sedges, and the presence in some sites of spatulate-tipped bone tools that are typical of basket-making toolkits (Olszewski 1993; Rosen 2004). It is very likely, then, that Natufian "sickle blades" were used to cut reeds and rushes for basketry materials, rather than for wild cereal harvesting. Olszewski (1993) notes that indeed, the largest numbers of sickles are found at sites near lowland marshes, well away from the range of wild cereals.

The subsequent Late Natufian phase coincided with the Younger Dryas event. It marked a distinct change in settlement pattern with smaller more ephemeral sites, and all appearances of a more mobile population (Goring-Morris 1998; Valla 1998). In the Negev Desert to the south, a new cultural tradition appeared, the Harifian. It is characterized by a new toolkit that includes a unique type of projectile point, the Harifian point. Presumably, this point was used by the Harifians following new hunting strategies, perhaps indicating a focus on smaller game animals and birds. Some researchers have suggested that the Harifians came about as an adaptation to the drier climate and resulting decrease in woodland resources (Goring-Morris 1998; Goring-Morris and Belfer-Cohen 1998).

Unfortunately, archaeobotanical information for Natufian sites in the Southern Levant is scarce. Natufian toolkits contain large numbers of sickles and more grinding stones compared to the earlier Kebaran and Geometric Kebaran periods, leading some researchers to argue that the Natufians intensively collected wild cereals, and possibly planted them as well (Bar-Yosef and Belfer-Cohen 1991; Henry 1989; McCorriston and Hole 1991; Unger-Hamilton 1989). However, as mentioned above, sickles may have functioned primarily as tools for harvesting basketry materials, and grinding equipment can be used for a wide variety of tasks including preparing minerals for pigment, and processing nuts and legumes as well as grass seeds (Olszewski 1993; Wright 1994).

A number of researchers have developed models suggesting that the direct effects of climatic forcing placed Natufian society on a path towards agriculture in the PPNA. All of these models have elements of climatic determinism. Some suggest that diminished rainfall in the Younger Dryas created hard times for the Natufian foragers, which led them to begin exploiting wild cereals in their native habitats and then planting them in areas where they did not grow on their own (Bar-Yosef and Belfer-Cohen 2002; Henry 1989; Moore and Hillman 1992). Others argued that the YD episode expanded the cereal resources and thus the Late Natufians experienced an abundant increase which encouraged more intensive exploitation of cereals and eventually led to agriculture (Bottema 2002; McCorriston and Hole 1991). However, closer examination of the early Neolithic sites in the Levant suggests there is little *direct* evidence for cultivation even though those settlements are commonly considered the world's first agricultural communities.

The Pre-Pottery Neolithic A period, beginning around 11,700 BP, saw the renewal of widespread village life which had its short-lived beginnings in the Early Natufian. The largest PPNA sites in the Southern Levant are from the Jordan Valley on both sides of the Jordan River. They include Jericho, Netiv Hagdud, Wadi Feynan, and Dhra, all located near springs. The sites are characterized by oval house structures made of stone foundations with a superstructure of mudbrick. Toolkits contained microliths, points, sickles, and milling stones. Population began to increase noticeably, and villages became substantial in the later phase of the PPNA, known as the Sultanian period. Some sites also included impressive public architecture such as the Jericho tower and storage installations (Bar-Yosef 1995; Kuijt and Finlayson 2009; Kuijt and Goring-Morris 2002).

Macrobotanical remains from PPNA sites have yielded a wide variety of plant taxa, including abundant grains of wild barley from Jordan Valley sites such as Netiv Hagdud, and wild emmer from sites in Syria such as Jerf el-Ahmar (Bar-Yosef and Kislev 1989; Willcox 2004). There has been much debate and speculation whether these wild cereals were cultivated or collected from wild stands. Bar-Yosef and others (Bar-Yosef and Kislev 1989) have argued that Sultanian villagers were taking advantage of the alluvial fans near the sites of Jericho and Netiv Hagdud to plant and irrigate stands of cereals that were the primary subsistence support for these large villages in the Jordan Valley. However, phytolith work conducted on these Jordan Valley sites indicates that the wild barley found in abundance there could not have grown on the moist alluvial fans, due to a complete lack of multicell phytolith forms which are indicative of grasses grown under moist alluvial conditions. On the contrary, they appear to come from grasses that were rain-fed in well-drained hillslope soils (Rosen, personal observation). Thus, if the barley had been cultivated it would have had to have been dry-farmed in upland areas distant from the site. It seems more reasonable to assume that it was collected from wild stands at higher elevations. Kislev, Weiss, and Hartmann (2004) have shown that a large amount of wild wheat and barley could be collected by simply picking up fallen spikelets from the ground throughout the summer season, well past the actual ripening period of the cereal. In relatively short periods of time a family of foragers could collect enough barley grains to feed themselves over many months, and could even have enough to last throughout the year.

Willcox (2004), working at the site of Jerf el-Ahmar in Syria, found evidence for fully domesticated emmer wheat very early in the PPNB deposits. He argued that there must have been a lengthy period of evolution from the wild to the domestic species of wheat. He suggested that this period could have been as long as 1000 years, and therefore the process of cultivation would have had to have begun early in the PPNA. This challenges the work by Hillman and Davis (1990), who argued for a very short period of evolution, possibly lasting only about 100 years. However, at Jerf el-Ahmar, Willcox had no macrobotanical remains showing transitional stages between wild emmer in the early PPNA and domestic emmer in the early PPNB. Previous reports of domestic emmer early in the PPNA at Tel Aswad in the Damascus Basin were shown to be invalid after those levels were redated to the PPNB (Harris 2003; Nesbitt 2002). Although some cultivation of wild cereals might have taken place on a small scale, there is still no conclusive evidence that *cultivation* rather than *collection* of wild cereals was a significant part of the plant exploitation strategy for PPNA populations.

THE ROLE OF CLIMATE CHANGE IN NATUFIAN AND PPNA ADAPTATIONS TO CHANGING ENVIRONMENTS

The Natufians occupy a privileged place in our perception of hunter-gatherer societies in marginal environments, due to their temporal positioning as the social group on the threshold of change from complex hunter/gathering to true village societies, and presumably at the turning point on the road to cultivation. However, as I have argued elsewhere (Rosen 2007a), it is more informative to put them in the perspective of other hunter-gatherers in similar environments who had to cope with shifting habitats and resource availability in the face of pronounced climatic change. Given that foragers respond to changes in resources more directly than to changes in temperature and precipitation, it is most helpful to reconstruct the impact of environmental change on the distribution of key elements in the subsistence economy of these societies, based on findings from the archaeological record. Human behavioral ecologists (HBE) have suggested a number of ways in which hunter/gatherers typically respond to adverse environmental change in order to manage the risk of relying on desirable, but declining, subsistence resources (Gremillion 2004; Kennett and Kennett 2000; Kennett and Winterhalder 2006; Winterhalder and Goland 1997). Several recurrent principles are useful to consider in the case of the Natufians.

Two elements of HBE models are particularly useful for understanding how Natufian and PPNA peoples would have responded to climate change: "resource choice" and "risk minimization." The models predict that foragers will choose to limit "booms" and "busts" in their food supply by selecting resources with lower average yields, but greater stability. They will concentrate on foods that are readily and dependably obtained, thereby minimizing the risk of starvation or hunger (Low 1990). They may broaden their resource base by becoming more mobile and by using a variety of lower-rank resources, which would be considered "famine food" under normal circumstances. They may also expand their relations with other social groups, and use different technologies in order to maximize the efficiency of hunting (Minnis 1985; Winterhalder and Goland 1997). Although there are numerous ways in which foragers can minimize risk, it is also important to acknowledge the unique idiosyncrasies of the social system, history, cultural tradition, and technology that may account for the varying responses on the part of different groups to similar environmental circumstances (Minnis 1985; Kennett and Winterhalder 2006:18).

Ethnographic studies of hunter-gatherers around the world contrast the exploitation of nuts and acorns with that of grass seeds. Many foragers rank nuts over seeds due to their high nutritional value, their ease of collection and processing, and the lack of need for complex toolkits for their exploitation (Keeley 1999; Lee 1979; Mason 1995). In contrast, grass seeds are given a lower ranking, since they require more energy to collect and process, and processing often involves specialized toolkits such as grinding stones, beaters, and baskets. Researchers have looked for a change in environmental conditions to explain how the values placed on a typically high-ranked plant resource, such as nuts or acorns, and that of a low-ranked one, such as grass seeds, can be reversed. Perhaps most relevant to the Natufian situation, Winterhalder and Goland (1997) found that if a resource with a low ranking of preference but high density switches to one of high ranking—as a consequence of environmental change—then this will lead to intensive exploitation.

A number of case studies provide analogies to the situation faced by Natufians during times of environmental change. In keeping with the HBE model, ethnohistorical and archaeological evidence from Australia indicates that in higher rainfall areas, foraging populations prefer to exploit fruits, nuts, and tubers over seeds due to the specialized tool kits and more intensive labor required for seed exploitation. However, when drier conditions set in, or when populations move into more arid regions, grass seeds become more heavily exploited because of their reliability and robust storability (Haberle and David 2004; O'Connell and Hawkes 1981; Smith 1989). The drier climatic conditions that occurred after 3500 BP in southeastern Cape York led to increasingly open vegetation and a broader subsistence base with more intensive use of grasses. In addition, aboriginal populations began to manage the landscape more intensively; among other practices, they maintained the open grassland regions by intentional burning (Haberle and David 2004).

A similar situation occurred on the North American Great Plains during the middle Holocene episode of drying climatic conditions. Populations of bison diminished, surface and groundwater sources became scarcer, and vegetation cover became less dense as the region shifted to more xeric grassland vegetation. According to Meltzer (1999), human adaptations to these changing environmental conditions included concentration of settlements around permanent water sources, the inclusion of lower-ranked/higher-cost resources, and the introduction of new technologies for intensive seed exploitation, processing, and storage.

Thus ethnographic and archaeological evidence corroborates the HBE model of hunter-gatherer foraging strategies: grass seeds are often a lower-ranked resource than nuts; nut use takes precedence over the exploitation of seeds; the use of grass seeds and other plants with high processing costs will tend to increase when environmental conditions or population increases reduce the availability of nuts (Keeley 1999).

This common hunter-gatherer strategy for managing risk seems very relevant to Early Natufian adaptations throughout the post-LGM Bølling-Allerød warming and the Late and Final Natufian during the Younger Dryas climatic deterioration. The expansion of the woodland during the post-LGM would have provided Natufians living in the Mediterranean area with abundant woodland resources from oak, almond, pistachio, and olive trees. With the Younger Dryas, there was a decrease in the woodland and expansion of the grasslands in the Levant. This situation might have led to diminishing returns from the exploitation of woodland resources and made it more profitable for the Natufian hunter-gatherers to turn to the formerly lower-ranked resources such as grass seeds in spite of the fact they would have required a larger investment of time and a shift in technology.

As indicated above, we have very little archaeobotanical evidence for Early or Late Natufian plant exploitation in the Mediterranean Core Area. However, we do have abundant well-preserved plant remains from a much earlier site in the Galilee called Ohalo II. This site was occupied by complex hunter-gatherers at ca. 23,000 BP, during the LGM, and thus at the apex of cool dry conditions in the Levant. Here the macrobotanical remains were well-preserved in waterlogged condition on the shore of Lake Kinneret. Predictably, the terminal Upper Paleolithic/early Epipaleolithic occupants of this site heavily exploited a variety of grasses, especially large-seeded grasses such as wild emmer wheat (*Triticum dicoccoides*), barley (*Hordeum spontaneum*), and goatgrass (*Aegilops* sp.). This earlier adaptation is likely to be a good analogy for the Late Natufians occupying the region during the dry Younger Dryas period, and is supported by the increase in milling stones from the Early to the Late Natufian time period (Wright 1994).

The fact that there was an increasing emphasis on grass seeds from the Early Natufian to the Late Natufian has been noted by numerous different authors beginning with Dorothy Garrod in the 1930s (Garrod and Bate 1937), and continuing on through the present with more in-depth studies by current researchers (Bar-Yosef 2002; Bar-Yosef and Belfer-Cohen 1991; Henry 1989; Hillman 1996). These studies focus on the Natufians as on the way to being agricultural communities, and they are seen as having primarily targeted wild cereals, namely wheat and barley. However, phytolith evidence from the large Natufian settlement of Eynan (Ain Mallaha) shows that cereals were only a portion of the wild grasses exploited by the Natufians. Their adaptation was to grass seeds in general and not exclusively cereals (Rosen 2007c, 2010) (Fig. 5.5).

Although the Natufians seem to have followed a strategy of changing resource ranking with changing environmental regimes, this alone was not enough to set them on the path to agriculture. In fact, the switch to wild grass seed exploitation seems to have been such a successful adaptation to the Younger Dryas drought that it continued to persist for about 1500 years. However, there were other social and technological shifts that were just as

Sample Contexts of Eynan Phytoliths

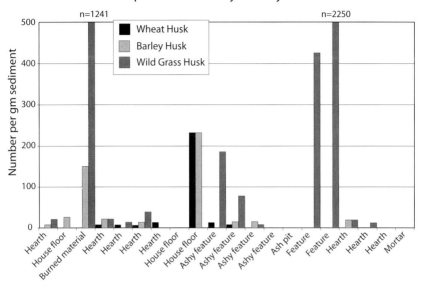

5.5 Grass and cereal phytolith densities from the Late Natufian levels at Eynan (Ain Mallaha) by archaeological context.

important as the subsistence changes. These other adaptations such as new hunting technologies on the part of the Harifians in the Negev, and shifts in land management, with the possible inclusion of fire to manipulate the ecology, took place across much of the Near East. It is only in the Levant that plant cultivation and domestication leading to agriculture developed, and that was much later in time. Thus the role of the Younger Dryas climate change as a forcing mechanism for the development of agriculture was much less important than many have argued.

Other researchers have suggested that the roots of a fully agricultural life took place in the early Pre-Pottery Neolithic A (PPNA), which occurred at the very beginning of the Holocene when climatic conditions were warming and wetting up. This idea has proponents among both paleoclimatologists (Burroughs 2005) and archaeologists (Bar-Yosef 1995; Colledge 2001; Willcox 2004). Burroughs presents a very strong climatic determinist thesis and maintains that not only did the climate preclude any agriculture in the Pleistocene due to large fluctuations in the climatic record (what he refers to as the "long grass"), but the "short grass" or low fluctuation curves in the Holocene made it almost inevitable that agriculture would begin with the onset of a warmer/wetter climate. This proposition much overemphasizes the climatic factor and underemphasizes the social and technological factors.

As argued above, there is no clear evidence for domesticated cereals during the PPNA, a period of time which lasted for a full 1000 years into the early Holocene. Even more telling, there is little to indicate that wild cereals were intensively planted rather than collected at this time. But in spite of this lack of evidence for cultivation in the Natufian and PPNA periods, cores from Lake Hula and Lake Ghab in the northern Levant contain significantly high quantities of microcharcoal (Turner et al. 2009; Yasuda, Kitagawa, and Nakagawa 2000). The charcoal from these two lakes is most likely the result of human land use practices involving the burning of woodlands at the beginning of the Holocene in the PPNA (Ghab) and the terminal Pleistocene (Hula). This suggests that even before cultivation, foragers were actively manipulating the plant ecology of the region to maintain the grasslands for a number of important resources, including cereals and other wild grass seeds. Grassland management also would have created a habitat for small game as well. This is in keeping with an earlier suggestion by Roberts (2002) that the late incursion of woodlands into central Anatolia might have been the result of human manipulation of the landscape. It is also consistent with archaeological examples of hunter/gatherer groups in Australia and how they responded to environmental change (Haberle and David 2004).

CONCLUSIONS

In the study of human adaptations to the major climatic changes of the terminal Pleistocene and early Holocene, evidence suggests that Natufian adaptations to the dry conditions of the Younger Dryas were extremely successful. This adaptation led to stabilization in patterns of plant resource exploitation, rather than a secular change towards agriculture. This is something also noted in the faunal record by Munro (2004). However, from a social point of view, permanent settlement around water sources in the PPNA and developing social institutions encouraged more social cohesion and population growth. Although the PPNA communities became more sedentary and lived in the first large villages, they still relied heavily if not exclusively on foraging for plant foods. Nevertheless, evidence from lake cores suggests people increasingly manipulated the plant ecology through burning and maintenance of open steppic vegetation.

The first evidence for true agriculture, in the sense of primary reliance on cultivated crops for the vegetal portion of the diet, occurred early in the PPNB about 10,500 BP, a full 1200 years after the first PPNA communities appeared. It is probably no coincidence that this development is associated with much larger populations and the wettest climatic conditions of the Holocene. The moist climate would have significantly decreased the risk of farming, encouraging incipient agriculturalists to "take the plunge" into increasing dependence on food production. Thus it is most likely that agriculture became an attractive and viable lifestyle only at the time that the climatic conditions provided a relatively low-risk environment for plant cultivation. In the scenario proposed here, there are both "pull" and "push" factors in the social and climatic realms with rising populations, increasing sedentism, the desire for material wealth, etc. "pushing" PPNB populations on the one hand, and the ameliorating climate "pulling" them on the other. Thus the role of climate is not only a matter of climatic change forcing social change. It must be viewed in terms of the interaction of pushing and pulling factors on both the social and environmental stages.

NOTE
1. All dates cited are in calibrated years before present.

REFERENCES CITED

Bar-Matthews, M., A. Ayalon, A. Kaufman, and G. J. Wasserburg. 1999. The Eastern Mediterranean Paleoclimate as a Reflection of Regional Events: Soreq Cave, Israel. *Earth and Planetary Science Letters* 166(1–2): 85–95.

Bartov, Y., M. Stein, Y. Enzel, A. Agnon, and Z. Reches. 2002. Lake Levels and Sequence Stratigraphy of Lake Lisan, the Late Pleistocene Precursor of the Dead Sea. *Quaternary Research* 57(1): 9–21.

Baruch, U., and S. Bottema. 1999. A New Pollen Diagram from Lake Hula: Vegetational, Climatic and Anthropogenic Implications. In *Ancient Lakes: Their Cultural and Biological Diversity*, ed. H. Kawanabe, G. W. Coulter, and A. C. Roosevelt, pp. 75–86. Brussels: Kenobi.

Bar-Yosef, O. 1995. Earliest Food Producers: Pre-pottery Neolithic (8000–5500). In *The Archaeology of Society in the Holy Land*, ed. T. E. Levy, pp. 190–204. London: Leicester University Press.

——— 1996. The Impact of Late Pleistocene–Early Holocene Climatic Changes on Humans in Southwest Asia. In *Humans at the End of the Ice Age: The Archaeology of the Pleistocene-Holocene Transition*, ed. L. G. Straus, B. V. Eriksen, J. M. Erlandson, and D. R. Yesner, pp. 61–78. New York: Plenum.

——— 2002. Natufian: A Complex Society of Foragers. In *Beyond Foraging and Collecting: Evolutionary Change in Hunter-Gatherer Settlement Systems*, ed. B. Fitzhugh and J. Habu, pp. 91–149. New York: Kluwer.

Bar-Yosef, O., and A. Belfer-Cohen. 1991. From Sedentary Hunter-Gatherers to Territorial Farmers in the Levant. In *Between Bands and States*, ed. S. A. Gregg, pp. 181–202. Carbondale, IL: Center for Archaeological Investigations.

——— 2002. Facing Environmental Crisis: Societal and Cultural Changes at the Transition from the Younger Dryas to the Holocene in the Levant. In *The Dawn of Farming in the Near East*, ed. R. T. J. Cappers and S. Bottema, pp. 55–66. Berlin: Ex Oriente.

Bar-Yosef, O., and M. E. Kislev. 1989. Early Farming Communities in the Jordan Valley. In *Foraging and Farming: The Evolution of Plant Exploitation*, ed. D. R. Harris and G. C. Hillman, pp. 632–42. London: Unwin Hyman.

Bottema, S. 1995. The Younger Dryas in the Eastern Mediterranean. *Quaternary Science Reviews* 14(9): 883–91.

——— 2002. The Use of Palynology in Tracing Early Agriculture. In *The Dawn of Farming in the Near East*, ed. R. T. J. Cappers and S. Bottema, pp. 27–38. Berlin: Ex Oriente.

Burroughs, W. J. 2005. *Climate Change in Prehistory: The End of the Reign of Chaos*. Cambridge: Cambridge University Press.

Cappers, R. T. J., S. Bottema, and H. Woldring. 1998. Problems in Correlating Pollen Diagrams of the Near East: A Preliminary Report. In *The Origins of Agriculture and Crop Domestication*, ed. A. B. Damania, J. Valkon, G. Willcox, and C. Q. Qualset, pp. 160–69. Rome: IPGRI.

Colledge, S. 2001. *Plant Exploitation on Epipalaeolithic and Early Neolithic Sites in the Levant*. BAR International Series 986. Oxford.

Garrod, D. A. E., and D. M. A. Bate, eds. 1937. *The Stone Age of Mount Carmel: Excavations at the Wady el-Mughara Vol. I*. Oxford: Clarendon.

Goldberg, P. 1986. Late Quaternary Environmental History of the Southern Levant. *Geoarchaeology: An International Journal* 1:225–44.

Goring-Morris, A. N. 1998. Complex Hunter-Gatherers at the End of the Paleolithic (20,000–10,000 BP). In *The Archaeology of Society in the Holy Land*, ed. T. E. Levy, pp. 141–68. London: Leicester University.

Goring-Morris, A. N., and A. Belfer-Cohen. 1998. The Articulation of Cultural Processes and Late Quaternary Environmental Changes in Cisjordan. *Paléorient* 23(2): 71–93.

Gremillion, K. J. 2004. Seed Processing and the Origins of Food Production in Eastern North America. *American Antiquity* 69:215–33.

Haberle, S. G., and B. David. 2004. Climates of Change: Human Dimensions of

Holocene Environmental Change in Low Latitudes of the PEPII Transect. *Quaternary International* 118/119:165–79.

Harris, D. R. 2003. Climatic Change and the Beginnings of Agriculture: The Case of the Younger Dryas. In *Evolution on Planet Earth: Impact of the Physical Environment*, ed. L. Rothschild and A. Lister, pp. 379–94. London: Academic Press.

Hassan, F. 1997. Nile Floods and Political Disorder in Early Egypt. In *Third Millennium BC Climate Change and Old World Collapse*, ed. H. N. Dalfes, G. Kukla, and H. Weiss, pp. 1–23. Berlin: Springer Verlag.

Henry, D. O. 1989. *From Foraging to Agriculture: The Levant at the End of the Ice Age*. Philadelphia: University of Pennsylvania Press.

Hillman, G. 1996. Late Pleistocene Changes in Wild Plant-foods Available to Hunter-Gatherers of the Northern Fertile Crescent: Possible Preludes to Cereal Cultivation. In *The Origins and Spread of Agriculture and Pastoralism in Eurasia*, ed. D. R. Harris, pp. 159–203. Washington, DC: Smithsonian Institution Press.

Hillman, G. C., and M. S. Davis. 1990. Measured Domestication Rates in Wild Wheat and Barley under Primitive Cultivation, and Their Archaeological Implications. *Journal of World Prehistory* 4(2): 157–222.

Issar, A. S. 2003. *Climate Changes during the Holocene and Their Impact on Hydrological Systems*. Cambridge: Cambridge University Press.

Keeley, L. R. 1999. The Use of Plant Foods among Hunter-Gatherers: A Cross-cultural Survey. In *Prehistory of Agriculture: New Experimental and Ethnographic Approaches*, ed. P. C. Anderson, pp. 6–14. Los Angeles: UCLA Press.

Kennett, D. J., and J. P. Kennett. 2000. Competitive and Cooperative Responses to Climatic Instability in Coastal Southern California. *American Antiquity* 65:379–95.

Kennett, D. J., and B. Winterhalder. 2006. *Behavioral Ecology and the Transition to Agriculture*. Berkeley: University of California Press.

Kislev, M. E., E. Weiss, and A. Hartmann. 2004. Impetus for Sowing and the Beginning of Agriculture: Ground Collecting of Wild Cereals. *Proceedings of the National Academy of Sciences of the United States of America* 101:2692–95.

Klinger, Y., J. P. Avouac, D. Bourles, and N. Tisnerat. 2003. Alluvial Deposition and Lake-level Fluctuations Forced by Late Quaternary Climate Change: The Dead Sea Case Example. *Sedimentary Geology* 162(1–2): 119–39.

Kuijt, I., and B. Finlayson. 2009. Evidence for Food Storage and Predomestication Granaries 11,000 Years Ago in the Jordan Valley. *Papers of the National Academy of Sciences* 106(27): 10966–70.

Kuijt, I., and N. Goring-Morris. 2002. Foraging, Farming, and Social Complexity in the Pre-Pottery Neolithic of the Southern Levant: A Review and Synthesis. *Journal of World Prehistory* 16:361–440.

Lee, R. B. 1979. *The !Kung San*. Cambridge: Cambridge University Press.

Low, B. S. 1990. Human Responses to Environmental Extremeness and

Uncertainty: A Cross-cultural Perspective. In *Risk and Uncertainty in Tribal and Peasant Economies*, ed. E. Cashdan, pp. 229–55. Boulder, CO: Westview.

Machlus, M., Y. Enzel, S. L. Goldstein, S. Marco, and M. Stein. 2000. Reconstructing Low Levels of Lake Lisan by Correlating Fan-delta and Lacustrine Deposits. *Quaternary International* 73/74:137–44.

Mason, S. L. R. 1995. Acornutopia? Determining the Role of Acorns in Past Human Subsistence. In *Food in Antiquity*, ed. J. Wilkins, D. Harvey, and M. Dobson, pp. 12–14. Exeter: Exeter University Press.

McCorriston, J., and F. Hole. 1991. The Ecology of Seasonal Stress and the Origins of Agriculture in the Near East. *American Anthropologist* 93:46–69.

McGovern, T. H. 1994. Management for Extinction in Norse Greenland. *Historical Ecology*, ed. C. Crumley, pp. 127–54. Santa Fe, NM: School of American Research Press.

Meltzer, D. J. 1999. Human Responses to Middle Holocene (Altithermal) Climates on the North American Great Plains. *Quaternary Research* 52(3): 404–16.

Minnis, P. E. 1985. *Social Adaptation to Food Stress: A Prehistoric Southwestern Example*. Chicago: University of Chicago.

Moore, A. M. T., and G. C. Hillman. 1992. The Pleistocene to Holocene Transition and Human Economy in Southwest Asia: The Impact of the Younger Dryas. *American Antiquity* 57:482–94.

Munro, N. D. 2004. Zooarchaeological Measures of Hunting Pressure and Occupation Intensity in the Natufian: Implications for Agricultural Origins. *Current Anthropology* 45:S5–S33.

Nesbitt, M. 2002. When and Where Did Domesticated Cereals First Occur in Southwest Asia? In *The Dawn of Farming in the Near East*, ed. R. T. J. Cappers and S. Bottema, pp. 113–32. Berlin: Ex Oriente.

O'Connell, J., and K. Hawkes. 1981. Alyawara Plant Use and Optimal Foraging Theory. *Hunter-Gatherer Foraging Strategies*, ed. B. Winterhalder and E. A. Smith, pp. 99–125. Chicago: University of Chicago Press.

Olszewski, D. I. 1993. Subsistence Ecology in the Mediterranean Forest: Implications for the Origins of Cultivation in the Epipaleolithic Southern Levant. *American Anthropologist* 95:420–35.

Roberts, N. 2002. Did Prehistoric Landscape Management Retard the Postglacial Spread of Woodland in Southwest Asia? *Antiquity* 76:1002–10.

Rosen, A. M. 1995. The Social Response to Environmental Change in Early Bronze Age Canaan. *Journal of Anthropological Archaeology* 14:26–44.

—— 2004. Phytolith Evidence for Plant Use at Mallaha/Eynan. In "Les fouilles à Mallaha en 2000 et 2001: 3ème rapport préliminaire" by F. R. Valla. *Journal of the Israel Prehistoric Society* 34:189–201.

—— 2007a. *Civilizing Climate: Social Responses to Climate Change in the Ancient Near East*. Lanham, MD: Altamira.

—— 2007b. The Role of Environmental Change in the Development of

Complex Societies in China: A Study from the Huizui Site. *Indo-Pacific Prehistory Association Bulletin* 27:39–48.

—— 2007c. Phytolith Remains from Final Natufian Contexts at Mallaha/Eynan. *Journal of the Israel Prehistory Society* 37:340–55.

—— 2010. Natufian Exploitation: Managing Risk and Stability in an Environment of Change. *Eurasian Prehistory* 7(1):117–31.

Smith, M. A. 1989. Seed Gathering in Inland Australia: Current Evidence from Seed-grinders on the Antiquity of the Ethnohistorical Pattern of Exploitation. In *Foraging and Farming: The Evolution of Plant Exploitation*, ed. D. R. Harris and G. C. Hillman, pp. 305–17. London: Unwin Hyman.

Turner, R., N. Roberts, W. J. Eastwood, E. Jenkins, and A. Rosen. 2009. Fire, Climate and the Origins of Agriculture: Micro-charcoal Records of Biomass Burning during the Last Glacial-interglacial Transition in Southwest Asia. *Journal of Quaternary Science* 25:371–86.

Unger-Hamilton, R. 1989. The Epi-Paleolithic Southern Levant and the Origins of Cultivation. *Current Anthropology* 30:88–103.

Valla, F. 1998. The First Settled Societies: Natufian (12,500–10,200 BP). In *The Archaeology of Society in the Holy Land*, ed. T. E. Levy, pp. 169–87. London: Leicester University.

Willcox, G. 2004. Measuring Grain Size and Identifying Near Eastern Cereal Domestication: Evidence from the Euphrates Valley. *Journal of Archaeological Science* 31:145–50.

Winterhalder, B., and C. Goland. 1997. An Evolutionary Ecology Perspective on Diet Choice, Risk and Plant Domestication. In *People, Plants, and Landscapes: Studies in Paleoethnobotany*, ed. K. J. Gremillion, pp. 123–60. Tuscaloosa: University of Alabama Press.

Wright, H. E., and J. L. Thorpe. 2003. Climatic Change and the Origin of Agriculture in the Near East. In *Global Change in the Holocene*, ed. A. Mackay, R. Battarbee, J. Birks, and F. Oldfield, pp. 49–62. London: Arnold.

Wright, K. I. 1994. Ground-Stone Tools and Hunter-Gatherer Subsistence in Southwest Asia—Implications for the Transition to Farming. *American Antiquity* 59:238–63.

Yasuda, Y., H. Kitagawa, and T. Nakagawa. 2000. The Earliest Record of Major Anthropogenic Deforestation in the Ghab Valley, Northwest Syria: A Palynological Study. *Quaternary International* 73/74:127–36.

Zohary, M. 1973. *Geobotanical Foundations of the Middle East*. Stuttgart: FischerVerlag.

6

Explaining the Structure and Timing of Formation of Pueblo I Villages in the Northern U.S. Southwest

TIMOTHY A. KOHLER AND CHARLES REED

Human interactions with the environment structure society in many different ways. Longstanding cultural practices likewise have a structuring effect on the environment. On appropriate time scales, then, practices affect societies through a feedback mechanism provided by the environment (Odling-Smee, Laland, and Feldman 1996). Climate change provides exogenous signals that may affect these interactions because of responses in either the society or the environment. Human population movements and sociopolitical strife play the roles of sometimes endogenous, sometimes exogenous, factors that on small spatial scales may seem inexplicable but which on longer temporal and wider spatial scales may have understandable rhythms (Turchin and Korotayev 2006).

This chapter makes some suggestions about the trajectory of early Pueblo society as seen primarily through a window into prehispanic southwestern Colorado provided in part by recent research through the Village Ecodynamics Project (VEP: Kohler et al. 2007; Varien et al. 2007). That project analyzed the long sweep of Pueblo history in this area, from AD 600–1300. Here we focus on the first half of that period, the Basketmaker III and Pueblo I occupations from about AD 600–900. This makes the research undertaken by the Dolores Archaeological Project (DAP: Breternitz, Robinson, and Gross 1986), which concentrated on those periods, critical to our purposes.[1]

THE BMIII AND PI PERIODS IN SOUTHWESTERN COLORADO: BRIEF DESCRIPTION

Probably through immigration of farmers rather than adoption of farming by local hunter-gatherers, farming lifeways became evident in our area (Fig. 6.1) in an important way around AD 600, in the Basketmaker III (BMIII) period. These first local farmers inhabited small sites, called hamlets, composed of relatively shallow round, squarish, or D-shaped pitstructures with antechambers, that may be isolated farmsteads or grouped into loose "neighborhoods" of perhaps half a dozen pitstructures whose contemporaneity is typically difficult to assess (pitstructure use-life appears to be short). Surface facilities including ramadas and small, disconnected round or oval rooms may appear in an arc north and west of the pitstructures (Kane 1986:363). Kane and most other archaeologists interpret these pitstructures as the residences of nuclear families. Pottery vessels are present, with small grayware forms such as seed jars and other jars most common;

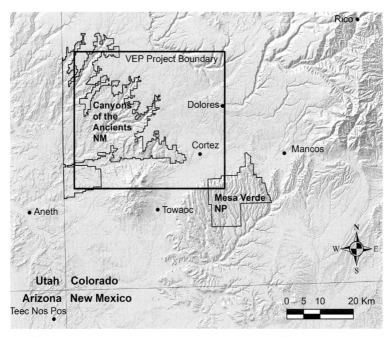

6.1 The Village Ecodynamics Project study area in southwestern Colorado. (From Kohler et al. 2007:fig. 4.1).

bowls and decorated vessels are relatively uncommon (Rohn 1977:233–34). Trough metates, relatively simple manos, and stemmed projectile points are all common. By AD 600 maize had been an important component of the Puebloan diet for well over a millennium south and southwest of our study area, whereas beans, the bow and arrow, and ceramic vessels were relatively recent additions (Gumerman and Dean 1989:114–15; Gumerman and Gell-Mann 1994:19).

Beginning around AD 725, roughly the beginning of the Pueblo I (PI) period, the appearance of various decorated ceramics, including local and non-local redwares, began to add variability to the ceramic assemblages (Blinman 1986:72–73). Small bowls became more common at the same time. Later in the PI period, around AD 800, a considerably larger bowl form (with a volume of at least 13 liters) appeared. By about AD 840, this was joined by a jar form with a volume of at least 7 liters, which was also substantially larger than earlier jars (Blinman 1986:87). Ceramic deposition rates and arguments from structure replacement suggest increasing duration of occupation for all sites during this period, but especially in the villages (Kohler and Blinman 1987; Varien and Ortman 2005). Increasing durations of structure use, and site longevity, probably allowed more intergenerational transfers of material, embodied, and relational wealth, augmenting possibilities for inequalities in wealth (Borgerhoff Mulder et al. 2009) and allowing some subtle movement towards economic and power differentials in PI societies.

In the Dolores area, architectural changes from earlier practices became pronounced by about AD 760, and included the construction of double-row surface roomblocks north and west of pitstructures, which greatly increased storage capacity. This increase may have been related to the appearance of new and possibly more productive varieties of maize at about this time, as well as to generally increasing use-lives for structures. The standard DAP interpretation was that by this time pitstructures were shared by two to three households (nuclear families) who lived primarily in the surface structures; or to put it slightly differently, pitstructures after AD 760 were probably shared spaces for extended families. Flannery has recently suggested that the emergence of extended family households is a regular feature of early village life, following on the heels of "true villages of rectangular households" occupied by nuclear families (2002:417), but in the DAP area these developments may be essentially simultaneous.[2]

One "oversized" pitstructure on Grass Mesa is known for the pre-AD 800 period in the DAP. Kane interprets this as a "corporate" structure (following Hayden and Cannon's [1982] use of this term) and notes that by AD 840 (the beginning of the McPhee Phase) roomblocks became increasingly large, housing up to 20 nuclear families: "This aggregation of household architecture into larger complexes suggests social organization above the household level was a prominent force within . . . communities" (1986:369). Kane infers that the emergence of these corporate groups implies that "unencumbered land in the local area was becoming scarce and competition for croplands probably occurred" and suggests that these corporate groups controlled the transmission of land holdings (1986:369; see also Kohler 1992). By this analysis the leaders of these corporate groups would have overseen the construction and controlled the use of oversized pitstructures which, with their ritual features, would have facilitated group-oriented activities probably including communication and reproduction of social structure and practices, and economic activities. In short these structures would have been key loci for the display and use of structural and organizational power as defined by Schachner (2001).[3]

Around AD 800 an even larger class of pitstructure, the great kiva, also appears on Grass Mesa (Kane 1986:367; Lightfoot 1988). These structures presumably served functions analogous to those of the over-sized pitstructures, and presented analogous opportunities for aspiring leaders or factions, but at the community or intercommunity level rather than the smaller level of Kane's corporate groups. (Lipe et al. [1988:1221] suggested that Grass Mesa's mid-8th century oversized pitstructure [Pitstructure 93] might better be interpreted as an early great kiva of community or intercommunity scope.) It is interesting and possibly significant that within the DAP area, oversized pitstructures, great kivas, and households that are relatively more clustered than elsewhere all appeared first on Grass Mesa. In the context of our argument here, we suggest that its placement on the north side of the Dolores River, from where it enjoyed easy access to the uninhabited, deer-rich highlands to the north, helps explain this precocity.

The village is the most famous characteristic of the later Pueblo I period in the northern Southwest. Pueblo I villages are notable both for their size—they are much larger than earlier sites in the Puebloan Southwest[4]—and for their configuration. In their description of the later portions of the AD 600–850 period in the northern Southwest, Gumerman and Gell-Mann

(1994:20) are struck by the modularity of the larger villages, and note that these "communities were made up of smaller social elements. Since the components of the larger sites are similar in size and morphology, they may represent a common social order for much of the northern region." Recent research, however, has shown that the spatial organization of PI villages was quite different east of the DAP area, near Durango (Potter and Chuipka 2007), so it seems likely that there were contrasting social organizational principles at work in the eastern and western portions of the northern Southwest during the 8th and 9th centuries AD that may well have their roots in the differing origins and histories of the first farmers west and east of the central Mesa Verde area (Lekson 2009:45–46; Matson 2006).

In the remainder of this chapter we move from these descriptions, and these (mostly) DAP-era discussions of them, to put these phenomena into a wider spatial and temporal explanatory context. We'll suggest that unprecedented population expansion throughout the Puebloan world (and in fact throughout the Southwest) beginning in the mid-1st millennium AD, abetted by favorable climatic conditions that opened up some of the most productive lands ever cultivated by Pueblo farmers, led to decreased per capita availability of the locally most important big game, mule deer, which in turn led to intensification in hunting (Spielmann and Angstadt-Leto 1996). Social strategies facilitating this intensification included the strengthening and possibly redefining of kinship systems as a way of forming trustworthy groups of hunters who could be relied on for increasingly long-distance deer hunting. Byproducts (or co-evolutions) of these social changes were trustworthy groups of men for warfare. New opportunities for the emergence of persistent social inequalities in these villages stemmed from increased longevity of site use (at least for villages) fostering the conditions for intergenerational transmission of wealth, an inferred increased importance of balanced reciprocal exchanges across roomblocks, status-enhancing provisioning of big game, and defense of village and territory.

CLIMATIC AND DEMOGRAPHIC CONTEXTS

In August 2005, VEP researchers re-cored Beef Pasture, a peaty fen located at an elevation of 10,000 ft (ca. 3000 m) in the La Plata Mountains some 40 km northeast of Mesa Verde National Park that was previously sampled and analyzed by Petersen and Mehringer (1976; Petersen 1988). With 72 closely spaced stratigraphic pollen samples anchored by 16 ^{14}C dates, this research provides one of the most precisely dated pollen records for the last 2000 years in North America (Wright 2006). Aaron Wright devised pollen ratios from this core—building in part on earlier work by Petersen—that reflect temperature, and summer and winter precipitation (Fig. 6.2, after Wright 2006: Fig. 21). Given that the central Mesa Verde region in which the largest PI villages developed is both north of, and higher in elevation than, much of Puebloan Southwest, these farmers were probably particularly sensitive to fluctuations in temperature. Although it is difficult to calibrate these pollen records against temperature, it seems likely that the late arrival of farmers in the VEP study area (which includes the DAP area)—relative to the much earlier presence of farming further south, and at lower elevations—was partly controlled by the long, slow upward trend in temperature from 100

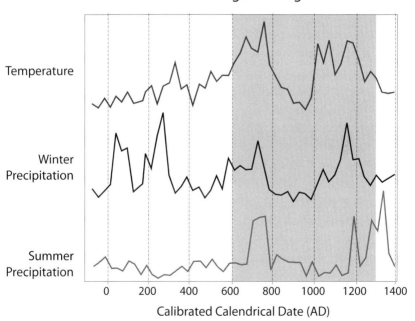

6.2 Low-frequency climatic trends in southwestern Colorado from about 100 BC to AD 1400, as reconstructed using pollen indices derived from a core drawn from Beef Pasture, Colorado (Wright 2006). The shaded area identifies the period during which Pueblo farmers occupied the VEP study area. (Figure courtesy of Aaron Wright)

BC to AD 800 that perhaps crossed a threshold where maize agriculture was locally reliable midway through the 1st millennium AD. Likewise, it seems probable that the trough in temperatures in the AD 900s contributed—at the very least—to the partial depopulation of the DAP and VEP areas during that century. Finally, the long-term perspective provided by this record makes it clear that low-frequency temperature and precipitation conditions during the two centuries from AD 600 to almost 800 were unusually propitious for agriculture.

We suspect that when temperatures permitted their use, the high-elevation portions of the central Mesa Verde region, with their deep blanket of fertile loess and orographic precipitation, provided farmers with yields that they could not hope to achieve in other portions of the Pueblo world. A portion of this area today claims to be the "pinto bean capital of the world."

Our recent attempts to understand the demography of the prehistoric Southwest, and of the Pueblo area, employ a ratio pioneered by Bocquet-Appel (2002). In its numerator is the number of individuals in a site, or in contemporaneous sites within a locality, aged 5–19 years. The denominator contains the count of all individuals from the same population 5 years of age or older. By means of empirical analyses and simulation, Bocquet-Appel has shown that this ratio is reliably positively correlated with both birthrates and with the instantaneous coefficient of population growth r.

Kohler et al. (2008) have graphed this proxy using skeletal data from throughout the Southwest, showing that the earliest maize agriculture, which dates to slightly before 2000 BC, seems to have had a negligible effect on growth rates. In fact growth rates do not markedly accelerate in the Pueblo portions of the Southwest until about AD 600 (Kohler and Varien 2010), more or less as the upland portions of the central Mesa Verde region opened to dry farmers. The Pueblo world underwent rapid population growth from about AD 600 to 1200, by which time the related processes of climatically induced spatial retrenchment and aggregation conspire to lower the demographic boom.

This spatially general process of population growth is central to our argument. To oversimplify in the interest of making the larger argument clearer, we suspect that population growth among Archaic populations in the Southwest was typically limited by access to carbohydrates. This was alleviated to some extent by the cultivation of maize, which not only contributes general carbohydrates but is also a high-glycemic index food, which according to Kakos (2003) promotes an insulin response causing the body to store fat, ultimately increasing women's fertility. For some reason, however, pan-Southwestern population growth remained relatively slow for more than two millennia after maize appeared on the southern Colorado Plateau. Possibly that effect can be explained by a low glycemic index for early maize. Or perhaps populations remained relatively mobile and thus limited their family size. Or perhaps some combination of the bow and arrow, more productive maize, beans, ceramic vessels, dry farming, and the increasing climatic availability of productive uplands that could be dry-farmed "completed" the Neolithic package around the middle of the 1st millennium AD and allowed high population growth rates. Most likely all these explanations contributed in some measure to the delayed but vigorous population expansion.

EFFECTS OF GROWING POPULATIONS ON LARGE GAME

Whatever the causes of population growth of the 1st millennium AD, recent simulations undertaken by the VEP demonstrate that it can be expected to have a serious impact on densities of the local highest-ranked game species, mule deer. Using agent-based models that represent key aspects of the paleolandscapes of an 1816-km² area in southwestern Colorado, Bocinsky et al. (2011) show that even when we use relatively conservative assumptions about how much protein from meat people seek, and varying several other parameters that relate to hunting strategies and game abundance, severe deer depletion is very likely once local population levels become as high as those supported in our area at the PI population peak.

We can see evidence for this effect in the faunal bone analyses conducted by DAP investigators. Taking the large assemblage (17,236 analyzed fragments of nonhuman bone) from Grass Mesa as an example, *Odocoileus hemionus* (mule deer) represents, overall, 8.4% of the total assemblage by Number of Identifiable Specimens (NISP), and bone identified only to the level of Cervidae—of which nearly all can be expected to be mule deer—represents another 14.2% of the total (Neusius and Gould 1988:table 15.2). By contrast, three-quarters of the Pueblo III sites tabulated by Driver (2002) contain fewer that 10% artiodactyls by NISP, which demonstrates not only the importance of deer to PI populations, but also the eventual depression of high-ranked game on this landscape.

The PI population history of Grass Mesa roughly parallels that of the DAP and VEP areas as a whole. Kohler (1988:table 3.7) estimates a momentary population for the AD 725–800 period of about 22 households, dipping slightly to 17 households from AD 800–840, then increasing markedly to 92 households from AD 840–880, and again to 124 households between AD 880 and 910. This last period contains the enigmatic Grass Mesa Subphase, in which surface structures disappeared and pitstructures decreased radically in size (Lipe et al. 1988:1272–76).

Over the course of this occupation, Neusius and Gould (1988:fig. 15.19) report that the percentage (by NISP) of the pitstructure faunal assemblages identified as lagomorphs increases regularly from 11.1 to 51.3. Among all of the identifiable bone recovered, the summed total of lagomorphs and rodents constitutes about half of the early assemblages, rising regularly through time to make up about 68% of the latest assemblages (Neusius and Gould 1988:fig. 15.13). In Table 6.1 we present our own tabulation of DAP fauna from Grass Mesa, using only those specimens (numbering over 5000) that can be securely dated to a specific period. Organized in this way, deer and related large game, plus other large mammals, declined from over 36% of the NISP in the AD 725–800 period to about 26% of NISP from 880–920.

Table 6.1. Changes in Fauna through Time at Grass Mesa Village

(a) Cell entries contain column percentages; marginals present raw frequencies (NISP). (b) Median polish of raw frequencies, after log transform. Tables compiled from DAP data organized by Wilshusen et al. (1999) and maintained at http://golem.anth.wsu.edu/databases/.

(a)

CATEGORY	725–800	800–840	840–880	880–920	TOTAL
		PERIOD (AD)			
Deer & related large game spp.[a]	18.0	13.6	8.5	8.3	518
Large mammal[b]	18.4	15.0	21.8	17.6	982
Medium mammal[c]	4.9	5.5	6.3	9.6	401
Other mammal[d]	7.9	4.7	9.6	7.8	423
Leporidae[e]	19.7	30.1	16.3	17.5	974
Other small mammal[f]	24.7	24.7	28.8	30.3	1500
Bird[g]	3.0	2.7	4.0	4.5	191
Turkey	0.0	0.8	0.5	0.4	23
Other[h]	2.1	1.5	2.1	2.4	115
Uncertain	1.5	1.5	2.1	2.3	108
Total	534	528	1672	2501	5235

Table 6.1 cont'd.

(b)

CATEGORY	PERIOD (AD)				ROW EFFECTS
	725–800	800–840	840–880	880–920	
Deer & related large game spp.[a]	0.23	0.13	-0.16	-0.14	0.20
Large mammal[b]	0.02	-0.04	0.03	-0.03	0.42
Medium mammal[c]	-0.06	0.02	-0.02	0.19	-0.06
Other mammal[d]	0.01	-0.18	0.04	-0.03	0.06
Leporidae[e]	0.04	0.24	-0.11	-0.05	0.44
Other small mammal[f]	-0.01	0.01	-0.01	0.04	0.58
Bird[g]	-0.02	-0.05	0.02	0.03	-0.30
Turkey	-0.40	0.33	0.05	-0.06	-1.16
Other[h]	0.04	-0.06	-0.04	0.05	-0.51
Uncertain	-0.04	-0.01	0.01	0.07	-0.56
Column effects	-0.27	-0.30	0.28	0.43	

Notes:

a. Artiodactyla, *Odocoileus hemionus,* Cervidae, *Antilocapra americana, Ovis canadensis,* and *Cervus elaphus*

b. Large mammal and *Ursus* spp.

c. Medium mammal

d. "Mammalia NFS" and "medium or large mammal"

e. Leporidae, *Sylvilagus audobonii, S. nuttallii, Sylvilagus* spp., *Lepus townsendii, L. californicus, L. americanus,* and *Lepus* spp.

f. Canidae, *Canis latrans, C. lupus, Canis* spp., *Vulpes vulpes, Vulpes* spp.; *Lynx rufus, Lynx* spp.; Mustelidae, *Mephitis mephitis, Mustela frenata, Mustela* spp., *Spilogale putorius, Taxidea taxus;* Sciuridae, *Cynomys gunnisoni, Marmota flaviventris, Spermophilus lateralis; Erethizon dorsatum;* Cricetidae, *Microtus montanus, Microtus* spp., *Neotoma mexicana, Neotoma* spp., *Onychomys leucogaster, Peromyscus* spp., *Thomomys bottae, Thomomys* spp., and small mammal

g. Bird, large bird, medium bird, small bird, passeriformes, *Bubo virginianus, Grus canadensis,* falconiformes, Accipitridae, *Accipiter* spp., *Aquila chrysaetos, Buteo* spp., *Cathartes aura;* Corvidae, *Corvus brachyrhynchos, C. corax, Corvus* spp., *Turdus migratorius, Zenaida macroura,* Tetraonidae, galliformes, *Branta canadensis,* and *Anas* spp.

h. "Mammal or bird," fish, reptiles, and snakes

SOCIAL RESPONSES TO DEER DEPLETION

Kohler and Van West (1996) argued that Pueblo villages formed under climatic conditions in which households benefited from sharing maize with other households, and tended to disband under conditions in which it was advantageous for households to hoard.[5] We now wish to argue that the specific *forms* of these villages can also be explained. To preview our argument, as population growth—coupled closely with the introduction of the bow and arrow which represented a significant advance in hunting technology—led to deer depletion, especially near larger settlements such as Grass Mesa, groups in which hunters could reliably form the larger parties required for hunting longer distances were at an advantage relative to those who could

not. Coordination failures in forming successful hunting parties were mini-
mized by drawing on kin, identified in such a way that kinship was unambiguous, thereby rewarding groups which emphasized strong unilineal
kinship bonds. These strongly defined kin systems were localized within
roomblock units that were highly visible in most Pueblo I villages. The
resultant societies would have resembled the segmentary lineage systems
identified by Sahlins (1961) as "organizations of predatory expansion."

The Stag Hunt

If local depression in mule deer populations created conditions in which
individual hunting for deer was becoming less reliable and profitable, the potential advantages for cooperative hunting would have generated the sort of
social dilemma depicted by Jean-Jacques Rousseau in his *Discourse on Inequality* (1755/1950). In a metaphorical scenario which turns out to literally depict
the situation that we believe obtained in the PI villages, Rousseau imagined a
society in which hunters must decide whether to hunt stag, which cannot be
successfully hunted by individuals, or to hunt hare, which can be successfully
hunted by individuals but with a lower return. Group hunting of stag results
in higher returns for all individuals involved compared to the sum of individual hare returns, *so long as these hunting groups can be reliably formed*. In seeking
to create such cooperative hunting parties that could go on longer and more
successful hunting expeditions, Pueblo I populations were faced with a collective action problem of the sort known as an assurance game.[6] The general
payoff structure for such games is shown in normal form in Table 6.2.

In such situations, hunting stag is unambiguously the highest-payoff
alternative, but it is only possible when all participants have a shared understanding of what is expected as a result of their cooperation (Alvard
2003:152; Alvard and Nolin 2002:537). Creating the type of cooperative
group needed to participate in risk-sharing activities required forming
groups with unambiguous membership and responsibilities within which
individuals could rely on shared norms and behavioral expectations. To participate, individuals must be assured that the potential benefits of cooperating outweigh the negative potentials of not receiving their fair share, and
that the system cannot be subverted by free riders. This need for shared
normative behavior creates a coordination problem which we argue, following a parallel example by Alvard (2003), favored reliance on a unilineal
descent system.

Table 6.2. The Assurance Game (two-person, one round)*

The generalized payoff matrix is to left, an example with specific payoffs (from Alvard and Nolin 2002:535) is on the right.

	HUNT STAG (COOPERATE)	HUNT HARE (DEFECT)	HUNT STAG (COOPERATE)	HUNT HARE (DEFECT)
Hunt Stag (Cooperate)	R_1, R_2	S_1, T_2	5,5	0,1
Hunt Hare (Defect)	T_1, S_2	P_1, P_2	1,0	3,3

* The first entry in each cell is the payoff to the row player; the second, the payoff to the column player. Plays are simultaneous. Assurance games have payoffs ranked as follows: R (reward) > T (temptation); P (punishment) > S (sucker's payoff); and R > P. Note that while both hunting stag is the Pareto optimum (it maximizes the group benefit), there is a risk to this choice: for example, if row player hunts stag and column player hunts hare, row player gets the lowest payoff (S=0).

Unilineality

One might expect that any kinship system, or even knowledge of degree of genetic relatedness, would be equally efficient in identifying members of an in-group (kin) vs. an out-group (non-kin). This is not the case. Figure 6.3 shows an example from Alvard (2003:fig. 6.1) in which Ego, if drawing on either genetic relatedness or the bilateral (kindred, cognatic) model of kinship that is its closest cultural analogue, should want to cooperate equally with both A and B, with whom he shares a coefficient of relatedness of 0.125. A and B, however, are unrelated to each other and would have no motivation to cooperate with each other by the logic of kin selection. The bilateral system thus creates overlapping groups with fuzzy boundaries, whereas unilineal descent unambiguously assigns each individual to one group only (Fox 1967:49).

We suggest that whether or not the unilineal principle was present prior to Pueblo I times, it became dominant in the DAP populations at least during this period. By focusing on one side of Ego's lineage, unilineal systems create an unambiguous descent group that facilitates the formation of work groups of whale hunters (Alvard 2003:131–32) or deer hunters. Within such groups "sentiments of common membership, expressed and reinforced by informal institutions of sharing, gift giving, ritual and participation in dangerous collective exploits" readily develop (Richerson and Boyd 1999:254). Because we hypothesize that these unilineal descent groups formed under pressures favoring large and reliable hunting groups, we suppose that they were patrilineal. This keeps related males together, since in such systems, as Fox (1967:114) points out, "almost inevitably the residential group is a

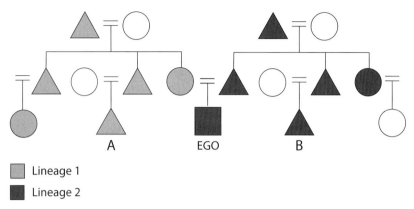

6.3 In a society reckoning kinship by degree of relatedness, Ego would be equally related to A and B, and hence might like to hunt with both of them, but A and B are unrelated and would have no incentive to hunt together. In a patrilineal system, Ego and B are unambiguously in the same group, and A is unambiguously excluded. (After Alvard 2003: fig. 1)

patrilocal unit." The roomblocks within Pueblo I villages therefore, we suggest, represent these patrilineal, patrilocal [virilocal] units. These are the "smaller social units" of Gumerman and Gell-Mann (1994:20)—alluded to above—by which these large villages were organized. They are likewise the "corporate units" postulated by Kane (1986) and Lipe et al. (1988:1268).

By this same logic, we expect that the "oversized" pitstructures that became common in the 9th-century villages represent the houses of senior lineage members—by our analysis, hunting leaders in spirit if not in body. The ritual features in these structures result from the fact that they doubled as assembly houses for the male lineage members. Fox notes the key point that patrilineal, patrilocal systems "manage to combine residence, descent, and authority very neatly" (1967:114).

Segmentary Lineage Organizations

What, if anything, can we infer about whether the lineage members residing in different roomblocks within a village also would have considered themselves to be related at a more general level? Some unilineal systems, which Sahlins (1961) called segmentary lineage organizations, exhibit special properties. He considered the Nuer and the Tiv to be the purest examples. These societies are composed of autonomous primary segments with no permanent organized leadership above that level. At the time of their ethnographic descriptions, both were expanding into areas occupied by other peoples, and were successful in this competition because their segmentary lineage system provided them with a mechanism for large-scale political "consolidation" despite the absence of permanent higher-level organizations (Sahlins 1961:328).

This capability seems to be due in great measure to the fact that all (or almost all) of the lineages in these societies considered themselves to be on a single patriline, so that at increasing social, spatial, and temporal distance, all the Tiv and most of the Nuer considered themselves relatives. Our Figure 6.4 reproduces a figure used by Sahlins (1961:fig. 1) to show how kinship and geography are related in such systems; Sahlins in turn borrowed this from Paul Bohannon (1954). It is clear that these systems pertain

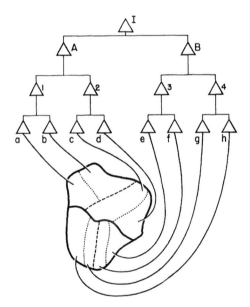

6.4 The idealized relationship between descent and territory among the Tiv, as represented by Bohannon and reproduced by Sahlins (1961: fig. 1). All lineages descend from an apical male ancestor I; his sons A and B divided his territory into two adjacent territories, as did their sons, and so forth. The result, as Bohannon says, is that "the geographical position of territories follows the genealogical division into lineages" (Bohannan 1954:3).

to expanding societies. Sahlins suggested that their organizations allowed them to expand in competitive environments because they could draw on a "lineage system uniting local groups" (Sahlins 1961:330). It is probable, we believe, that such organizations could also arise in circumstances where lineages were undergoing rapid population growth and local lineage splitting, without the specific historical circumstances of intrusion into areas occupied by other groups that Sahlins considered typical of such groups. We think, for example, that early adopters of productive maize agriculture would be excellent candidates for having these characteristics. Glenn Stone (1996:63–73) presents a relevant analysis of the "geometry of social affiliation" among the virilocal Kofyar as they spread into an agricultural frontier.

If this analysis is correct, the implication is that the residents of various roomblocks in a village such as Grass Mesa probably considered themselves very closely related to residents of their own roomblock, but also related, though more distantly, to residents of neighboring roomblocks within the village, and still more distantly related to residents of other villages within their own "tribe" (perhaps including most or all of the peoples on the northeast side of the Dolores River). This is the principle that Sahlins (1961) calls "segmentary sociability."

An implication of this system, in turn, is what Sahlins calls complementary opposition (or the massing effect). Joint mobilization for defense, or for exercise of privileges such as access to hunting territories, will be determined by the social distance of the threat or competition. Quarrels between members of socially adjacent lineages will pit just those lineages against each other, whereas quarrels between anyone in the largest social unit recognized (the tribe) and anyone outside of this social unit will result in the automatic mobilization of the entire tribe against the common enemy. For Sahlins, this characteristic is not part of the political system: it *is* the political system (1961:333) and if the opposition that evoked the unified response dissipates, the high-order structure and any temporary leadership that it may have permitted will dissolve once more into its component parts, or disappear.

There is osteological evidence that social strife in the VEP area was increasing during the AD 800s as the Pueblo I villages reached their population peak (Cole 2006). Given the importance we have alleged for hunting and the near certainty that much of this would have been non-local, conflict over hunting territories between villages (or possibly between larger tribal groups) was a likely source of animosity. This might only have added another foundation to the emerging social power of the hunt/lineage heads. There may have been no essential difference between the form of the organizations promoted by efficient response to warfare and efficient long-distance hunting. Depending on the social distance of the threat, temporary positions of leadership beyond that of the corporate heads could have emerged in both cases.

AGENT-BASED MODELS PROVIDE EVIDENCE FOR THE SOCIAL IMPORTANCE OF EARLY PUEBLO DEER HUNTING

The suggestion that deer hunting was instrumental in structuring PI villages in a particular manner may be a little inflammatory. Southwestern archaeologists (including the senior author) have typically focused on how the variable success and particular characteristics of maize agriculture can explain everything from village formation and dissolution, to local and regional migration, to fundamental structures in the Pueblo worldview. Yet we need to remember that at some point in Pueblo history, a primacy for agriculture was not a given. Older practices such as hunting of large mammals had developed authority structures surrounding them which by the Pueblo I period can be thought of as vested interests.

Some readers might grant the importance of deer in the early Pueblo diet, as attested by the zooarchaeological data presented above, and may also accept the suggestions from simulation and the data from zooarchaeology that deer was declining in availability during the Pueblo I period, without being willing to grant deer hunting the potency for structuration suggested here. For these readers we briefly mention another line of evidence speaking to the depth of influence of deer hunting and presumably of deer hunters in early Pueblo society.

Village Ecodynamics Project modeling efforts focused on agent-based models in which we reconstruct, as best we can, the spatial and temporal distribution of those aspects of the natural environment that seem most likely to affect the spatial positioning of human use of this landscape. These include potential maize productivity, fuelwood growth and availability, water availability, and the spatial distributions of three key game animals: deer, hare, and rabbits. These resources are modeled at a spatial resolution of 200 x 200 m, except for deer, which are modeled within "deer cells" one km on a side. The availability of these resources changes annually both because of exogenous inputs (precipitation as proxied by mid-elevation tree rings for all resources, plus, for maize, temperature as proxied by high-elevation tree rings) and human use. Locally realistic spatial variability is introduced into the model through use of soils maps documenting differential productivity that affects all resource types except water. Estimated water availability is derived from a MODFLOW model that simulates groundwater flows in the primary hydrogeological layer in our study area.

Of the infinite rulesets for household positioning that we could explore, we have been focusing on rules that require agents—which represent households—to approximately and myopically locate themselves so as to minimize their caloric costs for obtaining enough protein through hunting, calories through farming, water, and fuelwood to support their members. Households are seeded randomly onto the landscape at the beginning of the simulation, at AD 600. They remain where they are as long as they can satisfy their needs. Otherwise, they seek a new location within a tunable radius (currently 20 cells, or 4 km) that provides the necessary amounts of these resources with the least travel cost, calculated over all four resources. We give maize production some priority in this calculation, in the sense that households must be able to meet their needs from farming either within their home cell, or within the first row of cells surrounding their home cell.

Without going into details here, we can quantify the degree of fit between the archaeological record in the VEP study area and the agent behavior in the simulation for each of 14 periods between AD 600 and 1280. We can also experiment with various parameters in our simulations, such as how much meat from hunting agents seek, and how far they are willing to go to hunt. Here we report a series of runs examining the effects of varying seven parameters (Table 6.3) on simulated locational behavior. Figure 6.5 (and Table 6.4) display the behavior through time of two measures of spatial efficiency against our three paleodemographic estimates for the VEP study area (Varien et al. 2007). These measures are (1) the proportion of 348 (128 runs x 3 measures of goodness of fit for each) measures of goodness of fit r that are positive (in black); and (2) the proportion of positive correlation coefficients where the probability that r is not zero is less than or equal to .05 (in red).[7]

For our purposes here, it is most significant that settlements throughout

Table 6.3. The Seven Parameters Varied in the Runs Reported Here (v2.72)

PARAMETER	VALUES	
Interhousehold exchanges in meat and maize (both generalized and balanced reciprocity)*	Implemented (COOP=4) (runs 1–64)	Not implemented (COOP=0) (runs 65–128)
Paleoproductivity dataplane used	First principal component ("PRIN1") of Almagre and San Francisco Peaks tree-ring series used for temperature proxy (runs 1–32 & 65–96)	Almagre series only ("ALMA") used for temperature proxy (runs 33–64 & 97–128)
Protein consumption goal from meat (g/person)	15 (runs 1–16, 33–48, 65–80, & 97–112)	25 (runs 17–32, 49–64, 81–97, & 113–128)
Need meat (protein move) (see Bocinsky et al. 2011)	0 (may move to protein-depleted area if costs are otherwise low) (runs 1–8, 17–24, 33–40, 49–56, 65–72, 81–88, 97–104, 113–120)	1 (may not move to protein-depleted area, regardless of other costs) (runs 9–16, 25–32, 41–48, 57–64, 73–80, 89–96, 105–112, 121–128)
Maximum hunting radius	30 cells (6 km) (runs 1–4, 9–12, 17–20, 25–28, 33–36, 41–44, 49–52, 57–60, 65–68, 73–76, 81–84, 89–92, 97–100, 105–108, 113–116, & 121–124)	50 cells (10 km) (runs 5–8, 13–16, 21–24, 29–32, 37–40, 45–48, 53–56, 61–64, 69–72, 77–80, 85–88, 93–96, 101–104, 109–112, 117–120, & 125–128)
Maize harvest adjustment (acts as denominator to final production estimate for each cell)	1 (runs 1–2, 5–6, etc.)	0.8 (increases maize production by 25%) (runs 3–4, 7–8, etc.)
Soil degradation	1 (moderate: soils under continuous use eventually lose up to 30% of their productive potential) (odd-numbered runs)	2 (severe: soils under continuous use eventually lose up to 60% of their productive potential) (even-numbered runs)

*See Kohler et al. 2007:89–96

Settlement Efficiency Indices and Population History

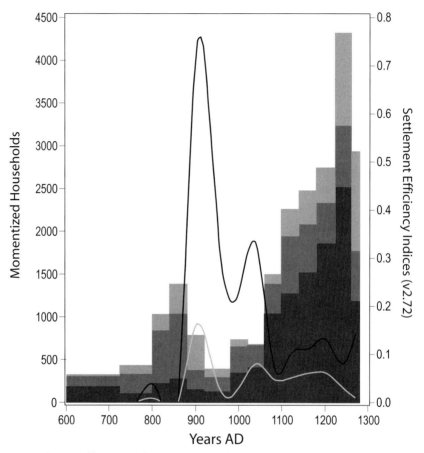

6.5 Settlement efficiency indices (see text and Table 6.3) calculated across 128 runs of the "Village" agent-based model and spline-fit, in relation to population history of the VEP area (histograms).

the first cycle of occupation (the Basketmaker III and Pueblo I periods) were well outside what we might call the optimal niche as estimated by the agent-based model. Clearly it was possible to live and even thrive outside the optimal niche as defined by our agents, perhaps in part because the total population on the landscape remained relatively low and the climates fairly forgiving for most of this period. But if the Pueblo I populations were not globally optimizing their access to all these resources, what were they up to?

Table 6.4. Measures of Settlement Efficiency of 128 Runs of the "Village" Agent-based Model

PERIOD	MIDPOINT (AD)	P POSITIVE ASSESSMENTS OF FIT (r)[a]	P SIGNIFICANT POSITIVE ASSESSMENTS OF FIT (r)[b]	HIGHEST r (RUN ID)	P OF HIGHEST r
6	663	0	0	-.0000 (89)	.9923
7	763	0	0	-.0002 (45)	.9872
8	820	0	0	-.0002 (52)	.9907
9	860	0	0	-.0007 (56)	.9588
10	900	.72	.16	.0471 (116)	<.0001
11	950	.38	.04	.0379 (3)	.0012
12	1000	.23	.03	.0626 (35)	<.0001
13	1040	.33	.08	.0704 (35)	<.0001
14	1080	.08	.05	.0658 (35)	<.0001
15	1120	.10	.05	.0706 (19)	<.0001
16	1160	.11	.06	.0678 (115)	<.0001
17	1203	.13	.06	.0778 (35)	<.0001
18	1243	.08	.03	.0310 (99)	.0108
19	1270	.14	.01	.0313 (3)	.0125

a. Three assessments of goodness-of-fit (r) were made for each run. One of these was calculated on the relationship between the unsmoothed simulated household years in each 200-x-200 m cell, and the same value for each cell in the archaeological record. This comparison is made only for cells that are either (1) within the block survey areas, or (2) have non-zero household years in the empirical record. The other two assessments were made (1) on a uniform smoothing of the empirical record, so that the contents of each central cell in a 3-x-3 block of cells is apportioned evenly across all 9 cells, and (2) on a kernel smoothing across the same local neighborhood, which retains a higher peak in the central cell than does the uniform smoothing. The denominator for all these proportions is 3 assessments of fit x 128 runs = 348.
b. The proportion of positive Pearson product-moment correlation coefficients r where $p \le .05$. The denominator for all these proportions is 3 assessments of fit x 128 runs = 348.

Figure 6.6 shows the known distribution of sites between AD 840 and 880, when our local PI villages were in their prime, against the settlement pattern created by the best-fitting agent-based model during those years. The real populations appear to be located more densely in the northeastern portions of the study area, alongside the Dolores River, than we would expect if they were minimizing their simultaneous access costs to all four of the resource categories we model. This area is at the local northeastern extreme of Pueblo occupation; beyond it, to the northeast, lie unoccupied highlands with dense deer populations.[8]

This visual impression is reinforced by examining the specific parameters that generated the best-fit simulation for each period (Table 6.5). Granting that none of our models fits the first four periods well at all, the least

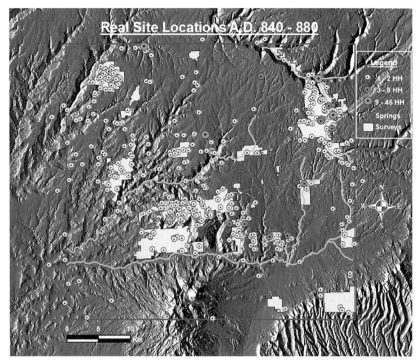

6.6a Real and simulated locations of households from AD 840–880 in the VEP area, a, real, b, simulated. Goodness of fit between the two maps is assessed for the areas of block survey, shown in a lighter color.

Table 6.5. Parameters for the Best-Fitting Model in Each Period

MIDPOINT (AD)	RUN	COOP	TEMP. PROXY	PROTEIN (G/PERS)	NEED MEAT	HUNT RADIUS	PROD. DIVISOR	SOIL DEGRADE
663	89	0	PRIN1	25	1	30	1	1
763	45	4	ALMA	15	1	50	.8	2
820	52	4	ALMA	25	0	30	.8	2
860	56	4	ALMA	25	0	50	.8	2
900	116	0	ALMA	25	0	30	.8	2
950	3	4	PRIN1	15	0	30	.8	1
1000	35	4	ALMA	15	0	30	.8	1
1040	35	4	ALMA	15	0	30	.8	1
1080	35	4	ALMA	15	0	30	.8	1
1120	19	4	PRIN1	25	0	30	.8	1
1160	115	0	ALMA	25	0	30	.8	1
1203	35	4	ALMA	15	0	30	.8	1
1243	99	0	ALMA	15	0	30	.8	1
1270	3	4	PRIN1	15	0	30	.8	1

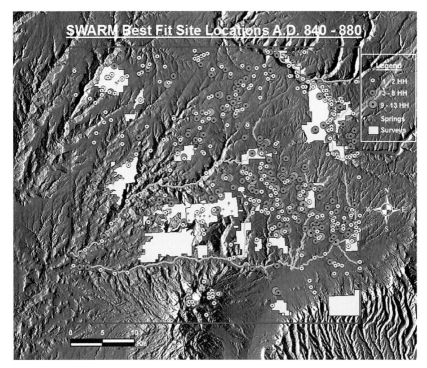

6.6b Simulated.

bad fit for the earliest farming occupation from AD 600–725 is to a model (89) that is unusual in that it does not have interhousehold exchange. It has high protein needs that can be satisfied within a small hunting radius, with no movement to areas of protein depletion allowed, and a low production landscape for maize. For all periods after this, the best-fit models always have the higher maize-productivity landscapes, perhaps reflecting the use of more productive maize, or an increase in ability to use the landscape in a more productive fashion. The first two periods (AD 600–800) are the only periods in our sequence in which the archaeological settlement patterns fit best to models that do not allow relocation to protein-depleted areas. Apparently that luxury was not possible in later periods.

As population grew, the three periods from AD 725–880 all fit best to a model with exchange and high protein needs, and the four periods from AD 725–920 are the only periods in the sequence that fit best to models having high soil degradation rates, reflecting the dominance of a shifting farming regime during this period (as Kohler and Matthews [1988] inferred from macrobotanical data). The two periods from AD 725–800 and AD 840–880 are the only two periods in the sequence that fit best to models with the larger hunting radius.

To summarize, the models that provide the best fit to the Pueblo I settlement practices (that is, the four periods from AD 725–920) are unusual, relative to those providing the best fit for later periods, in that they tend to exhibit a larger hunting radius, a higher soil degradation rate, an absolute refusal to move to areas that are protein depleted, and high protein consumption goals.

In light of these results, we think it is clear that site location in the Pueblo I period was biased towards those areas providing the best prospects for deer hunting, even though this increased the global costs for making a living on this landscape. The strength of this bias is possibly a measure of the power of those corporate leaders—the male lineage and hunt leaders whom we would locate in the protokivas—to influence residential location towards those areas that best served their own needs.

DISCUSSION AND CONCLUSIONS: DANCING WITH GHOSTS

We have argued that the continued and even increasing importance of big game hunting in an early southwestern agricultural population favored unilinear reckoning of descent. In our specific example (and it might be otherwise where the tradition of agriculture was longer) we suggest that this reckoning was specifically patrilineal, since patrilineal, patrilocal groups co-locate related male hunters. This organization seemingly provides the best chance of arriving at a favorable outcome in the "assurance game" of hunting deer in increasingly depleted landscapes.

From the perspective of the long-term fate of the early Pueblo way of life, we might argue that this degree of emphasis on deer hunting turned out to be maladaptive, not only because it relied on a depletable resource, but also since in this case it encouraged populations to live in areas that were unusually susceptible to the cold conditions that, as it happened, characterized the 10th century AD. Indeed, local population sizes fell precipitously in the early AD 900s, and those populations who remained employed a radically different settlement strategy more closely resembling the optima as discovered by our agents (Fig. 6.5). We might also suggest that the PI village location strategy was maladaptive in that it appears to depart so radically from the least-cost settlement poise estimated by the agents. Our results suggest that practices that are far from globally efficient can endure, at least for a while, if they serve the interests of sufficiently powerful members of the society, or if they are so deeply embedded in other aspects of social practice that changing them would have effects that cascade far beyond how much deer one eats.

David Sloan Wilson (2007:51–57) applied the evocative phrase "dancing with ghosts" to the mismatch between behavior and environment that happens whenever a species encounters a new environment. Of course, for humans such adaptational lags will be slight compared to species in which adaptation is mainly achieved by genetic change. Nevertheless, the environment of the PI villagers was different from the environment of their recent ancestors in one most important respect: the number of people. To maintain traditional levels of deer hunting in the face of these increased numbers required ever larger hunting radii and larger hunting groups; these in turn favored changes in social organization that we suspect began with strengthening patrilineal / virilocal structures but eventually contributed to making permanent the temporary leadership structures that arise in segmentary social organizations.

BEYOND DAP AND PI

It might be tempting to conclude that the male hunting-based authority structures inferred here expired along with the Pueblo I villages and their settlement strategies, especially since there is evidence from the DAP (reviewed in Wilshusen and Van Dyke 2006:245) that some adult couples were killed and buried in (their?) oversized pitstructures as the PI villages were being abandoned in the late AD 800s or early 900s. Still, many of the occupants of the northern PI villages may have ended up in the Chaco Canyon area by about AD 925, via intermediary locations along the San Juan River (Wilshusen and Van Dyke 2006). The fundamental basis of social power in Chaco Canyon was probably related to regional connections, perhaps involving warfare. The possibility that Chacoan leadership was polygynous is implied by female-biased sex ratios in San Juan basin burial assemblages that were especially strong in the Central San Juan subregion (Kohler and Kramer Turner 2006). Polygyny in turn is most characteristic of patrilineal organizations. We suggest that the deep connections between power, hunting, warfare, and sex (Potter 2004), which flow particularly easily along the lines provided by patrilineal organizations, were not ruptured by the collapse of the PI villages, but somehow became strengthened in the next century, and in a different location. How that was achieved would be a nice topic for a different paper.

NOTES

1. A note on spatial taxonomies: the DAP area is in the northeastern corner of the VEP area, which in turn is a part of the much larger central Mesa Verde region, which in turn is nested within the northern San Juan region.

2. Unlike those of the DAP, VEP estimates of population assume that each pitstructure represents a single household, presumably a nuclear family (Ortman, Varen, and Gripp 2007). If the VEP used DAP conventions, our estimates of numbers of households after AD 760 would be at least twice as high as they are.

3. Schachner (2001:179) however misreads Kane (1986) as suggesting that oversized pitstructures were involved in "community-wide" ritual participation. Kane would have agreed with Schachner (2001:179) that communal ritual conducted in oversized pitstructures was probably restricted to segments of the village or community which are the "corporate groups" of Kane's analysis.

4. Lekson (2009:65–66) points to two very large BMIII sites with Great Kivas in Chaco Canyon as models for later Pueblo villages. It is difficult though to assess the degree of contemporaneity of the pitstructures in these complexes, and their momentized populations may have been considerably smaller than a large DAP PI village such as Grass Mesa or McPhee Village.

5. We meant this argument to apply to villages from the Pueblo I through Pueblo III periods. In retrospect, Kohler believes that the model is most successful for the PI period, and that by PII/III times Pueblo people had developed institutions that tended to keep communities from dissolving into hamlets under conditions in which PI villages might have done so.

6. Or trust dilemma. See Bowles (2004:42) for an example analyzing planting-time strategies among sharecroppers in India. Wilson (2007:129–32) provides an entertaining account of how the cellular slime mold *Dictyostelium discoideum* solves the coordination game under food stress to move impressive distances and reproduce in a new habitat. Brian Skyrms (2004) discusses many ways in which the basic two-person stag hunt can be complicated, and shows that (as in the prisoner's dilemma) it is generally easier to achieve cooperation when players are interacting within a local neighborhood, than randomly within a larger population—though much depends on the details of the dynamics of interaction.

7. These runs are based on a version of the simulation that we call version 2.72. We have since completed a new 512-run parameter sweep with a modified model. Please consult chapters in Kohler and Varien (2011) for an update to this discussion.

8. Eventually it would be interesting to try to disentangle two possible reasons for the large size of these PI villages that butt up against uninhabited highland forests northeast of the Dolores River. If we envision population growth as a spatially random process from the inhabited areas, populations can be expected to pile up against the boundaries

of uninhabitable regions. The other possibility—more likely in our view although we would not rule out some role for the first—is the specific attraction of locations in which it is possible to farm, but from which relatively difficult-to-deplete areas for deer hunting are still convenient.

Acknowledgments

An early version of part of this paper was presented at the "Early Pueblo World" conference in August 2007; we thank the organizers, Jim Potter and Richard Wilshusen, for the opportunity to attend and participate. A draft of another portion was presented in a November 2007 AAA panel entitled "Computational Models in Anthropology: What are they good for, and why should you care?" and we also thank Lawrence Kuznar and Laura McNamara, who organized that panel, for the invitation to participate. Kohler also gratefully acknowledges support from NSF BCS-0119981, fellow members of the VEP, especially Sarah Cole, Jason Cowan, David Johnson, Ziad Kobti, Scott Ortman, Mark Varien, and Aaron Wright, without whom various portions of this analysis would not have been possible, and Bill Lipe, for drafting Kohler to work on the DAP in the first place.

REFERENCES CITED

Alvard, Michael S. 2003. Kinship, Lineage, and an Evolutionary Perspective on Cooperative Hunting Groups in Indonesia. *Human Nature* 14:129–63.

Alvard, Michael S., and David A. Nolin. 2002. Rousseau's Whale Hunt? Coordination among Big–Game Hunters. *Current Anthropology* 43:533–59.

Blinman, Eric. 1986. Additive Technologies Group Final Report. In *Dolores Archaeological Project: Final Synthetic Report*, compiled by D. A. Breternitz, C. K. Robinson, and G. T. Gross, pp. 53–101. Denver, CO: USDI Bureau of Reclamation.

Bocinsky, R. Kyle, Jason A. Cowan, Timothy A. Kohler, and C. David Johnson. 2011. Hunting Results: How Hunting Changes the VEP World, and How the VEP World Changes Hunting. In *Emergence and Collapse of Early Villages: Models of Central Mesa Verde Archaeology*, ed. T. A. Kohler and M. D. Varien. Berkeley: University of California Press. In press.

Bocquet-Appel, Jean-Pierre. 2002. Paleoanthropological Traces of a Neolithic Demographic Transition. *Current Anthropology* 43:637–50.

Bohannan, Paul. 1954. The Migration and Expansion of the Tiv. *Africa* 24:2–16.

Borgerhoff Mulder, Monique, Samuel Bowles, Tom Hertz, Adrian Bell, Jan Beise, Greg Clark, Ila Fazzio, et al. 2009. Intergenerational Wealth Transmission and the Dynamics of Inequality in Small-scale Societies. *Science* 326:682–88.

Bowles, Samuel. 2004. *Microeconomics: Behavior, Institutions, and Evolution*. Princeton, NJ: Princeton University Press.

Breternitz, David A., Christine K. Robinson, and G. Timothy Gross, compilers. 1986. *Dolores Archaeological Project: Final Synthetic Report*. Denver, CO: USDI Bureau of Reclamation.

Cole, Sarah. 2006. Population Dynamics and Sociopolitical Instability in the Central Mesa Verde Region, A.D. 600–1280. Master's thesis, Dept. of Anthropology, Washington State Univ., Pullman.

Driver, Jonathan C. 2002. Faunal Variation and Change in the Northern San Juan Region. In *Seeking the Center Place: Archaeology and Ancient Communities in the Mesa Verde Region*, ed. Mark D. Varien and Richard H. Wilshusen, pp. 143–60. Salt Lake City: University of Utah Press.

Flannery, Kent V. 2002. The Origins of the Village Revisited: From Nuclear to Extended Households. *American Antiquity* 67:417–33.

Fox, Robin. 1967. *Kinship and Marriage: An Anthropological Perspective*. Baltimore: Penguin Books.

Gumerman, George J., and Jeffrey S. Dean. 1989. Prehistoric Cooperation and Competition in the Western Anasazi Area. In *Dynamics of Southwest Prehistory*, ed. Linda S. Cordell and George J. Gumerman, pp. 99–148. Washington, DC: Smithsonian Institution Press.

Gumerman, George J., and Murray Gell-Mann. 1994. Cultural Evolution in the Prehistoric Southwest. In *Themes in Southwest Prehistory*, ed. George J. Gumerman, pp. 11–31. Santa Fe, NM: School of American Research Press.

Hayden, Brian, and Aubrey Cannon. 1982. The Corporate Group as an Archaeological Unit. *Journal of Anthropological Archaeology* 1:132–58.

Johnson, C. David. 2006. Critical Natural Resources in the Mesa Verde Region, A.D. 600–1300: Distribution, Use, and Influence on Puebloan Settlement. PhD diss., Dept. of Anthropology, Washington State Univ., Pullman.

Kakos, Peter J. 2003. Living in the Zone: Basketmaker Food Packages, Hormonal Responses, and the Effects of Population Growth. In *Anasazi Archaeology at the Millennium: Proceedings of the Sixth Occasional Anasazi Symposium*, ed. Paul F. Reed, pp. 34–47. Tucson, AZ: Center for Desert Archaeology.

Kane, Allen E. 1986. Prehistory of the Dolores River Valley. In *Dolores Archaeological Project: Final Synthetic Report*, compiled by D. A. Breternitz, C. K. Robinson, and G. T. Gross, pp. 353–435. Denver, CO: USDI Bureau of Reclamation.

Kohler, Timothy A. 1988. The Probability Sample at Grass Mesa Village. In *Dolores Archaeological Program. Anasazi Communities at Dolores: Grass Mesa Village*, 2 vols., compiled by W. D. Lipe, J. N. Morris, and T. A. Kohler, pp. 51–74. Denver, CO: USDI Bureau of Reclamation.

—— 1992. Field Houses, Villages, and the Tragedy of the Commons in the Early Northern Anasazi Southwest. *American Antiquity* 57:617–35.

Kohler, Timothy A., and Eric Blinman. 1987. Solving Mixture Problems in

Archaeology: Analysis of Ceramic Materials for Dating and Demographic Reconstruction. *Journal of Anthropological Archaeology* 6:1–28.

Kohler, Timothy A., Matt Pier Glaude, Jean-Pierre Bocquet-Appel, and Brian M. Kemp. 2008. The Neolithic Demographic Transition in the U.S. Southwest. *American Antiquity* 73:645–69.

Kohler, Timothy A., C. David Johnson, Mark Varien, Scott Ortman, Robert Reynolds, Ziad Kobti, Jason Cowan, Kenneth Kolm, Schaun Smith, and Lorene Yap. 2007. Settlement Ecodynamics in the Prehispanic Central Mesa Verde Region. In *The Model-based Archaeology of Socionatural Systems*, ed. T. A. Kohler and S. van der Leeuw, pp. 61–104. Santa Fe, NM: School of American Research Press.

Kohler, Timothy A., and Kathryn Kramer Turner. 2006. Raiding for Women in the Pre-Hispanic Northern Pueblo Southwest? A Pilot Examination. *Current Anthropology* 47:1035–45.

Kohler, Timothy A., and Meredith H. Matthews. 1988. Long-term Anasazi Land-Use Patterns and Forest Reduction: A Case Study from Southwest Colorado. *American Antiquity* 53:537–64.

Kohler, Timothy A., and Carla R. Van West. 1996. The Calculus of Self Interest in the Development of Cooperation: Sociopolitical Development and Risk among the Northern Anasazi. In *Evolving Complexity and Environment: Risk in the Prehistoric Southwest*, ed. J. A. and B. B. Tainter, pp. 169–96. Santa Fe Institute Studies in the Sciences of Complexity, Proceedings Vol. 24. Reading, MA: Addison-Wesley.

Kohler, Timothy A., and Mark D. Varien. 2010. A Scale Model of Seven Hundred Years of Farming Settlements in Southwest Colorado. In *Becoming Villagers: Comparing Early Village Societies*, ed. Matthew S. Bandy and Jake R. Fox, pp. 37–61. Tucson: University of Arizona Press.

Kohler, Timothy A., and Mark D. Varien, eds. 2011. *Emergence and Collapse of Early Villages: Models of Central Mesa Verde Archaeology*. Berkeley: University of California Press. In press.

Lekson, Stephen H. 2009. *A History of the American Southwest*. Santa Fe, NM: School of American Research Press.

Lightfoot, Ricky. 1988. Roofing an Early Anasazi Great Kiva. *Kiva* 53:253–72.

Lipe, William D., Timothy A. Kohler, Mark D. Varien, James N. Morris, and Ricky Lightfoot. 1988. Synthesis. In *Dolores Archaeological Program: Anasazi Communities at Dolores: Grass Mesa Village,* 2 vols., compiled by W. D. Lipe, J. N. Morris, and T. A. Kohler, pp. 1213–76. Denver, CO: USDI Bureau of Reclamation.

Matson, R. G. 2006. What Is Basketmaker II? *Kiva* 72:149–66.

Neusius, Sarah W., and Melissa Gould. 1988. Faunal Remains: Implications for Dolores Anasazi Adaptations. In *Dolores Archaeological Program: Anasazi Communities at Dolores: Grass Mesa Village,* 2 vols., compiled by W. D. Lipe, J. N. Morris, and T. A. Kohler, pp. 1049–1135. Denver, CO: USDI Bureau of Reclamation.

Odling-Smee, F. John, Kevin N. Laland, and Marcus W. Feldman. 1996. Niche Construction. *American Naturalist* 147:641–48.

Ortman, Scott G., Mark D. Varen, and T. Lee Gripp. 2007. Empirical Bayesian Methods for Archaeological Survey Data: An Application from the Mesa Verde Region. *American Antiquity* 72:241–72.

Petersen, Kenneth L. 1988. *Climate and the Dolores River Anasazi: A Paleoenvironmental Reconstruction from a 10,000-Year Pollen Record, La Plata Mountains, Southwestern Colorado*. University of Utah Anthropological Papers No. 113. Salt Lake City: University of Utah Press.

Petersen, Kenneth L., and Peter J. Mehringer, Jr. 1976. Postglacial Timberline Fluctuations, La Plata Mountains, Southwestern Colorado. *Arctic and Alpine Research* 8:275–88.

Potter, James M. 2004. The Creation of Person, the Creation of Place: Hunting Landscapes in the American Southwest. *American Antiquity* 69:322–28.

Potter, James M., and Jason Chuipka. 2007. The Animas-La Plata Project and Durango Archaeology: An Update. *Kiva* 72:419–42.

Richerson, Peter, and Robert Boyd. 1999. The Evolutionary Dynamics of a Crude Super Organism. *Human Nature* 10:253–89.

Rohn, Arthur. 1977. *Cultural Change and Continuity on Chapin Mesa*. Lawrence: Regents Press of Kansas.

Rousseau, Jean-Jacques. 1755/1950. A Discourse on the Origin of Inequality. In *The Social Contract, and Discourses*, tr. G. D. H. Cole, pp. 173–282. Baltimore: Penguin Books.

Sahlins, Marshall D. 1961. The Segmentary Lineage: An Organization of Predatory Expansion. *American Anthropologist*, n.s., 63:322–45.

Schachner, Gregson. 2001. Ritual Control and Transformation in Middle-Range Societies: An Example from the American Southwest. *Journal of Anthropological Archaeology* 20:168–94.

Skyrms, Brian. 2004. *The Stag Hunt and the Evolution of Social Structure*. Cambridge: Cambridge University Press.

Spielmann, Katherine A., and Eric A. Angstadt-Leto. 1996. Hunting, Gathering, and Health in the Prehistoric Southwest. In *Evolving Complexity and Environmental Risk in the Prehistoric Southwest*, ed. J. A. Tainter and B. B. Tainter, pp. 79–106. Reading, MA: Addison-Wesley.

Stone, Glenn Davis. 1996. *Settlement Ecology: The Social and Spatial Organization of Kofyar Agriculture*. Tucson: University of Arizona Press.

Turchin, Peter, and Andrey Korotayev. 2006. Population Dynamics and Internal Warfare: A Reconsideration. *Social Evolution and History* 5:112–47.

Varien, M. D., and S. G. Ortman. 2005. Accumulations Research in the Southwest United States: Middle-Range Theory for Big-Picture Problems. *World Archaeology* 37:132–55.

Varien, Mark D., Scott G. Ortman, Timothy A. Kohler, Donna M. Glowacki, and C. David Johnson. 2007. Historical Ecology in the Mesa Verde Region: Results from the Village Ecodynamics Project. *American Antiquity* 72:273–99.

Wilshusen, Richard H., Karin Burd, Jonathan Till, Christine G. Ward, and Brian Yunker. 1999. The Dolores Legacy: A User's Guide to the Dolores Archaeological Program Data. Self-published in spiral binding. On file, Dept. of Anthropology, Univ. of Colorado, Boulder.

Wilshusen, Richard H., and Ruth M. Van Dyke. 2006. Chaco's Beginnings. In *The Archaeology of Chaco Canyon: An Eleventh-Century Pueblo Regional Center*, ed. S. H. Lekson, pp. 211–59. Santa Fe, NM: School of American Research Press.

Wilson, David Sloan. 2007. *Evolution for Everyone: How Darwin's Theory Can Change the Way We Think about Our Lives*. New York: Delacorte Press.

Wright, Aaron M. 2006. A Low-Frequency Paleoclimatic Reconstruction from the La Plata Mountains, Colorado, and Its Implications for Agricultural Productivity in the Mesa Verde Region. Master's thesis, Dept. of Anthropology, Washington State Univ., Pullman.

7

Mitigating Environmental Risk in the U.S. Southwest

**KATHERINE A. SPIELMANN, MARGARET NELSON,
SCOTT INGRAM, AND MATTHEW A. PEEPLES**

It is a challenging task to contribute something new to the literature on risk and subsistence in the U.S. Southwest. For the past 25 or 30 years Southwestern archaeologists have modeled, investigated, and published on this topic in entire volumes devoted to the issue (e.g., Gumerman 1988; Tainter and Tainter 1996) and in individual books and articles (e.g., Anschuetz 2006; Braun and Plog 1982; Ford 1992; Minnis 1985; Rautman 1993). In reviewing this literature, however, one area that appears to be in need of further consideration is the link between specific risks regarding agricultural production and specific strategies to mitigate those risks. Southwestern archaeologists, some of us authors included, have tended to trot out a list of coping strategies, such as storage, exchange, and migration, that prehistoric Southwestern farmers might have used to avoid the risk of shortfall in food or other resources. Rarely, however, have we identified the utility of these strategies in the face of the specific kinds of environmental variation experienced by Southwestern farmers.

In this chapter we discuss the nature of the environmental risks that prehistoric Ancestral Pueblo farmers of the Colorado Plateau and Rio Grande regions faced (Fig. 7.1). We then consider the archaeological record and conceptual models concerning the different strategies used to mitigate these risks at different social and spatial scales. Using this information we make the following points: (1) at the local scale, household-based, multi-year storage and at the community scale, restricted sharing of stored food were effective primary strategies for mitigating interannual variation in precipitation and stream flow; (2) short-term emigration from settlements to villages in adjacent regions, which is documented in some ethnographic agricultural groups (such as the Fringe Enga and Gwembe Tonga), is not common in the cases we document, and perhaps in the Southwest in general; and (3) sustained drought conditions in the context of relatively high population levels and resource depletion were addressed primarily through permanent emigration from affected areas. We conclude that, given these facts, regional-scale exchange systems are unlikely to have developed primarily for buffering short-term food shortages, but may have supported permanent emigration. At the scale of the entire Colorado Plateau/Rio

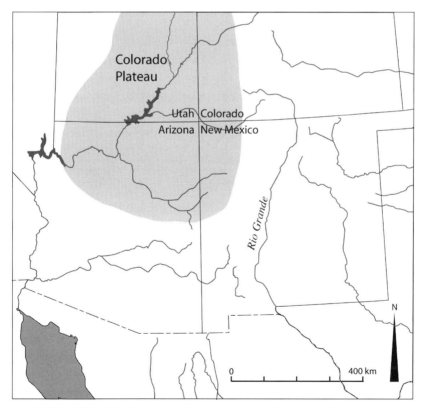

7.1 Map of the Southwest showing the location of areas mentioned in text.

Grande region, migration was a resilient strategy for farmers to cope with intense drought conditions.

VULNERABILITIES IN PREHISTORIC
SOUTHWESTERN FARMING

Prehistorically, corn was the Southwestern dietary staple. Although beans and squash were grown and other plants encouraged, and while some wild plants (e.g., agave, piñon) were important supplements, corn was the primary food eaten by all Southwestern agricultural populations. Bone chemistry data from several later prehistoric Southwestern populations (e.g., Spielmann, Schoeninger, and Moore 1990; Spielmann and Schoeninger 1992) document that corn probably constituted 80–90% of Southwestern diets in the period of interest in this chapter. There were no draft animals in the Southwest prehistorically, and thus no plow and no manure for fertilization; nor were there beasts of burden to transport food and other commodities from place to place. The societies of the late prehistoric Southwest were nonhierarchical in terms of both lifestyle and mortuary treatment. Although ethnographic data (e.g., Brandt 1994) caution us that significant power differences characterize modern Pueblo populations in the absence of material evidence of such distinctions, even in these cases the abilities of individuals to mobilize resources beyond reciprocal social and ritual obligations are limited. Thus the corn that was grown in the Southwest was for subsistence, social, and ritual consumption controlled largely by households.

Given its arid climate and paucity of perennial streams, water is the limiting factor in corn production across the Southwest (e.g., Muenchrath and Salvador 1995). Prehistoric farmers were thus vulnerable to variations in the timing and quantity of precipitation and stream flow. Much of Southwestern landscape modification, in fact, has to do with aspects of water control that reduce this vulnerability, from check dams (Sandor 1990), to terraces and waffle gardens (Anschuetz 1998, 2006), to reservoirs and irrigation ditches (Herrington 1979), to full-blown irrigation systems (Howard 2006). These constructions serve to concentrate available water onto agricultural fields, reducing but not eliminating the impact of spatial and temporal variability in precipitation.

Southwestern farmers had to cope with significant variation in precipitation within a growing season and on a year-to-year basis in the form of less frequent, sustained periods of low moisture, or drought. We acknowledge that drought is a complex phenomenon that defies simple definition and identification. More than 150 definitions of drought have been identified (Wilhite and Glantz 1985), reflecting both regional differences in impacts, and various disciplinary perspectives. In brief, however, drought is a condition of "insufficient water to meet needs" (Redmond 2002:1144), a definition which acknowledges the dynamic relationship between water supply and demand. The impact of a drought on a population depends upon a variety of factors including population size, resource depletion, and patterns of land use (Varien 1999:Ch. 5). In this chapter we contrast a context in which droughts result in an acute risk of shortfall and a context in which environmental conditions buffer against such shortfall.

Southwestern archaeologists are blessed with strong dendroclimatic data that permit the reconstruction of annual variation in precipitation (Dean 2000). With these data in hand, we can document the nature of short- and long-term variation in precipitation and then evaluate Ancestral Pueblo responses to the risks of food resource shortfall likely created by this variability.

STRATEGIES FOR COPING WITH VARIABILITY IN PRECIPITATION

Storage and Pooling

Ancestral Pueblo farmers solved the problem of variation in annual rainfall in part through the development of multiyear, household-scale storage capacity. We note that households also diversified field locations and crop varieties (e.g., Anschuetz 1998, 2006; Ford 1992: Ch. 6; Van West and Dean 2000), but do not discuss these strategies here. In this arid environment, corn can be stored for several years, allowing farmers to mitigate the effects of the high frequency variation in rainfall. An individual poor year or two could thus be ameliorated through the stored products of better years. Barney Burns' (1983) simulation of Anasazi household storage behavior suggests that storage technology could be used successfully to cope with high frequency variation in rainfall as long as approximately two to three years worth of corn was available for storage. In his investigation of drought and famine in the Southwest, Edwin Slatter (1979:80, 84) used historic data to suggest that Pueblo households kept two years of corn in storage, although there were incidences in which corn was stored sufficient for three to four years consumption.

That storage was a critical strategy for coping with variability in crop production was recently documented archaeologically by Jeffrey Dean (2006) in his analysis of changes in household storage capacity during the mid-1200s in northeastern Arizona. In this case, Pueblo farmers used a coping strategy traditionally aimed at high frequency variation to address a novel, low frequency process, a marked decline in the water table and a prolonged drought. Dean focused his analysis on changing storage capacity in Kiet Siel, a cliff dwelling of about 155 rooms in Tsegi Canyon. In the mid-1200s, as conditions for agriculture worsened, household granaries increased in number and total volume, even as living space decreased (Fig. 7.2). The fact that people chose to expand storage capacity suggests its central function in grappling with environmental perturbation in the Southwest. Ultimately, however, increasing storage proved unsuccessful under prolonged conditions of water deficit, and people left the canyon. Migration, as we discuss below, is a persistent response to severe drought in the Southwest.

Not all households, however, would be able to meet a target of two to three years of corn storage consistently enough to buffer all high frequency variation. Ethnographic data suggest that community-scale sharing of food is an effective strategy for evening out imbalances in food supply among households (e.g., Ford 1972). Michelle Hegmon (1991) evaluated this hypothesis through a simulation of Hopi agriculture. Her model demonstrated patterns of shortfall in storage; more than half the households did not survive when there was no sharing of food across households (Fig. 7.3). When the model was run with restricted sharing (households met their own needs first and then shared any surplus they had available), over 80% of the households survived if living in communities of at least six to eight households. Further work by Hegmon (1996) and Kohler and Van West (1996) substantiates the importance of selective pooling of household supplies to reduce the risk of shortfall.

Hegmon's work focused on sharing within villages. Pooling, however, also is likely to have occurred within clusters of hamlet settlements. For example, across much of the Colorado Plateau from roughly AD 800–1100 small, dispersed settlements predominated. By AD 1000, these Ancestral Pueblo sites were highly standardized and often are referred to as

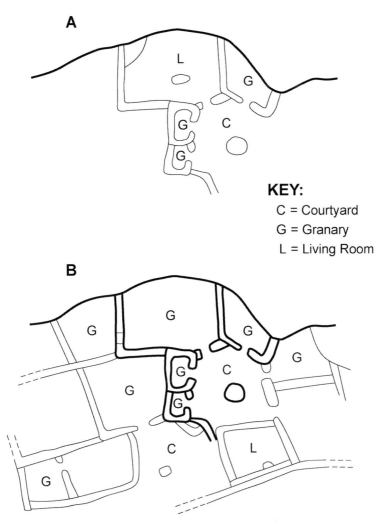

KEY:
C = Courtyard
G = Granary
L = Living Room

7.2 Room Cluster 2 at Kiet Siel: (a) in AD 1271 with three fairly small granaries, and (b) in AD 1276 with eight granaries, two of which were vacated living rooms. (After Dean 2006: fig. 8.3)

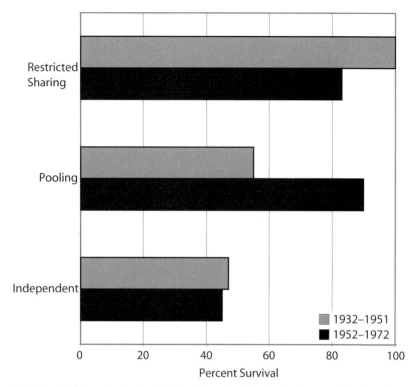

7.3 Household survival rates for the three sharing strategies over the two time periods. (After Hegmon 1996: fig. 1)

unit pueblos. From 8–12 contemporaneous units are clustered on the landscape within a quarter mile (ca. 0.4 km) of each other (Rohn 1989; Cordell 1997:285; Varien 1999). They probably functioned as communities within which food could have been shared.

In sum, at the local scale, household-based, multiyear storage and community-scale restricted sharing of stored food are likely to have been resilient strategies for mitigating interannual variation in precipitation and stream flow. In times when there were more than three or four consecutive years of drought, however, these strategies were insufficient for maintaining household food supplies.

Regional Exchange

Southwestern archaeologists have also proposed that regional-scale exchange networks were important for coping with variation in crop production. The archaeological data on this strategy are equivocal. In 1982, David Braun and Stephen Plog argued that on the Colorado Plateau beginning roughly in the AD 900s, increasingly regionalized patterns of stylistic homogeneity and exchange documented region-wide social networks that allowed agriculturalists to deal with the risks associated with dry farming. They did not specify in what ways these social networks mitigated risk, and their data did not allow them to investigate how these social networks were actually used. That same general argument (exchange, social networks, and buffering resource shortfalls) was also proposed in a study by Fred Plog and colleagues (1988), who noted a general temporal correlation between what they called "alliances" (exchange networks) and high spatial variability in precipitation on the Colorado Plateau. More recently, Alison Rautman (1993, 1996) used modern climate data to explicitly evaluate where on the central New Mexican landscape pithouse-dwelling farmers would have preferentially maintained social connections, if buffering resource shortfalls were a primary consideration in creating regional-scale social networks. Unlike the earlier studies, Rautman specifically considered the possibility of short-term population movement from villages experiencing shortfalls to villages with surpluses. Lacking exchange data, however, she was not able to fully evaluate her hypothesis, and thus like Braun and Plog focused on the general benefits of regional-scale social networks in mitigating agricultural risk.

The question then remains, what exactly is the relationship between regional scale interactions documented by commonalities in ceramic styles and exchange of ceramics, and agricultural risk in the Southwest? The ethnographic cases that Southwest archaeologists have cited in positing a relationship between regional-scale stylistic and exchange ties and variability in crop production are either relatively sedentary farmers such as the Gwembe Tonga of central Africa and the Fringe Enga of Papua New Guinea, or highly mobile hunter-gatherers, such as the San or Walbiri (as discussed, for example, in Wiessner 1977; Yengoyan 1976). In neither situation (farmers or hunter-gatherers), however, is multiyear storage feasible. As we discuss below, in the case of the Enga, sweet potatoes are not conducive to long-term storage; in the case of the Tonga, stored grains last a few months at best due to spoilage and infestation (Colson 1979). And, mobile hunter-gatherers living in arid lands do not store food for appreciable amounts of time. In all these cases, unlike the Southwest (Burns 1983:152), a single year or season of crop or resource failure *does* result in famine. When a single bad season leads to catastrophe, social ties maintained through regional-scale exchange networks are critical for redistributing people to locales where resources are more abundant.

In eastern, central, and southern Africa, crop production was poor one out of every four to five years at the time Elizabeth Colson was writing (1970s; Colson 1979). Given the frequency of bad years and the inability to rely on multiyear storage, cultivating social relations to tap food resources in other regions was an important strategy (Colson 1979; Scudder 1962). Among the Gwembe Tonga of the Zambezi valley, recurrent famine was due to drought, land degradation, and raiding (Scudder 1962:147), and was severe enough to cause high adult mortality. In the face of this high frequency of resource shortfall locally, Gwembe Tonga families maintained kin ties with Tongans on the Northern Rhodesian Plateau as a refuge during famine years (Scudder 1962:242–43). Younger and older members of families were sent to relatives to reduce household consumption during drought (Colson 1979), and in some cases entire villages were abandoned for a time.

What caught Southwesternists' attention in this case is the link between craft production, regional-scale exchange, and crop failure. Valley Tongans intensified production of craft items prior to emigrating, and brought with them baskets, tobacco, palm fronds, ceramics, mats, and salt to trade for grain with kin and trade partners (Scudder 1962:243–44). In this ethnographic case, craft production, exchange, and the social relations exchange entails are strategies that agriculturalists use to mitigate risk.

The Fringe Enga (Waddell 1975; Wohlt 2004) present a different sort of example of regional-scale exchange relations allowing for periodic, short-term migrations in the face of sweet potato crop failure. Several thousand people live in the upper elevations of the Papua New Guinea Highlands in dispersed settlements of several hundred people. In the Fringe Enga case, killing frosts occur every one to three decades, within the memory of living people, but at a much lower frequency than droughts for the Tonga. Nonetheless, sweet potatoes cannot be stored for long periods of time and rot in the ground two months after a killing frost. Therefore, when crops completely fail, people must leave their villages and walk for several days to villages at lower elevations. As with the Gwembe Tonga, relations with relatives and trade partners are reinforced through exchange, in this case of pandanus nut and high-quality pig meat. In addition, the Fringe Enga are middlemen in exchanges between the highlands and the central Enga. While exchange maintains sociality between episodes of crop failure, the actual move to kin and trade partners is also preceded by trade, as Enga families kill their pigs and trade meat to central Enga. Again, what intrigued Southwesternists about this case is the link between crop failure, regional-scale exchange relations, and short-term emigration.

Although the ethnographically recorded accordion-like pattern—emigration in the face of famine and return when conditions improve—might be difficult to see given the coarse-grained resolution of the archaeological record, we doubt that the stylistic and exchange patterns documented in Southwestern archaeology are evidence of this strategy. Instead, storage and inter-household pooling could have addressed interannual variation in crop production, as could diversifying farming practices, maintaining multiple residences, and relying on varied plant and animal resources.

Shortfalls resulting from periodic severe and prolonged droughts could not have been alleviated with these strategies. In the Southwest, these more acute perturbations appear to have been addressed through long-, rather than short-term emigration. In some cases migration streams may have been facilitated by exchange relations (e.g., Cordell et al. 2007); in others, as in the Mimbres case discussed below, there is no evidence of this process.

We do not contend that Ancestral Pueblos never used distant social connections to temporarily escape famine conditions, only that this was not a primary strategy for grappling with resource shortfall. Emigration is certainly facilitated by exchange and other relationships with those at destination locations (Anthony 1990). And there are examples in the Southwestern ethnographic record of some households emigrating from aggregated villages for a short time to another pueblo during times of famine. In these cases, emigration is one among a large number of outcomes, which include starvation. Talayesva (1942:52), for example, discusses the variety of different actions that Hopi took in the face of famine, including theft, hunting and gathering, and some families moving to Santo Domingo. Stevenson (1904:353) mentions that in general, starvation had caused some Zuni to move to other pueblos and vice versa.

Other Explanations for Stylistic Uniformity and Regional-scale Exchange

Two other practices could be contributing to the archaeological record of stylistic uniformity and regional-scale exchange beyond the originally inferred food buffering function. On the one hand, there is a pattern of relatively frequent abandonment of the small hamlet sites/unit pueblos in the earlier part of the Ancestral Pueblo archaeological record (AD 900–1100) that does not appear to coincide with patterns of variation in climatic variables but that could have resulted in an archaeological pattern of spatially homogenous ceramic styles. Ceramic accumulation analyses for one of these settlements, the Duckfoot site in southwestern Colorado, indicate an occupation of about 25 years (Lightfoot 1994). Others have also suggested that unit pueblos were occupied for about a generation, leading Powell (2002) to refer to this pattern as "generational mobility." Similarly, Nelson and LeBlanc (1986) refer to these relatively frequent movements of agriculturalists in the Southwest as "short-term sedentism." Thus, regional-scale social interaction (via exchange) was likely important for identifying and gaining access to productive areas to live as new generations of farmers sought new places to farm, not because people moved back and forth between their own villages and those of distant trade partners and kin (e.g., Dean 1996:45; Powell 2002).

Researchers have not identified the particular reasons for this generational mobility (Powell 2002). Death of the older generation and the 10–20 year life span of structures are two possibilities that have been suggested (Powell 2002). Depletion of soil fertility, game resources, and/or various plant resources may be another cause for settlement shifting. Thus, regional-scale exchange networks, evident in the distribution of different ceramic wares and types, most likely represent actions aimed at creating and maintaining a social landscape that allowed permanent, rather than short-term, migration or settlement shifting.

On the other hand, stylistic uniformity may not solely be the result of social networks, but may instead result from the demand for specific decorative treatments on the basis of their relationship to communal rituals. The years during which the exchange buffering model was developed were those when the Southwestern archaeological community generally interpreted commonalities in artifact style as passive or active reflections of interaction within a social community. The sociality of gifting was privileged over an explicit demand for certain types of ceramic vessels. More recently, a new explanatory model, one of active adherence to and participation in religious cults, has been proposed to explain some patterns of strong ceramic stylistic homogeneity. Crown (1994) postulated that in the 13th century pan-Pueblo adherence to the Pinedale style in general and the Gila Polychrome ceramic type in particular reflected adherence to a Southwestern fertility cult. Spielmann (1998) has suggested that the adoption of a particular style of red-slipped ceramic in the Rio Grande area reflects the development of a region-specific version of this cult. And Mobley-Tanaka (1998) has proposed that the Galisteo Basin was a primary exporter of glaze-decorated vessels because people in Galisteo Basin villages developed the Rio Grande sect of the Southwestern cult. More recently, in her analysis of Chupadero Black-on-white, Clark (2006) has documented a remarkable adherence to the same decorative style in the two primary areas of production, the Sierra Blanca and Salinas areas, despite the complete absence of ceramic exchange between the two. This region-wide similarity in design style may reflect the iconic importance of the decorations on Chupadero Black-on-white (but see Clark 2006). Thus, we cannot assume that commonalities in design style always resulted from the buffering strategies that Southwestern archaeologists have inferred in the past.

Migration

Severe droughts presented novel challenges for aggregated Ancestral Pueblo farmers (Dean 1988, 1996). Sharp and persistent reductions in precipitation and stream flow created a landscape of vulnerability that was not conducive to periodic dispersion and return, nor could it be addressed with storage and use of diverse resources and farming strategies. Instead, when faced with persistent famine conditions, as in the case of Tsegi Canyon mentioned above, people permanently left their villages.

Population movements and abandonments in the prehistoric U.S. Southwest have been closely examined and correlated at some places and times with changes in climate conditions, especially multiyear droughts (e.g., Adams 1998; Ahlstrom et al. 1995; Cordell 1975; Cordell et al. 2007; Crown, Orcutt, and Kohler 1996; Dean et al. 1985; Euler et al. 1979; Gumerman 1988; Judge 1989; Lipe 1995; Minnis 1985; Orcutt 1991; Schlanger 1988; Van West and Dean 2000). Cameron (1995:112) argues that "Movements of communities within a region, even when such movements have a lengthy periodicity, can be expected to be a normal part of a regional environmental adaptation that involves adjustment of a group's home range." Similarly, Dean and colleagues (1985) argue that mobility is the least costly strategy used to cope with environmental change when groups are not heavily invested in residential and agricultural facilities and when mobility is not restricted by population density.

Migration is motivated by both adverse conditions *pushing* people from where they live and favorable conditions *pulling* them to a new place (Anthony 1990; Herberle 1938; Lee 1966). Multiyear, intense droughts are frequently important push factors for migration at various spatial scales. Such droughts likely led to relatively low and/or variable resource productivity and, were thus strongly related to the risk or realization of resource shortfalls. Due to the high degree of spatial variability across the American Southwest, there are likely to be areas experiencing greater resource productivity than others during even the most widespread droughts. The promise of greater productivity in a different portion of the landscape would have provided a strong pull for migration into other areas. This push-pull framework was developed in migration studies and has been productively applied in previous archaeological research (Ahlstrom et al. 1995; Cameron 1995; Kohler 1993; Lipe 1995). For example, with regard to the Mesa Verde migration, Alhstrom and colleagues (1995) and Cordell and colleagues (2007) have argued that less severe drought conditions in the Rio Grande Valley compared to Mesa Verde, and greater annual precipitation, contributed to an environmental gradient or climatic pull, and thus migration into the Rio Grande area in the late 1200s.

In the following discussion we compare the Mimbres area of southwestern New Mexico and the Salinas area of central New Mexico. In the former, reduced precipitation and stream flow in the context of aggregated populations are likely to have resulted in acute shortfalls in the food supply. Many people permanently emigrated from the central Mimbres area, and this region never returned to pre-migration population levels. The Salinas case presents a much rarer situation in the Southwest in that high water tables allowed farming to continue through even the most severe droughts. Long-term residential stability characterizes this area. The contrast between these two cases illustrates how availability of water for crop production played a crucial role in the stability of populations on the Southwestern landscape.

THE CASE STUDIES

The Long-term Vulnerability and Transformation Project

The data that we discuss below were collected and analyzed over the course of the Long-term Vulnerability and Transformation project (NSF #0508001). This project involves the compilation and analysis of demographic, floral, faunal, climatic, and ceramic data from roughly AD 450–1600 for five case studies across the U.S. Southwest and northern Mexico (Phoenix Basin Hohokam, Zuni, Mimbres, Salinas, and Malpaso Valley). The goal of the project is the comparative analysis of resilience and vulnerability across these cases with respect to changing environmental circumstances. This chapter represents one of several comparisons (e. g., Hegmon et al. 2008) that the project has made possible. The databases upon which we focus here are the dendroclimatic and demographic databases from the Mimbres and Salinas cases (Fig. 7.4).

Scott Ingram was responsible for compiling and analyzing the paleoclimatic data for the project. In this chapter he uses the Southwestern tree-ring record to identify relatively rare and prolonged periods of low moisture, or drought. In this research, droughts are identified by smoothing the interannual variability of tree-ring retrodicted annual precipitation values and selecting threshold values. To smooth interannual variability, a 9-year centered moving average duration was selected as a compromise between shorter durations, which would not as accurately identify trends in the proxy climate data, and longer durations which would obscure climate variation that would have been potentially meaningful for human behavior. Nine-year interval averages are ranked from lowest to highest and assigned a percentile value to the middle of each interval (Year 5). The beginning, end, and duration of each drought are identified (and presented in the case study graphs below) with this middle year. Threshold values are used to identify the 9-year intervals that are classified as drought years. Droughts are defined as those 9-year intervals in the first quartile (moderate drought) and first decile (severe drought) of the distribution of interval averages during the entire length of the retrodicted record (at least 700 years). These threshold values are arbitrary but are assumed to represent droughts with sufficient rarity to have substantially influenced potential resource productivity and human behavior (e.g., Dean 1988).[1]

Matthew Peeples compiled and analyzed the paleodemographic data for

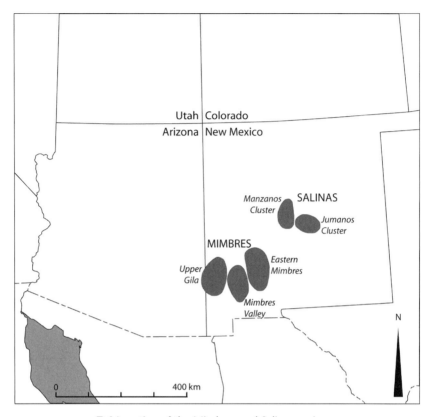

7.4 Location of the Mimbres and Salinas regions.

the project. He derived population estimates for each case from recorded room counts by placing sites in each time period into several size classes that were defined based on the best known and recorded components in the database. Components where less information was available were placed in rough size classes based on the best available information, and were then assigned the average room count of sites in their size class for a particular time period. Room counts were converted to population estimates using conversion factors defined from previous studies in each region.[2] For both the Mimbres and Salinas areas, the databases are likely missing a large proportion of sites dating to the earliest time periods (Late Pithouse Period and Jacal Period, respectively). Thus, population estimates for the earliest periods in both cases were defined based on the rates of growth for the best known portions of each region (Blake, LeBlanc, and Minnis 1986; Chamberlin 2008).

Mimbres

The Mimbres region is centered in southwest New Mexico, extending south into the Mexican state of Chihuahua and west into eastern Arizona. Our study focuses on the central Mimbres region encompassing three major rivers, which was the most densely occupied portion of the greater Mimbres region (Fig. 7.4). The region has a Chihuahuan Desert, basin, and range landscape cut by major rivers. The portion of the region on which we focus includes the upper watershed of the Gila River in the west, the Mimbres River at its center, and the Rio Grande and its western tributaries in southwest New Mexico at its eastern edge. Primary field locations for farming were on the floodplains along rivers and tributary drainages (Minnis 1985). In addition, small alluvial fans and checkdam fields were farmed (Sandor 1990).

The Mimbres archaeological sequence is marked by two major emigrations. The best known is at the end of the Classic Mimbres period (AD 1130). The second marks the end of Pueblo occupation of the region, a poorly understood depopulation that we believe occurred around AD 1450. A few smaller emigrations as well as immigrations occurred between the mid-12th and the mid-15th centuries. We focus on the depopulation near the mid-12th century. The depopulation of Mimbres villages around AD 1130 is associated with an extreme dry period (Fig. 7.5), although equally dry periods of equivalent length occurred before and after that event. As Nelson (1999) and others (e.g., Minnis 1985) have argued, a coalescence of social and environmental conditions contributed to the 12th-century depopulation of all villages in the region. Although some people remained in the Mimbres region, especially in the eastern Mimbres area, by dispersing

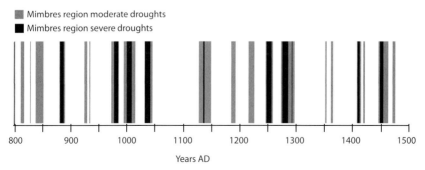

7.5 Mimbres climatic data.

into small hamlet settlements (Nelson 1999), the population of the region declined to about 25% of its Classic period maximum (Fig. 7.6). Inadequate local precipitation may have contributed a push for some to migrate out of the area, while better conditions elsewhere could have been one of various pull factors. We examine this transformation, considering the role of exchange in local and regional changes.

For well over a millennium, up until the late 10th century, people in the Mimbres region lived in small pithouse clusters in diverse settings, and moved residence frequently (Anyon, Gilman, and LeBlanc1981; Diehl 1994; Swanson 2009). While riverine locales were favored, pithouse settlements are also found away from rivers and perennial streams in both upland and lowland settings (Blake, LeBlanc, and Minnis 1986; Swanson 2009). Over these centuries, farming became gradually more important to the diet and by at least the 10th century settlements became more stable

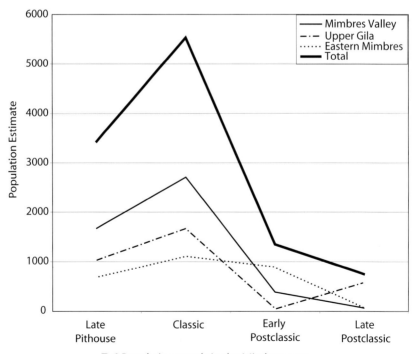

7.6 Population trends in the Mimbres area.

along the major rivers and their tributaries (Diehl 1996). During this period of pithouse occupation, many of the sites that appear to be large villages are actually the result of a sequence of settlement of prime locales by small groups, separated in time for long enough that the previously occupied houses had collapsed. Sometimes that time gap is broad enough that ceramic styles had changed between settlement periods (Swanson 2009). During this long period of low population density and dispersed population, people appear to have addressed potential resource shortfalls due to depletion of soils and local wild resources, or declining precipitation and stream flow, by storing, by using diverse field areas, and by shifting settlement within the region, the latter on a longer time scale than the former two strategies. Near the start of the 11th century, the beginning of the Classic Mimbres period, people in the Mimbres region settled into villages, which were built primarily along the rivers and near sections of perennial streams (Blake, LeBlanc, and Minnis 1986; LeBlanc 1983; Minnis 1985). It is this period of time on which we focus our comparison with the Salinas area.

Precipitation and population in the Mimbres area. The dendroclimatological data presented in Figure 7.5 document that the initial aggregation into the Classic Mimbres pueblos coincides with an extremely severe drought in the early 1000s. Initially the population of villages was relatively low, as was the regional population, so low precipitation did not have the substantial effect on population-resource balance that it did in the next century. The subsequent hundred years from roughly AD 1040 to 1125 was an especially wet period (Minnis 1985; note long-term absence of drought in Fig. 7.5). This moisture allowed people to farm upland alluvial fans and checkdam fields and expand the extent of irrigation agriculture on floodplains. The continuous farming of floodplain fields resulted in the removal of much of the riparian vegetation in the Mimbres Valley (Minnis 1985), the richest and most densely populated portion of the Mimbres region. In addition, the growing population depleted most of the large game—artiodactyls—from the main settlement areas (Cannon 2000, 2001; Nelson and Schollmeyer 2003; Schollmeyer 2009).

Storage became more formalized during the Classic Mimbres period, shifting from subfloor and extramural pits to rooms integrated into dwellings. All storage is associated with individual houses. A common house style includes one dwelling and one storage room, but many houses have multiple storage rooms (Shafer 1982; Hegmon, Brady, and Nelson 2006).

After about AD 1125, an extreme dry period ensued, challenging the provisioning of the largest population ever to live in the region. The challenge was likely greater than the local subsistence regime could support; every large village in the Mimbres Valley was depopulated and large numbers of people emigrated, especially from the Mimbres Valley (Fig. 7.6). In the less densely populated eastern Mimbres area, much of the population remained and reorganized into the previously dispersed settlement pattern, continuing to farm floodplain and upland alluvial fan fields (Nelson 1999).

Exchange relations with others outside the Mimbres region was not a strategy used to buffer either short-term fluctuations or the severe drought in the early 12th century (Minnis 1985; Nelson 1999). The people in the Mimbres region, in fact, seem not to have developed strong external exchange relations during the Classic Mimbres period when population was at its height. That period is known for its beautiful Mimbres Black-on-white ceramic tradition (Brody 1977; LeBlanc 1983). Ceramic vessels painted with naturalistic and geometric designs on a white background so dominated the painted ceramic tradition that fewer than 2% of painted assemblages from Mimbres villages were from outside the region (Hegmon, Nelson, and Ruth 1998). Other material categories of exchange items are similarly rare from Classic Mimbres villages (Minnis 1985). Hegmon and Nelson have argued that the homogeneity of painted ceramics may result from and support a social conformity important to the organization of Mimbres villages and regional coherence (Hegmon, Nelson, and Ruth 1998; Nelson et al. 2006). Thus, buffering shortfalls would have been accomplished by relations within the region, the kind of pooling of stored resources described above and simulated by Hegmon (1991).

We do not know the destination of those who migrated from the region. This invisibility perhaps also results from the lack of external exchange ties. At small hamlet sites in the Mimbres region that immediately postdate the Classic period, we find the continued use of Mimbres Black-on-white pottery and its merging with new styles (Hegmon, Nelson, and Ruth 1998), but outside the area the Mimbres Black-on-white tradition of naturalistic and geometric designs is no longer found after the Classic Mimbres period.

Salinas

The Salinas case study presents an instance of enduring economic, social, and settlement stability. The longevity of occupation of specific portions of the Salinas landscape is unusual in Southwestern prehistory and is likely an indicator of the reliability of crop production in this area, due to localized occurrences of a high water table.

The Salinas region is located in central New Mexico (Fig. 7.4), east of the Rio Grande valley and the Manzanos and Los Pinos Mountains. The Manzanos Mountains, with piñon-juniper woodland at the lower elevations and ponderosa pine and Gambel's oak on the upper slopes, supply water in the form of ephemeral streams. Chupadero and Jumanes mesas lie to the south and east of these ranges. Piñon-juniper woodland dominates the mesa tops and slopes, while sandy plains of rolling grasslands and sage extend to the east. There is now no permanent source of surface water in the vicinity of these mesas, although seasonal playas and springs were common prior to groundwater pumping.

Salinas sites occur in two clusters, referred to as the Manzanos and Jumanos clusters. The Manzanos cluster lies in the eastern foothills of the Manzanos Mountains in the northwestern portion of the province. The Jumanos cluster lies to the south, on and east of Chupadera and Jumanes mesas, and includes Gran Quivira, Pardo, Colorado, and Blanco (Tabira) pueblos. Since our best data pertain to the Jumanos cluster, we focus our discussion on this portion of the region.

In the Jumanos cluster, although few are known, pithouse sites (currently dated to late AD 800–1200s; Ice 1968; Rautman 1990) lie at the same locations as later jacal villages. Jacal structures are comprised of upright stone footings with a mud and thatch superstructure. They are provisionally dated to the AD 1000s–1200s; however, none have been excavated and thus there are no absolute dates associated with them. In his dissertation research, Matthew Chamberlin (2008) has documented that in the late 1200s people living in these jacal villages then aggregated largely *in place* into plaza-oriented masonry pueblos. In the early 1400s, there was then another aggregation (Spielmann 1996) during which the majority of early masonry locations were abandoned, and the Jumanos cluster population nucleated into a few large masonry pueblos built at the locations of some of the early masonry pueblos. This final aggregation focused on lower-elevation, eastward-extending fingers of Chupadera Mesa and basins between these fingers. Figure 7.7 maps the locations of the known pithouse, jacal, and early and late masonry Jumanos sites. While the icons are necessarily placed next to each other, the actual sites are often on top of one another (e.g., late masonry superimposed over early masonry, which are over jacal villages).

Matthew Peeples (2007) has recently documented that aggregation within the Salinas area consisted solely of the reorganization of the local population with no apparent immigration from elsewhere (see Fig. 7.9). Based on data from all full-coverage surveys greater than 500 contiguous acres across the entire Salinas region (more than 38,000 acres—ca. 150 km²—of survey) and New Mexico ARMS site records, much of the Salinas area is devoid of habitation sites. Given that there has been a great deal of survey across the entire region, it seems that the clustering of prehistoric sites is not a result of uneven survey coverage.

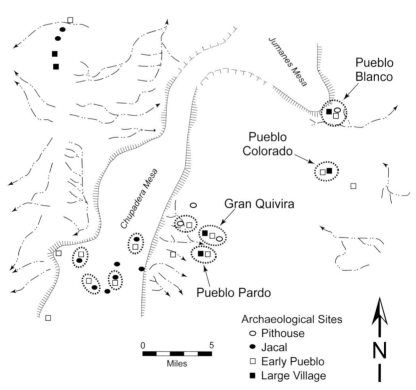

7.7 Jumanos sites in Salinas area; note juxtaposition of pithouse, jacal, early masonry and late masonry site locations.

Precipitation and population in the Salinas area. Figure 7.8 documents several periods of severe drought from the mid-1300s to the mid-1600s, yet as the demographic data in Figure 7.9 indicate, there are no marked population changes in the Salinas area. Thus, although the Salinas dendroclimatic data document widely spaced, severe droughts of the sort that led to depopulation in the Mimbres area, there is no evidence that people left the Salinas area in significant numbers.

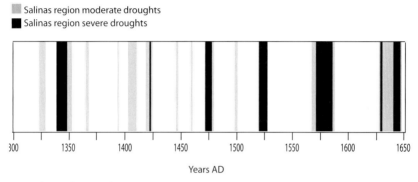

7.8 Salinas climatic data.

The tightly clustered and remarkably stable settlement pattern is likely due to the unique configuration of the water supply in the Salinas area. First, precipitation in this region averages about 15 inches per year (ca. 380 mm/yr), higher than many other parts of the Southwest. Second, in the early 20th century, before drilling for water had taken place, hydrogeological studies documented the presence of highly localized, perched water tables and artesian well conditions in the Quaternary alluvium east of Chupadera Mesa and the Manzanos Mountains (Meinzer 1911; Neel 1926; Spiegel 1955). Localized water tables at or near the ground surface would have sustained some crop production and domestic water supplies even through prolonged droughts. For example, despite a severe drought in the area in the late 1890s–early 1900s, the water table in places remained at ground level and could be tapped for ditch irrigation. Likewise, the shallow water belt identified by Meinzer (1911) in 1910 was still in place during a drought from 1921–1925 (Neel 1926).

While perched water tables allowed Salinas residents to remain in

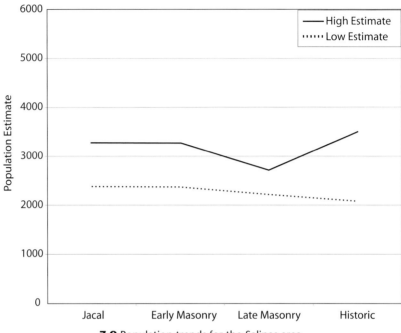

7.9 Population trends for the Salinas area.

place, there is some evidence that they may have reacted to severe droughts through some level of internal strife. The mid-1300s drought and potential difficulties with crop production, for example, may have resulted in inter-village conflicts. Alison Rautman and Matthew Chamberlin have discovered heavy burning at one of the early masonry sites, and Rautman's research has previously documented burning at another (Rautman 1995; Rautman and Chamberlin 2008). Recurring drought conditions in the early 1400s may have been in part responsible for the final, large-scale aggregation into Gran Quivira, Pueblo Pardo, Pueblo Colorado, and Pueblo Blanco on the lower fingers of the mesas, where water would have been more accessible. The depopulation of Pueblo Colorado in the 1500s likely corresponds with the extreme drought of the 1570s. Unlike the other three aggregated Jumanos pueblos, Pueblo Colorado was positioned in the middle of a basin rather than up against a portion of Chupadera Mesa. It is possible that the water table dropped too low due to the drought. Contemporaneous growth of nearby Pueblo Blanco suggests that residents of Pueblo Colorado may have moved there.

Despite the clearly favorable hydrological conditions of the Salinas area, the Jumanos population estimates reveal no marked increases from when our data begin (around the 1100s) to Spanish contact in the early 1600s (Fig. 7.9; Peeples 2007). Thus even though large numbers of migrants moved into the Rio Grande valley in the late 1200s, including the Rio Abajo south of Albuquerque, they did not venture further east into the Salinas area. Strong social mechanisms must have been in place to prevent such immigration.

CONCLUSION

The Ancestral Pueblo Southwest is characterized by robust strategies for mitigating the risk of shortfall in agricultural production. Spatially, at the local scale, household-based, multiyear storage and community-scale restricted sharing of stored food were resilient responses to high frequency environmental variation. At the regional scale, migration was a resilient strategy for maintaining a farming adaptation in the Southwest in the face of periodic, severe droughts. Thus, the farming practices of Southwestern people appear to have been adaptable from one setting to another. The social and cultural practices and beliefs that allowed for flexibility in access to different Southwestern landscapes for much of prehistory constitute a fundamental component of this resilience. Social relations established through exchange may have supported or facilitated the many migrations that have been documented across the Southwest landscape.

These conclusions are consistent with Naranjo's (1995) statement that movement is a part of life among Pueblo people. Further, the common use of movement by prehistoric people to address severe climate conditions and other social and environmental perturbations helps explain the many settlements that now stand as ruins throughout the Southwest. For decades, researchers and museum exhibitors have explained the abundance of village ruins as failed adaptations and seen the "abandonments" as evidence of collapse, loss, and disappearance (see Nelson 1999 for a discussion of this issue). Migration, however, is in fact a resilient approach at a regional scale that sustained Southwestern populations for millennia.

NOTES

1. Moving averages have been used in a number of studies to identify multiyear droughts and wet intervals (e.g., Benson et al. 2007; Cordell et al. 2007; Ni et al. 2002; Parks, Dean, and Betancourt 2006; Van West and Grissino-Mayer 2005; Woodhouse 2001) and they are easily understood and replicated. Eight to 20-year overlapping and non-overlapping intervals have also been used in numerous paleoclimatic studies examining relationships between climate and human behavior (Dean 1988; Larson et al. 1996; Parks, Dean, and Betancourt 2006; Reid, Graybill, and Siferle-Valencia 2006; Rose, Dean, and Robinson 1981). Record length has little impact on the identification of extreme periods based on Ingram's evaluation of the proposed method. Similar percentile approaches have been used by Hirshboeck and Meko (2005), Steinemann, Hayes, and Cavalcanti (2005), and Simaldtin (2001). When four or fewer years of separation exist between the middle years of identified drought intervals, the intervals are merged into a single period because the 9-year intervals substantially overlap. The tree-ring precipitation reconstructions used to represent climate conditions in the Mimbres region are the Central Rio Grande chronology (Grissino-Mayer, Baisan, and Swetnam 1997) and the Chupadero chronology (Dean and Robinson 1978) for the Salinas region.

2. For the Mimbres region, following Nelson and Schollmeyer (2003), every 2.5 rooms were assumed to represent one nuclear family household of approximately four individuals. For the Salinas region, each room was assumed to represent two individuals. For both cases, room use-life estimates were assumed to be roughly 50 years.

REFERENCES CITED

Adams, E. Charles. 1998. Late Prehistory in the Middle Little Colorado River Area: A Regional Perspective. In *Migration and Reorganization: The Pueblo IV Period in the American Southwest*, ed. K. A. Spielmann, pp. 53–63. Arizona State University Anthropological Research Paper 51. Tempe.

Ahlstrom, Richard V. N., Carla R. Van West, and Jeffrey S. Dean. 1995. Environmental and Chronological Factors in the Mesa Verde–Northern Rio Grande Migration. *Journal of Anthropological Archaeology* 14:125–42.

Anschuetz, Kurt. 1998. Not Waiting for Rain: Integrated Systems of Water Management by Pre-Colombian Pueblo Farmers in North-Central New Mexico. PhD diss., Dept. of Anthropology, Univ. of Michigan, Ann Arbor.

——— 2006. Tewa Fields, Tewa Traditions. In *Canyon Gardens: The Ancient Pueblo Landscapes of the American Southwest*, ed. V. B. Price and B. H. Morrow, pp. 57–73. Albuquerque: University of New Mexico Press.

Anthony, David W. 1990. Migration in Archaeology: The Baby and the Bathwater. *American Anthropologist* 92:895–914.

Anyon, Roger, Patricia A. Gilman, and Steven A. LeBlanc. 1981. The Re-evaluation of the Mogollon-Mimbres Archaeological Sequence. *The Kiva* 46:209–25.

Benson, Larry V., Michael S. Berry, Edward A. Jolie, Jerry D. Spangler, David W. Stahle, and Eugene M. Hattori. 2007. Possible Impacts of Early-11th-,

Middle-12th-, and Late-13th-Century Droughts on Western Native Americans and the Mississippian Cahokians. *Quaternary Science Reviews* 26:336–50.

Blake, T. Michael, Steven A. LeBlanc, and Paul E. Minnis. 1986. Changing Settlement and Population in the Mimbres Valley, SW New Mexico. *Journal of Field Archaeology* 13:439–64.

Brandt, Elizabeth. 1994. Egalitarianism, Hierarchy, and Centralization in the Pueblos. In *The Ancient Southwestern Community: Models and Methods for the Study of Prehistoric Social Organization*, ed. W. H. Wills and Robert Leonard, pp. 9–23. Albuquerque: University of New Mexico Press.

Braun, David, and Stephen Plog. 1982. Evolution of "Tribal" Social Networks: Theory and Prehistoric North American Evidence. *American Antiquity* 47:504–25.

Brody, J. J. 1977. *Mimbres Painted Pottery*. Santa Fe, NM: School of American Research Press.

Burns, Barney. 1983. Simulated Anasazi Storage Behavior Using Crop Yields Reconstructed from Tree Rings: A.D. 652–1968 (Colorado). PhD diss., Dept. of Anthropology, Univ. of Arizona, Tucson.

Cameron, Catherine M. 1995. Migration and the Movement of Southwestern Peoples. *Journal of Anthropological Archaeology* 14:104–24.

Cannon, Michael D. 2000. Large Mammal Relative Abundance in Pithouse and Pueblo Period Archaeofaunas from Southwestern New Mexico: Resource Depression among the Mimbres-Mogollon? *Journal of Anthropological Archaeology* 19:317–47.

—— 2001. *Large Mammal Resource Depression and Agricultural Intensification: An Empirical Test in the Mimbres Valley, New Mexico*. Ann Arbor, MI: University Microfilms.

Chamberlin, Matthew. 2008. Evaluating the Cultural Origins of Complexity in the Ancestral Pueblo World. PhD diss., School of Human Evolution and Social Change, Arizona State Univ., Tempe.

Clark, Tiffany C. 2006. Production, Exchange, and Social Identity: A Study of Chupadero Black-on-white Pottery. PhD diss., Dept. of Anthropology, Arizona State Univ., Tempe.

Colson, Elizabeth. 1979. In Good Years and Bad: Food Strategies of Self-Reliant Societies. *Journal of Anthropological Research* 35:18–29.

Cordell, Linda S. 1975. Predicting Site Abandonment at Wetherill Mesa. *Kiva* 40:189–202.

—— 1997. *Archaeology of the Southwest*. 2nd ed. San Diego, CA: Academic Press.

Cordell, Linda S., Carla R. Van West, Jeffrey S. Dean, and Deborah A. Muenchrath. 2007. Mesa Verde Settlement History and Relocation: Climate Change, Social Networks, and Ancestral Pueblo Migration. *Kiva* 72:379–405.

Crown, Patricia. 1994. *Ceramics and Ideology*. Albuquerque: University of New Mexico Press.

Crown, Patricia L., Janet D. Orcutt, and Timothy A. Kohler. 1996. Pueblo Cultures in Transition: The Northern Rio Grande. In *The Prehistoric Pueblo World, A.D. 1150–1350*, ed. M. Adler, pp. 188–204. Tucson: University of Arizona Press.

Dean, Jeffrey S. 1988. A Model of Anasazi Behavioral Adaptation. In *The Anasazi in a Changing Environment*, ed. G. Gumerman, pp. 25–44. Cambridge: Cambridge University Press.

——— 1996. Demography, Environment, and Subsistence Stress. In *Evolving Complexity and Environmental Risk in the Prehistoric Southwest*, ed. J. A. Tainter and B. B. Tainter, pp. 25–56. Reading, MA: Addison-Wesley.

——— 2000. Complexity Theory and Sociocultural Change in the American Southwest. In *The Way the Wind Blows*, ed. J. A. Tainter, R. J. McIntosh, and S. K. McIntosh, pp. 89–118. New York: Columbia University Press.

——— 2006. Subsistence Stress and Food Storage at Kiet Siel, Northeastern Arizona. In *Environmental Change and Human Adaptation in the Ancient American Southwest*, ed. D. E. Doyel and J. S. Dean, pp. 160–79. Salt Lake City: University of Utah Press.

Dean, Jeffrey, Robert C. Euler, George J. Gumerman, Fred Plog, Richard H. Hevly, and Thor N. V. Karlstrom. 1985. Human Behavior, Demography, and Paleoenvironment on the Colorado Plateaus. *American Antiquity* 50:537–54.

Dean, Jeffrey S., and William J. Robinson. 1978. *Expanded Tree-Ring Chronologies for the Southwestern United States*. Chronology Series 3. Tucson: Laboratory of Tree-Ring Research, University of Arizona.

Diehl, Michael W. 1994. *Subsistence Economics and Emergent Social Differences: A Case Study from the Prehistoric North American Southwest*. Ann Arbor, MI: University Microfilms.

——— 1996. The Intensity of Maize Processing and Production in Upland Mogollon Pithouse Villages, A.D. 200–1000. *American Antiquity* 61:102–15.

Euler, Robert C., George J. Gumerman, Thor N. V. Karlstrom, Jeffrey S. Dean, and Richard H. Hevly. 1979. The Colorado Plateaus: Cultural Dynamic and Paleoenvironment. *Science* 205(4411): 1089–1101.

Ford, Richard I. 1972. An Ecological Perspective on the Eastern Pueblos. In *New Perspectives on the Pueblos*, ed. A. Ortiz, pp. 1–17. Albuquerque: University of New Mexico Press.

——— 1992. *An Ecological Analysis Involving the Population of San Juan Pueblo, New Mexico*. New York: Garland.

Grissino-Mayer, Henri D., Christopher H. Baisan, and Thomas W. Swetnam. 1997. A 1,373 Year Reconstruction of Annual Precipitation for the Southern Rio Grande Basin. Final report submitted to the Directorate of Environment, Natural Resources Division, Fort Bliss, Texas, for the Legacy Program. Electronic document, https://docs.google.com/viewer?url=http://web.utk.edu/~grissino/downloads/Legacy%2520Final%2520Report.pdf (accessed November 5, 2010).

Gumerman, George J. 1988. *The Anasazi in a Changing Environment*. Cambridge: Cambridge University Press.

Hegmon, Michelle. 1991. The Risks of Sharing and Sharing as Risk Reduction: Interhousehold Food Sharing in Egalitarian Societies. In *Between Bands and States*, ed. S. A. Gregg, pp. 309–29. Carbondale: Southern Illinois University Center for Archaeological Investigations.

—— 1996. Variability in Food Production, Strategies of Storage, and Sharing, and the Pithouse-to-Pueblo Transition in the Northern Southwest. In *Evolving Complexity and Environmental Risk in the Prehistoric Southwest*, ed. J. A. Tainter and B. B. Tainter, pp. 223–50. Reading, MA: Addison-Wesley.

Hegmon, Michelle, Jennifer A. Brady, and Margaret C. Nelson. 2006. Variability in Classic Mimbres Room Suites: Implications for Household Organization and Social Differences. In *Mimbres Society*, ed. V. S. Powell-Marti and P. A. Gilman, pp. 45–65. Tucson: University of Arizona Press.

Hegmon, Michelle, Margaret C. Nelson, and Susan Ruth. 1998. Abandonment, Reorganization, and Social Change: Analysis of Pottery and Architecture from the Mimbres Region of the American Southwest. *American Anthropologist* 100:148–62.

Hegmon, Michelle, Matthew A. Peeples, Ann P. Kinzig, Stephanie Kulow, Cathryn M. Meegan, and Margaret C. Nelson. 2008. Social Transformation and Its Human Costs in the Prehispanic Southwest. *American Anthropologist* 110:313–24.

Herberle, R. 1938. The Causes of Rural–Urban Migration: A Survey of German Theories. *American Journal of Sociology* 43:935–50.

Herrington, Laverne. 1979. *Settlement Patterns and Water Control Systems of the Mimbres Classic Phase, Grant County, New Mexico*. Ann Arbor, MI: University Microfilms.

Hirschboeck, Katherine K., and David M. Meko. 2005. A Tree-Ring Based Assessment of Synchronous Extreme Streamflow Episodes in the Upper Colorado and Salt-Verde-Tonto River Basins: A Collaborative Project between the University of Arizona's Laboratory of Tree-Ring Research and the Salt River Project. Electronic document, http://fp.arizona.edu/kkh/srp.htm (accessed November 5, 2010).

Howard, Jerry. 2006. Hohokam Irrigation Communities: A Study of Internal Structure, External Relationships and Sociopolitical Complexity. PhD diss., Dept. of Anthropology, Arizona State Univ., Tempe.

Ice, Ronald. 1968. A Report on 1964 Excavations at Gran Quivira. Report on file at Salinas Pueblo Missions National Monument, Mountainair, New Mexico.

Judge, W. James. 1989. Chaco Canyon—San Juan Basin. In *Dynamics of Southwest Prehistory*, ed. Linda S. Cordell and George J. Gumerman, pp. 209–61. Washington, DC: Smithsonian Institution Press.

Kohler, Timothy A. 1993. News from the Northern American Southwest: Prehistory on the Edge of Chaos. *Journal of Archaeological Research* 1:267–321.

Kohler, Timothy A., and Carla Van West. 1996. The Calculus of Self-Interest in the Development of Cooperation: Sociopolitical Development and Risk among the Northern Anasazi. In *Evolving Complexity and Environmental Risk in the Prehistoric Southwest*, ed. J. A. Tainter and B. B. Tainter, pp. 169–96. Reading, MA: Addison-Wesley.

Larson, Daniel O., Hector Neff, Donald A. Graybill, Joel Michaelsen, and Elizabeth Ambos. 1996. Risk, Climatic Variability, and the Study of Southwestern Prehistory: An Evolutionary Perspective. *American Antiquity* 61:217–41.

LeBlanc, Steven A. 1983. *The Mimbres People, Ancient Pueblo Painters of the American Southwest*. New York: Thames and Hudson.

Lee, E. S. 1966. A Theory of Migration. *Demography* 3:47–57.

Lightfoot, Ricky R. 1994. *The Duckfoot Site*. Vol. 2, *Archaeology of the House and Household*. Cortez, CO: Crow Canyon Archaeological Center.

Lipe, William D. 1995. The Depopulation of the Northern San Juan: Conditions in the Turbulent 1200s. *Journal of Anthropological Archaeology* 14:143–69.

Meinzer, O. E. 1911. *Geology and Water Resources of Estancia Valley, New Mexico*. United States Geological Survey Water-Supply Paper 275. Washington, DC.

Minnis, Paul E. 1985. *Social Adaptation to Food Stress: A Prehistoric Southwestern Example*. Chicago: University of Chicago Press.

Mobley-Tanaka, Jeannette. 1998. An Analysis of Design on Glaze Ware Sherds from the Salinas Area, New Mexico. Ms. on file, Dept. of Anthropology, Arizona State Univ., Tempe.

Muenchrath, Deborah A., and R. J. Salvador. 1995. Maize Productivity and Agroecology: Effects of Environment and Agricultural Practices on the Biology of Maize. In *Soil, Water, Biology, and Belief in Prehistoric and Traditional Southwestern Agriculture*, ed. H. S. Toll, pp. 303–33. New Mexico Archaeological Council Special Publication, Vol. 2. Albuquerque.

Naranjo, Tessie. 1995. Thoughts on Migration by Santa Clara Pueblo. *Journal of Anthropological Archaeology* 14:247–50.

Neel, George M. 1926. *Seventh Biennial Report of the State Engineer of New Mexico*. Santa Fe: Sun Publishing.

Nelson, Ben A., and Steven A. LeBlanc. 1986. *Short-term Sedentism in the American Southwest: The Mimbres Valley Salado*. Albuquerque, NM: Maxwell Museum of Anthropology.

Nelson, Margaret C. 1999. *Mimbres during the Twelfth Century: Abandonment, Continuity, and Reorganization*. Tucson: University of Arizona Press.

Nelson, Margaret C., and Karen Gust Schollmeyer. 2003. Game Resources, Social Interaction, and the Ecological Footprint in Southwest New Mexico. *Journal of Archaeological Method and Theory* 10:69–110.

Nelson, Margaret C., Michelle Hegmon, Stephanie Kulow, and Karen G. Schollmeyer. 2006. Archaeological and Ecological Perspectives on Reorganization: A Case Study from the Mimbres Region of the US Southwest. *American Antiquity* 71:403–32.

Ni, Fenbiao, Tereza Cavazos, Malcolm K. Hughes, Andrew C. Comrie, and Gary Funkhouser. 2002. Cool-Season Precipitation in the Southwestern

USA since AD 1000: Comparison of Linear and Nonlinear Techniques for Reconstruction. *International Journal of Climatology* 22:1645–62.

Orcutt, Janet D. 1991. Environmental Variability and Settlement Changes on the Pajarito Plateau, New Mexico. *American Antiquity* 56:315–32.

Parks, James A., Jeffrey S. Dean, and Julio L. Betancourt. 2006. Tree Rings, Drought, and the Pueblo Abandonment of South-Central New Mexico in the 1670s. In *Environmental Change and Human Adaptation in the Ancient American Southwest*, ed. David E. Doyel and Jeffrey S. Dean, pp. 214–27. Salt Lake City: University of Utah Press.

Peeples, Matthew. 2007. Report on Salinas Demography. On file, School of Human Evolution and Social Change, Arizona State Univ., Tempe.

Plog, Fred, George J. Gumerman, Robert C. Euler, Jeffrey S. Dean, Richard H. Hevly, and Thor N. V. Karlstrom. 1988. Anasazi Adaptive Strategies: The Model, Predictions, and Results. In *The Anasazi in a Changing Environment*, ed. G. Gumerman, pp. 230–76. Cambridge: Cambridge University Press.

Powell, Shirley. 2002. The Puebloan Florescence and Dispersion: Dinnebito and Beyond, A.D. 800–1150. In *Prehistoric Culture Change on the Colorado Plateau: Ten Thousand Years on Black Mesa*, ed. S. Powell and F. E. Smiley, pp. 79–117. Tucson: University of Arizona Press.

Rautman, Alison. 1990. The Environmental Context of Decision-making: Coping Strategies among Prehistoric Cultivators in Central New Mexico. PhD diss., Dept. of Anthropology, Univ. of Michigan, Ann Arbor.

—— 1993. Resource Variability, Risk, and the Structure of Social Networks: An Example from the Prehistoric Southwest. *American Antiquity* 58:403–24.

—— 1995. Final Report on the Excavation of Pueblo de la Mesa. Report on file with the USDA, Forest Service, Cibola Branch, Albuquerque, NM.

—— 1996. Risk, Reciprocity, and the Operation of Social Networks. In *Evolving Complexity and Environmental Risk in the Prehistoric Southwest*, ed. J. A. Tainter and B. B. Tainter, pp. 197–222. Reading, MA: Addison-Wesley.

Rautman, Alison, and Matthew Chamberlin. 2008. When Is a Defensive Site? Coping with Conflict in Central New Mexico. Paper presented at the 73rd annual Meetings of the Society for American Archaeology, Vancouver.

Redmond, Kelly T. 2002. The Depiction of Drought: A Commentary. *Bulletin of the American Meterological Society* 83(8): 1143–47.

Reid, J. Jefferson, Donald A. Graybill, and Ann Clair Siferle-Valencia. 2006. Subsistence Management Strategies in the Grasshopper Region, East-Central Arizona. In *Environmental Change and Human Adaptation in the Ancient American Southwest*, ed. David E. Doyel and Jeffrey S. Dean, pp. 124–35. Salt Lake City: University of Utah Press.

Rohn, Arthur. 1989. Northern San Juan Prehistory. In *Dynamics of Southwestern Prehistory*, ed. L. S. Cordell and G. J. Gumerman, pp. 149–78. Washington DC: Smithsonian Institution Press.

Rose, Martin R., Jeffrey S. Dean, and William J. Robinson. 1981. *The Past Climate of Arroyo Hondo, New Mexico, Reconstructed from Tree Rings.* Arroyo Hondo Archaeological Series, Vol. 4. Sante Fe, NM: School of American Research Press.

Sandor, Jonathan. 1990. Prehistoric Agricultural Terraces and Soils in the Mimbres Area, New Mexico. *World Archaeology* 22:70–86.

Schlanger, S. H. 1988. Patterns of Population Movement and Long-term Population Growth in Southwestern Colorado. *American Antiquity* 53:773–93.

Schollmeyer, Karen Gust. 2009. Resource Stress and Settlement Pattern Change in the Eastern Mimbres Area, Southwestern New Mexico. PhD diss., Arizona State University, Tempe.

Scudder, Thayer. 1962. *Ecology of the Gwembe Tonga.* Manchester: University of Manchester Press.

Shafer, Harry, J. 1982. Classic Mimbres Phase Households and Room Use Patterns. *Kiva* 48:17–37.

Slatter, Edwin. 1979. Drought and Demographic Change in the Prehistoric Southwest United States: A Preliminary Quantitative Assessment. PhD diss., Dept. of Anthropology, Univ. of California at Los Angeles.

Smakhtin, V. U. 2001. Low Flow Hydrology: A Review. *Journal of Hydrology* 240:147–86.

Spiegel, Zane. 1955. *Geology and Ground-Water Resources of North-eastern Socorro County, New Mexico.* New Mexico Bureau of Mines and Mineral Resources Ground-water Report 4. Socorro.

Spielmann, Katherine A. 1996. Impressions of Pueblo III Settlement Trends among the Rio Abajo and Eastern Border Pueblos. In *Pueblo Cultures in Transition*, ed. M. Adler, pp. 177–87. Tucson: University of Arizona Press.

—— 1998. Ritual Influences on the Development of Rio Grande Glaze A Ceramics. In *Migration and Reorganization: The Pueblo IV Period in the American Southwest*, ed. K. A. Spielmann, pp. 253–62. Arizona State University Anthropological Research Paper 51. Tempe.

Spielmann, Katherine A., and Margaret Schoeninger. 1992. Multi-Disciplinary Studies of Trade in Meat at Gran Quivira Pueblo, New Mexico. Paper presented at the Conference on Paleonutrition, Center for Archaeological Investigations, Southern Illinois University, Carbondale.

Spielmann, Katherine A., Margaret Schoeninger, and Katherine Moore. 1990. Plains-Pueblo Interdependence and Human Diet at Pecos Pueblo, New Mexico. *American Antiquity* 55:745–65.

Steinemann, Anne, Michael J. Hayes, and Luiz F. N. Cavalcanti. 2005. Drought Indicators and Triggers. In *Drought and Water Crises: Science, Technology, and Management Issues*, ed. Donald Wilhite, pp. 71–92. Boca Raton, FL: CRC Press.

Stevenson, Matilda Coxe. 1904. *The Zuni Indians.* Bureau of American Ethnology 23rd Annual Report. Washington, DC

Swanson, Steven. 2009. The Ecology of Early Farming: A Mogollon Case Study.

PhD diss., School of Human Evolution and Social Change, Arizona State Univ., Tempe.

Tainter, Joseph A., and Bonnie Bagley Tainter. 1996. *Evolving Complexity and Environmental Risk in the Prehistoric Southwest.* Reading, MA: Addison-Wesley.

Talayesva, Don. 1942. *Sun Chief: The Autobiography of a Hopi Indian.* New Haven, CT: Yale University Press.

Van West, Carla R., and Henri D. Grissino-Mayer. 2005. Dendroclimatic Reconstruction. In *Fence Lake Project: Archaeological Data Recovery in the New Mexico Transportation Corridor and First Five-Year Permit Area, Fence Lake Coal Mine Project, Catron County, New Mexico.* Vol. 3, *Environmental Studies*, ed. Edgar K. Huber and Carla R. Van West, pp. 33.1–33.129. Statistical Research Inc., Technical Series 84. Tucson: SRI Press.

Van West, Carla, and Jeffrey S. Dean. 2000. Environmental Characteristics of the A.D. 9900–1300 Period in the Central Mesa Verde Region. *Kiva* 66:19–44.

Varien, Mark D. 1999. *Sedentism and Mobility in a Social Landscape: Mesa Verde and Beyond.* Tucson: University of Arizona Press.

Waddell, Eric. 1975. How the Enga Cope with Frost: Responses to Perturbations in the Central Highlands of New Guinea. *Human Ecology* 3:249–72.

Wiessner, Pauline W. 1977. Haxro: A Regional System of Reciprocity for Reducing Risk among the !Kung San. PhD diss., Dept. of Anthropology, Univ. of Michigan, Ann Arbor.

Wilhite, Donald, and Michael H. Glantz. 1985. Understanding the Drought Phenomenon: The Role of Definitions. *Water International* 10(3): 111–20.

Wohlt, Paul B. 2004. Descent Group Composition and Population Pressure in a Fringe Enga Clan, Papua New Guinea. *Human Ecology* 32:137–61.

Woodhouse, Connie A. 2001. A Tree-Ring Reconstruction of Streamflow for the Colorado Front Range. *Journal of the American Water Resources Association* 37:561–69.

Yengoyan, Aram. 1976. Structure, Event, and Ecology in Aboriginal Australia. In *Tribes and Boundaries in Australia*, ed. N. Peterson, pp. 121–32. Canberra: Australian Institute of Aboriginal Studies.

8

Farmers' Experience and Knowledge: Utilizing Soil Diversity to Mitigate Rainfall Variability on the Taraco Peninsula, Bolivia

MARIA C. BRUNO

INTRODUCTION

As many chapters in this volume demonstrate, unpredictable rainfall is a common reality for farmers worldwide, past and present. During my ethnographic study of farming practices among indigenous Aymara communities on the Taraco Peninsula, Bolivia, I had many conversations about rain. When I arrived in October 2003, the farmers said the planting season was delayed because the rains had not yet come. When the rain finally fell in November, they complained that it was too much. Despite anxiety voiced about too much or too little rain, I found that the Taraco farmers have practices that mitigate risks presented by variability in precipitation. The previous chapters have provided examples of risk reduction strategies such as exchange, storage, and economic diversification. In this chapter, I take a detailed look at how farmers in the Lake Titicaca basin of the Andes reduce the risk of crop failure due to unpredictable rainfall through knowledge of the water-retention qualities of the local soils. Using this knowledge they have developed a planting schedule and land-use strategy that usually results in a successful harvest even in the face of drought or flooding.

Detailed, ethnographic study of generational farming practices that develop in response to short-term climatic variations are important for investigators interested in responses to long-term or larger magnitude climatic events. The particular practices will often dictate whether a society can successfully adjust to the new conditions or not. While many of the chapters in this volume provide examples of how past societies dealt with large magnitude climatic changes, this chapter provides data for testing hypotheses about how the future farmers of the Lake Titicaca basin may respond to our current climate change predicament, but may also aid archaeologists in understanding how and why past inhabitants succeeded or failed in the face of climate change in antiquity.

CLIMATE CHANGE AND FARMING IN THE LAKE TITICACA BASIN, PAST AND PRESENT

Farming began in the Lake Titicaca basin (Figs. 8.1, 8.2) about 2000 years ago (Binford, Brenner, and Leyden 1996:95; Binford et al. 1997:242; Bruno 2006:43), approximately the same time that the current climatic regime and

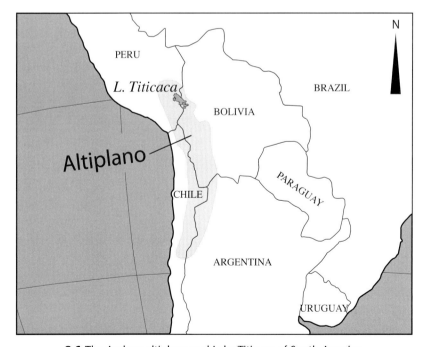

8.1 The Andean altiplano and Lake Titicaca of South America.

lake level were established (Baker et al. 2001:642; Tapia et al. 2003:160; Wir-rmann 1992: 46; Wirrmann and Oliverira-Almeida 1987:320). Prior to this period, the lake basin was extremely dry and the lake may have dropped to 100 m below its modern level (Cross et al. 2000:30; Mourguiart et al. 1998:60; Rigsby, Baker, and Aldenderfer 2003:180; Rowe et al. 2002:194; Seltzer et al. 1998:169; Tapia et al. 2003:160; Wirrmann and Mourguiart 1995:352; Wirrmann and Oliverira-Almeida 1987:322). There is very little evidence for human occupation of the immediate lake basin during this time (Albarracín-Jordan and Mathews 1990:51; Bandy 2006:215; Lémuz-Aguirre 2001:13; Stanish et al. 1997:50).

While the basin has never returned to the extremely dry state it ex-perienced in the mid-Holocene, the late Holocene climate has fluctuated

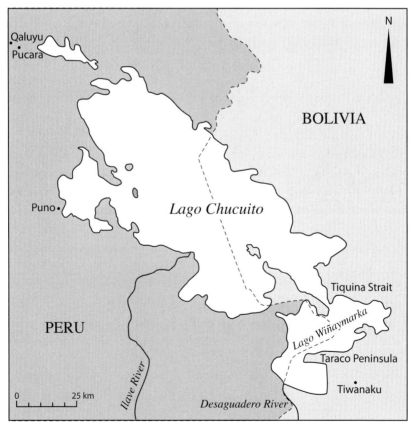

8.2 The Lake Titicaca Basin.

between wetter and drier periods (Abbott et al. 1997). Lake cores taken by the Abbott team in Lake Wiñaymarka suggest there may have been extended dry periods from 2900–2800 BP, 2300–2200 BP, 1850–1650 BP, and 900–500 BP. Three of these dry spells fell in the Formative period (approximately 3500–1500 BP), and the last occurred at the end of the Tiwanaku period (approximately 1500–800 BP) (Table 8.1).

Archaeologists working in the Lake Titicaca basin are interested in understanding how these shifts affected human populations and their various economic activities (Binford et al. 1997; Janusek 2004:126; Rigsby, Baker, and Aldenderfer 2003:166). In particular, the Taraco Archaeological Project examines how these fluctuations impacted the prehistoric inhabitants of the Taraco Peninsula (Bandy 2001:140; Capriles Flores, Domic, and Moore 2007). In the following chapter, Moore examines zooarchaeological data to discuss changes in herding and fishing on the peninsula. As part of this team, I am interested in how these shifts may have affected agricultural production.

Currently, settlement (Bandy 2001) and archaeobotanical data (Bruno 2008; Whitehead 2007) demonstrate that agricultural production contributed to the Taraco Peninsula economy throughout the Formative period. In fact, the available archaeological data do not suggest abandonment of farming during the hypothesized dry periods. While this may suggests problems with the interpretation of the paleoclimatic data (Calaway 2005:784–86) and/or correlating them to the archaeological record (Bruno 2008:482–84), it may also indicate that farmers were able to adjust their farming practices to adapt to the shifting climatic conditions.

As part of my investigation of Lake Titicaca basin agriculture, I conducted a 13-month ethnoarchaeological study of modern-day Aymara farming communities on the Taraco Peninsula (October 2003 to November 2004). A major objective of this study was to document how the physical landscape and local climate shape agricultural land use. There are many differences between past and present Taraco Peninsula farmers, including crops, technologies, and even variation in the relative distribution of soils on the landscape. They do, however, share a very similar physical environment particularly in the basic geology of the peninsula, climatic regime, and shifting dynamic of the lake. Recognizing these differences and similarities, I suggest that it is possible to use relational analogy (Wylie 2002:147–48) to hypothesize about how past farmers may have reacted to long-term

TABLE 8.1. LAKE TITICACA BASIN CHRONOLOGY WITH RELATIVE CLIMATIC CONDITIONS (BASED ON ABBOTT ET AL. 1997)

	Lake Titicaca Chronology	Relative Climatic Conditions
1500	Late Horizon (Inca/Pacajes)	Wet
	Late Intermediate Period (Pacajes)	Dry
1000	Middle Horizon (Tiwanaku IV-V)	Wet
500		
	Late Formative (Tiwanaku I-III)	Dry
0 BC/AD		Wet
		Dry
500	Middle Formative (Late Chiripa)	Wet
		Dry
1000	Early Formative (Early/Middle Chiripa)	Wet
1500		

shifts in rainfall and lake level based on modern-day use of the landscape for agriculture.

In the following section, I describe the general characteristics of the climate in the Lake Titicaca basin with particular attention to the rainfall patterns and their effect on lake level. This description is pertinent to my discussion of farming practices and also provides the background to Moore's chapter on the impact of shifting rainfall and lake level on herding and fishing during the Formative period.

CLIMATE OF THE ANDEAN ALTIPLANO AND LAKE TITICACA BASIN

Lake Titicaca is located on the altiplano, or high plain, which extends between the eastern and western ranges of the Andes (Fig. 8.1). The altiplano is one of the coldest and driest regions of the Andes. The mean annual temperature ranges from 7°–10°C (Montes de Oca 1995:363), with warmer temperatures in the austral summer (December, January, February) and cooler temperatures in the austral winter (June, July, August). Rainfall varies on a north to south gradient with an average of 800 mm per year in the northern basin and 200 mm per year in the southern basin (Vuille, Bradley, and Keimig 2000:12447).

Today, the altiplano, particularly the drier southern portion, is only suitable for camelid pastoralism and limited cultivation of cold and drought-tolerant crops such as the Andean pseudocereals quinoa (*Chenopodium quinoa*), kañawa (*Ch. pallidicaule*), potatoes (*Solanum tuberosum*), and barley (*Hordeum vulgare*). The Lake Titicaca region (Fig. 8.2), however, is more productive, supporting cultivations of maize (*Zea mays*), fava beans (*Vicia faba*), and a wider range of Andean tubers (such as *Oxalis tuberosa*, *Ullucus tuberosus*, and *Tropaeolum tuberosum*). Agriculture thrives in the Titicaca basin because it receives more moisture and has slightly warmer, more stable temperatures. On average, the lake area receives about 600–900 mm of rain annually (PROSUKO 1996; Roche, Bourges, and Mattos 1992:68). Figure 8.3 shows that two communities near the lake (Taraco and Pillapi) receive more monthly rainfall than the community about 20 km from the lake (Tiwanaku). Temperatures around the lake are still cold, averaging around 8°C (Roche, Bourges, and Mattos 1992:66) (Fig. 8.3), but fluctuate less than the surrounding areas and experience fewer frosts. According to a study by

8.3 Total monthly precipitation (1960–1990) at three locations in the southern Lake Titicaca Basin. Taraco and Pillapi are communities on the Taraco Peninsula near the lake. Tiwanaku located in valley about 15 km from lake. (Based on PROSUKO 1996)

Vacher, de Thuy, and Liberman (1992:514–15), lakeshore weather stations had 320 frost-free days versus 100–150 frost-free days in non-lake stations.

Two primary factors contribute to the more temperate microclimate of the Lake Titicaca basin. First, the lake is in the northern sector of the altiplano, which receives more precipitation than the south because of atmospheric circulation patterns (Lenters and Cook 1997). Second, the large body of water (approximately 8562 km²) absorbs a great deal of solar radiation and is warmer (10–14°C) than the surrounding air temperature (Wirrmann 1992:18). "The lake is therefore continuously giving out heat to its surroundings" (Roche, Bourges, and Mattos 1992:70). This radiation of warmth generates "thermal effects" (Boulange and Aquize 1981) producing more rainfall, warmer mean temperatures, and fewer frosts. This makes the Titicaca basin more agriculturally productive than the surrounding altiplano.

Although the lake environment provides better conditions for farming than the wider altiplano, farmers here still face several risks that can destroy their crops. While frost, hail, and pests are risks, the greatest limiting factor for production is rainfall. Unlike other regions of the Andes (Guillet 1987; Netherly 1984; Williams 2006), Titicaca farmers do not utilize irrigation systems to water their fields. Instead they depend entirely on yearly rainfall, which is limited to three or four months a year. The quantity of rainfall received in this small window of time can make or break the yearly harvest.

Dynamics of Rainfall and Lake Level

The Andean region has one rainy and one dry season. The altiplano, in particular, receives most (70–90%) of its rainfall in the austral summer and is dry in the austral winter. The most precipitation occurs between December and February (Roche, Bourges, and Mattos 1992:71–72) (see Fig. 8.3).

While the large body of water influences local climate, the seasonal pattern of rainfall also influences the amount of water present in Lake Titicaca. The lake is approximately 8562 km^2 and consists of two basins (Fig. 8.2). The larger (7132 km^2) northern basin is called Lago Chucuito. The smaller (1470 km^2) southern basin is called Lago Wiñaymarka (Wirrmann 1992:19–21). The two basins are connected by the Strait of Tiquina, which has a sill about 20 m below the modern lake level at 3788 masl (Abbott et al. 1997:170; Wirrmann 1992:18). The mean modern lake level is considered to be 3810 masl. The lakes drain into the Lago Poopó basin to the south via the Desaguadero River. The sill of this outlet is about 5 m below the modern lake level at 3804 masl (Wirrmann 1992:21).

The lake level is dependent upon the balance of water input and output via various sources. The primary input sources are runoff and rainfall. Rivers from the eastern and western mountain ranges drain into the lake and account for about 53% of yearly input. Rainfall accounts for 47% of the yearly input (Roche, Bourges, and Mattos 1992:82–83). Although runoff is slightly greater, rainfall is more variable and thus has a greater influence on total yearly input.

The lake loses water by outflow and evaporation. When the lake is higher than the Desaguadero River sill (>3800 m), water drains out to the south. Outflow, however, only accounts for 9% of annual water loss while evaporation accounts for 91% (Roche, Bourges, and Mattos 1992:82–83). Given these variables, the balance between precipitation and evaporation largely determines the lake level (Abbott et al. 1997:170; Baker et al. 2001:642; Roche, Bourges, and Mattos 1992:65, 81).

Seasonal fluctuation in rainfall causes the lake to rise and fall during the year. The lake rises to its highest point at the end of the rainy season and after the peak of river runoff, usually in April. Evaporation occurs throughout the remaining eight months of sunny, dry weather and the lake drops, usually reaching its lowest point in December (Roche, Bourges, and Mattos 1992:79). Based on modern records, the lake shifts approximately 0.7 m annually (Cross et al. 2001:3).

While this change may not be as noticeable in Lake Chucuito, such a shift is very obvious in the shallow Lake Wiñaymarka, where I conducted my research. The two photographs in Figure 8.4 show the same point in the community of San José in January 2004 and April 2004. The exposed land where fava beans grew in January was inundated by April. In the area I worked, a strip of land approximately 10 m wide is covered and exposed during these seasonal shifts. As I will describe below, this dynamic plays an important role in agricultural land-use strategies of farmers living near the lakeshore.

In addition to the seasonal fluctuation of rainfall, there is also inter-annual variation. Current research suggests that interannual variability of rainfall in the altiplano correlates strongly with the El Niño–Southern Oscillation (ENSO) phenomenon (Garreaud, Vuille, and Clement 2003; Lenters and Cook 1999; Ronchail 1995; Vuille 1999; Vuille, Bradley, and Keimig 2000) (see Roberts, this volume). During warm ENSO phases (El Niño periods), the altiplano is drier and during cool ENSO phases (La Niña periods), it is wetter.

These fluctuations in interannual rainfall affect the average height of the lake causing the lake to lose or gain water overall. Between 1914 and 1989, Roche et al. (1992:79,fig. 10) monitored the lake level near Puno and found a total interannual range of 6.37 m (Fig. 8.5). The lake reached its lowest absolute level in December 1943 when it was –3.72 m below the datum (3809.93 masl) and reached its highest absolute level in April 1986 when it was 2.56 m above the datum. Thus, in addition to the seasonal fluctuations, there may be more drastic shifts in the average shoreline depending on the overall rainfall for a given year.

This discussion demonstrates how the Lake Titicaca basin landscape is shaped by oscillations between wet and dry periods, and high and low lake levels on a seasonal and annual basis. As a consequence, these fluctuations in rainfall and lake level influence the manner in which people farm this region. As with other arid regions discussed in this volume, the amount of rainfall dictates whether or not the plants will have enough moisture to thrive. In the Lake Titicaca basin, the quantity of rainfall and shifting

8.4 (a) Top photo shows a growing fava bean field in January 2004 with Lake Titicaca waters approaching. Note the mostly exposed dirt pile to the right. (b) Bottom photo shows the harvested fava bean field in April 2004 with waters covering most of the field. The dirt pile is completely surrounded by water.

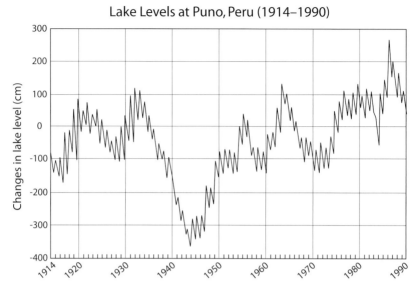

8.5 Documented lake level changes at Puno, Peru, between 1914 and 1989. The zero datum on the Y-axis is 3809.93 m. Lake level serves as a proxy for fluctuations in rainfall. Low lake levels indicate drier conditions and high lake levels indicate wetter conditions. (Based on Roche et al. 1992: fig. 10)

lake level also dictate where farmers can cultivate. I now turn to the ethnographic information I collected on the Taraco Peninsula to describe how farmers take advantage of soil diversity to account for rainfall variability.

FARMING THE TARACO PENINSULA, BOLIVIA

The Taraco Peninsula is a relatively low-lying (maximum 3810–4100 m) mountain range of approximately 100 km² that extends west into the southern portion of Lake Wiñaymarka (Fig. 8.2). From October 2003–2004, I lived in and conducted ethnobotanical research on farming and plant use in four Aymara communities located on the peninsula: Chiripa (pop. 313), Coa Collu (pop. 596), San José (pop. 205), and Santa Rosa (pop. 132) (Fig. 8.6). The communities consist of families that own between 2 to 7 ha of land where they build their homes and farm. Current landholdings are based upon the redistribution of land to highland indigenous populations during Bolivia's 1953 Agricultural Reform (Benton 1999:88; Klein 2003:215). Today,

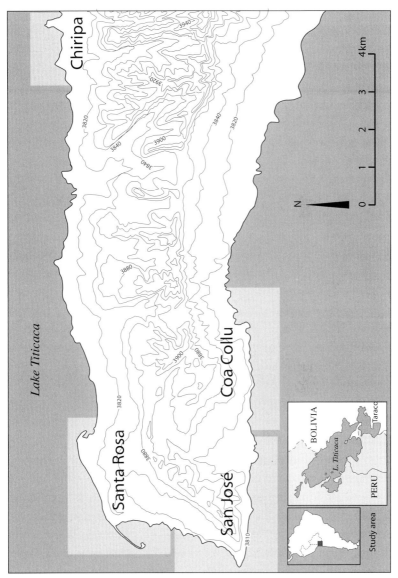

8.6 The Taraco Peninsula, Bolivia and the participating communities.

most households consist of extended families with grandparents, spouses, and grandchildren. Smaller households of only nuclear families (two to four people) are becoming more common as people move to the cities of El Alto and La Paz.

Families practice a mixture of subsistence farming, herding, and fishing. They consume most of their produce, but they also sell portions of it to earn money for purchased items such as cooking gas, vegetables, bread, rice, and other household necessities. A typical day consists of recovering fish from nets set in the lake, tending to animals (typically cows, sheep, and pigs), cooking, and completing seasonal agricultural tasks. During my year on the peninsula and in subsequent visits, I participated in and observed each of these activities. The focus of my research was on farming so I conducted more detailed investigation on these practices.

Research Methods

I lived with a family in San José, which was in walking distance or a short bus ride to the neighboring communities. I collected information on the agricultural cycle, plant and land use through participant observation and interviews. Participation in this project was voluntary and therefore my sampling was opportunistic; however, I made a concerted effort to interview people from a range of socioeconomic levels, women and men, young and old, wealthy and poor. The data presented here derive primarily from 74 semistructured interviews that asked participants to recount an average agricultural year, describing the crops that are cultivated and the activities carried out each season. I included questions related to land use, soil types, and field maintenance, particularly crop rotation and fallow. I also completed 17 more detailed interviews that focused on the landholdings and cultivation practices of individual families. For these interviews, my research assistant mapped fields of individual landholders with a Garmin Geographic Positioning System 12, while I interviewed the farmer about the "life history" of each field. I asked what crops had been planted over the past several years and how long the field had been or would be fallowed. In total, we recorded 226 fields. These data are the basis for the descriptions provided below.

Crops, Rotation, and Fallow

Modern-day farming on the Taraco Peninsula and the greater Andean region is a combination of practices deriving from the pre-Hispanic Andes, colonial Eurasia, and modern agronomic science. Farmers are constantly experimenting with new products, particularly crops, fertilizers, and pesticides, while also utilizing long-standing cultivation and land-use practices. The primary crops on the peninsula today are the Andean cultigens: potato (*Solanum tuberosum*), oca (*Oxalis tuberosa*), isañu (*Trapeolum tuberosum*), ullucu or *papa lisa* (*Ullucus tuberosa*), quinoa (*Chenopodium quinoa*), tarwi (*Lupinus mutabilis* Sweet), and maize (*Zea mays*). The Eurasian cultigens include: fava beans (*Vicia faba*), peas (*Pisum sativum* L.), barley (*Hordeum vulgare*), wheat (*Triticum* sp.), and oats (*Avena sativa* L.). They cultivate most of the barley, wheat, and oats to feed livestock while the remaining crops are for human consumption.

In a typical year, farmers dedicate each of their fields to one of the major crops based on a fairly standardized system of crop rotation and fallow (Table 8.2). The system that the Taraco farmers follow is very similar to those collected in other regions of the basin (Orlove and Godoy 1986:191–90, Appendix 1).

Fallow is an essential part of the rotation. Although it has been said that fields near the lake can be continuously cropped (Buechler 1969:181; Vacher, de Thuy, and Liberman 1992:517), most people fallow fields for at least 1 or 2 years, but sometime up to 10 years. The only people I found who did not fallow were those with holdings too small to leave fields out of cultivation.

The potato is always first in the cycle immediately following the fallow. According to the farmers, the potatoes need many nutrients to grow and the rested soil provides them. The fallow also reduces the number of pests in the soil that can damage the underground tuber (Orlove and Godoy 1986:184).

Fertilizer is always added to the planted potatoes. Sheep dung is the most common fertilizer used, but people now frequently employ some chemical products. Because of the altiplano's relatively low vegetation cover, the soils are relatively low in nutrients needed for sustaining crops. Farmers throughout the region use animal fertilizer, traditionally camelid dung, to augment soil nutrients and fertility, especially for potato production (Winterhalder, Larsen, and Thompson 1974:96–97).

Oca (a tuber) usually follows the potatoes. Although oca will occupy

Table 8.2. Examples of crop rotation and fallow in the fields of two families on the Taraco Peninsula, Bolivia, based on interviews conducted in 2004. The number associated with "rest" is the years a field was in fallow.

INT24				
Field	2003	2004	2005	2006
1	rest 4	rest 5	potato	oca
2	rest 2	potato/ullucu	oca	fava bean
3	rest 2	faba bean/peas/maize	barley	rest
4	rest 4	potato/ullucu	oca	
5	rest 3	rest 4	potato	
6	barley	rest 1	rest 2	rest 3
7	fava bean	barley	rest 1	rest 2
8	potato	oca/ullucu/isañu/maize/fava	fava bean	
9	rest 6	rest 7	potato	
10	maize	rest 1	rest 2	fava bean/maize
11	barley	rest 1	rest 2	rest 3
12	barley	rest 1	potato	
13	barley	rest 1	rest 2	
14	fava bean/maize	barley	rest 1	rest 2
15	rest 3	potato/barley	oca	
16	potato	rest 1	barley	barley
INT71				
1	oca	fava bean	barley	
2	fava bean	rest 1	potato	
3	fava bean	rest 1	rest 2	potato
4	rest 2	rest 3	potato	
5	rest 1	rest 2	rest 3	rest 4
6	rest	barley	rest	
7		fava bean	barley	rest 1
8	rest 4	rest 5	potato	oca
9		potato	oca	fava bean
10	fava bean	barley	rest	
11	rest 4	rest 5	potato	
13	rest 2	rest 3	potato	fava bean
14	potato	fava bean/quinoa	oats	
15	potato	oca	fava bean	
16		rest	maize	potato

most of the field, farmers often also include rows of isañu (also a tuber), peas, and even potatoes. Fertilizers are not used with the oca. The farmers commented that the soil still maintains a lot of nutrients after the potatoes and the oca do not need as many nutrients as the potatoes do.

Fava beans generally follow oca, but are often planted with other crops, especially maize and quinoa. Fava beans do not need fertilizer either, and most farmers recognize that the legume actually gives nutrients back to the soil. The final year of production is a grain, commonly one of the Eurasian crops such as barley, oats, or wheat. In some cases, people placed quinoa in this position.[1] Others will grow two years of barley and then leave the field to rest ending the cycle.

With this system of rotation and fallow, a family will have at least one field with each crop and several fields in fallow. This provides a yearly harvest of a range of products and also serves to reduce the risk of total crop failure. Usually at least one of these crops will produce even if some are attacked by a malady such as hail, frost, worms, drought, or flood.

Agricultural Calendar

When asked to describe the yearly agricultural cycle, almost all respondents began by describing a series of plowings that must be completed before planting. These can begin as early as February, but they conduct them primarily in July, August, and September. Field preparation usually begins by turning over the earth with an ox-drawn plow to loosen the soil and pull up plants (Fig. 8.7). Today, it is also common to hire a tractor, particularly for fallowed fields that have a thick mat of grasses and bushes.

After the plow passes, people follow along breaking up dirt clods with wooden sticks and metal picks or shovels. The dirt clods often form around plant roots, especially those of the introduced chixi grass (*Pennisetum clandestinum* Chiov.). In breaking up the dirt clod, they remove the dry plants and place them in a pile. After they finish removing the dried plants, they burn them. This not only removes the unwanted weedy plants, but creates ash that they till back into the soil as a type of fertilizer. Farmers usually plow the soil two or three times before planting. The farmers explain that this process is necessary for making the earth soft for planting, to expose nutrients that are beneath the surface, and also to kill insects and weeds.

Planting is the next task and is accomplished between the months of September and November, when rainfall is sporadic and light. People follow a fairly systematic order based on the crop, but also on the type of soil and location of the field. I will explain these last two variables in the following section. In general, farmers begin planting in September with the crops that take longest to mature. These include fava beans, quinoa, and maize. In October and November, they plant the tubers. To plant, a man or other strong individual directs the ox-drawn plow to make furrows, and women follow behind either placing the tuber seed in the furrow or broadcasting grains. The farmer draws the plow back through to cover the seeds.

From December to March, the plants grow watered by the summer rains. Along with the crops, wild plants flourish during this time and it is necessary to remove them from the fields. Usually farmers conduct a major weeding effort in January or February, when the non-crop plants are young and easy to remove (Fig. 8.8). With a small pick, farmers (usually the women) walk through the rows of growing crops and manually pick and pull up the weedy species. Occasionally they use the plow to loosen the weeds and improve the drainage furrows. They also attend to the tubers at this time, mounding up the dirt around the plant. They state that this helps the tubers grow. After this weeding, people usually do not enter the fields again until harvest time.

The harvest starts as early as January for some crops, but mostly occurs between March and April. Farmers usually harvest the tubers first, as they allow many of grain crops to dry in the field. Row by row, they use small metal picks to dig up the tubers. They harvest the grains either by pulling up the whole plant (quinoa) or cutting the base with a sickle. They make piles of the harvested crops and spend the dry months, June through August, processing them to eat or to store. As this occurs, the time for preparing the field approaches again and a new agricultural cycle begins.

This description provides a general view of how seasonal rainfall shapes the timing of the agricultural cycle. The farmers plan each step in the process so that the seed is planted before the rains come and that they mature before the rains leave. Obviously, insufficient rain will leave the plants without the water they need to grow, so a season with little rainfall could ruin a crop. Conversely, abundant rainfall is especially damaging to tuber crops that will rot or not mature if there is too much water.

There have been studies in the Andes that found farmers have methods to predict wetter versus drier years. As mentioned above, drought years often correlated with El Niño events. Based on his own observations and review of the Andean ethnographic literature, Benjamin Orlove found that several central Andean communities observe the brightness and position of the Pleiades in June to predict these dry spells (Orlove, Chiang, and Cane 2000:68, 2002). If the farmers find the stars of the Pleiades to be dim and/or fewer in number, they predict that it will be a dry year and set tuber planting back several weeks. According to studies completed by two

8.7 Planting on the Taraco Peninsula with ox-drawn plow.

8.8 Weeding a fava bean field.

climatologists, John Chiang and Mark Cane, a warm phase ENSO causes greater high cloud cover. These clouds are barely visible to the naked eye, but would be enough to dim the Pleiades stars (Orlove, Chiang, and Cane 2000:69, 2002:432).

During my study, I did not meet anyone on the Taraco Penisula who made such observations and predictions. It is possible that this practice exists since several of the examples Orlove et al. (2000:68) cite are in the Titicaca basin. Even if they did not use the Pleiades to predict the timing of the summer rainfall, I found that farmers paid close attention to general weather patterns and would set back planting of particular crops until enough rain was available. I did observe people rushing out to buy the yearly Farmer's Almanac, available for only one Boliviano (about 0.14 USD) in the town market and on the streets of El Alto. They read the small booklet for predictions about the year's weather patterns. I did not find, however, that this directly impacted their decisions about when to plant. Through my interviews and observations, however, I learned that farmers take additional steps to account for the potential variation in rainfall by utilizing different types of soils present on the landscape. This is the focus of my discussion here.

SOILS OF THE TARACO PENINSULA

Based on a geological map of the peninsula (IGM 1994), the Taraco peninsula consists of a range of different soils types (Fig. 8.9). A rocky Pliocene conglomerate called the Taraco Formation (Ttc) forms the peninsula's mountain range. The shores, plains, and gentle slopes of the peninsula contain gravel, sand, silt, and clay created by deep Pleistocene lakes and modern erosional processes (Qfl & Qcf). Colluvial deposits (Qc) of boulders and gravel occur in small pockets in hilltop valleys. Finally, alluvial deposits (Qa) of pebbles, gravel, sand, silt, and clay form where rivers have dissected the landscape. Thus, from a geological perspective, there is a range of soil types on the peninsula from deep silty clay deposits near the shore to very rocky (cobbles) deposits in the hills.

The residents of the Taraco peninsula also recognize these distinct geological deposits. In the interviews, they described four common soil types on the peninsula: *laq'a*, *k'ink'u*, *ch'alla*, and *q'ala laq'a/ch'ata*. Harry Tschopik (1963:513) and Luperio Onofre Mamani (1997) recorded similar

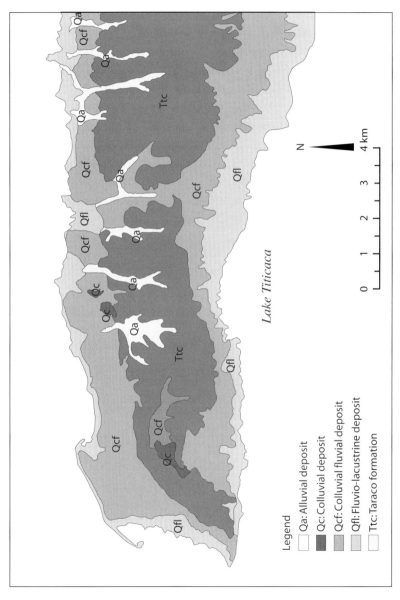

8.9 Geological map of the Taraco Peninsula. (Based on IGM map 1994)

soil categories in other areas of the lake basin. Below I present each soil category provided by the Taraco farmers, along with the descriptions of their characteristics, distribution, and productive potential (Table 8.3).

The most desirable soil is *laq'a* in Aymara or *tierra* in Spanish. This can be directly translated as earth or the lay term soil in English. This tends to be silty clay that is moist and loose. These soils are distributed near the lakeshores but also in some patches on the hillsides. They are easy to till and rich in organics, thus preferred by most of the farmers. *K'ink'u* is clay. It is bright red or yellow in color and is also found near the lakeshores and eroding out of ravines. I received a mixture of responses regarding its cultivation potential. It is cultivated, but as clay, it can become very hard in dry conditions but very slick in wet conditions. Thus, it is only cultivatable with a moderate quantity of rainfall. *Ch'alla* is sandy soil and usually found on the hill slopes. While some complained about the high quantity of stones that can be found in this soil, many described it as relatively easy to till and as productive. It is especially good for tubers because it drains well. Finally, *q'ala laq'a*, also called *ch'ata*, is a rocky soil. It is found mostly on the eroded hilltops but can also grade into the *ch'alla* on the hillslopes. This is the least desirable area for agricultural production because the loose soil component is thin and the abundant stones make it difficult to till.

Table 8.3. Soil Terms, Distribution, and Qualities Based on Interviews with Taraco Farmers

AYMARA	SPANISH	ENGLISH	LOCATION	POSITIVE QUALITIES	NEGATIVE QUALITIES
Laq'a	Tierra	Earth, soil	Milli/Slopes	Moist, easy to till	Poor with heavy rains
Chi'ara Laq'a	Tierra negra	Black soil	Milli	Moist, easy to till, fertile	Poor with heavy rains
K'ink'u	Arcilla	Clay	Patchy	Can be moist	Too hard or too soft
Ch'alla	Arena	Sand	Slopes	Well-drained, fertile	Poor in drought
Q'ala Laq'a/ Ch'ata	Tierra pedregosa	Rocky	Hilltop	Well-drained	Difficult to till, uncultivatable in drought

Altitudinal Distribution of Soils and Timing of Planting

While some of these soils types, such as the clays, are patchy across the landscape, the descriptions show that there is a general vertical distribution from the lakeshore to the hilltop: the laq'a and k'ink'u are most common along the lakeshore, ch'alla and laq'a on the slopes, and q'ala laq'a/ch'ata on the hilltops. The agricultural cycle interviews revealed that farmers usually begin planting the soils along the shoreline first and make their way upslope. The logic of this order is based on timing of the rains, water retention qualities of the soils, and seasonal fluctuations of the lake level.

The farmers told me that the first soils to be planted, usually in August, are those near the lakeshore. The farmers call this land *milli*, which according to the *Diccionario Practico Aymara-Castellano Castellano-Aymara* (De Lucca D. 1987:112) literally means "first potato." The milli is the swath of land along the shore that is inundated by the lake during its high stand between the months of April and July. The lake begins to fall in July and eventually exposes tracts of land that are moist and fertile. These conditions permit planting before the rains begin in October. I was told that any crop could be planted in the milli, but the most common crops were potatoes, fava beans, and grains.

It is necessary to plant the milli early for the crop must be ready to harvest before the lake rises again in late February or March. This zone is particularly important in years with little rainfall, as the soil moisture is often sufficient to produce a crop. According to Vacher et al. (1992:516), these moist lakeshore soils do continue to be productive during droughts. The crop can be in peril, however, in very wet years, as the plants may not mature before the water rises (Buechler 1969:181).

The soils of the milli are thick and can support dense vegetation such as grasses and sedges. Near the shoreline, the rising lake clears this vegetation making the area easy to cultivate. In areas where there is little slope directly above the shoreline, the dense vegetation and thick soils are difficult to manipulate without a tractor. These areas are often left uncultivated and instead used for pasture.

The second fields to be planted are those on the slopes above the milli. While I commonly heard this area referred to as pampa (plain) or *laderas* (slopes), it did not have a specific designator such as milli. This is the largest area of cultivation and has a variety of soil types. The most common type, however, is ch'alla. These soils are not moistened by lake or groundwater;

therefore, farmers wait for the early rains in October and November to plant here. In a year of average rainfall, these fields will yield an excellent crop. These sandy soils drain well so even with abundant rainfall the crops here will succeed. Unfortunately, in a very dry year, the crops here will have difficulty.

The final fields to be cultivated are in the *q'ullu* or hilltops. Many published maps, such as the IGM 1:50,000 map (IGM 1991), indicate that these areas are not cultivated, but this is not the case currently. Several farmers I interviewed had fields in these areas. People with access to these areas cultivate them if the weather conditions permit. Rocky and thin soils, q'ala laq'a or ch'ata, occur here and require plentiful rain to successfully produce. For this reason, they are the last to be planted, in December or January, when there appears to be sufficient rain. In dry years, they may not be planted at all. These areas, however, will be successful in the very wet years.

I found that most farmers had landholdings in all of the soil types. Some seem to have obtained long swaths of land during the agricultural reform, but some gain access to different soils through familial connections. Additionally, many families share plots with friends and neighbors. If people outside of the immediate family help prepare and plant a field, they are often given a few furrows to plant their own seed (Carter and Mamani 1982:136). Through these informal exchanges, people get access to types of soils they may not own themselves. The politics of landholding certainly shapes the modern mosaic of land use on the Taraco Peninsula, and likely did so in the past. Access to different soil types, however, may have always been important to Taraco farmers and the manner in which this was regulated likely changed with shifts in population densities and political organization.

Crops and Soil Types

In some regions of the Andes, particular crops are associated with particular ecological zones (Brush 1977; Goland 1991; Hastorf 1993; Mayer 1979; Orlove 1977). For example, within the Mantaro Valley of Peru, farmers have fields in low elevation, warm valleys exclusively for maize, as well as fields in high elevation, cold hilltops exclusively for potatoes (Mayer 1979:12–13). This is not the case on the Taraco Peninsula. According to my interviews, people follow the crop rotation across the entire landscape. Of course, certain crops do better in certain soils; for example, the fava beans

I saw growing on the hilltop were quite short, while those growing in the milli were lush and tall.

The only potential crop-soil correlation I encountered was for the small, uncommon tuber, ullucu. Many people mentioned that it grows best in the rocky soils on the hilltops. One might also expect to find a particular distribution for maize, as it is susceptible to frosts and low temperatures in general. While people did not correlate maize with any particular soil type, they plant it in protected areas such as small valleys or hillsides. It is almost never planted in the open plain for these areas experience strong frosts.

The ability to plant all crops across various soils and elevations on the Taraco Peninsula is likely due to the relatively low relief of the peninsula and the moderate climatic conditions of the lake region. In other Andean regions, such as the Mantaro Valley, steep topography presents distinct climatic zones (warm valley bottoms versus cold mountain tops) within a day's walk. Although there are altitudinal differences in soils on the peninsula, they only vary by a few hundred meters in elevation compared to thousands of meters in the central and coastal Andean valleys.

The elevation of the Taraco Peninsula (3800–4000 m) actually falls within the range of what is considered to be the cool, potato-growing regions of the Andes (Pulgar Vidal 1972; Troll 1968). As mentioned earlier, however, the thermal effects of the lake create moderate conditions similar to the lower Andean valleys where maize can be grown. Thus, the Taraco Peninsula is unique for the Andes in that a wide range of crops can be planted in a single area.

A MODEL FOR UNDERSTANDING RESPONSES TO LARGE MAGNITUDE CHANGES IN RAINFALL

This case study demonstrates how generations of farmers working on a particular landscape with particular risks develop knowledge and practices that enable them to minimize possible losses and shift their strategies if necessary. The practices detailed above show how Taraco farmers reduce the risk of crop failure due to unpredictable rainfall by taking advantage of soil diversity in their landscape. Each year, they plant a range of crops across each soil type. In addition to assuring that at least a few of their crops are successful, the recognition of how different soils behave in different conditions prepares people to shift practices if one type of rainfall pattern (drought or flooding) begins to persist. I suggest that this ethnographic documentation of how farmers have adapted to short-term climatic fluctuations can provide insight into how farmers might respond to persistent periods of drought or flooding. Below, I present a hypothetical model of land use under longer-term dry and wet conditions. This could be used to predict how populations might react in the future to such conditions, but also serves as a model to be tested with archaeological data for understanding past responses to the documented climatic shifts mentioned at the beginning of the chapter (Table 8.1).

The lakeshore is much like a riverine floodplain, with the waters rising and falling on a seasonal basis creating moist, loose soils. Under persistent dry conditions or a long-term drought the lake level would drop (see Fig. 9.2 in Moore, this volume) and the population could follow the diminishing lake shore to take advantage of the remaining moist, cleared soils. In modern times, there are stories of farmers moving onto exposed lakebed after severe droughts in the 1860s and 1940s (Erickson 1999:637). The lands left behind by the lake would eventually become dry, grassy, and difficult to till. This area may lose its agricultural significance and become more important for pasture, as the flat pampas are used on the peninsula today.

During dry years, the slopes of the Taraco peninsula may continue to be cultivatable, as long as there is some yearly rainfall. Archaeologically, we know that there continued to be rather dense populations in this area even during documented dry periods (Bandy 2001:101; 2006:229). This suggests the slopes soils are still cultivatable during droughts. The hilltops, however, would probably become uncultivatable.

Under wetter conditions, the tendency of land use would reverse from that practiced under drier condtions. When the rains increase the lake will fill again. Any lands that were in the lakebed would be lost and the higher areas would become more important. With the loss of potential agricultural lands in the lake bottom, the hilltop may provide needed terrain. Additionally, the well-drained soils of the slopes and hilltops would be more productive in seasons with greater precipitation than the clay-rich, flood-prone soils in the lower elevations.

In the past, the use of raised fields may have also been a solution to recovering lands lost to higher lake levels. Archaeologists have documented approximately 82,000 km^2 of ancient raised fields throughout the Lake Titicaca basin (Smith, Denevan, and Hamilton 1968:355). While most of them appear to date to the Tiwanaku period (Janusek and Kolata 2004; Kolata and Ortloff 1996; Stanish 1994), there is evidence that they first appeared in the Formative period (Erickson 1988; Stanish 1994). Although the focus of raised field research has been on their potentially superior productive capabilities (Erickson 1996; Kolata 1991), they also provide an important technology for making the inundated lakeshore productive.

This hypothetical model is a very general scheme that only accounts for climate and land use. In order to determine the actual dynamics of a response to large magnitude climate changes, we would also have to take into account other economic activities such as herding and fishing as well as the social and political entities that regulate access to land and the coordination of agricultural activities. As several of the chapters in this volume point out, the ability to successfully respond to climate change may have more to due with social and political responses than economic decisions or adaptations. My goal in presenting this land-use model based on ethnographic data is to provide researchers a baseline with which to add more data sets. More complex models of behavior could be used for future planning in the face of climate change, but also to better understand responses to past climate change.

CONCLUSIONS

In this paper, I have discussed how farmers on the Taraco Peninsula, Bolivia, have used soil diversity on the landscape to deal with the risk of variable rainfall. Farmers plan the yearly planting schedule around the timing of summer rains and distribute their fields across different soil types with distinct water retention/drainage properties. Dispersal of fields in all soil types and a staggered planting schedule ensure farmers of at least a few successful crops regardless of abundant or scarce rainfall. This case demonstrates how farmers, confronted with annual climatic uncertainty, develop regular practices that account for these irregularities. In fact, such practices may prepare them to successfully respond to longer-term shifts in rainfall patterns thus reducing the possibility of catastrophic failure of the farming system. This type of flexible land use and inclusion of other complementary economic activities such as herding and fishing may explain why the Taraco Peninsula, and the greater Titicaca basin, has successfully sustained farmers for over 2,000 years.

Acknowledgments

I am very grateful to the people of the four communities—Chiripa, Coa Collu, San José, and Santa Rosa—that participated in my project and kindly shared their knowledge of farming the Taraco Peninsula. Permission to conduct the ethnobotanical research was granted by the Herbario Nacional de Bolivia and the Dirección General de Biodiversidad. IIE Fulbright, the Wenner-Gren Foundation (Small Grant #7073), and the National Science Foundation (Dissertation Improvement Grant #0321720) provided funds for this research. I wish to thank Eduardo Machicado for his help with the data collection and creation of the maps presented here. He also provided useful advice in the revision process. I thank the organizers of the Forces of Nature conference for inviting me to contribute and thank the other participants for their useful feedback. I am especially grateful to Katherine Moore for her feedback in revisions of this paper, as well as her close collaboration over the years.

NOTE

1. It is worth mentioning that it seems fava beans have nearly replaced quinoa as a major crop on the peninsula. Based on studies of rotations in other parts of the altiplano, quinoa usually was the third year crop. I only met a few families who dedicated entire fields to quinoa and if they had, the next year they would not plant it again. From my questioning, I gathered that quinoa is not as important a food anymore. Instead people eat more fava beans, rice, pasta, and bread. Also, fava beans are a cash crop that is sold to vendors in the La Paz and the Peruvian cities across the lake. Thus, for a variety of reasons, quinoa and its relatives are no longer an important part of the Taraco landscape, although it was prehistorically (Bruno and Whitehead 2003; Wright, Hastorf, and Lennstrom 2003:387).

REFERENCES CITED

Abbott, M., M. Binford, M. Brenner, and K. Kelts. 1997. A 3500 14C Yr High-resolution Record of Water-level Changes in Lake Titicaca, Bolivia/Peru. *Quaternary Research* 47:169–80.

Albarracín-Jordan, J., and J. Mathews. 1990. *Asentamientos prehispánicos del Valle de Tiwanaku*. La Paz: Producciones CIMA.

Baker, P. A., Geoffrey O. Seltzer, Sherilyn C. Fritz, Robert B. Dunbar, Matthew J. Grove, Pedro M. Tapia, Scott L. Cross, Harold D. Rowe, and J. P. Broda. 2001. The History of South American Tropical Precipitation for the Past 25,000 Years. *Science* 291:640–43.

Bandy, M. S. 2001. Population and History in the Ancient Titicaca Basin. PhD diss., Univ. of California, Berkeley.

—— 2006. Early Village Society in the Formative Period in the Southern Lake Titicaca Basin. In *Andean Archaeology III: North and South*, ed. W. Isbell and H. Silverman, pp. 210–36. New York: Springer Science & Business Media.

Benton, J. 1999. *Agrarian Reform in Theory and Practice: A Study of the Lake Titicaca Region of Bolivia*. Brookfield, VT: Ashgate.

Binford, M. W., A. L. Kolata, M. Brenner, J. W. Janusek, M. T. Seddon, M. Abbott, and J. H. Curtis. 1997. Climate Variation and the Rise and Fall of an Andean Civilization. *Quaternary Research* 47:235–48.

Binford, M. W., Mark Brenner, and B. W. Leyden. 1996. Paleoecology and Tiwanaku Agroecosystems. In *Tiwanaku and Its Hinterland: Archaeology and Paleoecology of an Andean Civilization*. Vol. 1, *Agroecology*, ed. A. L. Kolata, pp. 89–108. Washington, DC: Smithsonian Institution Press.

Boulange, B., and J. E. Aquize. 1981. La sédimentation actuelle dans le lac Titicaca et de son bassin versant. *Revue Hydrobiologie Tropical* 14:269–87.

Bruno, M. C. 2006. A Morphological Approach to Documenting the Domestication of *Chenopodium* in the Andes. In *Documenting Domestication: New Genetic and Archaeological Paradigms*, ed. Melinda A. Zeder, D. G. Bradley, Eve Emshwiller, and Bruce D. Smith, pp. 32–45. Berkeley: University of California Press.

—— 2008. Waranq Waranqa: Ethnobotanical Perspectives on Agricultural Intensification in the Lake Titicaca Basin. PhD dissertation, Washington Univ., St. Louis.

Bruno, M. C., and W. T. Whitehead. 2003. *Chenopodium* Cultivation and Formative Period Agriculture at Chiripa, Bolivia. *Latin American Antiquity* 14:339–55.

Brush, S. B. 1977. *Mountain, Field, and Family: The Economy and Human Ecology of an Andean Valley*. Philadelphia: University of Pennsylvania Press.

Buechler, H. C. 1969. Land Tenure and Use. In *Land Reform and Social Revolution in Bolivia*, ed. D. B. Heath, Charles J. Erasmus, and H. C. Buechler, pp. 176–99. Praeger Special Studies in International Economics and Development. New York: Frederick A. Praeger.

Calaway, M. J. 2005. Ice-cores, Sediments, and Civilisation Collapse: A Cautionary Tale from Lake Titicaca. *Antiquity* 79:778–90.

Capriles Flores, J., A. I. Domic, and K. M. Moore. 2007. Fish Remains from the Formative Period (1000 BC–AD 400) of Lake Titicaca, Bolivia: Zooarchaeology and Taphonomy. *Quaternary International* 180:115–26.

Carter, W., and M. Mamani. 1982. *Irpa Chico: individuo y comunidad en la cultura Aymara*. La Paz: Libreria Editorial Juventud.

Cross, Scott L., Paul A. Baker, Geoffrey O. Seltzer, Sherilyn C. Fritz, and Robert B. Dunbar. 2000. A New Estimate of the Holocene Lowstand Level of Lake Titicaca, Central Andes, and Implications for Tropical Palaeohydrology. *The Holocene* 10:21–32.

—— 2001. Late Quaternary Climate and Hydrology of Tropical South America

Inferred from an Isotopic and Chemical Model of Lake Titicaca, Bolivia and Peru. *Quaternary Research* 56:1–9.

De Lucca D., M. 1987. *Diccionario practico: Aymara-Castellano Castellano-Aymara.* La Paz: Editorial Los Amigos del Libro.

Erickson, C. L. 1988. Raised Field Agriculture in the Lake Titicaca Basin. *Expedition* 30(3): 8–16.

—— 1996. Investigación arqueológica del sistema agricola de los camellones en la cuenca del Lago Titicaca del Perú. La Paz: PIWA and El Centro de Información para el Desarrollo.

—— 1999. Neo-environmental Determinism and Agrarian "Collapse" in Andean Prehistory. *Antiquity* 73:634–42.

Garreaud, R., Mathias Vuille, and A. C. Clement. 2003. The Climate of the Altiplano: Observed Current Conditions and Mechanisms of Past Changes. *Palaeogeography, Palaeoclimatology, Palaeoecology* 194:5–22.

Goland, C. 1991. *Cultivating Diversity: Field Scattering as Agricultural Risk Management in Cuyo Cuyo, Department of Puno, Peru.* Production, Storage, and Exchange in a Terraced Environment on the Eastern Andean Escarpment, Vols. 1 and 2. Chapel Hill: University of North Carolina.

Guillet, D. 1987. Terracing and Irrigation in the Peruvian Highlands. *Current Anthropology* 28:409–30.

Hastorf, C. A. 1993. *Agriculture and the Onset of Political Inequality before the Inka.* Cambridge: Cambridge University Press.

IGM. 1991. Taraco. In Series H731, Sheet 5844 IV. 2-IGM ed. Instituto Geográfico Militar, La Paz, Bolivia.

—— 1994. Carta geológica de Bolivia, Hoja Tiahuanacu. Instituto Geografico Militar, La Paz, Bolivia.

Janusek, J. W. 2004. Tiwanaku and Its Precursors: Recent Research and Emerging Perspectives. *Journal of Archaeological Research* 12:121–83.

Janusek, J. W., and A. L. Kolata. 2004. Top-down or Bottom-up: Rural Settlement and Raised Field Agriculture in the Lake Titicaca Basin, Bolivia. *Journal of Anthropological Archaeology* 23:404–30.

Klein, H. S. 2003. *A Concise History of Bolivia.* Cambridge: Cambridge University Press.

Kolata, A. L. 1991. The Technology and Organization of Agricultural Production in the Tiwanaku State. *Latin American Antiquity* 2:99–125.

Kolata, A. L., and C. Ortloff. 1996. Tiwanaku Raised-Field Agriculture in the Lake Titicaca Basin of Bolivia. In *Tiwanaku and Its Hinterland: Archaeology, and Paleoecology of an Andean Civilization.* Vol. 1, *Agroecology,* ed. A. Kolata, pp. 109–52. Washington, DC: Smithsonian Institution Press.

Lémuz-Aguirre, C. 2001. Patrones de asentamiento arqueológico en la Península de Santiago de Huatta, Bolivia. Tesis de Licenciatura, Universidad Mayor de San Andrés, La Paz.

Lenters, J. D., and K. H. Cook. 1997. On the Origin of the Bolivia High and

Related Circulation Features of the South America Climate. *Journal of the Atmospheric Sciences* 54:656–77.

—— 1999. Summertime Precipitation Variability over South America: Role of the Large-Scale Circulation. *Monthly Weather Review* 127:409–31.

Mayer, E. 1979. *Land Use in the Andes: Ecology and Agriculture in the Mantaro Valley of Peru with Special Reference to Potatoes*. Lima: International Potato Center (CIP).

Montes de Oca, I. 1995. Geografía y clima de Bolivia. *Bulletin de l'Institut Français d'Études Andines* 24:357–68.

Mourguiart, P., Thierry Corrège, Denis Wirrmann, Jaime Argollo, M. E. Montenegro, M. Pourchet, and P. Carbonel. 1998. Holocene Palaeohydrology of Lake Titicaca Estimated from an Ostracod-based Transfer Function. *Palaeogeography, Palaeoclimatology, Palaeoecology* 143:51–72.

Netherly, P. 1984. Management of Late Andean Irrigation Systems on the North Coast of Peru. *American Antiquity* 49:227–54.

Onofre Mamani, L. 1997. Contemporary Aymara Agricultural Soil Categories. In *Archaeological Survey in the Juli-Desaguadero Region of Lake Titicaca Basin, Southern Peru*, ed. C. Stanish, pp. 125–27. Fieldiana. Anthropology, n.s., no. 29. Chicago: Field Museum of Natural History.

Orlove, B. 1977. Integration through Production: Use of Zonation in Espinar. *American Ethnologist* 4:84–101.

Orlove, B. S., J. C. H. Chiang, and M. A. Cane. 2000. Forecasting Andean Rainfall and Crop Yield from the Influence of El Niño on Pleiades Visibility. *Nature* 403:68–71.

—— 2002. Ethnoclimatology in the Andes. *American Scientist* 90:428–35.

Orlove, B., and R. Godoy. 1986. Sectoral Fallowing Systems in the Central Andes. *Journal of Ethnobiology* 6:169–204.

PROSUKO. 1996. Evaluacion de parametros microclimaticos e hidricos en el sistema suka kollus: comportamiento de la precipitacion y temperatura en zonas sukakolleras de Peru y Bolivia. PROSUKO.

Pulgar Vidal, J. 1972. *Ocho regiones naturales del Perú*. Lima: Editorial Universo.

Rigsby, C. A., Paul A. Baker, and M. S. Aldenderfer. 2003. Fluvial History of the Rio Ilave Valley, Peru, and Its Relationship to Climate and Human History. *Palaeogeography, Palaeoclimatology, Palaeoecology* 194:165–85.

Roche, M., J. Bourges, J. Cortes, and R. Mattos. 1992. Climatology and Hydrology of the Lake Titicaca Basin. In *Lake Titicaca: A Synthesis of Limnological Knowledge*, ed. C. Dejoux and A. Iltis, pp. 63–83. Dordrecht: Kluwer.

Ronchail, J. 1995. Variabilidad interanual de la precipitaciones en Bolivia. *Bulletin de l'Institut Français d'Études Andines* 24:369–78.

Rowe, H. D., Robert B. Dunbar, David A. Mucciarone, Geoffrey O. Seltzer, Paul A. Baker, and S. C. Fritz. 2002. Insolation, Moisure Balance, and Climate Change on the South American Altiplano since the Last Glacial Maximum. *Climate Change* 52:175–99.

Seltzer, G. O., P. A. Baker, S. L. Cross, R. B. Dunbar, and S. C. Fritz. 1998. High-resolution Seismic Reflection Profiles from Lake Titicaca, Peru-Bolivia; Evidence for Holocene Aridity in the Tropical Andes. *Geology* 26:167–70.

Smith, C. T., William M. Denevan, and P. Hamilton. 1968. Ancient Ridged Fields in the Region of Lake Titicaca. *Geographical Journal* 134:353–66.

Stanish, C. 1994. The Hydraulic Hypothesis Revisited: Lake Titicaca Basin Raised Fields in Theoretical Perspective. *Latin American Antiquity* 5:312–32.

Stanish, C., Edmundo de la Vega, Lee Steadman, Cecilia Chávez J., Kirk L. Frye, Luperio Onofre M., Matthew Seddon, and P. Calisaya Chuquimia. 1997. *Archaeological Survey in the Juli-Desaguadero Region of Lake Titicaca Basin, Southern Peru.* Fieldiana: Anthropology, n.s., no. 29. Chicago: Field Museum of Natural History.

Tapia, P. M., S. C. Fritz, P. A. Baker, G. O. Seltzer, and R. B. Dunbar. 2003. A Late Quaternary Diatom Record of Tropical Climatic History from Lake Titicaca (Peru and Bolivia). *Palaeogeography, Palaeoclimatology, Palaeoecology* 194:139–64.

Troll, C. 1968. The Cordilleras of the Tropical Americas: Aspects of Climate, Phytogeographical and Agrarian Ecology. In *Geo-Ecology of the Mountainous Regions of the Tropical Americas*, ed. C. Troll, pp. 15–56. Colloquium Geographicum, Band 9. Bonn: Ferd. Dümmlers Verlag.

Tschopik, H. 1963. The Aymara. In *Handbook of South American Indians*, vol. 2, ed. J. H. Steward, pp. 501–73. Washington DC: Cooper Square Publishers.

Vacher, J., E. Brasier de Thuy, and M. Liberman. 1992. Influence of the Lake on Littoral Agriculture. In *Lake Titicaca: A Synthesis of Limnological Knowledge*, ed. C. Dejoux and A. Iltis, pp. 511–22. Dordrecht: Kluwer.

Vuille, M. 1999. Atmospheric Circulation over the Bolivian Altiplano during Dry and Wet Periods and Extreme Phases of the Southern Oscillation. *International Journal of Climatology* 19:1579–1600.

Vuille, M., R. S. Bradley, and F. Keimig. 2000. Interannual Climate Variability in the Central Andes and Its Relation to Tropical Pacific and Atlantic Forcing. *Journal of Geophysical Research* 105(D10): 12447–460.

Whitehead, W. T. 2007. Exploring the Wild and Domestic: Paleoethnobotany at Chiripa, a Formative Site in Bolivia. PhD diss., Univ. of California, Berkeley.

Williams, P. R. 2006. Agricultural Innovation, Intensification, and Sociopolitical Development: The Case of Highland Irrigation Agriculture on the Pacific Andean Watersheds. In *Agricultural Strategies*, ed. J. Marcus and C. Stanish, pp. 309–33. Los Angeles: Cotsen Institute of Archaeology, UCLA.

Winterhalder, B., R. Larsen, and R. B. Thomas. 1974. Dung as an Essential Resource in a Highland Peruvian Community. *Human Ecology* 2:89–104.

Wirrmann, D. 1992. Morphology and Bathymetry. In *Lake Titicaca: A Synthesis of Limnological Knowledge*, ed. C. Dejoux and A. Iltis, pp. 16–22. Dordrecht: Kluwer.

Wirrmann, D., and P. Mourguiart. 1995. Late Quaternary Spatio-temporal

Limnological Variation in the Altiplano of Peru and Bolivia. *Quaternary Research* 43:344–54.

Wirrmann, D., and L. Oliverira-Almeida. 1987. Low Holocene Level (7700–3650 Years Ago) of Lake Titicaca (Bolivia). *Paleogeography, Paleoclimatology, and Paleoecology* 59:315–23.

Wright, M. F., C. A. Hastorf, and H. A. Lennstrom. 2003. Pre-Hispanic Agriculture and Plant Use at Tiwanaku: Social and Political Implications. In *Tiwanaku and Its Hinterland: Archaeological and Paleoecological Investigations of an Andean Civilization*. Vol. 2, *Urban and Rural Archaeology*, ed. A. L. Kolata, pp. 384–403. Washington, DC: Smithsonian Institution Press.

Wylie, A. 2002. *Thinking from Things: Essays in the Philosophy of Archaeology*. Berkeley: University of California Press.

9

Grace Under Pressure:
Responses to Changing Environments
by Herders and Fishers in the Formative
Lake Titicaca Basin, Bolivia

KATHERINE M. MOORE

This chapter describes long-term adaptation to dramatically fluctuating landscapes in the basin of Lake Titicaca, Bolivia. Fine-grained zooarchaeological analysis is used to track shifting reliance on a key, but risky, resource: fish. From the first known occupation of the region, around 1500 BC, lacustrine resources including fish, birds, and lake-edge plants were important to residents. Yet the combined effects of the topography, climate, and vegetation around this high altitude lake produce noticeable changes in the position of the shoreline over just a few years. Continuous occupation over lengthy periods during which the lake virtually dried up show the deep-seated resiliency of this social and economic system. Despite the risks, specialized fishing settlements persisted while the landscape transformed around them. During these periods, fishing did decline in importance compared to herding, hunting, and agriculture, but the technical skills and ecological expertise of fishers were transmitted and maintained over hundreds of years. When lake levels rose, fishing again became an important economic activity, and some deposits of this period show evidence of even more intensive fishing than had been the case 800 years before.

This case example is set in the "medium" time scales discussed in this volume (1500–200 BC; Table 9.1). It offers a glimpse of an intensive and specialized economy that periodically undergoes extreme environmental stress. Although it is often difficult to use archaeological data to precisely estimate changes in the economic importance of a resource over time, the archaeobiological remains allow us to see the constellation of resources shift on a broader, presence-absence basis. Thus, archaeologists can "see" the resource disappear from a site's deposits, or "see" a site's occupants disappear from the landscape after abandonment. Here, we see the resource, fish, sag in importance and then recover, using both dietary remains and evidence of craft production linked to those dietary remains. The fact that the residents did return to fishing should not minimize our impression of the costs of this response. By analogy, we know that the integration of fishing with other economic activities is carefully managed, and involves rights to fishing grounds as well as availability of labor and the material culture of fishing. The marked nature of the decline of fishing also directs our attention to the less archaeologically visible stresses that would have impinged on crop production, control of grazing land, and animal husbandry.

Table 9.1. Taraco Peninsula Chronological Scheme and Components of Four Sites Included in this Study (Bandy and Hastorf 2007)

TITICACA BASIN PERIODS	CERAMIC PHASES	CALENDAR YEAR	CHIRIPA	KALA UYUNI	SONAJI	KUMI KIPA
Late Intermediate	Early Pacajes	AD 1100–1450	x*		x*	
Middle Horizon	Tiwanaku IV/V	AD 500–1100	x	x	x	x
Late Formative	Tiwanaku III	AD 300–500		x	x	x
	Tiwanaku I	200 BC–AD 300		x	x	x
Middle Formative	Late Chiripa	800–200 BC	x**	x		
Early Formative	Middle Chiripa	1000–800 BC	x	x		
	Early Chiripa	1500–1000 BC	x	x		

*Material from this period not included in this discussion
** Includes the "Latest Late Chiripa" levels examined separately in some of the datasets

The southern basin of Lake Titicaca in the Central Andes has produced a long record of adaptation to a dynamic environment. Very early complex societies are found in this relatively well-studied region. The best known of these centers is the massive ceremonial complex at Tiwanaku. The Formative period Chiripa culture (1800 BC to AD 500), forerunner of the Tiwanaku civilization, arose along the shores of Lake Titicaca (Stanish 2003). The archaeological site of Chiripa, and many Chiripa culture sites with related ceramics, architecture, and iconography, are located on the gentle slopes above the lake. The sites are particularly concentrated in the study area of the Taraco peninsula. The scale and internal organization of these sites around sunken, stone-lined courts has drawn attention to public activities including ceremonial consumption of food and drink (Bandy and Hastorf 2007; Hastorf 1999).

LAKE TITICACA SETTING

The sites discussed in this chapter are spaced near the present-day shores of the Taraco peninsula, a finger of low hills that now extends into the southern section of Lake Titicaca. (See Bruno, this volume, for a more comprehensive treatment of this area's climate and political and social history.) The lake basin is surrounded by mountains rising to 6000 m and is one of the broadest expanses of plateau in the Andes. This densely populated region depends today on subsistence agriculture, pastoral production, and fishing for household use and urban markets. Archaeobiological remains from both ceremonial and domestic spaces in these sites indicate early dependence on tubers, cereals, wild plant resources, fish, game, and the meat of domesticated camelids (Bruno and Whitehead 2003; Logan 2006; Moore, Steadman, and deFrance 1999). The constituents of the cropping and herding systems in this region deserve special attention as elements in the intensification of prehistoric economies. The traditional economies of the Andes are an archetype of tightly organized and interdependent systems of practice, strategies, and symbols across diverse local environments (Gade 1999; Winterhalder and Thomas 1974). Observations of current traditional practice have been a useful guide for understanding some aspects of the prehistoric adaptive system and its material correlates (Erickson 2000). Even so, ethnoarchaeological research shows that modern material culture has been transformed by introduced species and technologies, particularly at the fine-grained detail studied by archaeobiologists in flotation and micromorphology samples (Moore et al. 2007). Over the past 5,000 years, the Titicaca basin has fluctuated between its Holocene maximum (close to its modern extent) and periods where the lake would have shrunk to a saline marsh with several shallow pools. One goal of archaeobiological research in the Lake Titicaca basin is to evaluate the role of climatic change on local subsistence adaptation, and by extension, its role in local and regional political and ideological organization.

Lake Titicaca is one of a series of lakes situated between the eastern and western cordilleras of the Central Andes in South America, all relics of much larger Pleistocene lakes (Fig. 9.1). The larger, northern part of the lake reaches a maximum depth of 200 m, but the smaller and much shallower part to the south has a maximum depth of 37 m and is only 5–20 m deep over most of its extent. It is this portion of Lake Titicaca that surrounds the Taraco peninsula and is the focus of this chapter. The drainage of the southern lake separates from that of the northern part when lake levels drop to the sill, 30 m below current levels. A small volume of Lake Titicaca water flows south via the Rio Desaguadero, first to Lake Poopo, shallow and much more saline than Lake Titicaca, and then to the Salar Uyuni, today the world's largest salt flat. Studies of shoreline features, seismic data, and lakebed cores show that the levels of Lake Titicaca have fluctuated repeatedly since the lake filled in the early Holocene (Fig. 9.2) (Abbott et al. 1997; Abbott et al. 2003; Fritz et al. 2006). Yearly fluctuations during the 20th century are within ± 3 m of the modern mean level of 3810 masl. Fluctuations of even greater intensity occurred during periods of dense settlement, which would have seriously affected food procurement strategies.

A minor decline in lake levels (to 10 m below modern levels) took place between 1200 BC and 800 BC, apparently coinciding with most of the Middle Chiripa ceramic phase of the Early Formative. Persistent lower lake stands (as much as 17 m below levels observed today) prevailed between 300 and 100 BC (during the Middle Formative), between AD 100 and 400 (during the early Late Formative or Tiwanaku I period), and most recently during the period AD 1100–1500 (during the Pacajes phase) (Fig. 9.2) (Abbott et al. 1997; Baker et al. 2001). The climatic conditions that lead to the periodic rapid evaporation of Lake Titicaca may include reduced precipitation in the mountain ranges draining into the lake due to large-scale changes in sea surface temperatures, reduced local precipitation (Rigsby et al. 2005), or increased evaporation due to increased temperatures. The emerging consensus is that very long cycles in solar radiation drive rainfall variation across most of South America (Abbott et al. 2003; Baker et al. 2005). Abbott et al. (2003) suggest that the northern part of the lake may have experienced lake level declines of up to 100 m. There, the first stages of lake level decline would look like one of the ordinary small-scale fluctuations to people living around the lake. In the southern lake, the area covered by water fluctuates

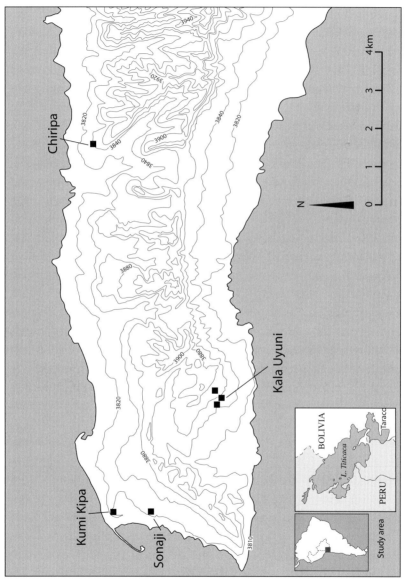

9.1 Taraco Peninsula in the Lake Titicaca setting.

broadly with relatively small changes in level, because there is a smaller inflow, and so it responds more quickly to precipitation changes once it has been cut off from the northern part. In contrast to the north, the first 10 to 15 m of decline in lake level would produce dramatic changes in the shoreline of the southern lake, leaving lakeside settlements several kilometers from open water. Once the area around the peninsula had been drained, subsequent lake level declines would have produced fewer changes in the topography, though the water table would have been lower. More persistent dry periods gradually would have stretched familiar strategies for adjusting to shoreline vegetation and soil moisture to the limit. The prehistoric subsistence practices of the southern basin are likely to have been strongly affected by these changes.

AQUATIC RESOURCES

With the lake at its current depth, extensive reed beds (*totorales*) are a prominent feature of the shoreline at the eastern end of the Taraco peninsula. Traditional fishermen use reed boats, and totora is commonly used for roofing, matting, containers, and fodder. The reeds provide nesting and feeding grounds for dense populations of migratory and resident birds. Coots, grebes, and ducks are common in the reed beds; there are also ibis, cormorants, gulls, geese, and tinamous in the low pampa above the reed beds (Kent, Webber, and Steadman 1999). Flamingos are seen in the shallow part of the lake today on an irregular basis, but are more common in the shallower and more saline Lake Poopo. Hunting is a minor activity along the lakeshore today, though ducks are eaten and many people collect eggs. Parsons (2006:227) notes that strikingly little use is made of the available aquatic invertebrates in communities along the Titicaca shoreline compared to many other regions where reedy marshes are exploited.

The fish in Lake Titicaca are too small to take a hook and are generally taken in nets and traps. Scoop nets can be used in the shallow areas, but most fish in the Taraco region today are taken in seine and gillnets set by boat. The waters of the lake also harbor two groups of native fish: more than ten species of killifish (*carachi*) of the genus *Orestias* and a small catfish (*mauri*) of the genus *Trichomycterus*. Different species feed along the lakeshore and school in the open water in the middle of the lake. Most extended households farming along the Taraco peninsulas own fishing gear and are

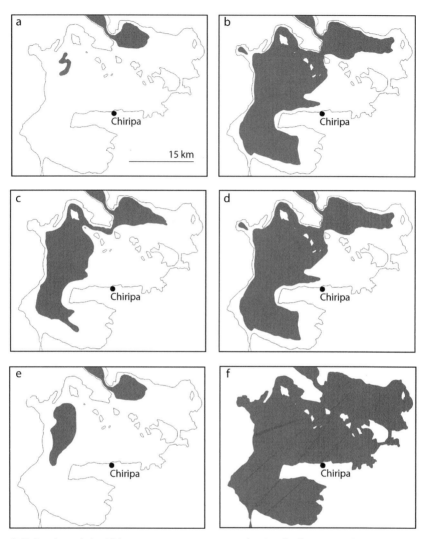

9.2 Southern Lake Titicaca extent reconstructed using bathymetric data and lake core data in Abbot and Seltzer (2003) and Cross et al. (2000). (a) Extent of lake before occupation of Chiripa, ca. 2500 BC: 20 m below 20th-century levels; (b) extent of lake during Early Chiripa phase: 5 m below 20th-century levels; (c) extent of lake during Middle Chiripa phase: 11–14 m below 20th-century levels; (d) extent of lake during early part of Late Chiripa phase, ca. 800 BC: 5 m below 20th-century levels; (e) extent of lake during later part of Late Chiripa phase, ca. 200 BC: 15–18 m below 20th-century levels; (f) modern lake level.

involved in fishing a part of the lake over which they have inherited rights (Orlove 2002). Fishermen know each other's boats, gear, and traditional fishing areas and carefully monitor activity on the lake, limiting the possibility that any one fisherman will be able to increase his haul at the expense of others. A rapid decline in water levels in the lake would disrupt social as well as economic practice.

Fishermen, despite social regulation on catches, have considerable flexibility in how much time and effort they invest in fishing. Fishing can be scheduled around agricultural tasks, pastoral busy times such as shearing and marking of young animals, trips, and school schedules. Fishing can be laid aside for short periods at little cost, and can also be intensified for short terms. When labor is relatively abundant in the dry season, two different fishermen can use the same boat to set their own nets in a single day.

PASTORALISM

While the Lake Titicaca basin was famous for its extensive herds of llamas and alpacas at the time of the Spanish chroniclers in the 16th century, virtually no camelid herding takes place in the Taraco region today. Thus, the model of the impact of lake level changes on pastoral strategies presented here rests on analogies between local conditions and the ecology of native camelids observed in similar regions elsewhere.

The two wild camelid species have distributions that overlap in the Central Andes, but their ability to tolerate environmental extremes differs (Franklin 1983). The larger guanaco (*Lama guanaco*) has a wide tolerance for altitude, temperature, fodder, and dry conditions. The smaller vicuña (*Vicugna vicugna*) tolerates the highest altitudes, prefers a narrower range of forage species, and cannot survive under dry conditions where there is no surface water. The guanaco is the ancestor of the llama (*Lama glama*); the llama and guanaco both can consume a wide variety of plant species and crop waste and can survive on moisture contained in fodder if no surface water is available. The smaller domesticated alpaca (*Lama pacos*) is descended from the guanaco or llama, but both genetic (Wheeler, Chikhi, and Bruford 2006) and archaeological data (Moore 1989) suggest that the vicuña is a partial ancestor of the alpaca. The alpaca today is restricted to regions at relatively high altitude compared to the llama, to relatively cool regions, and to regions with perennial springs, streams, or wet meadows.

Llamas can be used as pack animals, for meat, and are sheared for fiber; alpacas provide meat and abundant fine fiber for textiles, but are generally too small to carry a load. In contrast to fishing, responsibility for herds demands constant vigilance of individual animals and an unending need to provide fodder. Taking these factors into account, the dramatic changes to the landscape of the Taraco region over the course of the Formative period must have offered different advantages to herders (and hunters) of different camelid forms.

Camelid herding is intrinsically risky for smallholders in the Andes (Flannery, Marcus, and Reynolds 1989; Flores Ochoa 1979; Nachtigall 1966). In particular, Flannery, Marcus, and Reynolds (1989) examine some risks of herding camelids, taking into account their relatively slow development (3 years to maturity) and long reproductive cycles (11 months gestation). In addition, predation, infectious diseases and parasites, exposure to cold and snow, lightning, and falls in rugged terrain are significant mortality factors in herds. While attentive pastoral care increases herding success, giving animals as gifts creates ties that reduce risk by insuring aid and support of families outside the local community. In the Titicaca basin, the interrelated system of animals, products, activities, and obligations would have operated beyond pastoral activities to include fishing, agriculture, and craft production.

As our understanding of lake level fluctuations improves, the implications for camelid herders also emerge. In 2010, at relatively high lake levels, the Titicaca basin has many more alpaca than llama, but this pattern is strongly influenced by the history of agrarian reform, the world wool market, regional urban demand for beef, and the availability of truck transport. In the early 16th century, also at high lake levels, chroniclers mentioned large herds of both llamas and alpacas. In the Tiwanaku V period (AD 900–1100, also at high lake levels), the ritual and political center of the Tiwanaku state (approximately 25 km from the Taraco sites) was provisioned mostly by camelids of a body size similar to llamas, with fewer distinctly smaller animals in the alpaca range (Webster 1993). For a complex polity stretching across hundreds of kilometers from warm valleys in the east to arid valleys and deserts in the west), different herd and pack animals are likely to have been optimal in different regions.

Most Taraco landholders raise sheep, cattle, pigs, and use donkeys for transport. Along the Taraco peninsula, pastoral activities are closely managed in a landscape of fields, household compounds, and areas used as pasture. Herders take cattle, sheep, and pigs to lower pastures each day and return to upland corrals each evening. They supplement natural forage with fodder they raise, threshing waste, and totora reeds cut from stands along the lake edge where animals cannot graze by themselves.

In the Taraco region, ruminant animals feed on stubble and waste of crop plants but such fodder may not be abundant. Herders on Taraco would have also needed periodic grazing rights in upland regions off the peninsula where herds would not compete for water and soil in areas that are suitable for cultivation. At some time during the periods discussed here, camelids began to carry cargo, lowering the costs and risks of exchange with other regions. Textiles of camelid wool would have been locally important exports and a source of valuables in that exchange. In addition, the rich fishing resources in the Titicaca basin would have buffered the Titicaca herds in times of climate stress.

PREDICTIONS FOR THE ARCHAEOLOGY OF RESOURCE STRESS

Bathymetric data indicate a dramatically reduced area of open water in the southern part of the lake during prehistoric extreme low stands. The impact of evaporation on lake water quality and the local ecology can be partly understood by looking at the contemporary regions around Lake Poopo. Today, Lake Titicaca is fresh but Lake Poopo to the south ranges between 30 and 100 times more saline depending on season and distance from the mouth of the river. In a reduced Lake Titicaca, the remnant pools would have become increasingly saline (Abbott et al. 2003; Cross et al. 2000), perhaps twice as salty as under present-day conditions, leaving a crust of evaporated minerals along the receding edge (Sylvestre et al. 1995). The extensive reed beds would have died back along the former lake edge and shifted farther into the lake each year. Even though the reed beds would have followed the shallow water, the human use of totora and the continuing harvest and manipulation of the plants might have affected the extent or density of the beds during any period. Archaeologically, resource stress under conditions of low lake levels would show up in reduced proportions of fish and other aquatic resources and increased reliance on crops, gathered foods, and food from herds and game.

Archaeological data were collected between 1992 and 2006 at four sites: Chiripa, Kala Uyuni, Sonaji, and Kumi Kipa. The site of Chiripa has a substantial mounded center and has been well known as a prehistoric site for many decades (Bandy 1999). The other sites were chosen based on an intensive survey of the entire peninsula study area (Bandy 2001). Previous work at the site showed that archaeobiological remains were abundant and diverse (Erickson and Horn 1979; Kent 1982). Even so, estimating the changing importance of subsistence activities over time required intensive recovery and analysis. In an earlier study (Moore, Steadman, and deFrance 1999), I estimated available biomass to compare the economic significance of mammals and fish. Here, the quantitative estimates of the relative amount of different animal foods are from density of large mammal bone, fish, and bird remains from bulk flotation samples (weight compared to volume of deposit). Detail on the use of camelids comes from larger samples of bone scrap recovered using screens. To show patterns in animal husbandry, I use NISP of measured long bones and teeth from camelids and summaries of those measurements as a proxy for body size. In the following sections, I outline the evidence for changing animal use: fish, birds and other aquatic resources, and camelids across the Formative in the context of landscape change. I compare the evidence for changing use with predictions of how such changes would have affected the availability of the resources and risks associated with depending on each resource.

FISH

Evidence for the Use of Fish

Fish remains are common at each of the sites in this study. Preliminary research on flotation samples from early Chiripa phase deposits at the site of Chiripa indicated that fishing had been more important than animal herding and hunting by some measures. The majority of animal biomass at the site came from fish even though the bones of camelids were ubiquitous and visible in the deposits (Moore, Steadman, and deFrance 1999). Two measures are used to track the importance of fish: relative density of fish bones and scales from heavy fraction flotation samples compared to density of mammal bone, and the remains of fishing gear: stone net weights and fish net gauges made from bone. The flotation samples were processed using a modified SMAP machine with a 1-mm mesh insert to collect the heavy fraction (Whitehead 1999). The heavy fractions, including all mammal bone as well as fish remains, were sorted to 1 mm to recover all bones and the very tough scales of *Orestias* (*Trichomycterus*, a catfish, has no scales). It is likely that fish were caught with nets throughout the sequence, as they are today. There are no remains of the nets themselves, but archaeological traces of net fishing include pecked stones probably used as net weights. In addition, polished bone pieces used to manufacture the nets have been recovered from many Formative deposits (Moore 1999). Bandy (2006) summarized the evidence for net weights from Chiripa (primarily Middle Formative), and two predominately Late Formative sites, Kala Uyuni and Sonaji.

Data on the abundance of fish remains comes from flotation samples from four sites and six time periods (n=315 samples). This chronology used here is slightly different from that used by the rest of the Taraco Archaeological Project (Bandy and Hastorf 2007) in that the relatively lengthy Late Chiripa phase (800–200 BC) is broken into two samples at the site of Chiripa on stratigraphic grounds. No information on the absolute chronological spread is available for these units at this time. These samples are referred to in the figures as Late Chiripa and Latest Late Chiripa. In other comparisons, all the Late Chiripa phase material is considered together in chronological comparisons.

Bone density varies between archaeological contexts (plastered or packed surfaces, pit fill, etc.). In a detailed analysis of a small sample of fish remains from Kala Uyuni, Capriles (2006) showed the diversity of fish taken in terms of fish species, body size, and possible fishing practice for most of the Formative period. A cruder measure of fish abundance is used here so that more of the archaeological sequence could be included. Relative density of fish bone varies between 0 and 0.96 for the 314 individual flotation samples that made up the sample in this study. Fish remains lay in dense patches in some contexts, so individual samples were pooled to produce averages for each component.

Table 9.2 summarizes the average relative fish (scale and bone) density over time. The shifts in relative abundance sites are plotted together (Fig. 9.3). The slope and direction of the trend in fish density over the course of the Early through Latest Chiripa at Chiripa and Kala Uyuni is striking. The two sites are approximately 12 km from each other and on opposite sides of the peninsula. Both are approximately 1.5 km from the current lake edge. The differences between the Formative phases are significant. The mean differences between the EC and MC (t=2.38, d.f.=81, p=.019), the MC and the LC (t=–4.36, d.f.=80, p=.00003), the LC and the Late Formative (t=5.91, d.f.=135, p=.0000) are all significant. The subsequent further decline from the Late Formative components at three sites to the Tiwanaku IV/V components also appears consistent. The Tiwanaku IV/V samples are relatively small and these differences are not statistically significant.

Table 9.2. Relative Density of Fish Remains (gm fish remains/gm all bone remains/l sediment) from Flotation Samples at Four Taraco Sites

	CHIRIPA	KUMI KIPA	KALA UYUNI	SONAJI	TOTAL
Early Chiripa	0.366	—	0.569	—	0.391
Middle Chiripa	0.248	—	0.406	—	0.283
Late Chiripa	0.436	—	0.576	—	0.506
Latest Late Chiripa	0.309	—	—	—	0.309
Late Formative (Tiwanaku I and III)	—	0.234	0.2795	0.434	0.274
Tiwanaku IV/V	0.080	0.136	0.1835	0.180	0.166
No. samples	168	30	100	7	305

Fishing Technology

A second, independent indicator of the decline in fishing over the course of the Early and Middle Formative comes from the archeological signatures of fish nets. Two measures summarize preliminary analysis of bone tool and stone tool assemblages from Chiripa and Kala Uyuni (Table 9.3). Small pecked net weights are compared to the total debitage in the same samples for the stone tool values, and fine camelid bone net gauges are compared to the entire bone tool assemblage. The trend in fishing gear has the same result as the trend in fish between the Early Chiripa and Late Formative. An intriguing difference can be noted in the Late Chiripa phase, when the importance of fish in the diet was as high as in the Early Chiripa phase, but the tools to bring in those fish declined sharply. Several explanations might explain this discrepancy: first, that the actual location of fishing gear storage or maintenance might have shifted to the lakeshore as the shore repeatedly eased away from the large sites; second, fish may have been caught/

collected in a different way; third, the organization of fishing activities may have changed. For instance, dip nets and basket traps used while standing in shallows would leave no weights and might involve less netting and repair of nets (Portugal 2002).

Table 9.3. Fishing Technology at Taraco Sites:
Bone Net Gauges and Net Weights

PHASE	BONE TOOLS (N)		NET WEIGHTS (N)	WORKED STONE (wt., g)	NET GAUGE/ BONE TOOL (%)		NET WEIGHT/ WORKED STONE (no./wt.)
	Kala Uyuni	Chiripa	Kala Uyuni Chiripa	Kala Uyuni Chiripa	Kala Uyuni	Chiripa	Kala Uyuni Chiripa
Late Formative	78	—	5	3963	1.5	—	0.001
Latest Chiripa	—	186	—	—	—	6.4	—
Late Chiripa	163	360	36	5053	6.5	1.4	0.007
Middle Chiripa	21	62	—	—	1.9	2.4	—
Early Chiripa	—	61	—	—	—	3.8	—

Changes in Fishing Practice in Early and Middle Formative Times

Lake shrinkage in the southern lake would have had two consequences for fishing: fish populations would have declined with lake volume, and the travel time to the water would have risen. The shoreline at lowest lake stands would have been 10–15 km from the known sites occupied at this time, rather than 1 km as it is for most farmers now. Fishing trips might have become less frequent, even if equipment and nets were stored farther out along the receding shore. Boating and fishing require relatively complex equipment and ongoing upkeep. The bone gauges used to make fish nets were the most elaborate utilitarian items made of bone at these sites (Moore 1999), and these delicate pieces were continually breaking and being discarded. A long period of decline in the importance of fish might reduce the number of people with these skills and lead to a loss of cultural knowledge. New combinations of agricultural and pastoral practices centered on the lakebed and fishing in the smaller lake might have emerged. Fishing would have been the loser in this situation, and is expected to have declined significantly during each period of persistent low lake levels.

The intensity of fishing during the Early Formative at Chiripa is difficult to place in regional context. Stanish et al. (2002) speculated that aquatic resources were important to settlements from Late Archaic through Formative on the Island of the Sun, referring to the position of the current lakeshore and the presumption of boating technology, but specifically citing only the Chiripa fish bone remains as characteristic of Formative occupations. Herhahn (2004) suggested that proximity to the lakeshore at Wiska-chuni (on the southwestern coast of the northern section of Lake Titicaca) would lead the Early and Middle Formative residents to rely on fish, based also on the material from Chiripa. In fact, the fine screen samples from Wis-kachuni show that fish made up less than 1% of faunal remains, though there were discrete clumps of fish bone in some deposits that appeared to approach densities seen at Chiripa and Kala Uyuni. Lemuz (2001) recovered abundant fish bones (without using flotation) from Early Formative levels at Santiago de Huata. This site is near abundant totora beds near the Straits of Tiquina leading from the northern to the southern parts of Late Titicaca, and while the recovery techniques did not produce comparable numbers, these assemblages do indeed appear to show an intensive reliance on fish.

As mentioned above, the Early and Late Chiripa included periods of historically high lake stands for that time, while the Middle Chiripa Phase appears to have coincided with a low stand from approximately 1000 BC to 800 BC. It appears that there was a general decline of fishing at this time as reflected in sites that were continuously occupied (based on the ceramic sequences). Following the refilling of the lake during the Late Chiripa phase, fish densities rebounded, including, for example, pits crammed with fish bone around the ritual center of Kala Uyuni (Capriles 2006). The Late Chiripa and Late Formative (Tiwanaku I) phases included two more 100–200 year long periods of low lake levels, but these appear to be reflected less directly in the pattern of fish density. One problem with these data is that the resolution of the ceramic dating used to assign phases is not precise enough to capture further short periods of time. Even so, it is clear that fishing declines in importance for good following the Late Chiripa phase. Limited data from other sites with Tiwanaku material, including the local center of Iwawe just outside the Taraco study area (Capriles 2003), two sectors at the imperial center of Tiwanaku itself (K. Gardella, pers.comm.; J. Capriles, pers. comm.), and at the early related center at Khonkho Wankarni (J. Po-koines, pers. comm.) suggest that fish were a minor part of the economic activity in the rural hinterland and negligible at the urban center.

Part of the consistency seen in the record of camelid and fish use at the Taraco sites may be due to the force of site formation processes on the archaeobiological assemblages. Since taphonomic forces and recovery processes produce a bias against the recovery of fish bones, though, the importance of fish throughout the Early and Middle Formative is a robust finding, and the response to the droughts of the Middle Chiripa period is a convincing pattern. More important in evaluating this pattern on a regional scale is the possible bias of the archaeological sample, since most excavations took place in the largest, most permanently occupied settlements, rather than in ephemeral or special purpose sites. We cannot directly address the possibility that the Taraco sites were periodically abandoned during the period when lake levels were lowest and fishing would have been too expensive a strategy to continue. In this view, the period of lowest lake levels is archaeologically invisible from these sites, and what is perceived here as a resilient adaptation was actually broken by periods during which the integration of fishing, herding, and farming yielded to a different way of life in different sites. Underwater sensing and survey (Hiebert, Frye, and Austermule 2006) of the lake bottom around the present-day peninsula may help to resolve this issue. Though the re-establishment of the fishing economy in the Middle Formative (Late Chiripa) took place with little perceptible break in the ubiquity of fish use, the technology used to obtain the fish seems to have shifted, leaving open the idea of a break.

BIRDS AND OTHER WILD RESOURCES

Evidence for Aquatic Birds

According to a preliminary study from Chiripa, 85% of the bird bones recovered were from birds living on open water, in the totora reed beds, or on mud flats and pools along the shore of the lake (based on data in Kent, Webber, and Steadman 1999). Estimates for density of bird bones in the flotation samples in this study are lower than in the sieved samples because birds are swamped by the importance of fish. Bird bones are present in all assemblages but were not common. When remains recovered in the one-quarter inch screen are compared, bird bones range from 1% to 15%

of total density of faunal remains recovered. Eggshell fragments are also common in Taraco sites, though they have not been identified to species. They appear to be from the large-bodied birds nesting along the lakeshore. During the Formative phases, eggshell fragments are generally associated with higher densities of bird bone, strengthening the argument for the importance of birds and the lakeshore habitat in subsistence.

As a measure of the availability of these wild foods and the intensity of their use, the relative density of bird remains to overall bone density was calculated from the heavy fractions of the flotation samples. The proportion of bird bone recovered using the standard one quarter inch screen was similar to the proportion of bird bone from the flotation samples, but the flotation samples are cited here for consistency and to avoid any bias in favor of relatively large-bodied birds.

Evidence for Hunting

Hunting was already uncommon by the time permanent settlements were established around the lake in Early Chiripa phase times. Vicuña remains make up 5–10% of all large mammals in the Formative deposits, based on their teeth (NISP). Deer, though important in the Andes in the periods before animal domestication, are extremely rare in Titicaca sites. Small game such as wild rodents and carnivores are also rare.

Changes in the Use of Birds and Other Wild Resources

The bird fauna of the Taraco sites represents the third-ranked animal resource after fish and camelids. Activities around fishing would have often brought fisherman into bird habitats. The trends in relative density of bird bone (Fig. 9.4) are based on the 305 flotation samples noted above. The trends also appear in the screened samples from many more contexts. Bird hunting appears to be unrelated to the pattern of fishing, net making (for either fish or birds), or lake levels. The assemblages around Late Formative (Tiwanaku I) structures and courtyards at Kala Uyuni were particularly dense in bird bones. Further comparison shows that this peak in abundance of birds is part of a longer-term increase for which we do not have a ready explanation. The importance of birds (and all wild food resources) declined in the small number of Tiwanaku IV/V samples. Even in Early Chiripa times, hunting seems to have been a minor activity around the lake, so it is notable that bird hunting increases in the Late Formative as fishing declined.

Relative Density of Fish Remains (g/liter), Taraco Sites

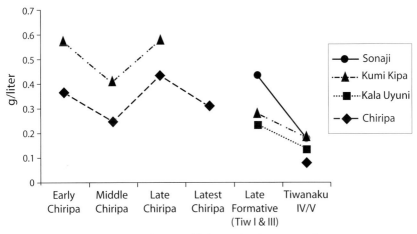

9.3 Relative density of fish remains for Taraco sites.

Density of Bird Bone (g/liter of deposit)

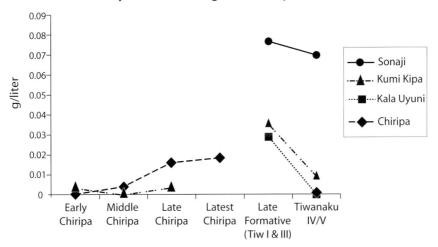

9.4 Density of bird bone from flotation samples, compared to overall density of bone from each sample.

It is possible that bird abundance actually reflects more intense exploitation of the totora reed beds than the lake itself, or activity in the managed reed bed in preference to the degraded quality of the lake resources after several episodes of evaporation and refilling. Allen (1921) noted some of the differences between the bird fauna of Lake Poopo and Lake Titicaca. The most notable was the large numbers of flamingos that feed in the saline shallows of Lake Poopo compared to their occasional presence in the southern part of Lake Titicaca. The other difference noted by Allen was the lack of diving ducks, cormorants, the flightless grebe, and geese, all of which need deeper water than Lake Poopo and more vegetation for nesting (see also accounts by Carricker 2006). The importance of bird bone may also point to some specific activities involving bird feathers, beads from bird bones, or other items, but the bulk of the bird bones from Sonaji and Kala Uyuni are clearly dietary remains based on the bones represented, the pattern of burning, and fragmentation.

Egg gathering was also a common activity based on finds of eggshells in the flotation samples. Some of these resources could be gathered as extras while fishing, but men without boats, women, or children could seek these foods on their own at other times, or in connection with gathering reeds for fodder, fuel, or craft material. The intensity of prehistoric use of this resource suggests management of the totora reeds themselves (see Bruno, this volume). It also suggests that the animal populations nesting and feeding in the reeds were familiar with humans and resistant to overexploitation.

LLAMAS AND ALPACAS

Evidence for the Context of Camelid Pastoralism

The Lake Titicaca basin is known for large herds of domesticated camelids; wild camelids also are native to the region. Camelids of the genus *Lama* (llama, alpaca, wild guanaco) and *Vicugna* (vicuña) dominate the faunal remains from the prehistoric Taraco sites. The abundance of camelid remains in sites does not indicate their economic significance. The density of camelid remains varied according to archaeological context, sedimentation rates, and post-occupation disturbances such as mound building and tomb construction. More detailed examination of the remains is necessary to determine their economic significance over time.

The camelid species are ordered in size (llama > guanaco > alpaca > vicuña) depending on the location within the geographic range of these species. Size distributions for single dimensions grade into one another, with greater differences in proportions in a few cases. Except for teeth, few postcranial remains can be assigned to genus. Body size and proportion were estimated for this study using dimensions of bones of the feet as a measure of size diversity within the camelid group. This measure allows the distribution of body sizes in the archaeological assemblage to be compared to the sizes of modern wild and domesticated camelids. The Taraco sites typically contain a mixture of camelid body sizes, indicating multiple species (potentially wild and domesticated) during all periods (Kent 1982; Moore 2006; Moore, Steadman, and deFrance 1999). The identity and relative abundance of these species holds some important clues for the way that ancient inhabitants managed their pastoral lives and landscapes.

Camelid pastoralism is traced using bones from all five of the Taraco sites. These bones, with a single exception of an apparent offering in the Middle Chiripa period deposits, represent food remains; however, the diversity of camelids in the Central Andes indicates that several different ecological and pastoral strategies may be represented. The first phalanx, or toe bone, of the camelids was chosen to study the general trends in body size and the specific differences in proportion between the different wild and domesticated forms. Overall, the bones from wild camelids are gracile, while the domestic forms are broader and more robust. Of the more than 400 phalanges measured, 237 were from deposits with secure ceramic phase dates.

Five dimensions of the first phalanx have been studied, but the breadth of the proximal end of the bone reflects the differences in proportion most clearly (Table 9.4, Fig. 9.5) Each assemblage of bones is a mixture of large and small animals drawn from a variety of populations, including wild populations. Over time from the Early Chiripa phase to the Middle and Late Chiripa phases, larger animals become more common. The largest animals in the regional sample cluster in the latest part of the Late Chiripa phase. From this peak, there are increasing numbers of smaller animals, ending up with the small sample from the Classic Tiwanaku IV/V component. These animals are too small to be compared with a modern llama.

Of these comparisons over time, the decrease between Latest Chiripa and Late Formative (Tiw I/III) is significant (t=3.62, d.f.=128, p=.0004).

**Table 9.4. Dimensions of Camelid First Phalanges,
mm (fore and hind combined) for Taraco Sites**

SITE/ LOCALITY	SAMPLE MEAN	EARLY CHIRIPA	MIDDLE CHIRIPA	LATE CHIRIPA	LATEST LATE CHIRIPA	LATE FORMATIVE (TIA I/III)	TIWANAKU IV/V	LOCALITY COMBINED
Chiripa	Length	63.5	65.0	69.7	73.5	—	—	70.3
	Prox Breadth	15.3	21.2	20.8	21.9	—	—	21.3
	Prox Depth	24.5	19.6	19.8	20.6	—	—	20.2
Kala Uyuni	Length	—	66.8	69.4	—	70.5	65.9	68.3
	Prox Breadth	21.7	20.6	21.8	—	21.1	18.6	20.7
	Prox Depth	19.2	18.5	19.4	—	19.2	17.8	18.7
Kumi Kipa and Sonaji	Length	—	—	—	—	68.7	66.8	68.6
	Prox Breadth	—	—	—	—	20.0	17.4	19.8
	Prox Depth	—	—	—	—	18.9	16.8	18.7
Sample mean Length		63.5	65.8	69.7	73.5	69.2	66.0	69.5
Sample mean Prox Breadth		17.4	21.0	20.9	21.9	20.3	18.1	20.8
Sample mean Prox Depth		21.9	19.2	19.8	20.6	18.9	17.4	19.6

(The combined Late Chiripa and Late Formative difference is significant as well.) The continued decline between Tiw I/III and Tiw IV/V is also a significant difference (t=2.89, d.f.=79, p=.004). The increase between Early and Middle Chiripa animals is not significant.

Changes in the Use of Llamas and Alpacas

For the southern Titicaca basin during the Formative period, local villagers are sure to have been familiar with the challenges of both dry and rainy years for keeping their animals. Dry years would have produced poor pasture conditions and an inadequate amount of crop waste for fodder. The resources of the emerging lake bed, important each dry season, would have been increasingly important. Not only are animals pastured on the seasonally dry lake edge right up to the beginning of the reed beds, the totora reed beds are cut for fodder and mats of aquatic vegetation raked up from

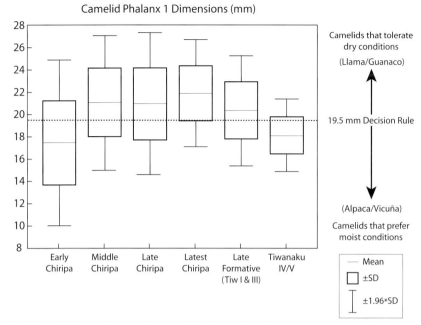

9.5 Camelid first phalanx (fore and hind combined) maximum proximal breadth, Taraco sites combined.

shoreline and shallows to feed animals. Successive dry years would have accentuated human dependence on the lakeshore strip as it followed the remaining open water to the north and west of the settlements. Accounts by Erickson (1999) of such a prolonged dry period during the 1940s suggest that the soil moisture retained in the emerging lakebed provided a relatively lush and productive expanse for both pasture and cropping. In addition, Erickson (2000) emphasizes the dynamic built environment of the Titicaca basin that enhanced the availability of water and plant growth along a transect from high pastures to the lakebed. The built features related directly to maintaining animal production in antiquity might have included manipulation of springs to increase flow and irrigate meadows in areas above settlements and cropland, and excavating sunken gardens (*q'ocha*) to capture and retain moisture. Investing in such hand-built features might not make sense during a typical dry year followed by typical wet years, but building a sunken garden might be a key method of extending pasture lands onto newly exposed pampa. From a slightly different perspective, Bruno's chapter in this volume suggests that the soils of the newly exposed pampa pasture would have been suited for pasture but not for traditional agriculture.

The traditional puna pastures would become increasingly dry and overgrazed with the onset of sustained dry periods. The extent of new, moist pastureland in the former lakebed might disrupt traditional herding practices that emphasized pasturelands at higher elevations. A key question about Formative pastoralism is whether a sustained dry period might have favored the larger, more drought resistant llamas or the smaller, more choosy and water-dependent alpacas. The domestic camelids of today are not a precise analog for the animals reconstructed for past herds, particularly the relatively ancient herds of the Formative. Even so, the association of body size and water needs is likely to have been consistent in the past, given that it holds between wild and domestic camelids. The landscape of the lowest lake stands would have expanded the moist pastures that are today used to raise alpacas, favoring small-bodied camelids generally. Grazing resources in the landscape of the dry upland pastures would be reduced for all herbivores but would probably favor the larger-bodied llamas (and wild guanaco) over the smaller camelid forms. Within the entire basin, small camelids might have experienced a relative advantage, leading to an expectation that their relative importance would increase during times of the lowest lake stands.

There are several issues to evaluate when comparing these initial expectations for animals in the archaeological record. First, animals in different size classes might have different age profiles. The younger the average age at slaughter of the animals in a particular herd, the greater their contribution to the animal bone assemblage. Generalized data for the Formative camelids (Moore 2006) showed that the smaller camelids lived longer than the larger camelids, accounting for some of the impression that larger, llama-sized camelids were more common. When the mix of sizes classes in an archaeological assemblage shifts toward the smaller end of the scale, this is a relatively robust signal that the smaller camelids have experienced an advantage, and/or that the size of larger animals has diminished. Second, the products and labor offered by the different size classes of Formative camelids might have been different from camelids of today. The economic or social significance of those products might have been different than they are today, especially the use of animals in ritual and exchange. In the Titicaca basin today, the high numbers of alpacas are the result of the world demand for alpaca wool for fine textiles, not their value for food or their success in modern environments. Other clues for the biological significance of body size as a descriptive measure (dental characters and wear, pathologies, age profiles, skeletal completeness, etc.) need to be considered when size changes are observed. These subtle indicators are traces of the prehistoric herder's detailed personal knowledge of the health and status of each animal.

Would the periodic dry periods have made raising smaller, water-dependent camelids too risky or expensive when agricultural fields also required scarce ground water and attention? No archaeological data suggest camelid body size changed according to deterioration of local upland pasture. Instead, several different economic and ecological factors produced the pattern of camelid body sizes. First, people of the Latest Late Chiripa had bred some of the larger animals for cargo use. These animals would have been an element of the interregional trade that Bandy (2004) proposes would have been facilitated by lowered lake levels. These large camelids would have offered an economic advantage for centralized authorities (not to mention a physically impressive symbol or highly appropriate sacrifice as is seen at Chiripa). The age profiles and records of skeletal pathology from these bones are consistent with such use. Second, the emergence of a fine fiber small camelid (perhaps an ancestor of the alpaca) is clear by Late Chiripa times. While no fiber exists for the open sites in the Titicaca basin, fiber of Formative date is known from dry contexts in Chile (Dransart 2002). Additionally, the small camelids have a distinctively old age at slaughter compared to larger camelids from the same deposits (Moore 2006), typical of herds kept for repeated shearing.

CONCLUSIONS

The archaeological measures for pastoralism and fishing over this sequence show changes in both intensity and organization. The landscape in which these remains were produced experienced profound changes and would have demanded both social and biological changes in agricultural and economic organization. The earliest Formative sites appear to hug the lakeshore and to have been based on an integrated fishing and agricultural economy, so the declining returns from fish must have disrupted foodways, craft organization, and land tenure. From the perspective of excavations at major sites where populations were maintained through this time, the effect of the changes in lake levels can be perceived as a clear, temporary decline in the use of fish. Yet, fishing did not disappear entirely. The integration of the entire agropastoral system and the flexibility and endurance of the animals appear to have provided a stable base over time to the local populations. In the Titicaca basin, even while times were tough the remaining water, the still-available marsh resources, and the moist soils would still have made this area richly productive compared to higher pampas and valleys. Long memories of changing but eventually improving conditions, while shaken by the persistence of the Formative period lake level declines, would have provided expectations of successful coping strategies. Successful strategies in shorter-term droughts would have rewarded the continuity of traditional practice, including maintaining ritual centers, springs, rights to grazing and fishing territories, and a diverse herd of breeding animals, through the longest periods of low lake levels. Much more profound changes in the population history and economy of the region followed the influence of new political and religious forms during the Tiwanaku expansion. The demands of participation in the world of the Tiwanaku center were apparently more stressful to the traditional life of the Taraco peninsula than were 200 years of sparse fish catches and poor harvests in a row.

REFERENCES CITED

Abbott, M., M. Binford, M. Brenner, and K. Kelts. 1997. A 3500 ^{14}C Yr High-resolution Record of Water-level Changes in Lake Titicaca, Bolivia/Peru. *Quaternary Research* 47:169–80.

Abbott, Mark B., Brent B. Wolfe, Alexander P. Wolfe, Geoffrey O. Seltzer, Ramon Aravena, Brian G. Mark, Pratigya J. Polissar, Donald T. Rodbell, Harry D. Rowe, and Mathias Vuille. 2003. Holocene Paleohydrology and Glacial History of the Central Andes Using Multiproxy Lake Sediment Studies. *Palaeogeography, Palaeoclimatology, Palaeoecology* 194:123–38.

Allen, William Ray. 1921. The Birds of Lake Poopo, Bolivia. *Auk* 38:340–43.

Baker, P. A., S. C. Fritz, J. Garland, and E. Ekdahl. 2005. Holocene Hydrologic Variation at Lake Titicaca, Bolivia/Peru, and Its Relationship to North Atlantic Climate Variation. *Journal of Quaternary Science* 20:655–62.

Baker, P. A., C. A. Rigsby, G. O. Seltzer, S. C. Fritz, T. K. Lowenstein, N. P. Bacher, and C. Veliz. 2001. Tropical Climate Changes at Millennial and Orbital Timescales on the Bolivian Altiplano. *Nature* 409:98–101.

Bandy, M. S. 2001. Population and History in the Ancient Titicaca Basin. PhD diss., Dept. of Anthropology, Univ. of California, Berkeley.

—— 2004. Trade and Social Power in the Southern Titicaca Basin Formative. In *Foundations of Power in the Prehispanic Andes*, ed. K. J. Vaughn, D. Ogburn, and C. A. Conlee, pp. 91–112. Archaeological Papers of the American Anthropological Association 14. Arlington, VA.

—— 2006. Analyses de artefactos liticas de siete temperadas de excavaciones en quatro sitios en Taraco y Santa Rosa. In "Taraco Archaeological Project: Report of the 2005 Excavations at the Sites of Sonaje and Kala Uyuni," ed. C. A. Hastorf, pp. 95–101. Report submitted to the Directorate Unidad Nacional de Arqueologia de Bolivia, La Paz.

Bandy, M. S., and Christine A. Hastorf, eds. 2007. *Kala Uyuni: An Early Political Center in the Southern Lake Titicaca Basin. 2003 Excavations of the Taraco Archaeological Project*. Contributions of the Archaeological Research Facility, University of California, No. 64. Berkeley.

Bruno, M. C., and W. T. Whitehead. 2003. *Chenopodium* Cultivation and Formative Period Agriculture at Chiripa, Bolivia. *Latin American Antiquity* 14:339–55.

Capriles F., J. M. 2003. Entre el valle y la península: variabilidad en la utilización de recursos faunísticos durante Tiwanaku (400–1100 d.C.) en el sitio Iwawi, Bolivia. Tesis de Licenciatura, Universidad Mayor de San Andrés, La Paz.

—— 2006. A Zooarchaeological Analysis of Fish Remains from the Lake Titicaca Formative Period (ca. 1000 B.C.–A.D. 500) Site of Kala Uyuni, Bolivia. Master's thesis, Dept. of Anthropology, Washington Univ., St. Louis.

Carriker, Melbourne A., Jr. 2006. *Experiences of an Ornithologist along the Highways and Byways of Bolivia*. Bloomington, Indiana: AuthorHouse.

Cross, Scott L., Paul A. Baker, Geoffrey O. Seltzer, Sherilyn C. Fritz, and Robert. B. Dunbar. 2000. A New Estimate of the Holocene Lowstand Level of Lake Titicaca, Central Andes, and Implications for Tropical Palaeohydrology. *The Holocene* 10:21–32.

Dransart, Penelope Z. 2002. *Earth, Water, Fleece and Fabric: An Ethnography and Archaeology of Andean Camelid Herding*. London: Routledge.

Erickson, C. L. 1999. Neo-environmental Determinism and Agrarian "Collapse" in Andean Prehistory. *Antiquity* 73:634–42.

——. 2000. The Lake Titicaca Basin: A Pre-Columbian Built Landscape. In *Imperfect Balance: Landscape Transformations in the Precolumbian Americas*, ed. D. L. Lentz, pp. 311–56. New York: Columbia University Press.

Erickson, C. L., and Darwin Horn. 1979. Domestication and Subsistence Implications of Plant and Animal Utilization in the Titicaca Basin. Unpublished manuscript on file with authors.

Flannery, K. V., J. C. Marcus, and R. G. Reynolds. 1989. *The Flocks of the Wamani. A Study of Llama Herders on the Punas of Ayacucho, Peru*. New York: Academic Press.

Flores Ochoa, Jorge A. 1979. *Pastoralists of the Andes: The Alpacas Herders of Paratia*, tr. R. Bolton. Philadelphia: Institute for the Study of Human Issues.

Franklin, William L. 1983. Contrasting Socioecologies of South America's Wild Camelids: The Vicuña and Guanaco. In *Advances in the Study of Mammalian Behavior*, ed. J. F. Eisenberg and D. G. Kleiman, pp. 573–629. American Society of Mammalogists, Special Publication 7.

Fritz, S. C., P. A. Baker, P. Tapia, and J. Garland. 2006. Spatial and Temporal Variation in Cores from Lake Titicaca, Bolivia/Peru during the Last 13,000 Years. *Quaternary International* 158:23–29.

Gade, Daniel W. 1999. *Nature and Culture in the Andes*. Madison, Wisconsin: University of Wisconsin Press.

Hastorf, C. A., ed. 1999. *Early Settlement at Chiripa, Bolivia: Research of the Taraco Archaeological Project*. Contributions of the University of California Archaeological Research Facility No. 57. Berkeley.

——, ed. 2005. Projecto Arqueologico Taraco: informe de las excavaciones de la temporada del 2004 en los sitios de Kumi Kipa, Sonaji y Chiripa. Report submitted to the Directorate Unidad Nacional de Arqueologia de Bolivia. La Paz.

——. 2006. Taraco Archaeological Project: Report of the 2005 Excavations at the Sites of Sonaje and Kala Uyuni. Report submitted to the Directorate Unidad Nacional de Arqueologia de Bolivia. La Paz.

Herhahn, Cynthia L. 2004. *Moving to Live: A Pastoral Mobility Model for the South Central Andes*. PhD diss., Univ. of California, Santa Barbara.

Hiebert, F. T., Kirk Frye, and Stefan Austermule. 2006. Sonar Research on Potential Ancient Settlements below Current Southern Titicaca Lake Levels in Bolivia. Poster presentation, 25th Northeast Conference on Andean Archaeology and Ethnohistory, Philadelphia.

Kent, Adam, T. Webber, and D. W. Steadman. 1999. Distribution, Relative Abundance, and Prehistory of Birds on the Taraco Peninsula, Bolivian Altiplano. *Ornitología Neotropical* 10:151–78.

Kent, J. D. 1982. *The Domestication and Exploitation of the South American Camelids. Methods of Analysis and Their Application to Circumlacustrine Archaeological Sites in Bolivia and Peru*. PhD diss., Dept. of Anthropology, Washington Univ., St. Louis.

Lémuz-Aguirre, Carlos. 2001. *Patrones de asentamiento arqueológico en la península de Santiago de Huata, Bolivia*. Tesis de Licenciatura, Universidad Mayor de San Andrés, La Paz.

Logan, A. L. 2006. The Application of Phytolith and Starch Grain Analysis to Understanding Formative Period Subsistence, Ritual, and Trade on the Taraco Peninsula, Highland Bolivia. Master's thesis, Dept. of Anthropology, Univ. of Missouri, Columbia.

Moore, K. M. 1989. *Hunting and the Origins of Herding in Prehistoric Highland Peru*. PhD diss., Dept. of Anthropology, Univ. of Michigan, Ann Arbor.

—— 1999. Chiripa Worked Bone and Bone Tools. In *Early Settlement at Chiripa, Bolivia: Research of the Taraco Archaeological Project*, ed. C. A. Hastorf, pp.

73–93. Contributions of the University of California Archaeological Research Facility No. 57. Berkeley.

—— 2006. Camelid Pastoralism and Early Complex Society in the Southern Lake Titicaca Basin. Paper presented at the 10th International Conference for Archaeozoology, Mexico City.

Moore, K. M., D. W. Steadman, and S. deFrance. 1999. Herds, Fish, and Fowl in the Domestic and Ritual Economy of Formative Chiripa. In *Early Settlement at Chiripa, Bolivia: Research of the Taraco Archaeological Project*, ed. C. A. Hastorf, pp. 105–16. Contributions of the University of California Archaeological Research Facility No. 57. Berkeley.

Moore, K. M., M. C. Bruno, J. Capriles F., and C. A. Hastorf. 2007. Integrated Contextual Approaches to Understanding Past Activities Using Plant and Animal Remains from Kala Uyuni. In *Taraco Archaeological Project Excavations at Kala Uyuni*, ed. M. Bandy and C. A. Hastorf, pp. 113–33. Contributions of the University of California Archaeological Research Facility No. 64. Berkeley.

Nachtigall, H. 1966. *Indianische Fischer, Feldbauer und Viehzüchter: Beiträge zur peruanischen Völkerkunde*. Berlin: Reimer.

Orlove, B. 1977. *Alpacas, Sheep, and Men: The Wool Export Economy and Regional Society in Southern Peru*. New York: Academic Press.

—— 2002. *Lines in the Water: Nature and Culture at Lake Titicaca*. Berkeley: University of California Press.

Parsons, Jeffrey R. 2006. *The Last Pescadores of Chimalhuacan, Mexico: An Archaeological Ethnography*. University of Michigan Museum of Anthropology Anthropological Paper 96. Ann Arbor.

Portugal Loayza, Jimena. 2002. *Los Urus: aprovechimento y manejo de recorsos acuáticas*. La Paz: Lidema.

Rigsby, C. A., J. P. Bradbury, P. A. Baker, S. M. Rollins, M. R.Warren. 2005. Late Quaternary Palaeolakes, Rivers, and Wetlands on the Bolivian Altiplano and Their Palaeoclimatic Implications. *Journal of Quaternary Science* 20:671–91.

Stanish, Charles. 2003. *Ancient Titicaca: The Evolution of Complex Societies in Southern Peru and Northern Bolivia*. Berkeley: University of California Press.

Stanish, Charles, Richard L. Burger, Lisa M. Cipolla, Michael D.Glascock, and Estaban Quelima. 2002. Evidence for Early Long-distance Obsidian Exchange and Watercraft Use from the Southern Lake Titicaca Basin of Bolivia and Peru. *Latin American Antiquity* 13:444–54.

Sylvestre, Florence, Simone Servant-Vildar, Marc Fournier, and Michel Servant. 1995. Lake Levels in the Southern Bolivian Altiplano (19°–21°S.) during the Late Glacial Based on Diatom Studies. *International Journal of Salt Lake Research* 4(4): 281–300.

Webster, A. D. 1993. The Role of Camelids in the Emergence of Tiwanaku. PhD diss., Dept. of Anthropology, Univ. of Chicago, Chicago.

Wheeler, J. C., L. Chikhi, and M. W. Bruford. 2006. Genetic Analysis of the

Origins of Domestic South American camelids. In *Documenting Domestication: New Genetic and Archaeological Paradigms*, ed. M. A. Zeder, D. G. Bradley, E. Emshwiller, and B. D. Smith, pp. 329–41. Berkeley: University of California Press.

Whitehead, W. T. 1999. Paleoethnobotanical Evidence. In *Early Settlement at Chiripa Bolivia: Research of the Taraco Archaeological Project,* ed. C. A. Hastorf, pp. 95–104. Contributions of the University of California Archaeological Research Facility No. 57. Berkeley.

Winterhalder, B., R. Larsen, and R. B. Thomas. 1974. Dung as an Essential Resource in a Highland Peruvian Community. *Human Ecology* 2:89–104.

10

Periodic Volcanism, Persistent Landscapes, and the Archaeofaunal Record in the Jama Valley of Western Ecuador

PETER W. STAHL

The northern Andes of Ecuador and southern Colombia is one of the world's most volcanically active regions. Extensive lowlands that lie directly to the west of the Andean chain were home to the early appearance and prolonged development of complex, agriculturally based human occupation. Although extending up to hundreds of linear kilometers beyond their nearest volcanic source, vast portions of these lowland habitats were subject to periodically severe environmental disturbance and protracted tephra fallout that emanated from at least three major eruptions since the 1st millennium BC (Isaacson and Zeidler 1999; Zeidler and Isaacson 2003).

Archaeological evidence suggests that human response to these volcanic events was variable, at least in one coastal valley system. Two earlier episodes may have been responsible for the truncation of Formative occupation, while clear evidence indicates that later post-Formative occupations endured the effects of potentially cataclysmic tephra fallout during the 1st millennium AD. The variable reactions to these successive events may have been precipitated by how evolving agricultural systems responded to the impact of ash fallout through time. A protracted regional program of archaeological research in the Jama River Valley of Ecuador's northern Manabí province has marshaled settlement and archaeobiological data that can address some of the issues involved in the diachronic relationship between prehispanic tropical agroecology, forest ecology, and intermittent but catastrophic environmental events.

Understanding the nature and evolution of indigenous agroecological systems in prehispanic time and space are important missions for archaeology, particularly considering their latent relevance to contemporary application in the neotropics. The long view of archaeology is essential for understanding environmental history, prehispanic landscape management, ecological inheritance, restoration ecology, and the elusive matter of sustainability (Stahl 2008). These issues are particularly relevant for areas prone to periodic risk and for studying how traditional ecological knowledge was, or at least could have been, used to foster cultural resilience in the face of cataclysmic change.

The fate of tropical forests is a global conservation priority, particularly in the neotropics where units of loss are recorded in football fields per minute and Belgiums per year. The proximate reasons for contemporary tropical deforestation are usually obvious; however, pinpointing ultimate causation is predictably complicated. The former usually implicate logging, road construction, land speculation, ranching, and industrial agriculture. The latter often include "economic teleconnections" linked to crop and livestock improvements, increased global demand for agricultural commodities, and rising petroleum prices, whose combined momentum ultimately pushes the agricultural frontier deeper into the forest (Fearnside 2005; Laurence et al. 2004; Nepstad et al. 2008).

Their fate is significant for connected reasons. The alarming disappearance of forests is linked to important issues of biodiversity conservation, water cycling, and the increasingly dire concern of carbon dioxide emission, which has assumed an ascendant position with enhanced public awareness of global climate change (Fearnside 2005:686). Tropical forests are also home to millions of people, many of whom are indigenous and lay at least moral claim to the occupation of ancestral lands. The time for remediation is certainly now, but who has both the competence and right to manage it effectively (Chomitz 2007)?

Current control of over 20% of the Brazilian Amazon has been transferred to indigenous communities under the increasing conviction that their management can provide an effective barrier to deforestation and serve as a decisive factor in the ultimate fate of Amazonian ecosystems (Schwartzman and Zimmerman 2005:722). The local control of forests by indigenous communities who possess both enhanced knowledge and historic claims can be a viable option, particularly when they practice an agroforestry that sustains human subsistence while promoting ecological functions (Chomitz 2007). Traditional agroforestry, which either simultaneously and/or sequentially combines agriculture and/or livestock with tree crops and/or forest plants, has long been recognized as an ecologically feasible management system (Denevan and Padoch 1988). Moreover, recent studies suggest that the incorporation of long fallow forest mosaics in various stages of succession by indigenous agriculture mitigates deforestation while also maintaining an acceptable degree of faunal integrity (Nepstad et al. 2006; Ohl-Schacherer et al. 2007; Stocks, McMahon, and Taber 2007; see also Ford and Nigh 2009).

In this chapter, I begin with a brief description of the volcanically active northern Andes in Ecuador and southern Colombia. I then focus attention on the Jama Valley in Ecuador's western coastal lowlands, and summarize our knowledge of the area's prehispanic settlement, particularly as it relates to three episodes of volcanic activity that are clearly marked by valley-wide tephra sediments deposited prior to the arrival of Europeans in the early 16th century. Next, I discuss some observations on the relationship between volcanic ash deposition, landscape features, and agricultural systems from areas recently affected by tephra fallout. I then review settlement and archaeobotanical data from the Jama Valley which suggest that later populations with diversified agricultural systems may have survived major volcanic impacts principally through the intensification of upland swidden farming. I conclude by examining a large and diverse archaeofaunal record recovered from 21 archaeological sites that can be contextually associated with volcanic events that impacted the valley system throughout its prehistory. I focus on the diachronic relationship between assemblage diversity, ubiquity, archaeofaunal representation, and agroecological systems before and after they were shocked by intermittent episodes of valley-wide tephra deposition. I am particularly interested in what clues these data provide about the relationship between forest fragmentation and volcanic events throughout the Jama Valley occupational sequence, and what these might tell us about prehispanic resilience to periodic disruption.

VOLCANISM IN THE NORTHERN ANDES

The uneven distribution of active volcanoes along the Andean cordillera is directly related to the angle at which the Nazca plate subducts its continental counterpart. Subduction angles that dip between 25 and 30 degrees generate volcanism and are typical of the geologically active Andes above 2° S lat. in southern Colombia and Ecuador. In particular, this is where the Carnegie Ridge, a 300 km wide by 3 km high mountainous feature of the Nazca plate, passes over the Galápagos hot spot and collides with the continental plate. This collision is likely responsible for increased geological uplift, a well-developed series of transverse faults, and the multiple rows of chemically diverse stratovolcanoes that characterize the Ecuadorian cordillera (Fig. 10.1). Areas to the south are volcanically quiet until steep subduction angles are once again encountered in southern Peru and again in southern Chile (Hall and Wood 1985; Isaacson 1987, 1994).

Ecuador is famous for its band of active and dormant stratovolcanoes that are arranged along an eastern Cordillera Real and a western Cordillera Occidental. Hall and Mothes (1999:31) mention some 30 eruptive centers that experienced volcanic activity since the terminal Pleistocene, and list 28 of the most important eruptions that took place during the Holocene. The western range of volcanoes forms a roughly 270 km continuous front of regularly spaced cones which often explode as strong plinian eruptions with columns of smoke and ash ejected high into the stratosphere. Although varied in composition, their pyroclastic material consists of relatively acidic silicic tephra which is distributed by upper atmospheric winds blowing across the eruption cloud, and eventually deposits in a fan-shaped pattern outward from the original source. The nature of the tephra fallout and its aerial extent are conditioned by the character and volume of ejected material, the height of the eruption column, and the velocity and direction of prevailing winds. As upper tropospheric winds in the northern Andes have been characterized by relatively stable easterlies at least since the Pleistocene, the western montaña and coastal plains have received the thickest deposition of pyroclastic materials from volcanic eruptions emanating in the Cordillera Occidental (Bullard 1979; Hall and Wood 1985; Isaacson 1987, 1994; Kittleman 1979).

Chemical characterization studies of tephra samples collected from various contexts throughout the northern highlands and western lowlands

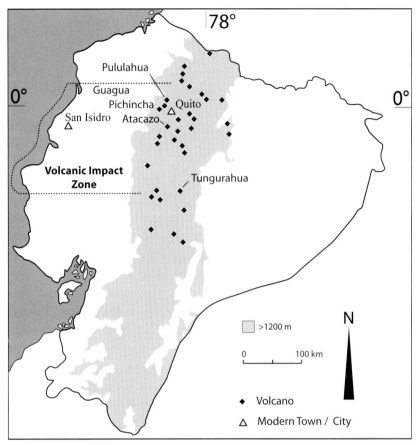

10.1 Ecuadorian volcanoes, the Western Lowland Volcanic Impact Zone, and possible eruptive sources mentioned in text.

have helped to delineate a volcanic impact zone that includes: the montaña of western Pichincha province; northern, central, and part of southern Manabí province; and, northern portions of Guayas and Los Ríos provinces (Fig. 10.1). As many as three major volcanic eruptions have left their imprint in the pre-Columbian archaeological record of the western lowlands. The second of three events can be conclusively identified with the eruption of Pululahua between 752 and 182 cal BC, an event whose strength ranks within the 99th percentile of global Holocene eruptions. Sources for the bracketing eruptions are less securely identified, but an earlier event around 1600 BC may be associated with the eruption of Guagua Pichincha, and a later event between AD 300 and 550 may be associated with the eruption of either Guagua Pichincha, Atacazo, or Tungarahua (Fig. 10.1). In all cases, their relative impact on human occupation would have been experienced in a clinal gradient from east to west and from north to south (Isaacson 1987, 1994; Isaacson and Zeidler 1999; Zeidler 2006; Zeidler and Isaacson 2003).

PREHISPANIC SETTLEMENT AND EPISODIC TEPHRA FALLOUT IN THE JAMA VALLEY

Located directly to the south of the equator, the 1,612 km² transverse valley system of the Río Jama and its tributaries forms the largest drainage basin of northern Manabí province in Ecuador's central coastal lowlands (Fig. 10.2). The main river channel flows through 75 km of rolling terrain that drops in elevation from 600 masl inland to 0 masl on the coast (Zeidler and Kennedy 1994:13). Lower-lying coastal areas experience a dry tropical climate with 500 to 1000 mm in seasonal precipitation primarily between January and April, and support Very Dry and Dry Tropical Forest life zones. Higher elevations in the middle and upper reaches of the valley retain double the amount of rainfall primarily between December and April and support dry and Humid Pre-Montane Forest life zones (Cañadas 1983). During the past century, logging, cattle grazing, and intensive agriculture have been the primary forces responsible for valley-wide landscape change. Over 93% of the valley contains nonforested land used for agriculture and grazing, with the remainder comprising a mosaic patchwork of secondary growth forests that today is principally confined to isolated ridgetops and slopes (Zeidler and Kennedy 1994).

Systematic archaeological reconnaissance and testing in the valley have revealed a lengthy, and on occasion interrupted, prehispanic human occupation spanning at least 3500 calendar years (Table 10.1). Some 239 archaeological sites have been recorded through stratified probabilistic survey of semiarid coastal plain (Stratum I), subhumid coastal cordillera (Stratum II), and humid upland valley (Stratum III), in a 785 km² area (Fig. 10.2; Zeidler 1995; Zeidler and Zeidler 2002). A seven-phase cultural sequence, based in part on 38 radiocarbon determinations from 17 of these sites, is proposed for the area. The chronological sequence is further supported by the superpositioning of three volcanic airfall strata that were deposited during temporally discrete prehispanic eruptions. Regularly encountered in

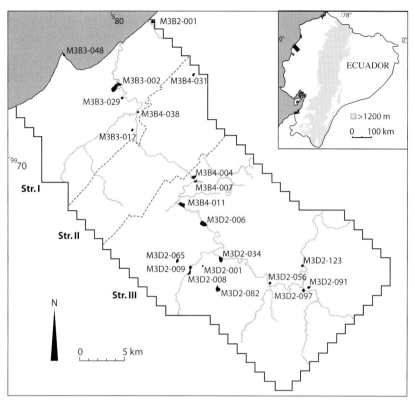

10.2 The Jama River Valley with major tributaries and archaeological sites examined in the study.

archaeological excavations and the exposed profiles of river cuts, these distinct layers of fine-grained tephra serve as convenient horizon markers for the occupational sequence (Zeidler, Buck, and Litton 1998). After centuries of compaction, these tephra layers of fluvially repositioned aeolian ash vary in depth from 0.05 m to 1.8 m throughout the valley (Donahue and Harbert 1994:49).

Prehispanic settlement of the valley began with an Early Formative Piquigua phase (Valdivia 8) occupation from 2030 to 1880 cal BC; however, it is possible that earlier material may lie deeply buried in alluvial contexts (Donahue and Harbert 1994:57). The first volcanic airfall (Tephra I) blanketed the valley during this 150-year occupation, dividing the Piquigua occupation into early and late phases. A late Piquigua occupation of the

Table 10.1. Prehispanic Cultural Occupation and Hiatus in the Jama Valley
(after Zeidler, Buck and Litton 1998; Zeidler and Isaacson 2003). All dates are calibrated.

CULTURAL SEQUENCE	CULTURAL COMPONENT	CERAMIC PHASE	95% PROBABILITY	MODAL VALUE	95% PROBABILITY
Historic	Campace?	Muchique 5	AD1360–1540	AD 1430–1640	AD 1620–1910
		Spanish Conquest (AD 1532)			
Regional Development	Jama-Coaque II	Muchique 4	AD 950–1360	AD 1290–1430	AD 1400–1620
		Muchique 3	AD 640–1108	AD 880–1260	AD 970–1430
		Muchique 2	AD 230–700	AD 420–790	AD 550–990
		Tephra III (hiatus)			
Regional Development	Jama-Coaque I	Muchique 1	620–50 BC	240–90 BC	100 BC–AD 350
		Tephra II (hiatus)			
Late Formative	Chorrera	Tabuchila	1730–1050 BC	1300–750 BC	1020–90 BC
		(hiatus)			
Early Formative	Valdivia 8	Piquigua (late)	2000 BC–?	1800 BC–?	1540 BC–?
		Tephra I			
EARLY FORMATIVE	Valdivia 8	Piquigua (early)	2320 BC–?	2030 BC–?	1880 BC–?

San Isidro site (M3D2-001) suggests some continued post-airfall occupation of the valley before it was abandoned for reasons probably unrelated to volcanic activity around 1900 cal BC. An occupational hiatus of some 600 years separates the Early Formative occupation of the valley from the Late Formative Tabuchila phase (Chorrera) reoccupation at 1300 cal BC. This second occupational phase was abruptly terminated at 750 cal BC with the appearance of a second volcanic airfall (Tephra II), which marks a major discontinuity in the cultural sequence. Over 500 years later the valley was repopulated with the appearance of a new Regional Development Jama-Coaque ceramic tradition, which is marked by the Muchique 1 phase beginning at 240 cal BC and ending at 90 cal AD. This same basic Jama-Coaque tradition continued after the appearance of a third volcanic airfall (Tephra III) which separates the Muchique 1 phase occupation from the subsequent Muchique 2 phase beginning 420 cal AD and ending at 790 cal AD. Muchique phase 3 began at 880 cal AD, although no occupational hiatus is inferred, and ended at 1260 cal AD. Muchique phase 4 began at 1290 cal AD and ended at 1430 cal AD. A final, but poorly understood Muchique phase 5 which began at 1430 cal AD and ended at 1640 cal AD may be associated with the historic Campace who inhabited the area at the time of the Spanish conquest (Zeidler, Buck and Litton 1998:173–75).

SOME OBSERVED EFFECTS OF RECENT
VOLCANIC TEPHRA FALLOUT

The principal environmental impact of volcanic activity on the Jama Valley system was caused by primary deposition of aeolian tephra with subsequent alluvial redeposition into secondary contexts. The repercussions of volcanic fallout can be gauged according to different environmental parameters of the event (Reycraft and Bawden 2000:1–2) and the varied responses of impacted organisms. These include: the event's magnitude, which directly implicates depth of tephra deposition; its frequency, duration, and temporal periodicity; the speed of the event's onset; the daily and seasonal timing of the event; the aerial extent and spatial dispersion of tephra fallout throughout the valley system; the location, topography, and condition of the impacted land surface; and, the ability of different organisms to cope with the variable parameters of the volcanic event. Published accounts of tephra fallout and its effects, gathered from historical records, firsthand observations, and actualistic studies can be used to understand its possible impact on the valley's prehispanic inhabitants.

Impacts of Primary Tephra Deposition

The initial depth and duration of aeolian tephra deposits is an important consideration for measuring organismic response. Burial in upwards of 1 m of tephra can kill all vegetation, whereas 150 mm of deposits can destroy herbaceous vegetation in some areas while not damaging shrubs and trees. The weight of ash accumulation alone can mechanically overload plants, and burial can alter photosynthesis, abrade leaves, and influence underground structures. Invertebrates and vertebrates can suffer heavy mortality, usually from burial, asphyxia, ingestion of tephra, desiccation, and topical contamination and abrasion (Anderson and MacMahon 1985; Antos and Zobel 1985; Burt 1961; Dale, Delgado-Acevedo, and MacMahon 2005; MacMahon 1982; Mack 1981; Rees 1979).

Impacts of Secondary Tephra Transport and Redeposition

Waterborne erosion of primary tephra deposits can have different affects on different habitats when ash is hydrodynamically removed from primary depositional contexts that are prone to erosive forces and subsequently transported and redeposited into areas of secondary accumulation. The former usually include sloped terrain at higher elevations, whereas the latter are often level floodplains at lower elevations. Redeposition of volcanic tephras can be a major step toward systemic recovery in eroded areas, yet may hinder or harm recuperation in areas of secondary accumulation. Erosive forces prevail in wet climates and on sloped terrain where removal of ash deposits can promote plant survival and stimulate plant regrowth through exposure of the original soil surface.

On the receiving end, eroded materials can destroy vegetation in lower-lying, particularly riparian, areas. Waterborne ash enters the watershed, where heavy silt loads can: block light penetration and inhibit primary production; alter aqueous habitats through scouring and deposition; and, kill fish outright through gill abrasion. As water velocity is reduced, suspended sediments eventually redeposit in riparian settings at lower elevations where they can further hinder or aggravate systemic recovery (Antos and Zobel 1985, 1987; Burt 1961; Crawford 1986; Dale, Delgado-Acevedo, and MacMahon 2005; del Moral 1981; Eggler 1963; Kiilsgaard et al. 1986;

Lucas 1986; Means et al. 1982; Phinney 1982; Rees 1979; Segerstrom 1950; Wissmar 1982).

Response and Recovery

The erosion of primary tephra deposits can accelerate, retard, or disrupt systemic recovery from volcanic events depending upon climatic and surface susceptibility to erosive forces and whether or not the area in question is on the giving or receiving end of tephra redeposition. Erosion plays a significant role in vegetation recovery, primarily because volcanic tephras are relatively deficient in nutrients available to plants, potentially toxic, and poor in water retention. Many buried plants are incapable of growing through deposits greater than 300 cm in depth. Eroded hill slopes expose underlying soil parent material, and areas with little or no tephra accumulation serve as refugia for plant survival which can be important for vegetation recovery. In impacted areas, surviving and pioneering invertebrates and vertebrates can include arthropods, beetles, and fossorial and semi-fossorial taxa. In either case, habitat generalists with broad ecological tolerances, especially those that characterize unstable and ruderal habitats, are expected, especially where structural heterogeneity is high. Mobile birds, especially insectivorous species, can quickly recolonize once ravaged areas. Intrinsically less stable floodplains are much slower to recover from ash deposition and redeposition. Low-relief cultivated areas at lower elevations are often buried in ash and can remain useless for agriculture for long periods of time (Adams et al. 1986; Anderson 1982; Anderson and MacMahon 1985; Antos and Zobel 1985, 1987; Burt 1961; Dale, Delgado-Acevedo, and MacMahon 2005; del Moral 1981; Edwards 2005; Edwards et al. 1986; Eggler 1963; Kiilsgaard et al. 1986; MacMahon 1982; MacMahon et al. 1989; Manuwal et al. 1987; Means et al. 1982; Nolan 1979; Olson 1983; Rees 1979; Segerstrom 1950; Sloniker 1986; Thornton et al. 1990; Ugolini and Zasoski 1979).

PREHISPANIC RESPONSES TO VOLCANIC EPISODES IN THE JAMA VALLEY

Various authors have highlighted the impact of volcanism on prehispanic cultural development in a region that was periodically affected by potentially catastrophic events originating in the geologically active northern Andes (Hall and Mothes 1999; Isaacson 1987, 1994; Isaacson and Zeidler

1999; Lathrap, Isaacson, and McEwan 1984; Zeidler and Isaacson 2003). The archaeological record in the Jama Valley suggests that the prehispanic response to tephra fallout was variable through time. Very limited evidence hints that the first eruptive event (Tephra I) was survived by Early Formative Piquigua phase occupants at San Isidro (M3D2-001). Shortly thereafter, the record suggests a roughly 600-year occupational gap until the appearance of the late Formative Tabuchila phase. This is followed by disruption and a lengthy hiatus after the deposition of Tephra II, which clearly marks the end of Formative culture in the valley. Over two centuries later, the earliest Muchique 1 phase of the long Jama-Coaque cultural sequence appears, and despite the potentially catastrophic occurrence of a major volcanic event (Tephra III), a subsequent Muchique 2 phase follows. At this time, if the valley had been abandoned at all, it would only have been for a potentially short period that was measured in decades rather than centuries (Zeidler 2006). Later phases in the same archaeological tradition continue uninterrupted for over a thousand years until after the arrival of Europeans. A major research question has developed out of the constructed valley-wide archaeological sequence: why did tephra from an earlier eruption signal the end of Formative occupation, while later Jama-Coaque occupations were able to persist throughout the valley system despite clear evidence of a potentially catastrophic volcanic event?

Interpretation of settlement and archaeobotanical data suggests that later Jama-Coaque populations were heavily invested in a much more extensive and diversified agroecological system that incorporated significant off-river cultivation. Earlier Formative agriculture, although implementing some off-river cultivation, tended to be focused on floodplain production. The potential impact of the sudden and unexpected deposition of volcanic tephra on hill slope cultivation can be dramatically different from that of floodplain farming. The mixing of silty clays with volcanic materials directly above and below the Jama Valley tephra layers suggests that these sediments were formed through rapid erosion likely induced by heavier rainfall before and after volcanic eruption (Donahue and Harbert 1994:49). Cultivating fields on sloping hillsides exposes erosional surfaces that augment the runoff of deposited volcanic tephra, which is subsequently transported to lower elevation floodplain habitats where it eventually accumulates.

While acknowledging the ever present caveat that earlier sites in any archaeological sequence can remain undetected because of deep burial or complete destruction, available evidence suggests that Formative and post-Formative occupations were characterized by different settlement strategies throughout the valley. The Early Formative Piquigua phase colonization appears to have been restricted to a few larger pockets of inland (Stratum II and III, Fig. 10.2) alluvial bottomland along the main river channel, particularly in the immediate vicinity of San Isidro. Mound building began here at two adjacent sites (M3D2-001, M3D2-002), which could have served as a central place in an early settlement hierarchy. Small sites begin to appear in nonalluvial areas at higher elevations during the Late Formative Tabuchila phase occupation; however, the densest concentrations overlie earlier Formative components in alluvial pockets, especially around San Isidro. Beginning in its earliest Muchique 1 phase, the post-Formative Jama-Coaque tradition is markedly pan-valley in orientation. Nevertheless, dispersion into nonalluvial areas is not appreciable until Muchique 2, shortly after the third volcanic event. Hereafter most of the noticeable valley infilling occurs, along with a dramatic increase in population density on nonalluvial uplands. Archaeological data suggest that during the Muchique 2 and 3 phases, three chiefly polities with notable settlement hierarchies became established throughout the valley system. Each is spaced roughly 16 km apart, and is marked by a large focal mound over 10,000 m^2 in basal area, at Santa Rosa in the lower valley, and San Isidro and Zapallo in the upper valley (Pearsall and Zeidler 1994; Zeidler 2005).

Diachronic changes in valley vegetation structure are suggested by botanical analyses of data recovered from superpositioned fluvial deposits, buried A-horizons, and transported tephra that had accumulated from before the Piquigua occupation up to the present. These layers are exposed in a deep 8.825 m sediment profile located on the left bank of the Jama River, at Río Grande, about 3.5 km northeast of San Isidro (M3D2-006, Fig. 10.2). Although maize (*Zea mays*) appears early in the sequence, it is not until the Tabuchila and Muchique 1 phases that major shifts in vegetation cover are recorded. In this stratum, previously predominant forest taxa are replaced by open area taxa, and particulate charcoal first becomes common or abundant. Both patterns are attributed to forest clearance by humans, when it is suggested that upland cultivation was well underway prior to the Tephra III event (Veintimilla 1998). Phytolith data from San Isidro (M3D2-001) reveal a consistent suite of cultivated and utilized plants from Early Formative through Muchique 4 phases which includes maize, arrowroot

(Marantaceae), achira (*Canna edulis*), palms and sedges (Cyperaceae), and wild grasses (Poaceae), especially bamboos. Although subject to further confirmation, maize appears to increase in abundance, relative to tree fruits, beans, and roots/tubers from the Muchique 1 phase to the early Muchique 2 phase. It is suggested that rapidly maturing annuals like maize were best adapted to the altered growing conditions that appeared after Tephra III. Slower maturing tree crops and underground tubers would have been hard hit, inaccessible, and out of production for lengthy periods of time. Furthermore, had specialized crop production been focused around alluvial bottomland ceremonial centers with staple cultivation primarily concentrated on hill slope farms, then later agroecological systems would have been more resilient in the face of volcanic disaster (Pearsall 1996, 2004).

Additional evidence from the Jama Valley's prehispanic record includes a large collection of over 85,000 archaeofaunal specimens recovered from 39 archaeological sites. Previous analyses of individual assemblages recovered from specific excavation contexts, and preliminary interpretations of the entire data set, suggest that the assorted faunas had originally accumulated through natural and cultural mechanisms within a mosaic environment of anthropogenic forest fragments (Stahl 1994, 2000, 2006). The relationship between forest fragmentation and volcanic events throughout the Jama Valley occupational sequence, and its implications for prehispanic resilience to periodic disruption, remain to be explored.

PERIODIC VOLCANISM AND THE ARCHAEOFAUNAL RECORD IN THE JAMA VALLEY

A total of 42 assemblages comprising 73,183 archaeofaunal specimens are clearly associated with the volcanic tephra layers at 21 archaeological sites throughout the Jama Valley. These include: 10 assemblages from Formative contexts below Tephra II; 13 from post-Formative contexts above Tephra II but below Tephra III; and, 19 from post-Formative contexts above Tephra III (Table 10.2). The overall character of the collection is strongly influenced by the intensive use of flotation recovery in the Jama Valley Archaeological-Paleoethnobotanical project (Pearsall 1995). The large collection is highly fragmented, taxonomically rich, and unevenly composed of preserved specimens from small-bodied animals. Unidentifiable fragments dominate the archaeofaunal specimens, and many more could not be reliably identified

Table 10.2. Archaeological Sites, Ceramic Affiliations, Relationship to Tephras, and Archaeofaunal Sample Size

SITE NUMBER	SITE NAME	CERAMIC PHASE	ABOVE TEPHRA	N
M3B2-001	Don Juan	M1	II	7257
M3B2-001	Don Juan	M3	III	28435
M3B3-001	La Mina	M2	III	190
M3B3-002	El Tape	M2	III	155
M3B3-012	Acrópolis	M3	III	4
M3B3-012	Acrópolis	M4	III	103
M3B3-029	Ladrillera	M2	III	3
M3B3-048	Punta La Cereza	M	II	1
M3B4-004	—	M	II	1
M3B4-007	La Isla	M2/3	III	234
M3B4-007	La Isla	M3	III	175
M3B4-011	Pechichal	M2	III	12572
M3B4-031	El Mocoral	T	I	963
M3B4-038	—	M	II	18
M3D2-001	San Isidro	M	II	214
M3D2-001	San Isidro	M1	II	373
M3D2-001	San Isidro	M2	III	1083
M3D2-001	San Isidro	M2/3	III	181
M3D2-001	San Isidro	P	I	424
M3D2-001	San Isidro	T	I	965
M3D2-001	San Isidro	T	0	83
M3D2-006	Río Grande	M	II	56
M3D2-006	Río Grande	M2	III	263
M3D2-008	Dos Caminos	M	II	2
M3D2-008	Dos Caminos	T	I	3142
M3D2-009	Finca Cueva	M	II	278
M3D2-009	Finca Cueva	M1	II	4138
M3D2-009	Finca Cueva	M1/2	II	471
M3D2-009	Finca Cueva	M2	III	3053
M3D2-009	Finca Cueva	M2/3	III	1549
M3D2-009	Finca Cueva	M3	III	3437
M3D2-009	Finca Cueva	T	I	23
M3D2-009	Finca Cueva	T/P	I	3
M3D2-034	Muchique	P	I	2
M3D2-056	Dislabón	M1	II	503
M3D2-056	Dislabón	M2	III	478
M3D2-065	Capaperro	M	II	111
M3D2-065	Capaperro	P	I	2199
M3D2-082	Cuadros	M2/3	III	3
M3D2-091	Eloy Alfaro	M2/3	III	2
M3D2-097	Doño Bajo	P	I	34
M3D2-123	Hacienda Paloma	M2/3	III	2

73183

beyond zoological class. Others include the ubiquitous tiny bones and teeth of small animals, whose skeletons tend to be preserved with greater completeness in the archaeological deposits. A minor and significant sample includes small fragments of larger animals that do not appear in proportion to their expected dietary importance, but are often preserved as isolated specimens of structurally dense bone. The preservation of archaeological bone throughout the Jama Valley contexts was likely the outcome of complex and interrelated variables. These are related to the natural disposition of neotropical vertebrate communities and various aspects of cultural exploitation and noncultural modification that are responsible for the differential alteration of bone specimens prior to and after burial (Stahl 1995).

Bone preservation was likely initiated along two distinct pathways. The sample is dominated by specimens from small eurytopic habitat generalists. Context and relative skeletal completeness implicate many of these ubiquitous specimens as incidental accumulations in and around locations of deposition. These animals could serve as potentially reliable proxies for understanding local conditions at the time of assemblage formation. In contrast, lesser numbers of isolated specimens from larger animals likely accumulated through intentional human consumption and cultural disposal. Many of these animals prefer cleared areas and their remains contribute important information about extra-local conditions as they were likely procured in and transported to areas somewhat removed from their location of eventual deposition.

Do zooarchaeological data support the interpretation of anthropogenic forest mosaics throughout the entire occupational sequence, particularly in light of major volcanic impacts? How do recovered archaeofaunal assemblages compare from contexts before and after sequential volcanic events? Is there evidence in the archaeofaunal record of different adaptive responses to periodic volcanism throughout the valley by Formative and post-Formative inhabitants? Do zooarchaeological data support a claim of Formative agroecological production characterized by floodplain farming prior to Tephra II with increased post-Formative utilization of hill slopes, especially following Tephra III?

The following discussion explores richness, evenness or equitability, and ubiquity within the archaeofaunal assemblage as they relate to volcanic impacts on the Jama Valley. Assemblage richness—the numbers of different kinds of preserved and identified taxa—is examined before and after volcanic events in order to evaluate whether a restricted or broad range of animals accumulated in archaeological deposits. What kinds of animals and inferred habitats are represented in these deposits? Assemblage Evenness—the numerical distribution of preserved specimens that constitute the different categories of identified taxa—is examined before and after volcanic events in order to evaluate whether archaeological deposits are dominated (low evenness) by certain animals or whether they include equitable distributions (high evenness) of different animals. What kinds of animals and associated habitats are represented? Relative ubiquity of specimens within archaeological contexts is examined before and after volcanic events. Did certain animals consistently accumulate in deposits, and possibly why?

Assemblage Richness and Tephra Contexts

Assemblage richness is explored at different and inclusive levels of zoological classification (Order, Family, Genus) in order to maximize the available data. Certain specimens may not be identifiable to increasingly precise levels of classification due to a lack of osteological features with finer grained diagnostic acuity and/or because of their condition of preservation. Sample sizes vary widely between contexts, from as little as one specimen (which may have little significance to this study) to over 28,000; therefore, assemblage richness is examined with two techniques, each of which is sensitive to the relationship between sample size and diversity measures. The first uses rarefaction analysis, which estimates differences in richness measures for smaller sample sizes through interpolation from larger samples (Holland 2003). The second is a popular simulation approach, which extrapolates from pooled smaller samples (Kintigh 1992). Both techniques carry their own assumptions and problems (e g., Birks and Line 1991; Gotelli and Colwell 2001; Orton 2000; Ringrose 1993), and are here used in tandem as analytical instruments for data exploration.

Whether analyzed with rarefaction or simulation, each tephra-associated assemblage displays depressed assemblage richness at the level of zoological Order (human specimens are removed from all analyses). Over 80% have richness values below the lower confidence intervals, and those that do not tend to have small sample sizes. A similar ranking of zoological orders dominates the Formative and post-Formative faunas: Rodentia (rodents); Artiodactyla (even-toed ungulates); Carnivora (carnivores); Xenarthra (sloths and armadillos); and Anura (frogs and toads).

Figures 10.3 and 10.4 illustrate rarefaction and simulation results respectively at the level of zoological Family. All assemblages display markedly depressed richness, as only a few appear above the lower confidence intervals of either technique. Many (n=48) zoological families (excluding Hominidae) are identified in the collection; however, most of the Jama assemblages tend to be characterized by relative few families regardless of temporal affiliation, notably Muridae (mice), Cervidae (deer), Dasypodidae (armadillo), and Leporidae (rabbits).

A trend of depressed richness continues in the rarefaction (Fig. 10.5)

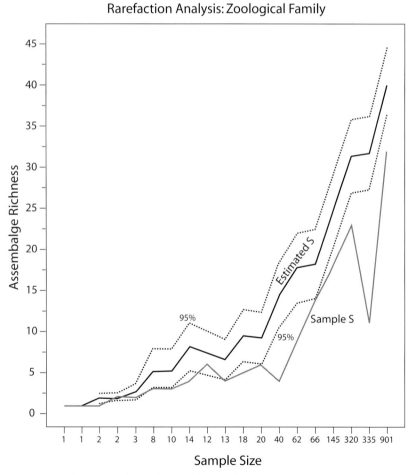

10.3 Rarefaction Analysis of assemblage richness: level of zoological family.

and simulation (Fig. 10.6) of assemblages at the level of zoological genera. However, some disparities may be attributed to differences in modes of accumulation. The Formative assemblage at San Isidro (M3D2-001) has higher than expected richness values which fall within the upper confidence intervals of either analysis. The large San Isidro mound incorporates a variety of sampled depositional contexts, and therefore likely accumulated a wider range of archaeologically recovered specimens than other sites. Pechichal (M3B4-011) is a large pit with very depressed richness values despite its large sample size. Specimens may have collected in this feature through relatively restricted modes of accumulation, particularly via the accidental entrapment of microfaunas (Stahl 2000). Similarly, many of the faunal specimens from Capaperro (M3D2-065) were recovered from a prominent human burial feature (Zeidler, Stahl, and Sutliff 1998), and likely reflect a restricted range of taxa. Nonetheless, certain genera stand out amongst these depressed richness values, regardless of temporal context: *Oryzomys* (rice rats), *Sigmodon* (cotton rats), *Odocoileus* (whitetail deer), *Dasypus*

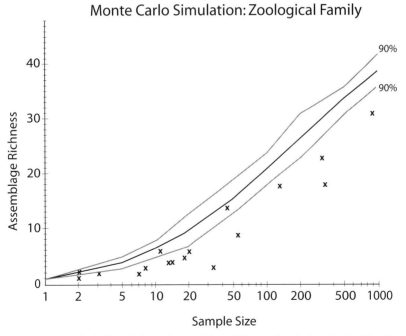

10.4 Monte Carlo Simulation of assemblage richness: level of zoological family.

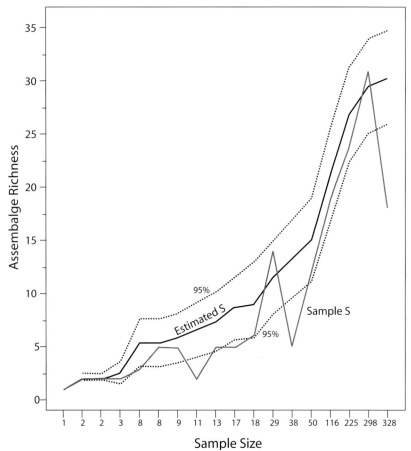

10.5 Rarefaction Analysis of assemblage richness: level of zoological genus.

(armadillo), *Proechimys* (spiny rats), and *Sylvilagus* (rabbits). These trends are further explored in examinations of evenness and ubiquity.

Assemblage Evenness and Tephra Contexts

Assemblage evenness is explored at inclusive levels of zoological classification (Order, Family, Genus) through simulation. Over 80% of the assemblages have evenness values lower than the 90% confidence interval at the ordinal level. Three sites with higher than expected evenness include two Formative contexts. One includes a burial feature (M3D2-065), and another

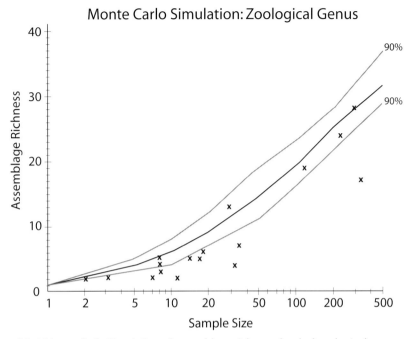

10.6 Monte Carlo Simulation of assemblage richness: level of zoological genus.

(M3D2-097) has a sample size of only two specimens. In ranked order, assemblage evenness is numerically dominated by the following zoological orders: Rodentia, Artiodactyla, Carnivora, Xenarthra, Anura, Serpentes (a Suborder of reptile but included at the ordinal level to distinguish snakes from lizards), and Lagomorpha (rabbits). The list is almost identical to the catalogue of zoological orders that dominate the depressed richness of most assemblages.

Figure 10.7 illustrates simulation results at the level of zoological family. Over 85% of the assemblages exhibit markedly depressed evenness values, as only a few appear above the lower confidence intervals. The M3D2-097 assemblage with two specimens shows higher than expected evenness, and the elevated value for M3D2-001 may again be explained by differences in modes of accumulation. This is corroborated by the depressed values of special contexts like M3B4-011 and M3D2-065. Despite the wide range of zoological families (excluding Hominidae) that contribute to the collection, a markedly redundant ranked list of families again contributes to

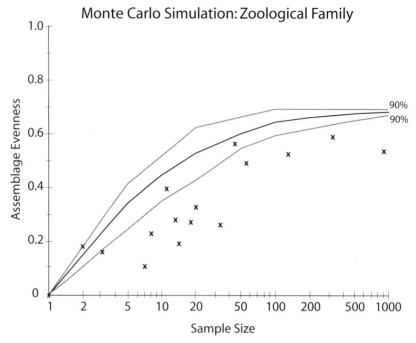

10.7 Monte Carlo Simulation of assemblage evenness: level of zoological family.

assemblage domination: Muridae, Cervidae, Dasypodidae, Echimyidae (spiny rats), and Leporidae.

The trend of depressed evenness continues in simulation (Fig. 10.8) of assemblages at the level of zoological genera, as again over 80% of the assemblages have values falling below the lower confidence intervals. The higher than expected richness value within the upper confidence interval of the Formative assemblage at M3D2-001 and the increased depression of values for M3B4-011 and M3D2-065 further suggest that they are heavily influenced by differences in modes of accumulation. A familiar ranked list of the most important genera includes *Oryzomys, Sigmodon, Odocoileus, Dasypus, Proechimys,* and *Sylvilagus*. Other notable taxa include *Akodon* (grass mouse), *Mazama* (brocket deer), *Dasyprocta* (agouti), and *Tayassu* (peccary).

Assemblage Ubiquity and Tephra Contexts

Table 10.3 (zoological family) and Table 10.4 (zoological genus) list the underlying numerical structure of richness and evenness values in relation

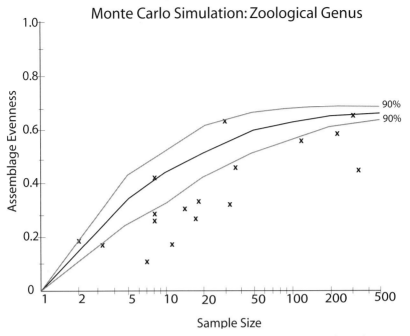

10.8 Monte Carlo Simulation of assemblage evenness: level of zoological genus.

to contextual associations with tephra layers throughout the valley. Each table records the total numbers of identified specimens (NISP) for each taxonomic category in the entire sample and their distribution where known within archaeological contexts positioned under Tephra II (N=107), above Tephra II but under Tephra III (N=101), and above Tephra III (N=172). Data in these tables should be interpreted with caution. The larger sample size of later post-Tephra III (N=51,922) contexts may include higher numbers of rare specimens simply as a factor of increased sampling, compared to post-Tephra II (N=13,423) and pre-Tephra II (N=7838) samples. The relatively small sample of Formative contexts may be an artifact of archaeological recovery if earlier evidence was either deeply buried or destroyed. Different contexts may be differentially preserved due to burial depth and time spent in exposed and burial environments. Different depositional contexts may have accumulated variable faunal signatures depending upon their unique configurations. However, the interpretation of assemblage composition through analyses of ubiquity, richness, and evenness reveals a broad pattern that makes a certain degree of ecological sense.

Table 10.3. Ubiquity of Vertebrate Families in Archaeological
Contexts with Tephra Affiliations

FAMILY (NISP)	NAME	UNDER TII (N=107)	ABOVE TII (N=101)	ABOVE TIII (N=172)
Accipitridae (1)	Hawks	0	0	1
Anatidae (2)	Ducks	1	0	1
Ardeidae (3)	Egrets, Herons, Bitterns	0	1	2
Ariidae (58)	Marine Catfish	0	4	23
Boidae (27)	Boas	0	4	12
Bradypodidae (5)	Sloths	1	0	4
Bufonidae (6)	Toads	1	1	3
Canidae (3)	Dogs	0	1	2
Caviidae (7)	Cuy	0	0	4
Cebidae (16)	Monkeys	0	1	10
Cervidae (90)	Deer	13	11	39
Carcharhinidae (21)	Shark	0	3	5
Columbidae (3)	Pigeons, Doves	0	1	1
Crotalidae (2)	Vipers	0	0	1
Cuculidae (1)	Cuckoos, Anis	0	0	1
Cunciculidae (9)	Pacas	1	2	4
Dasyatidae (1)	Rays, Skates	0	0	1
Dasypodidae (204)	Armadillos	13	12	38
Dasyproctidae (50)	Agoutis	1	4	29
Didelphidae (72)	Opossums	5	1	15
Echimyidae (82)	Spiny Rats	1	5	39
Emydidae (26)	Pond Turtles	1	0	3
Erethizontidae (1)	Porcupines	0	1	0
Felidae (18)	Cats	7	1	5
Iguanidae (21)	Iguanas	1	5	10
Leporidae (43)	Rabbits	5	2	18
Lutjanidae (21)	Snapper	0	2	10
Muridae (467)	Mice	20	22	84
Mustelidae (2)	Weasels, Otters	0	2	0
Myrmecophagidae (1)	Anteaters	0	0	1
Ophidiidae (1)	Cusk Eel	0	0	1
Phyllostomidae (7)	Leaf-nosed Bats	2	0	3
Pomadasyidae (219)	Grunts	0	7	28
Procyonidae (3)	Raccoons	0	1	2
Psittacidae (1)	Parrots	1	0	0
Rallidae (2)	Rails, Coots, Gallinules	0	0	2
Ranidae (3)	Frogs	0	0	2
Scaridae (1)	Parrotfish	0	0	1
Sciaenidae (285)	Drums, Croakers	1	8	32
Sciuridae (8)	Squirrels	0	1	4
Scolopacidae (1)	Sandpipers, Snipes	0	1	0
Serranidae (54)	Sea Bass, Groupers	0	3	14
Sphyraenidae (28)	Barracudas	0	5	14
Tapiridae (2)	Tapirs	2	0	0
Tayassuidae (23)	Peccaries	2	4	15
Tinamidae (2)	Tinamous	0	0	2

A group of zoological families is relatively ubiquitous in all contexts, regardless of association with specific tephra layers (Table 10.3). Greater ecological resolution is provided by considering which genera constitute these families (Table 10.4). These faunas are consistently the same taxa that contribute to low richness and evenness values in most of the assemblages. They include Sigmodontine or New World rats and mice, which at the genus level are comprised of rice rats (*Oryzomys*), cotton rats (*Sigmodon*), and grass mouse (*Akodon*). High numbers of specimens at the ordinal level indicate significant skeletal completeness, especially in contexts conducive to natural entrapment. Ubiquitous non-Sigmodontine rodents include spiny rat (*Proechimys*), agouti (*Dasyprocta*), and paca (*Cuniculus*). Deer (*Odocoileus* and *Mazama*) are omnipresent in the Jama Valley assemblages as they normally are everywhere. Armadillos (*Dasypus*), rabbits (*Sylvilagus*), and didelphid marsupials, including large (*Didelphis*) and mouse (*Marmosa*) opossum, are also common and ubiquitous. Felids, especially larger jaguars (*Panthera*), are conspicuous for their ceremonial significance, as are favored food items like peccaries (Tayassu). Anurans (frogs and toads), iguanas (*Iguana*), and snakes, especially boas (*Boa*), round out the menagerie of ubiquitous taxa.

Many rarer taxa were only recovered in later post-Formative contexts, above Tephra II. These include certain smaller mammals, birds, and marine fish. Cebid monkeys (Cebidae), raccoon (*Procyon*), squirrel (*Sciurus*), tree anteater (*Tamandua*), and the Andean domesticated cuy (*Cavia*) are restricted to post-Formative contexts. A few isolated bird specimens of egret, heron or bittern (Ardeidae), pigeon or dove (Columbidae), cuckoo or anis (Cuculidae), rail, coot or gallinule (Rallidae), sandpiper or snipe (Scolopacidae), and tinamou (*Crypturellus*) were recovered from later contexts. Available archaeological data suggest that coastal zones in the lower valley were only significantly inhabited after the end of the Formative and Tephra II. Although drums and croakers (Sciaenidae) were identified in one Formative context, the bulk of marine fish, including catfish (Ariidae), shark (Carcharhinidae), rays and skates (Dasyatidae), snapper (Lutjanidae), cusk eel (Ophidiidae), grunts (Pomadasyidae), parrotfish (Scaridae), sea bass and groupers (Sciaenidae), and barracuda (Sphyraenidae) are recorded in abundance from post-Formative and some interior valley contexts. The only recovered taxa restricted to Formative contexts were parrot (Psittacidae) and tapir (*Tapirus*).

Table 10.4. Ubiquity of Vertebrate Genera in Archaeological Contexts with Tephra Affiliations

GENUS (NISP)	NAME	UNDER TI (N=107)	ABOVE TII (N=101)	ABOVE TIII (N=172)
Akodon (9)	Grass Mouse	3	1	5
Alouatta (12)	Howler Monkey	0	0	7
Anolis (6)	Anole	0	1	4
Arius (1)	Sea Catfish	0	0	1
Artibeus (5)	Fruit Bat	2	0	1
Boa (27)	Boa	0	4	12
Bradypus (2)	Sloth	0	0	2
Brotula (1)	Brotula	0	0	2
Bufo (4)	Toad	0	1	2
Cavia (7)	Cuy	0	0	4
Cebus (2)	Capuchin Monkey	0	0	2
Coendou (1)	Porcupine	0	1	0
Crypturellus (1)	Tinamou	0	0	1
Cuniculus (9)	Paca	1	2	4
Dasyprocta (50)	Agouti	1	4	29
Dasypus (204)	Armadillo	13	13	29
Didelphis (59)	Opossum	0	1	18
Felis (9)	Cats	3	0	3
Iguana (5)	Iguana	0	2	2
Marmosa (13)	Mouse Opossum	7	0	7
Mazama (8)	Brocket Deer	2	1	5
Nasua (1)	Coati	0	0	1
Numenius (1)	Whimbrel	0	1	0
Odocoileus (62)	White-tailed Deer	7	6	31
Oryzomys (339)	Rice Rat	12	16	72
Panchomys? (1)	Leaf-eared Mouse (extinct)	1	0	0
Panthera (8)	Jaguar	4	1	1
Phyllostomus (1)	Leaf-nosed Bat	0	0	1
Proechimys (82)	Spiny Rat	1	5	33
Rana (2)	Frog	0	1	1
Rhinoclemys (26)	Wood Turtle	1	0	3
Rhipidomys (3)	Climbing Mouse	0	0	2
Scarus (1)	Parrotfish	0	0	1
Sciurus (3)	Squirrel	0	0	2
Sigmodon (105)	Cotton Rat	5	14	36
Sphyraena (28)	Barracuda	0	4	14
Sylvilagus (42)	Rabbit	5	2	17
Tamandua (1)	Tree Anteater	0	0	1
Tapirus (2)	Tapir	2	0	0
Tayassu (23)	Peccary	2	3	15
Zygodontomys (3)	Cane Mouse	1	0	2

DISCUSSION

Related aspects of archaeofaunal diversity from various spatial and temporal contexts suggest that the entire prehispanic sequence of human occupation in the Jama Valley was associated with a redundant array of animal taxa. Although the preserved faunal specimens had originally accumulated through different cultural and natural pathways, a repetitive list of associated faunas is to be anticipated. Humans and most predators are predisposed to select and consume a restricted catalogue of dietary items. The archaeological specimens also regularly include an often overlapping suite of animals whose remains had accumulated accidentally in and around human settlements. Both sets of dietary and non-dietary faunas are composed of taxa that frequent anthropogenic conditions, and represent archaeological evidence for a pervasive cultural footprint in the neotropics. They suggest forest clearance and the persistence of fragmented landscapes (Stahl 2000, 2006, 2008).

The animals that lived and died within the immediate vicinity of archaeological contexts are particularly useful for recording local conditions at the time of assemblage formation. Most of the recovered Jama specimens consist of small eurytopic generalists with broad niche requirements that are attracted to the unstable conditions of relatively open environments. When resource levels are high, low species richness and equitability are supported in unstable environments where large populations of rapidly reproducing r-selected generalists have a decided competitive advantage (Valentine 1971:57). Intermediate levels of environmental instability in neotropical forest ecosystems are critical for maintaining high species diversity (Colinvaux 1998; Connell 1978). Localized and intermediate grade perturbations caused by fire, treefall, disease, drought, flood, and animals including humans are frequent and commonplace.

Small and local habitat generalists dominate the archaeofaunal profile in most Jama Valley contexts. Preserved specimens of these taxa are generally ubiquitous, numerically abundant, and skeletally complete, and were likely accumulated inadvertently. Human disturbance favors ruderal or weedy species of frogs, snakes, insectivorous understory birds, and rodents which become superabundant with the disappearance of specialized animals (Malcolm 1998:48). Frogs and snakes are little affected by fragmentation and invade forest edges where they thrive on more secure food resources. Smaller mammals like rice rats, cotton rats, grass mice, and mouse opossums are especially prevalent in second growth, disturbed habitats, and human-made clearings.

The isolated fragments of specimens from a redundant set of larger animals likely represent the intentional byproduct of preferred human dietary selection. Favored prey items are composed of eurytopic taxa that thrive in edge conditions created through forest fragmentation. They include ubiquitous food sources such as deer, armadillo, collared peccary, and a range of larger rodents like spiny rat, agouti, and paca. These animals could have been procured in areas at varying distance from sites of eventual bone deposition, and strongly suggest the existence of fragmented landscape mosaics as a backdrop to the cleared settlements in and around which the local microfaunas had accumulated (see Stahl 2000, 2006, and 2008 for references).

Human activities are marked by vegetation clearance, particularly in the creation of agricultural fields and gardens. Humans are well aware of the many benefits that cleared land can bring to the menu. Gardens are exploited as much for intentionally sown, maintained, and conserved plant products as they are for the animals that are attracted to these culturally concentrated food sources. Neotropical archaeofaunal assemblages that are dominated by these taxa indicate vegetation clearance, which hints at the strong possibility of gardening. The archaeofaunal and botanical evidence suggests that farmers had inhabited the Jama Valley since the Early Formative. The settlement data indicate that early agricultural production was decidedly oriented toward riverine floodplains. Settlement and limited botanical data suggest that later post-Formative populations had intensified production by expanding agricultural effort into the expansive upland hill slopes. The animal bone data remain somewhat mute on this latter point as the entire sequence appears to have been characterized by a redundant set of habitat generalists. Although upland farming can not be excluded from the agricultural inventory of early Formative farmers, some clues in the archaeofaunal record might suggest its possible intensification later in the occupational sequence.

The zooarchaeological "staples" in later Jama-Coaque contexts are accompanied by additional taxa that frequent fragmented conditions, whether they were incidentally introduced commensal faunas and/or intentionally procured animals. Notable mammals include Cebid monkey, raccoon, squirrel, and tree anteater, which all utilize landscape fragments in their inhabited range. Highly mobile birds include the little tinamou which favors the habitats of agricultural landscapes, as do species of pigeons and cuckoos. The significance of these taxa is difficult to evaluate, as they may be rarer taxa fortuitously recovered in the greater sample size of post-Formative assemblages, or simply excluded from Formative assemblages due to an accident of preservation.

It may be important that coastal areas of the Jama Valley lack any Formative sites, but it is presently difficult to evaluate whether this pattern was real or due to the vagaries of burial and/or destruction. Post-Formative inhabitants definitely occupied the coast, and at times in spectacular fashion. It is of no surprise that the bulk of identified marine fish are recovered in Jama-Coaque contexts. Only one drum and croaker specimen was identified in a Formative context; otherwise, catfish, shark, rays and skates, snapper, cusk eel, grunts, parrotfish, sea bass and groupers, and barracuda were exclusively restricted to later Jama-Coaque assemblages. Although most are recovered from coastal contexts at Don Juan (M3B2-001), a number of interior sites were clearly provisioned at this time, including sites in the lower (El Tape M3B2-002, Ladrillera M3B3-029) and upper valley (Dos Caminos M3D2-008, Finca Cueva M3D2-009). Formative inhabitants were undoubtedly aware of the nearby ocean and its resource potential; however, the only significant evidence for its use is from coastal Jama-Coaque occupation. The later prevalence of marine taxa, especially at inland locations, might be evidence for the increased logistical capability of a multi-valley social organization that would also be able to manage a catastrophic event more effectively than its Formative predecessor.

The differential response of later Jama-Coaque societies to volcanic devastation within their valley may have resulted from a number of interrelated variables that might be interpreted from the archaeological record. In comparison to their Formative predecessors, Jama-Coaque occupations were certainly more substantial. Populations were larger and denser, the political-economic system was minimally valley-wide, the subsistence base was likely more extensive, and response to calamity may have been more easily coordinated by a centralized political hierarchy. Whereas abandonment may no longer have been an option, resiliency may have become practicable (Santley et al 2000; Zeidler 2006). What is clearly present in the archaeofaunal data are preserved specimens identified from a redundant set of animals whose ecologies strongly implicate the persistence of fragmented landscape mosaics throughout the Jama Valley's entire prehispanic occupation. Their significance should be considered as meaningful as the valley's durable and highly visible mounds which were deliberately reoccupied over the span of four millennia despite periodic volcanic disasters. Archaeological excavation confirms that the largest mounds were repeatedly occupied since the Early Formative. They appear to have served as persistent places that were repeatedly reconstituted with newer monuments, even after serial volcanic catastrophes had disrupted the ritual landscape (Zeidler and Zeidler 2002).

The archaeological data also suggest that there was more to the prehispanic world of the Jama Valley than just its durable and visible earthen mounds. The archaeological record documents a persistent landscape of vegetation mosaics created by humans over the course of the valley's entire occupational record. Both its longevity and persistence, even in the face of repeated devastation, indicate that it was the preferred landscape of choice. The idea of a culturally familiarized and constructed landscape was suggested years ago by Jack Harlan, a plant geneticist, breeder, and pioneer in the origin of plant domestication. Harlan (1992:63–64) considered the *domus* as "more than space or territory; it is an area intimately known and spiritually safe." It is where "the landscape can be thought of as being brought into the household" and a place where one could be "at home." It has been suggested that farmers are particularly invested in a deeper perspective of place because they rely on resources from the past to see them through to the next harvest which forms the basis for their future well-being. As a result, current generations are continuously indebted to an infrastructure that was provided by the past and that ensures their future (Meillassoux 1972). A common theme in neotropical America emphasizes that landscapes are gifts from the ancestors, and that the present is beholden to a past which maintains ultimate power over reproduction (e g., Rival 1998:239; Salomon 1995:325–26). Dependent upon memory and mnemonics, history is understood through genealogy, and in this regard monuments serve as powerful links to the past (Bradley 1998). Certainly of equal value and perhaps even more powerful in this sense is the landscape (Gosden and Lock 1998; Rumsey 1994), not simply for the messages it transmits about past generations but also for the indispensable gifts it continues to bestow on present and future generations.

Acknowledgments

I thank the organizers for generously including me in this symposium. This research was made possible through grants from the National Science Foundation (BNS-8709649, BNS-8908703, BNS-9108548) awarded to James A. Zeidler and Deborah M. Pearsall, with supplemental funding (for BNS-9108548) awarded jointly to James A. Zeidler and John S. Isaacson. I am indebted to John for reading an earlier draft of this paper, and for his stimulating research on prehistoric volcanism in Ecuador. Jim and Debby are once again thanked for their collegiality and continuous support. I remain solely responsible for the contents of this paper.

REFERENCES CITED

Adams, A. B., K. E. Hinckley, C. Hinzman, and S. R. Leffler. 1986. Recovery of Small Mammals in Three Habitats in the Northwest Sector of the Mount St. Helens National Volcanic Monument. In *Mount St. Helens: Five Years Later*, ed. S. A. C. Keller, pp. 345–58. Cheney: Eastern Washington University Press.

Andersen, Douglas C. 1982. Observations on *Thomomys talpoides* in the Region Affected by the Eruption of Mount St. Helens. *Journal of Mammalogy* 63:652–55.

Andersen, Douglas C., and James A. MacMahon. 1985. The Effects of Catastrophic Ecosystem Disturbance: The Residual Mammals of Mount St. Helens. *Journal of Mammalogy* 66:581–89.

Antos, Joseph A., and Donald B. Zobel. 1985. Recovery of Forest Understories Buried by Tephra from Mount St. Helens. *Vegetatio* 64:103–11.

—— 1987. How Plants Survive Burial: A Review and Initial Responses to Tephra from Mount St. Helens. In *Mount St. Helens, 1980: Botanical Consequences of the Explosive Eruptions*, ed. David E. Bilderback, pp. 246–61. Berkeley: University of California Press.

Birks, H. J. B., and J. M. Line. 1991. The Use of Rarefaction Analysis for Estimating Palynological Richness from Quaternary Pollen-analytical Data. *Holocene* 2:1–10.

Bradley, Richard. 1998. *The Significance of Monuments*. London: Routledge.

Bullard, Fred M. 1979. Volcanoes and Their Activity. In *Volcanic Activity and Human Ecology*, ed. Payson D. Sheets and Donald K. Grayson, pp. 9–48. New York: Academic Press.

Burt, William Henry. 1961. Some Effects of Volcan Parícutin on Vertebrates. *Occasional Papers of the Museum of Zoology, University of Michigan* 620:1–24.

Cañadas Cruz, L. 1983. *El mapa bioclimático y ecológico del Ecuador*. Quito: Banco Central del Ecuador.

Chomitz, Kenneth A. 2007. *At Loggerheads? Agricultural Expansion, Poverty Reduction, and Environment in the Tropical Forests*. Washington, DC: World Bank.

Colinvaux, Paul. 1998. The Ice-age Amazon and the Problem of Diversity. *Review of Archaeology* 19:1–10.

Connell, J. H. 1978. Diversity in Tropical Rain Forests and Coral Reefs. *Science* 199:1302–10.

Crawford, Bruce. 1986. The Recovery of Surviving Fish Populations within the Mount St. Helens Natural Volcanic Monument and Adjacent Areas. In *Mount St. Helens: Five Years Later*, ed. S. A. C. Keller, pp. 293–96. Cheney: Eastern Washington University Press.

Dale, Virginia H., Johanna Delgado-Acevedo, and James MacMahon. 2005. Effects of Modern Volcanic Eruptions on Vegetation. In *Volcanoes and the Environment*, ed. Joan Martí and Gerald Ernst, pp. 227–49. Cambridge: Cambridge University Press.

del Moral, Roger. 1981. Life Returns to Mount St. Helens. *Natural History* 90(5): 36–47.

Denevan, William M., and Christine Padoch. 1988. Introduction: The Bora Agroforestry Project. In *Swidden-fallow Agroforestry in the Peruvian Amazon*, ed. William M. Denevan and Christine Padoch, pp. 1–7. Advances in Economic Botany, Vol. 5. New York: New York Botanical Gardens.

Donahue, Jack, and William Harbert. 1994. Fluvial History of the Jama River Drainage. In *Regional Archaeology in Northern Manabí, Ecuador*. Vol. 1, *Environment, Cultural Chronology, and Prehistoric Subsistence in the Jama River Valley*, ed. James A. Zeidler and Deborah M. Pearsall, pp. 43–57. University of Pittsburgh Memoirs in Latin American Archaeology, No. 8. Pittsburgh.

Edwards, John S. 2005. Animals and Volcanoes: Survival and Revival. In *Volcanoes and the Environment*, ed. Joan Martí and Gerald Ernst, pp. 250–72. Cambridge: Cambridge University Press.

Edwards, John S., Rodney L. Crawford, Patrick M. Sugg, and Merrill A. Peterson. 1986. Arthropod Recolonization in the Blast Zone of Mount St. Helens. In *Mount St. Helens: Five Years Later*, ed. S. A. C. Keller, pp. 329–33. Cheney: Eastern Washington University Press.

Eggler, Willis A. 1963. Plant Life of Parícutin Volcano, Mexico, Eight Years after Activity Ceased. *American Midland Naturalist* 69:38–68.

Fearnside, Philip M. 2005. Deforestation in Brazilian Amazonia: History, Rates, and Consequences. *Conservation Biology* 19:680–88.

Ford, Anabel, and Ronald Nigh. 2009. Origins of the Maya Forest Garden: Maya Resource Management. *Journal of Ethnobiology* 29:213–36.

Gosden, Chris, and Gary Lock. 1998. Prehistoric Histories. *World Archaeology* 30:2–12.

Gotelli, Nicholas, and Robert K. Colwell. 2001. Quantifying Biodiversity: Procedures and Pitfalls in the Measurement and Comparison of Species Richness. *Ecology Letters* 4:379–91.

Hall, Minard L., and Patricia A. Mothes. 1999. La actividad volcánica del Holoceno en el Ecuador y Colombia austral. Impedimento al desarrollo de las civilizaciones pasadas. In *Actividad volcánica y pueblos precolombinos en el Ecuador*, ed. Patricia A. Mothes, pp. 11–40. Quito: Abya-Yala.

Hall, M. L., and C. A. Wood. 1985. Volcano-tectonic Segmentation of the Northern Andes. *Geology* 13:203–7.

Harlan, Jack R. 1992. *Crops and Man.* 2nd ed. Madison, WI: American Society of Agronomy.

Holland, Steven M. 2003. Analytic Rarefaction. Stratigraphy Lab, University of Georgia, Athens. http://www uga edu/strata/software/AnRareReadme.html (accessed Sept. 2007).

Isaacson, John S. 1987. Volcanic Activity and Human Occupation of the Northern Andes: The Application of Tephrostratigraphic Techniques to the Problem of Human Settlement in the Western Montaña during the Ecuadorian Formative. PhD diss., Dept. of Anthropology, Univ. of Illinois, Urbana.

—— 1994. Volcanic Sediments in Archaeological Contexts from Western Ecuador. In *Regional Archaeology in Northern Manabí, Ecuador*. Vol. 1, *Environment, Cultural Chronology, and Prehistoric Subsistence in the Jama River Valley*, ed. James A. Zeidler and Deborah M. Pearsall, pp. 131–39. University of Pittsburgh Memoirs in Latin American Archaeology, No. 8. Pittsburgh.

Isaacson, John S., and James A. Zeidler. 1999. Accidental History: Volcanic Activity and the End of the Formative in Northwestern Ecuador. In *Actividad volcánica y pueblos precolombinos en el Ecuador*, ed. Patricia A. Mothes, pp. 41–72. Quito: Abya-Yala.

Kiilsgaard, Christen W., Sarah E. Greene, Susan Stafford, and W. Arthur McKee. 1986. Recovery of Riparian Vegetation on the Northeastern Region of Mount St. Helens. In *Mount St. Helens: Five Years Later*, ed. S. A. C. Keller, pp. 222–30. Cheney: Eastern Washington University Press.

Kintigh, Keith W. 1992. Tools for Quantitative Archaeology. Programs for Quantitative Analysis in Archaeology. Keith W. Kintigh, Tempe, AZ.

Kittleman, Lawrence R. 1979. Geologic Methods in Studies of Quaternary Tephra. In *Volcanic Activity and Human Ecology*, ed. Payson D. Sheets and Donald K. Grayson, pp. 49–82. New York: Academic Press.

Lathrap, Donald W., John S. Isaacson, and Colin McEwan. 1984. On the Trail of the First Metallurgy of the Ancient New World: How Old Is the Classic Quimbaya Style? *Field Museum of Natural History Bulletin* 55(10): 11–19.

Laurence, William F., Ana K. M. Albernaz, Philip M. Fearnside, Heraldo L. Vasconcelos, and Leandro V. Ferreira. 2004. Deforestation in Amazonia. *Science* 304:1109.

Lucas, Robert E. 1986. Recovery of Game Fish Populations Impacted by the May 18, 1980, Eruption of Mount St. Helens: Winter-run Steelhead in the Toutle River Watershed. In *Mount St. Helens: Five Years Later*, ed. S. A. C. Keller, pp. 276–92. Cheney: Eastern Washington University Press.

MacMahon, James A. 1982. Mount St. Helens Revisited. *Natural History* 91(5): 14–24.

MacMahon, James A., Robert R. Parmenter, Kurt A. Johnson, and Charles M. Crisafulli. 1989. Small Mammal Recolonization on the Mount St. Helens Volcano: 1980–1987. *American Midland Naturalist* 122:365–87.

Mack, Richard N. 1981. Initial Effects of Ashfall from Mount St. Helens on Vegetation in Eastern Washington and Adjacent Idaho. *Science* 213:537–39.

Malcolm, Jay R. 1998. High Roads to Oblivion. *Natural History* 107(6): 46–49.

Manuwal, David A., Mark H. Huff, Michael R. Bauer, Christopher B. Chapell, and Karen Hegstad. 1987. Summer Birds of the Upper Subalpine Zone of Mount Adams, Mount Rainier, and Mount St. Helens, Washington. *Northwest Science* 61:82–92.

Means, Joseph E., W. Arthur McKee, William H. Moir, and Jerry F. Franklin. 1982. Natural Revegetation of the Northeastern Portion of the Devastated Area. In *Mount St. Helens: Five Years Later*, ed. S. A. C. Keller, pp. 93–103. Cheney: Eastern Washington University Press.

Meillassoux, Claude. 1972. From Reproduction to Production. *Economy and Society* 1:93–105.

Nepstad, D., S. Schwartzman, B. Bamberger, M. Santilli, D. Ray, P. Schtesinger, P. Lefebvre, A. Alencar, E. Prinz, G. Fiske, and A. Rolla. 2006. Inhibition of Amazonian Deforestation and Fire by Parks and Indigenous Lands. *Conservation Biology* 20:65–73.

Nepstad, Daniel C., Claudia M. Strickler, Britaldo Soare-Filho, and Frank Merry. 2008. Interactions among Amazon Land Use, Forests and Climate: Prospects from a Near-term Forest Tipping Point. *Philosophical Transactions of the Royal Society of London, Series B* 363:1737–46.

Nolan, Mary Lee. 1979. Impact of Parícutin on Five Communities. In *Volcanic Activity and Human Ecocology*, ed. Payson D. Sheets and Donald K. Grayson, pp. 293–338. New York: Academic Press.

Ohl-Schacherer, Julia, Glenn H. Shepard, Jr., Hillard Kaplan, Carlos A. Peres, and Douglas W. Yu. 2007. The Sustainability of Subsistence Hunting by Matsigenka Native Communities in Manu National Park, Peru. *Conservation Biology* 21:1174–85.

Olson, Gerald W. 1983. An Evaluation of Soil Properties and Potentials in Different Volcanic Deposits. In *Archaeology and Volcanism in Central America*, ed. Payson D. Sheets, pp. 52–56. Austin: University of Texas Press.

Orton, Clive. 2000. *Sampling in Archaeology*. Cambridge: Cambridge University Press.

Pearsall, Deborah M. 1995. "Doing" Paleoethnobotany in the Tropical Lowlands: Adaptation and Innovation in Methodology. In *Archaeology in the Lowland American Tropics. Current Analytical Methods and Recent Applications*, ed. Peter W. Stahl, pp. 113–29. Cambridge: Cambridge University Press.

—— 1996. Reconstructing Subsistence in the Lowland Tropics: A Case Study from the Jama River Valley, Manabí, Ecuador. In *Case Studies in Environmental Archaeology*, ed. Elizabeth J. Reitz, Lee A. Newsom, and Sylvia J. Scudder, pp. 233–54. New York: Plenum Press.

—— 2004. *Plants and People in Ancient Ecuador: The Ethnobotany of the Jama River Valley*. Belmont, CA: Wadsworth.

Pearsall, Deborah M., and James A. Zeidler. 1994. Regional Environment, Cultural Chronology, and Prehistoric Subsistence in Northern Manabí. In *Regional Archaeology in Northern Manabí, Ecuador*. Vol. 1, *Environment, Cultural Chronology, and Prehistoric Subsistence in the Jama River Valley*, ed. James A. Zeidler and Deborah M. Pearsall, pp. 201–15. University of Pittsburgh Memoirs in Latin American Archaeology, No. 8. Pittsburgh.

Phinney, Duane E. 1982. Overview of the Effects of the Mount St. Helens Eruption on Salmon Populations. In *Mount St. Helens: Five Years Later*, ed. S. A. C. Keller, pp. 125–27. Cheney: Eastern Washington University Press.

Rees, John D. 1979. Effects of the Eruption of Parícutin Volcano on Landforms, Vegetation, and Human Occupancy. In *Volcanic Activity and Human Ecology*, ed. Payson D. Sheets and Donald K. Grayson, pp. 249–92. New York: Academic Press.

Reycraft, Richard M., and Garth Bawden. 2000. Introduction. Environmental Disaster and the Archaeology of Human Response. In *Environmental Disaster and the Archaeology of Human Response*, ed. Richard M. Reycraft and Garth Bawden, pp. 1–10. Anthropological Papers No. 7, Maxwell Museum of Anthropology, Albuquerque.

Ringrose, Trevor J. 1993. Diversity Indices and Archaeology. In *Computing the Past. Computer Applications and Quantitative Methods in Archaeology CAA 92*, ed. Jens Andresen, Torsten Madsen, and Irwin Scollar, pp. 279–85. Aarhus: Aarhus University Press.

Rival, Laura. 1998. Domestication as a Historical and Symbolic Process: Wild Gardens and Cultivated Forests in the Ecuadorian Amazon. In *Advances in Historical Ecology*, ed. William Balée, pp. 232–50. New York: Columbia University Press.

Rumsey, Alan. 1994. The Dreaming, Human Agency and Inscriptive Practice. *Oceania* 65:116–30.

Salomon, Frank. 1995. "The Beautiful Grandparents": Andean Ancestor Shrines and Mortuary Ritual as Seen through Colonial Documents. In *Tombs for the Living: Andean Mortuary Practices*, ed. Tom D. Dillehay, pp. 315–53. Washington, DC: Dumbarton Oaks.

Santley, Robert S., Stephen A. Nelson, Bently K. Richardson, Christopher A. Pool, and Philip J. Arnold III. 2000. When Day Turned to Night: Volcanism and the Archaeological Record from the Tuxtla Mountains, Southern Veracruz, Mexico. In *Environmental Disaster and the Archaeology of Human Response*, ed. Garth Bawden and Richard Martin Reycraft, pp. 143–62. Anthropological Papers No. 7, Maxwell Museum of Anthropology. Albuquerque.

Schwartzman, Stephan, and Barbara Zimmerman. 2005. Conservation Alliances with Indigenous Peoples of the Amazon. *Conservation Biology* 19:721–27.

Segerstrom, Kenneth. 1950. *Erosion Studies at Parícutin, State of Michoacán, Mexico*. Geological Survey Bulletin 965-A. Washington, DC: U.S. Government Printing Office.

Sloniker, Eugene V. 1986. Mount St. Helens Volcano Reforestation: May 18, 1980 to Present. In *Mount St. Helens: Five Years Later*, ed. S. A. C. Keller, pp. 249–55. Cheney: Eastern Washington University Press.

Stahl, Peter W. 1994. Qualitative Assessment of Archaeofaunal Taxa from the Jama Valley. In *Regional Archaeology in Northern Manabí, Ecuador*. Vol. 1, *Environment, Cultural Chronology, and Prehistoric Subsistence in the Jama River Valley*, ed. James A. Zeidler and Deborah M. Pearsall, pp. 185–99. University of Pittsburgh Memoirs in Latin American Archaeology, No. 8. Pittsburgh.

—— 1995. Differential Preservation Histories Affecting the Mammalian Zooarchaeological Record from the Forested Neotropical Lowlands. In *Archaeology in the Lowland American Tropics. Current Analytical Methods and Recent Applications*, ed. Peter W. Stahl, pp. 154–80. Cambridge: Cambridge University Press.

—— 2000. Archaeofaunal Accumulation, Fragmented Forests, and Anthropogenic Landscape Mosaics in the Tropical Lowlands of Prehispanic Ecuador. *Latin American Antiquity* 11:241–57.

—— 2006. Microvertebrate Synecology and Anthropogenic Footprints in the Forested Neotropics. In *Time and Complexity in Historical Ecology. Studies in the Neotropical Lowlands*, ed. William Balée and Clark L. Erickson, pp. 127–49. New York: Columbia University Press.

—— 2008. The Contributions of Zooarchaeology to Historical Ecology in the Neotropics. *Quaternary International* 180:5–16.

Stocks, Anthony, Benjamin McMahon, and Peter Taber. 2007. Indigenous Colonists and Government Impacts on Nicaragua's Bosawas Reserve. *Conservation Biology* 21:1495–1505.

Thornton, I. W. B., T. R. New, R. A. Zann, and P. A. Rawlinson. 1990. Colonization of the Krakatau Islands by Animals: A Perspective from the 1980s. *Philosophical Transactions of the Royal Society of London. Series B, Biological Sciences* 328:131–65.

Ugolini, F. C., and R. J. Zasoski. 1979. Soils Derived from Tephra. In *Volcanic Activity and Human Ecology*, ed. Payson D. Sheets and Donald K. Grayson, pp. 83–124. New York: Academic Press.

Valentine, J. W. 1971. Resource Supply and Species Diversity Patterns. *Lethaia* 4:51–61.

Veintimilla B., César Ivan. 1998. Analysis of Past Vegetation in the Jama River Valley, Manabí Province, Ecuador. Master's thesis, Dept. of Anthropology, Univ. of Missouri, Columbia.

Wissmar, Robert C. 1982. Limnological Features of Lakes within the 18 May 1980 Mount St. Helens Blast Zone. In *Mount St. Helens: Five Years Later*, ed. S. A. C. Keller, pp. 119–23. Cheney: Eastern Washington University Press.

Zeidler, James A. 1995. Archaeological Survey and Site Discovery in the Forested Neotropics. In *Archaeology in the Lowland American Tropics. Current Analytical Methods and Recent Applications*, ed. Peter W. Stahl, pp. 1–41. Cambridge: Cambridge University Press.

—— 2005. Rank-size Relationships and Prehispanic Settlement Systems in the Jama Valley, Coastal Ecuador. Paper presented at the 70th annual meeting of the Society for American Archaeology, Salt Lake City, Utah.

—— 2006. Modeling Cultural Response to Volcanic Disaster in the Jama-Coaque II Culture, Coastal Ecuador. Paper presented at the 4th Cities on Volcanoes Conference, Quito.

Zeidler, James A., and John S. Isaacson. 2003. Settlement Processes and Historical Contingency in the Western Ecuadorian Formative. In *Archaeology of Formative Ecuador*, ed. J. Scott Raymond and Richard L. Burger, pp. 69–123. Washington, DC: Dumbarton Oaks Research Library and Collections.

Zeidler, James A., and Robin C. Kennedy. 1994. Environmental Setting. In *Regional Archaeology in Northern Manabí, Ecuador*. Vol. 1, *Environment, Cultural Chronology, and Prehistoric Subsistence in the Jama River Valley*, ed. James A. Zeidler and Deborah M. Pearsall, pp. 13–41. University of Pittsburgh Memoirs in Latin American Archaeology, No. 8. Pittsburgh.

Zeidler, James A., and Mary Jo Zeidler. 2002. Earthworks as Persistent Places in Jama-Coaque Political Geography. Paper presented at the 67th annual meeting of the Society for American Archaeology, Denver.

Zeidler, James A., Caitlin E. Buck, and Clifford D. Litton. 1998. Integration of Archaeological Phase Information and Radiocarbon Results from the Jama River Valley, Ecuador: A Bayesian Approach. *Latin American Antiquity* 9:160–79.

Zeidler, James A., Peter W. Stahl, and Marie J. Sutliffe. 1998. Shamanistic Elements in a Terminal Valdivia Burial, Northern Manabí, Ecuador. In *Recent Advances in the Archaeology of the Northern Andes*, ed. Augusto Oyuelo-Caycedo and J. Scott Raymond, pp. 109–20. Monograph 39. Los Angeles: Institute of Archaeology, University of California.

11

Managing Predictable Unpredictability: Agricultural Sustainability at Gordion, Turkey

NAOMI F. MILLER

Farming is a notoriously risky occupation, and is particularly so when climate conditions are very variable. The agropastoral economy that developed in west Asia about 10,000 years ago was one solution. It integrated a subsistence base of domesticated plants and animals: wheat, barley, pulses, sheep, goat, cattle, and pig. Depending on local conditions, this flexible system tolerated varying degrees of sedentism or mobility by allowing people to combine multiple strategies in exploiting a diverse group of taxa. By the time of the early civilizations (3rd millennium BC, the Early Bronze Age), technological advances, such as irrigation, and social developments, like the specialization of labor (including full-time nomadic pastoralism; see Beck, this volume), added even more options.

The archaeological site of Gordion, near the present-day village of Yassihöyük, is located at the upper edge of the central Anatolian steppe where dryfarming and herding have been practiced for over 6000 years (Kealhofer 2005). Famous as the home of King Midas and early waystation on Alexander the Great's conquest of Asia, Gordion was occupied long before and well after those two lifetimes. Located in the Sakarya river valley, about 90 km southwest of Ankara, the ancient settlement remains date as early as the 3rd millennium BC and extend through the Roman period; there is some Medieval occupation, and faint surface traces of military trenches date to the

Turkish War of Independence in 1921 (Fig. 11.1). The 1st millennium-BC occupation extends for over a kilometer on both sides of the river. Based on small mounds and sherd scatters, regional survey has securely documented settlement in the valley and surrounding uplands by the Early Bronze Age (Kealhofer 2005). The most visible remains of the region, however, are well over one hundred burial mounds, most of which seem to date to the Middle Phrygian period (Liebhart et al. n.d.). The largest of these, at a height of 53 m, is Tumulus MM, which dominates the landscape (Fig. 11.2).

Excavation (1950–present) has centered on the 13-ha Citadel Mound. The first phase of work, directed by Rodney Young, exposed several hectares of the early Phrygian "Destruction Level" (Sams 2005). In 1988, Mary Voigt directed smaller-scale excavations with the goal of refining the stratigraphic sequence (Table 11.1; DeVries et al. 2003; Voigt 2005) and obtaining archaeobotanical, zooarchaeological, and other samples for scientific analyses.

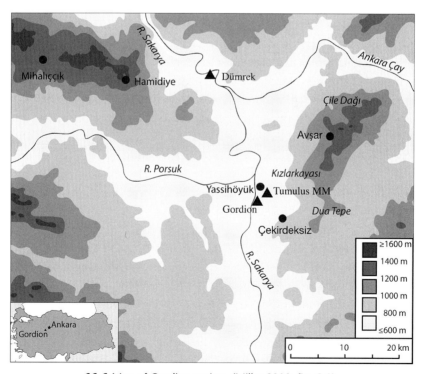

11.1 Map of Gordion region. (Miller 2010: fig. 2.1)

Naomi F. Miller

**Table 11.1. Yassıhöyük Stratigraphic Sequence, Approximate Dates
(source: Voigt 2005:27)**

	PHASE	DATE
YHSS 1	Medieval	13–14th century AD
YHSS 2	Roman [not in these samples]	early 1st–5th century AD
YHSS 3	Hellenistic	330–mid-2nd century BC
YHSS 4	Late Phrygian	540–330 BC
YHSS 5	Middle Phrygian	800–540 BC
YHSS 6	Early Phrygian, ending in "Destruction Level"	950–800 BC
YHSS 7	Early Iron Age	12th century–950 BC
YHSS 8–9	Late Bronze Age	1500–12th century BC
YHSS 10	Middle Bronze Age	2000–1500 BC
—	Early Bronze Age [not in these samples]	2500–2000 BC

Plant macroremains and animal bones from the 1988/1989 deep sounding at Gordion allow us to characterize ancient environment and land use within an ever-changing landscape (Miller 2010; Miller, Zeder, and Arter 2009; Zeder and Arter 1994). The remains discussed here date from Late Bronze Age to Hellenistic and also Medieval times (see Table 11.1 for the "Yassıhöyük Stratigraphic Sequence," YHSS 8/9 to YHSS 3 and YHSS 1; Voigt 1994). From the beginning, plant and animal husbandry focused on wheat, barley, sheep, goat, cattle, and pig. Variability within this broadly defined agropastoral system was a response to prevailing natural and social conditions. The archaeobiological evidence suggests that a strategy that flexibly incorporates dry-farming cereals, small-scale garden irrigation, and a strong pastoral component is the one that provides the most secure living in this environment.

CLIMATE AND NATURAL VEGETATION

In central Anatolia, precipitation declines with elevation. Annual precipitation at the nearest meteorological station in Polatlı (about 15 km to the southeast, elev. 885 m) averages about 350 mm/yr and interannual variability is high.[1] Average annual precipitation at Gordion is somewhat lower; at just under 700 m, the site lies at the upper edge of the steppe zone. It sometimes rains during our field seasons (June to August). Even more commonly, we see rain falling from storm clouds all around us, but not in the center of the valley. Although total grain crop loss from drought is rare, the conditions of dry-farming are marginal enough that relatively small shifts in

11.2 View across the excavated center of the Citadel Mound toward Tumulus MM (left) and other tumuli.

annual precipitation might have had strong effects on agricultural production. Our sequence is recent enough that major climate change is not an issue, but there are some hints of a moist phase dating to the mid-9th century across Eurasia (Morris 2004:730; van Geel et al. 2004). As Neil Roberts (this volume) points out, shorter-term fluctuations can affect the success of different agropastoral strategies; this Iron Age climate amelioration may help explain some of the changes we see in the archaeobiological record.

The present-day distribution of vegetation is the product of millennia of grazing, agriculture, and deforestation interacting with the geological substrate and climatic conditions. Healthy steppe vegetation includes dense growth of perennial grasses such as feathergrasses (*Stipa arabica, S. holosericea, S. lessingiana*), sheep's fescue (*Festuca ovina*), perennial brome grasses (*Bromus cappadocicus, B. tomentellus*), and many other plants. With overgrazing, sagebrush (*Artemisia* sp.) and wild thyme (*Thymus* spp.) become prominent. Today, the area within a kilometer of Gordion is covered with this degraded steppe vegetation, irrigated fields of wheat, barley, sugarbeet, onions, melon, and sunflower, and some poorly drained low-lying areas. A limited number of woody plant taxa grow along the Sakarya river (willow, tamarix), in watered gardens, and there are a few isolated elm trees allowed to grow in the midst of fields.

With elevation, open woodland of scrubby juniper (*Juniperus oxycedrus, J. excelsa*) and oak (*Quercus pubescens*) are established within 20 km of the site, at about 900 m, near Avşar. They may have grown closer to the settlement in antiquity; under moister conditions, all can grow to be full-sized trees. Closed-canopy pine forest (*Pinus nigra*) grows as close as 40 km northwest of Gordion at about 1100 m, near Hamidiye. A variety of other trees grows as part of these associations.

Analysis of the charred wood remains from Late Bronze Age to Medieval times provides a broad picture of changes in vegetation cover (Miller 1999a, 2010). Over time, juniper growing on the nearby rock outcrops declined. Oak increased, as did minor woods of riparian habitats and secondary forest. These general results suggest an overall decline in woody vegetation, but trees were readily available for fuel throughout the sequence. This conclusion is consistent with Ben Marsh's (2005) geomorphological work, which suggests the massive erosion we see today is a relatively recent phenomenon.

THE AGROPASTORAL CONTINUUM

The traditional mixed farming economy of west Asia is particularly adapted to unpredictable environments. People can respond to changing climatic or sociopolitical conditions by adjusting their reliance on the pastoral and agricultural elements of the subsistence economy, a fact well-recognized by the present-day inhabitants of Yassıhöyük (Gürsan-Salzmann 2005:176). The charred seed remains recovered in flotation samples provide insight into those choices made by the ancient inhabitants (Miller 2010).

Based on concentrations of seeds in burned buildings as well as remains scattered in other samples, the primary crop plants at Gordion were two- and six-row barley, bread wheat, lentil, and bitter vetch. Minor crops include flax and millet (*Setaria*); rice and cotton first appear in Medieval times. Seeds of wild plants, especially *Trigonella* (a clover-like legume), abound in the flotation samples from occupation debris.

Many seeds found in occupation debris from west Asian archaeological sites originated in animal dung used as fuel (Miller 1984), so seed remains are key to integrating plants and animals in the archaeological record. An earlier archaeobotanical study of Bronze Age sites along the Euphrates river pointed to the potential value of the ratio of wild seeds to cereal grains for monitoring shifts in the emphasis on herding and farming (Miller 1997). In particular, the dung of animals pastured on the steppe will have a higher proportion of the seeds of wild steppe plants relative to cultivated grain, and if that dung is burned for fuel, the resulting wild:cereal ratio will be relatively high. Insofar as the seeds of wild plants originated in dung from steppe grazers, and cereals were consumed by crop-fed or stubble-grazing animals, changes in the wild:cereal ratio serve as a proxy for changes in dependence on farming and herding. Not surprisingly, in areas with higher rainfall the economy relied more heavily on cultivation, with lower wild:cereal ratios and high proportions of cattle and pig bone. Cattle and pig both need ready access to water, and so in the context of west Asia, are penned closer to settlements than sheep and goat. Areas with lower rainfall show higher wild:cereal ratios and higher proportions of sheep and goat bone. Holding climate constant, the wild:cereal ratio can reflect change over time in the sociopolitical factors of herding strategies. At one of the Euphrates sites, Kurban Höyük, occupation phases characterized by higher wild:cereal ratios indicating steppe pasture were associated with higher proportions of sheep and goat (relative to cattle and pig).

Gordion shows even stronger associations in these measures (Figs. 11.3, 11.4). Zeder's faunal analysis (Miller, Zeder and Arter 2009; Zeder and Arter 1994) shows that sheep and goat were the most important food animals throughout the sequence, but in the Middle Phrygian period (YHSS 5), cattle and pig are of maximum significance (see Table 11.2 for absolute quantities on which figures are based). Consistent with this evidence for limited pastoralism compared to farming, the low point in the wild:cereal ratio also occurs in Middle Phrygian times. Two other plant indicators of agriculture and land use support the view that the Middle Phrygian period is anomalous in its high dependence on farming: the distributions of *Trigonella* and of indicators of irrigation. *Trigonella*, the most numerous wild seed, is a plant of healthy steppe that would be preferentially grazed; to this day, at least six species have been seen growing on or near the site. Its proportions in the seed assemblage generally follow the wild:cereal ratio, except at the end of the sequence by which time its numbers presumably had been reduced by overgrazing (Fig. 11.5). The proportion of indicators of irrigation generally follows the wild:cereal ratio, except during the Middle Phrygian

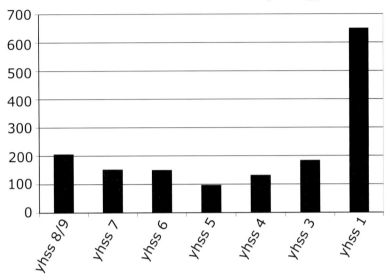

11.3 Median Wild:Cereal ratio (number/weight in grams). (Miller 2010: fig. 5.19b)

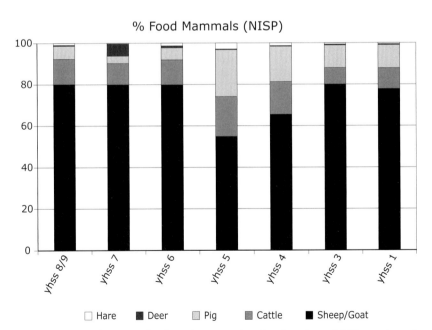

11.4 Percent food mammals: sheep/goat, cattle, pig, deer, hare (NISP: number of identified specimens). (Miller 2010: fig. 6.1)

period, when it has a high value (Fig. 11.6). The distribution of the ruderals, or herbaceous indicators of disturbance (mostly *Galium*, but also *Alhagi*, *Peganum harmala*, *Hordeum* cf. *murinum*, and others), is harder to explain, but may relate to small numbers recovered. They do, however, tend to increase over time, until the Medieval period (YHSS 1) (Fig. 11.7). The cumulative effects of disturbance to the native vegetation can also be seen in the results of the wood charcoal analysis; an overall decline in woods of primary forest (juniper, oak, and pine) corresponds to a gradual increase in riparian and secondary succession species (elm, pear/hawthorn, poplar/willow) (Miller 1999a; 2010:Fig. 4.1).

Table 11.2. Quantities on which Graphs Are Based (source: Miller 2010)

YHSS PHASE	8–9	7	6	5	4	3	1
No. samples	32	66	8	15	53	36	15
Wild & weedy							
(total no. per phase)	5060	7710	58	368	8765	6573	2557
Median Wild:Cereal							
(no./g)	206	152	150	97	132	184	650
NISP food mammals*	2269	3303	1628	1827	2169	1322	881
Italian millet							
(*Setaria italica*) (no.)	0	9	0	3	161	77	91
Naked wheat							
(*Triticum aestivum/*							
durum) (weight, g)	5.36	18.86	0.08	0.66	9.07	4.07	0.54
Two-row barley							
(*Hordeum vulgare* var.							
distichum) (weight, g)	7.90	12.41	0.13	1.53	18.33	6.27	0.68

*sheep/goat, cattle, pig, deer, hare

The Medieval period (YHSS 1) saw a qualitative change in the agropastoral economy, one that employed a new strategy: summer irrigation. The change may have been at least partly a response to the heavy deposition of sediments from eroded hillsides, which would have led to a more flood-prone, meandering river in the valley bottom (Marsh 2005:168). That new regime is closest to what became the traditional (i.e., 20th-century) base of the Yassıhöyük village economy (Gürsan-Salzmann 2005): sheep and goat herding and the cultivation of winter crops (wheat and barley) and summer-irrigated cash crops (onions, sugarbeet, melon, and, until the 1950s, rice). As in most of the archaeological sequence, relatively high

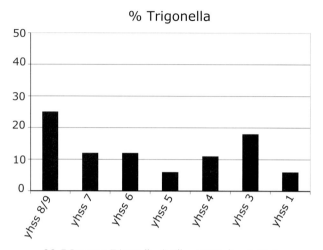

11.5 Percent *Trigonella*. (Miller 2010: fig. 5.20a)

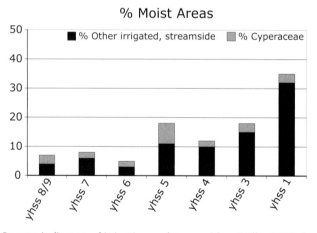

11.6 Percent indicators of irrigation and streamsides. (Miller 2010: fig. 5.26)

proportions of sheep and goat characterized the pastoral economy. Fall-sown wheat and barley were the primary cereals. But relative to those traditional grains, the proportion of millet, a summer-irrigated crop that had occurred in low but increasing amounts over the course of the Gordion occupation, reaches its maximum in the Medieval samples, which also contain the first evidence for summer-irrigated rice and cotton (Figs. 11.6, 11.8; see also Fig. 11.4).

% Galium, Ruderal and Overgrazed

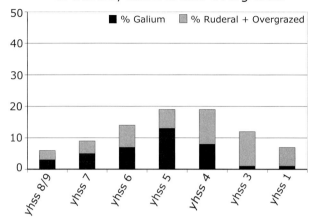

11.7 Percent ruderals: indicators of disturbance. (Miller 2010: fig. 5.23)

Italian Millet/(Barley + Naked Wheat), no./g

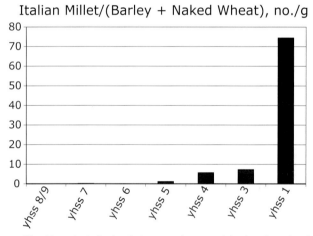

11.8 Italian millet (*Setaria italica*) relative to wheat and barley (number/weight in grams). (Miller 2010: fig. 5.8)

The results of the integrated archaeobiological analysis (Miller, Zeder, and Arter 2009) are fully consistent with the conclusions reached by other project members (Kealhofer 2005; Voigt 2005, 2007, 2009), and strongly suggest that people adjusted their agricultural strategies according to physical and social conditions. Sheep and goat herding expands the territory that can be turned to productive use (i.e., pasture), and irrigation, with its heavy use of human labor, expands the time put toward production. Both strategies can reduce year-to-year fluctuations in the food supply, and are discernible in the archaeobiological record.

A mid-9th century BC climate amelioration may have set the stage for the period of prosperity that culminated in the territorial state associated with King Midas during the 8th century BC (i.e., the Middle Phrygian period). During the 9th century the site was fortified and formal stone buildings were constructed (the Early Phrygian period, YHSS 6). By the time of a catastrophic fire dated to 800 BC, a massive building project involving the laying of clay fills as a foundation for new buildings in the palace quarter and a reorientation of the stone fortications had already begun. After the fire, workers covered the central area (the archaeological "Destruction Level") with several meters of clayey sediment, built up a second high mound adjacent to it, and laid fills in an adjacent Lower Town (Voigt 2007). As Marsh (2005) suggests, the spoil from canal digging may have provided the material that raised the level of the city. Irrigation of staple crops would have greatly enhanced food security as well as overall quantity; large, predictable surpluses would have allowed trade and craft production to flourish. The site of Gordion reached its greatest extent during Middle Phrygian times (Voigt and Young 1999), the regional settled population was at its greatest, and the maximum area of land was devoted to agriculture (Kealhofer 2005).

Gordion remained an economic center, but lost political autonomy in the Late Phrygian period (YHSS 4) (Voigt 1994:278; Voigt and Young 1999). Regional population seems to have declined (Kealhofer 2005). The rapid reversion toward pastoralism suggests the Middle Phrygian economy was not sustainable in the long run without serious input of labor; climate aridification would have intensified this shift in subsistence strategy.

Regional settled population in the Medieval period appears to have been relatively small (Kealhofer 2005), and sheep and goat herding reached levels not seen since the Early Iron Age (YHSS 7). Perhaps the human population was more transhumant than in earlier times. For those who remained in the settlement, the increased emphasis on summer irrigation represents a new strategy, though both irrigation and millet were known as early as the Iron Age at Gordion and elsewhere (Nesbitt and Summers 1988). The seeds of summer-irrigated crops represent a tiny proportion of the assemblage, but rice and cotton may have been grown as commodities (see Karaman 2009; Samuel 2001:428). Despite the overall decline in settlement in the valley, cultivation of these crops shows that medieval farmers worked harder during the summer months. Where Middle Phrygian summer irrigation of millet was almost certainly a strategy that would have increased the food supply or crop security, that strategy seems less likely in the more sparsely populated valley of medieval times. Whether to satisfy tax obligations or just supplement their income, this year-round system suggests that medieval farmers were participating in a supraregional economy.

LESSONS FOR TODAY

Over the past twenty years of my observation, the agricultural landscape continues to evolve. As Ayşe Gürsan-Salzmann (2005) has documented, the largely pastoral economy of the 19th century gave way to a mixed agricultural economy in the 20th. Today, the village of Yassıhöyük houses fewer farmers year round, as many residents seek economic opportunities for themselves or schooling for their children in Polatlı and beyond. Increasingly, migrant agricultural workers from southeastern Turkey camp on the outskirts of the village. Anecdotally, we (the archaeologists) have seen fluctuations in the proportions of sheep, goats, and cows. In the mid-1990s, the national government began an irrigation project that allows farmers to irrigate virtually all their fields. Farmers have told Gürsan-Salzmann (pers. comm.) that they keep growing onions and other cash crops even though they deplete the soil; any cash income is welcome, and the cost of the water is subsidized. As irrigation increased, we noticed a dramatic decline in sheep grazing on the landscape. As the zooarchaeological model would have predicted, we initially saw an increase in the number of cows. Pigs did not have a corresponding increase, now that the local population is Muslim. In the summer of 2006, herds of cattle predominated over flocks of sheep. The cows were a Dutch breed that produces a lot of milk and whose purchase was subsidized by the government (Gürsan-Salzmann, pers. comm.). Thus, recent history seemed to reflect many aspects of the past: the labor, cattle, and irrigation complex apparently was replacing the lower-intensity traditional agropastoral economy. And then, in the severe drought year of 2007, cows virtually disappeared from the village. Two villagers, Zekeriya Utgu and Remzi Yılmaz, told me that the drought had made it too expensive to hire cowherds (shepherds' wages are lower), so the only cows kept in the village were ones individual families could care for by themselves. Flocks of sheep and goat were again numerous.

The Gordion archaeological project has played an important role in the economy of the Yassıhöyük for over sixty years. In the early years, the project intensified dependence on the cash economy through the wages paid to local workmen. Tourism has had a smaller impact than might be expected, given Gordion's place in myth and history. Since the mid 1990s, I have been developing ways of using plants for conserving the archaeological monuments, with an eye on using archaeological and environmental preservation to enhance the touristic value of the region and to provide the village with another source of income (Miller 1999b, n.d.). In recent years, the Gordion project's goals have greatly expanded and now include this kind of work, too (Gürsan-Salzmann and Erder 2010).

The history of agricultural land use in the Sakarya valley near Gordion suggests alternative pathways for making a living in this precarious environment. For several thousand years, an agricultural economy based on sheep and goat herding and dryfarmed cereals was the norm. In different ways and for different reasons, the Middle Phrygian and Medieval periods represent novel variations on this theme. Agropastoralism is a very flexible system that allows people to respond quite quickly to rapidly changing conditions. No analogy is perfect, and natural and social environments are not static. Even if climate returns to some prior state after a long- or short-term shift, the land itself may change; it would not be possible, for example, to reestablish forest on eroded, soil-less slopes. It is even more obvious that social conditions do not revert to some prior state. To an even greater extent than was the case in Middle Phrygian times, present-day Yassıhöyük is embedded in a national and international economy that demands both agricultural productivity and monetary income. Finally, each succeeding generation has inherited the landscape of its predecessors, and the historical landscape itself is a resource that has survived over 2500 years, longer than any irrigation regime. If over-irrigation is allowed to change the water table and soil chemistry, the land may be permanently harmed. It is, however, still possible to create a sustainable economy that incorporates plant and animal husbandry along with ecotourism and archaeological tourism.

NOTE

1. I am grateful to Mr. Hüseyin Erdoğan of the Polatlı Meteoroloji Istasyonu for these data: 355.4 mm (41-year average).

Acknowledgments

This chapter benefitted greatly from the comments and insights of Katherine M. Moore, Ayşe Gürsan-Salzmann, and Mary M. Voigt. An earlier version of this paper was presented at the Gordion Symposium (April 20–21, 2007) organized by C. Brian Rose at the University of Pennsylvania Museum.

REFERENCES CITED

DeVries, K., P. I. Kuniholm, G. K. Sams, and M. M. Voigt. 2003. New Dates for Iron Age Gordion. *Antiquity* 77:296.

Gürsan-Salzmann, Ayşe. 2005. Ethnographic Lessons for Past Agro-Pastoral Systems in the Sakarya-Porsuk Valleys. In *The Archaeology of Midas and the Phrygians, Recent Work at Gordion*, ed. L. Kealhofer, pp. 172–89. Philadelphia: University of Pennsylvania Museum.

Gürsan-Salzmann, Ayşe, and Evin Erder. 2010. A Conservation Management Plan for Preserving Gordion and Its Environs. *Expedition* 52(1): 4–7.

Karaman, Kamil Kıvanç. 2009. Decentralized Coercion and Self-restraint in Provincial Taxation: The Ottoman Empire, 15th–16th Centuries. *Journal of Economic Behavior and Organization* 71:690–703.

Kealhofer, Lisa. 2005. Settlement and Land Use: The Gordion Regional Survey. In *The Archaeology of Midas and the Phrygians. Recent Work at Gordion*, ed. L. Kealhofer, pp. 137–48. Philadelphia: University of Pennsylvania Museum.

Liebhart, Richard, Gareth Darbyshire, Evin Erder, and Ben Marsh. n.d. A Fresh Look at the Tumuli of Gordion. In *Tumulus as Sema. Space, Politics, Culture and Religion in the First Millennium BC, Proceedings of the International Symposium Tumuli, Istanbul, 1–3 June 2009*, ed. O. Henry and U. Kelp. Berlin: De Gruyter.

Marsh, Ben. 2005. Physical Geography, Land Use, and Human Impact at Gordion. In *The Archaeology of Midas and the Phrygians. Recent Work at Gordion*, ed. L. Kealhofer, pp. 161–71. Philadelphia: University of Pennsylvania Museum.

Miller, Naomi F. 1984. The Use of Dung as Fuel: An Ethnographic Model and an Archaeological Example. *Paléorient* 10(2): 71–79.

—— 1997. Farming and Herding along the Euphrates: Environmental Constraint and Cultural Choice (Fourth to Second Millennia B.C.). *MASCA Research Papers in Science and Archaeology* 14, pp. 123–32. Philadelphia: Museum Applied Science Center for Archaeology, University of Pennsylvania Museum.

—— 1999a. Seeds, Charcoal and Archaeological Context: Interpreting Ancient Environment and Patterns of Land Use. *TÜBA-AR* 2:15–27.

—— 1999b. Erosion, Biodiversity, and Archaeology: Preserving the Midas Tumulus at Gordion/Erozyon, Bioçesitlilik ve Arkeoloji, Gordion'daki Midas Höyüğü'nün Korunması. *Arkeoloji ve Sanat* 93:13–19 and unnumbered plate.

—— 2010. *Botanical Aspects of Environment and Economy at Gordion, Turkey.* Philadelphia: University of Pennsylvania Museum.

—— n.d. Gordion: Historical Landscape as Park, Open-Air Archaeological Site as Garden. In *The Archaeology of Phrygian Gordion*, ed. C. Brian Rose. Philadelphia: University of Pennsylvania Museum. Forthcoming.

Miller, Naomi F., Melinda A. Zeder, and Susan R. Arter. 2009. From Food and Fuel to Farms and Flocks: Considering Context of Use in Reconstructing Ancient Agricultural Economies. *Current Anthropology* 50:915–24.

Morris, Ian. 2004. Economic Growth in Ancient Greece. *Journal of Institutional and Theoretical Economics* 160:709–42.

Nesbitt, Mark M., and Geoffrey D. Summers. 1988. Some Recent Discoveries of Millet (*Panicum miliaceum* L. and *Setaria italica* [L.] P. Beauv.) at Excavations in Turkey and Iran. *Anatolian Studies* 38:85–97.

Sams, G. Kenneth. 2005. Gordion. Explorations over a Century. In *The Archaeology of Midas and the Phrygians*, ed. L. Kealhofer, pp. 10–21. Philadelphia: University of Pennsylvania Museum.

Samuel, Delwen. 2001. Archaeobotanical Evidence and Analysis. In *Peuplement rural et aménagements hydroacrigoles dans la moyenne vallée de l'Euphrate fin VIIᵉ–XIXᵉ siècle* by S. Berthier, pp. 347–481. Damascus: Institut Français de Damas.

van Geel, B., N. A. Bokovenko, N. D. Burova, K. V. Chugonov, V. A. Dergachev, V. G. Dirksen, M. Kulkova, et al. 2004. Climate Change and the Expansion of the Scythian Culture after 850 BC: A Hypothesis. *Journal of Archaeological Science* 31:1735–42.

Voigt, Mary M. 1994. Excavations at Gordion 1988–89: The Yassıhöyük Stratigraphic Sequence. In *Anatolian Iron Ages 3: The Proceedings of the Third Anatolian Iron Ages Colloquium*, ed. A. Çilingiroglu and D. H. French, pp. 265–93. Ankara: British Institute of Archaeology.

—— 2005. Old Problems and New Solutions. Recent Excavations at Gordion. In *The Archaeology of Midas and the Phrygians*, ed. L. Kealhofer, pp. 22–35. Philadelphia: University of Pennsylvania Museum.

—— 2007. The Middle Phrygian Occupation at Gordion. In *Anatolian Iron Ages 6*, ed. A. Çilingiroğlu and A. Sagona, pp. 311–33. Leuven: Peeters.

—— 2009. The Chronology of Phrygian Gordion. In *Tree-Rings, Kings, and Old World Archaeology and Environment: Papers Presented in Honor of Peter Ian Kuniholm*, ed. S. W. Manning and M. J. Bruce, pp. 219–37. Oxford: Oxbow Books.

Voigt, Mary M., and T. C. Young, Jr. 1999. From Phrygian Capital to Achaemenid Entrepôt: Middle and Late Phrygian Gordion. *Iranica Antiqua* 34:191–241.

Zeder, Melinda A., and Susan R. Arter. 1994. Changing Patterns of Animal Utilization at Ancient Gordion. *Paléorient* 20(2): 105–18.

Index

(Page numbers in italics indicate figures)